# Managed Speech

*But freedom to differ is not limited to things that do not matter much. That would be a mere shadow of freedom. The test of its substance is the right to differ as to things that touch the heart of the existing order.*

—Justice Robert Jackson[1]

1. West Virginia State Board of Education v. Barnette, 319 U.S. 624, 642 (1943).

# Managed Speech

*The Roberts Court's First Amendment*

Gregory P. Magarian

OXFORD
UNIVERSITY PRESS

OXFORD
UNIVERSITY PRESS

Oxford University Press is a department of the University of Oxford. It furthers the University's objective of excellence in research, scholarship, and education by publishing worldwide. Oxford is a registered trademark of Oxford University Press in the UK and certain other countries.

Published in the United States of America by Oxford University Press
198 Madison Avenue, New York, NY 10016, United States of America.



Library of Congress Cataloging-in-Publication Data

Names: Magarian, Gregory P., author.
Title: Managed speech : the Roberts court's First Amendment / Gregory P. Magarian.
Description: New York : Oxford University Press, 2017. | Includes bibliographical references and index.
Identifiers: LCCN 2016041170 | ISBN 9780190466794 ((hardback) : alk. paper)
Subjects: LCSH: United States. Supreme Court. | Judicial process—United States. | Freedom of speech—United States. | United States. Constitution. 1st Amendment.
Classification: LCC KF8742 .M24 2017 | DDC 342.7308/53—dc23 LC record available at https://lccn.loc.gov/2016041170

3 5 7 9 8 6 4 2

Printed by Edwards Brothers Malloy, United States of America

**Note to Readers**

This publication is designed to provide accurate and authoritative information in regard to the subject matter covered. It is based upon sources believed to be accurate and reliable and is intended to be current as of the time it was written. It is sold with the understanding that the publisher is not engaged in rendering legal, accounting, or other professional services. If legal advice or other expert assistance is required, the services of a competent professional person should be sought. Also, to confirm that the information has not been affected or changed by recent developments, traditional legal research techniques should be used, including checking primary sources where appropriate.

*(Based on the Declaration of Principles jointly adopted by a Committee of the American Bar Association and a Committee of Publishers and Associations.)*

For Arnold T. Schoch and Horan Henry Magarian

# CONTENTS

# ACKNOWLEDGMENTS

Writing my first book has taught me that no one writes a book alone. My two Deans at the Washington University School of Law, Kent Syverud and Nancy Staudt, have encouraged and generously supported this project. My colleagues Lee Epstein and Brian Tamanaha have graciously shared their experience and wisdom while offering essential guidance and support. My colleagues John Inazu and Neil Richards have helped me think through my ideas while also advising me about the process. Lee and John, along with my colleagues Pauline Kim, Russell Osgood, and Liz Sepper, read the manuscript and gave me extensive and helpful comments. Ash Bhagwat, Leslie Kendrick, Heidi Kitrosser, and Tim Zick likewise read all or parts of the manuscript and provided great feedback. My colleague Marion Crain helped me to understand the intersection of labor law and the First Amendment.

I received valuable comments and criticism on earlier versions of various chapters of this book in faculty workshops at Aoyama Gakuin University Law School, Boston College Law School, and the Washington University School of Law; the First Amendment Roundtable at the Washington University School of Law; the Workshop in Politics, Ethics, and Society at the Washington University Department of Political Science; the U.S. Law Study Group at Waseda University Law School; the Symposium on the Contemporary First Amendment at William and Mary Law School; and the Freedom of Expression Scholars Conference at Yale Law School. I'm especially grateful to Jill Delston, Fred Schauer, and Mark Tushnet, who served as discussants or co-panelists at some of those events. An early version of Chapter 1 was published in the *William and Mary Law Review.*

Jamie Berezin, Alex Flach, Alden Domizio, and Elinor Shields at Oxford University Press adroitly shepherded the book through the review, editing, and production processes. Nancy Cummings provided first-rate administrative support. Gwenn Barney, Sean Craig, Katharine Finley, Alex Joyner, Julia Lang, Jonathan Schmalfeld, Brett Walker, and Nikki Windsor contributed outstanding research assistance. Students in my seminar on the Roberts Court's First Amendment challenged and sharpened my thinking on many points. The ace librarians in the Washington University Law Library helped track down all the materials I needed.

My deepest gratitude and highest love go to my family. My parents, Jean and Don Magarian, have shaped my values, my ideas, and my desire to write. My wife, Melissa Posten, has been endlessly patient, encouraging, and energizing. My daughter, Molly, is happy that her dad wrote a book, even if it sounds kind of boring. Melissa's mom, Pat Hughes, brings constant good cheer to our home.

Thanks, everyone.

# INTRODUCTION

If a democracy doesn't make noise, it dies. We in the United States are supposed to be a self-governing people. We pride ourselves on artistic creativity, economic innovation, and scientific vision. Self-government requires constant political debate. Creativity, innovation, and vision can arise only from ongoing cultural conversations. Those discourses can't just comprise polite expressions of mutual affirmation by wealthy and powerful elites. The discussion we need is boisterous, angry, and hopeful. It's aspirational, transgressive, and inclusive. It's the steady hum of ideas in laboratories and studios, in chat rooms and comment threads, and most of all in the streets. It's the shouts that forge the social movements that shape our society, from revolutionary battle cries to abolitionist prophecies, from labor pickets to civil rights sit-ins, from blessings of same-sex marriages to whatever our shared future holds. It's the exclamations, whispers, and laughter that make us the individuals we are, individuals who join together, govern ourselves, and form a communal culture. A democratic society needs to muster and sustain the broadest, deepest, noisiest public discussion we can all pull from our lungs.

The First Amendment to the United States Constitution makes legal space for our public discussion. It states: "Congress shall make no law . . . abridging the freedom of speech, or of the press; or the right of the people peaceably to assemble, and to petition the Government for redress of grievances."[1] The rights of speech, press, assembly, and petition mean to ensure that anyone can have conversations that pull in any direction, even—especially—conversations that other people, and the government we all empower, don't want to hear. The First Amendment isn't the whole story of our public discussion, or even most of the story. Public discussion is a tower built of radical activism, dogged journalism, inspired eccentricity, and much more. The First Amendment forms only the tower's deep foundation. Most of us don't have

1. U.S. Const. amend. I. This book uses the terms "free speech," "expressive freedom," and "First Amendment" more or less interchangeably to refer collectively to the rights of speech, press, assembly, and petition. The First Amendment's prohibition on making any law "respecting an establishment of religion, or prohibiting the free exercise thereof" is another subject for another book.

to think about the First Amendment as we argue, negotiate, banter, celebrate, criticize, satirize, teach, and learn our ways through daily life. Even so, First Amendment law has to support all those expressive interactions. If the foundation fails, the tower crumbles.

This book explores and critiques how the current U.S. Supreme Court, under the leadership of Chief Justice John Roberts, has reshaped First Amendment law. The Supreme Court influences the quality of our public discussion more than any other single institution. Despite the First Amendment's seemingly absolute wording, government abridges expressive freedom in all kinds of ways. You can't contract for a criminal act, reveal state secrets to a foreign government, or (says an old joke) yell "movie!" in a crowded firehouse. The words "no law" cannot mean exactly what they say, and the First Amendment therefore requires interpretation. That's the Supreme Court's job. Supreme Court decisions over the past century have given us many important answers about the First Amendment's scope and power. We know the amendment protects us if we make strong public criticisms of government officials, if we refuse to recite the Pledge of Allegiance at school, or even if we advocate violent insurrection. Constitutional lawyers sometimes make the mistake of claiming that the Supreme Court's pronouncements matter above and beyond all other things. In reality, legal doctrine only emerges and operates in political social context, and Supreme Court decisions only draw the broad outlines of legal doctrine as people experience it. Even so, the Court's First Amendment decisions serve a crucial function in shaping public discussion.

First Amendment protection for expressive freedom is durable, in the sense that our society continuously places great value on expressive freedom. First Amendment protection is also malleable, in the sense that expressive freedom means very different things to different people and in different circumstances. New First Amendment questions continually require the Supreme Court's interpretation. Just as bodies regenerate cells, each era's Court generates its own version of the First Amendment, building on precedent but reflecting the present justices' distinctive set of understandings about what expressive freedom means. Anyone who cares about the vitality of our democracy should take a great interest in what sort of First Amendment the present Court is giving us.

## THE ROBERTS COURT

The chief justice of the United States only has one vote in deciding Supreme Court cases, just like each of the Court's eight associate justices. Still, we conventionally use chief justices' names to label eras on the Court, because a chief's priorities and personality strongly influence the Court's identity. The chief justice has power to decide which justice will write the majority opinion in any case where the chief votes with the majority. The chief presides over the justices' conferences, deciding how discussion of petitions for review and argued cases will proceed. Chief justices also take primary responsibility for protecting the Court's institutional capital and public reputation.

John G. Roberts became chief justice in 2005, replacing his mentor, William H. Rehnquist. The Roberts Court, like the Court under Chief Justice Warren Burger in the 1970s and early 1980s, has welcomed multiple new justices after what had been a long period of consistency in the Court's makeup. For more than a decade, from 1994 until 2005, Chief Justice Rehnquist led an unchanging roster of associate justices. Since 2005 the Court has changed dramatically. Around the time President George W. Bush appointed Chief Justice Roberts, he also appointed Justice Samuel A. Alito to replace Sandra Day O'Connor. Over the next half decade, President Barack Obama appointed Justices Sonia Sotomayor and Elena Kagan to replace David Souter and John Paul Stevens. In five frenzied years, almost half the Court turned over, with the four new justices joining five Rehnquist Court holdovers: President Reagan's appointees Antonin Scalia and Anthony Kennedy, President George H.W. Bush's appointee Clarence Thomas, and President Clinton's appointees Ruth Bader Ginsburg and Stephen Breyer.

This book examines every decision about expressive freedom the Supreme Court handed down between Chief Justice Roberts' ascent in September 2005 and Justice Scalia's death in February 2016. During that time the Court issued more than 40 decisions about the First Amendment's speech protections. Those decisions form one of the most important parts of this Court's record and legacy.[2] They have inspired sharply divergent judgments.

Many free speech advocates revere the Roberts Court. Renowned First Amendment lawyer Floyd Abrams has said: "It is unpopular speech, distasteful speech, that most requires First Amendment protection, and on that score, no prior Supreme Court has been as protective as this."[3] Burt Neuborne, a leading academic and legendary civil liberties lawyer, concurs: "This court is the strongest First Amendment court in history. The current majority uses the First Amendment as a powerful tool of deregulation that eliminates virtually all government efforts to regulate anything to do with the flow of information."[4] Former judge and academic Kenneth Starr has called the Roberts Court

2. The major books on the Roberts Court all devote substantial attention to the Court's free speech decisions. *See* Marcia Coyle, The Roberts Court: The Struggle for the Constitution 197–278 (2013); Laurence Tribe & Joshua Matz, Uncertain Justice: The Roberts Court and the Constitution 88–153 (2014); Mark Tushnet, In the Balance: Law and Politics on the Roberts Court 215–80 (2013).

3. Adam Liptak, *Study Challenges Supreme Court's Image as Defender of Free Speech*, N.Y. Times (Jan. 8, 2012), at A25.

4. Greg Stohr, *Freedom of Speech Is Buttressed as U.S. Supreme Court Concludes Term*, Bloomberg (June 28, 2011), http://www.bloomberg.com/news/2011-06-28/speech-rights-triumph-as-u-s-high-court-limits-government-power.html.

"the most free speech Court in American history."[5] Such praise has persisted as the Roberts Court's First Amendment record has lengthened.[6]

In contrast, critics raise several different objections to the Roberts Court's free speech decisions. Some claim that the Roberts Court hasn't protected speech even-handedly. These critics bluntly contend that the Roberts Court majority has imposed its right-wing political ideology on First Amendment law.[7] On this critique, "[t]he Roberts court strongly protects speech that it likes, while allowing regulation of speech it disfavors."[8] Other critics agree with the Roberts Court's cheerleaders that the Court has vigorously protected speech, but they complain that the Court has protected too much speech that doesn't deserve protection.[9] A third critique holds that, although politics explains some of the Roberts Court's free speech rulings, an arguably excessive preference for concrete legal rules, as opposed to flexible legal standards, explains more.[10]

## MANAGED SPEECH

This book draws connections between and among the Roberts Court's free speech decisions in order to assess the decisions' significance for First Amendment law. This Court opposes many government restrictions on speech. It wants private money to flow freely in politics. It cares deeply about the speech rights of large commercial actors. On the other hand, this Court has approved restrictions on the speech of political dissenters, government workers, and students. In allocating expressive opportunities, it has favored wealthier and more powerful speakers. I find more in the Roberts Court's record to criticize than to praise. I don't, however, believe this Court has

5. A.E. Dick Howard, *Out of Infancy: The Roberts Court at Seven*, 98 VA. L. REV. IN BRIEF 76, 82 (2012) (quoting Kenneth Starr, President, Baylor Univ., Address at the Pepperdine Judicial Law Clerk Institute (Mar. 18, 2011)); *see also* Kenneth W. Starr, *The First Amendment Rights of the Disfavored*, 49 U. LOUISVILLE L. REV. 1, 4, 13 (2010).

6. *See, e.g.*, Nat Stern, *Secondary Speech and the Protective Approach to Interpretive Dualities in the Roberts Court*, 22 WM. & MARY BILL RTS. J. 133 (2013).

7. *See* Erwin Chemerinsky, *Not a Free Speech Court*, 53 ARIZ. L. REV. 723 (2011); Erwin Chemerinsky, *The Roberts Court and Freedom of Speech*, 63 FED. COMM. L.J. 579 (2011); Aziz Z. Huq, *Preserving Political Speech from Ourselves and Others*, 112 COLUM. L. REV. SIDEBAR 16 (2012); David Kairys, *The Contradictory Messages of Rehnquist-Roberts Era Speech Law: Liberty and Justice for Some*, 2013 U. ILL. L. REV. 195.

8. Professor Adam Winkler, quoted in Stohr, *supra* note 4.

9. Critiques of this sort appear in RANDALL P. BEZANSON, TOO MUCH FREE SPEECH? (2012); Vikram D. Amar & Alan Brownstein, *The Voracious First Amendment:* Alvarez *and* Knox *in the Context of 2012 and Beyond*, 46 LOY. L.A. L. REV. 491 (2013); and Andrew M. Koppelman, *Veil of Ignorance: Tunnel Constructivism in Free Speech Theory*, 107 NW. U. L. REV. 647 (2013).

10. *See* TUSHNET, *supra* note 2, at 237–46.

simply promoted a right-wing political agenda, overprotected speech indiscriminately, or indulged a preference for rigid rules. I contend, instead, that the Roberts Court's free speech jurisprudence fits a descriptive template that I call *managed speech.*

Managed speech describes a mode of First Amendment jurisprudence that seeks to reconcile substantial First Amendment protection for expressive freedom with aggressive preservation of social and political stability. Managed speech embodies three central tendencies of the Roberts Court's First Amendment decisions. First, the Roberts Court has continuously authorized powerful, established institutions—sometimes governmental, sometimes private—to exercise a strong measure of managerial control over public discussion. Second, the Roberts Court has routinely disregarded the expressive interests and First Amendment claims of *outsider speakers:* less powerful and lesser-financed speakers, political dissenters, and others outside the social mainstream. Third, the Roberts Court's decisions show a consistent preference for modes of public discussion that promote social and political stability, while disfavoring modes of public discussion that threaten to destabilize existing arrangements of social and political power.

Managed speech can work in several different ways. A speech manager may restrict the content of the discussion, dominate the discussion in a way that crowds out other speakers, or make structural decisions that determine which speakers and content may enter the discussion. The Supreme Court itself manages public discussion every time it decides a free speech dispute and makes First Amendment law. My primary concern is not with that inevitable, overarching mode of judicial management. Managed speech connotes, instead, judicial grants to other actors of managerial control over public discussion. Whenever an actor exerts strong, ongoing influence over the content or process of public debate, that actor has managerial authority in the sense I mean. In response to that managerial dynamic, a court might restrict the power of the government or powerful speakers to control the discussion, disaggregate or disperse managerial power, or facilitate a truly wide open, unmanaged discussion. Managed speech does none of those things. Instead, managed speech concentrates managerial power over public discussion in the government or in favored private actors. The Roberts Court, with a consistency and potency unique in the Supreme Court's history, has authorized established, powerful institutions strongly invested in the status quo to exercise managerial control over public discussion, with the apparent goal and typical result of pushing public discussion away from destabilizing, noisy margins and toward a stable, settled center.

This book treats the Roberts Court's free speech decisions as a text that operates as legal doctrine. The managed speech thesis provides a lens through which we can read and critique that text. Authorial intent presents a problem for any textual interpretation, and the presence of 9 alternating, collaborating, clashing authors (11 in total over the life of the Roberts Court to date) compounds the problem. Moreover, the Supreme Court as an institution faces limits in imposing whatever its collective will might be. The Court has substantial power to set its agenda by choosing which cases to review. On the other hand, the Court can only review cases that litigants file, and Congress has power to mandate review of particular sorts of cases. The justices work under constraints of past Courts' precedential decisions, the checking powers of the elected branches, and public scrutiny. I don't claim that managed speech describes the specific intent of the Roberts Court or that the justices would describe their free speech jurisprudence in the terms I use. Sometimes, notably in the campaign finance decisions discussed in Part III, managed speech may fairly describe the majority's intentions. My aim, however, is not to psychoanalyze the justices. Rather, managed speech offers a robust descriptor for this Court's collective approach to making First Amendment law, a best-fit line through a diverse, important set of legal decisions.

My account of the Roberts Court's free speech jurisprudence examines all the decisions' moving parts. Most of this Court's free speech decisions, like most Supreme Court decisions generally, have majority opinions, which carry the full force of law. When just a plurality of justices can agree on a lead opinion, only the result and whatever reasoning a majority shares across separate opinions has full precedential force. My discussion covers both majority and plurality decisions, accounting for the varying degrees of contention in the plurality cases. I also discuss major dissents and concurrences. These separate opinions show what ideas the majority isn't embracing. They often shed light on the majority's views and reveal important disagreements that help us understand the doctrine. The Court's degree of unity or division in a given case also indicates the potential durability or fragility of the holding. What the Court does, the decisions' legal holdings, forms the top line of my managed speech analysis, but what the various justices say also matters for understanding and evaluating the Court's free speech jurisprudence.

## DYNAMIC DIVERSITY

Beyond criticizing managed speech, this book advocates an alternative, very different model for First Amendment law. I call my preferred normative model *dynamic diversity*. Dynamic diversity isn't a wholly novel theory of expressive freedom. The model incorporates ideas long familiar from free speech debates. Dynamic diversity doesn't foreground every value that matters for expressive freedom. First Amendment law should, among other things, advance the search for truth, promote personal autonomy and self-fulfillment, and block government actors from making decisions they aren't well equipped to make.[11] Dynamic diversity, however, embodies the central values that, in my view, animate a normatively appealing account of expressive freedom.

Dynamic diversity seeks to maximize two related kinds of diversity in public discussion. First, constitutional speech protection should promote diversity of ideas. First Amendment doctrine should encourage a state of affairs where participants in public debate have more and more varied perspectives and information to consider. This *idea value* focuses on the interests of audiences. Second, constitutional speech protection should promote diversity of participation. First Amendment doctrine should enable and encourage more people with different perspectives, characteristics, and experiences to join in public discussions. This *participation value* focuses on the interests of speakers.

In valuing diversity of both ideas and participation, dynamic diversity harmonizes two tendencies that theorists sometimes place in opposition. Alexander Meiklejohn offers the classic argument for diverse ideas in public debate. His conception of collective self-government requires that "no suggestion of policy shall be denied a hearing because it is on one side of an issue rather than another . . . because someone in control thinks it unwise, unfair, un-American."[12] Professor Meiklejohn, though, dismisses the interest in diverse participation. "What is essential," he insists, "is not that everyone shall speak but that everything worth saying shall be said."[13] Conversely, election law scholar Spencer Overton, writing about campaign finance regulation, makes a paradigmatic case for the importance of widespread participation in electoral debates.[14] Professor Overton, though, denies the importance of ensuring that public debate includes a wide range of ideas, when he rejects leveling of candidates' resources as a proper goal of campaign finance law.[15] I think Professor Meiklejohn and Professor Overton are right to champion the free speech values they do but wrong to dismiss the values they do. At times the idea and participation values may clash in First Amendment disputes. Usually, though, the two values complement one another. Enabling broad-based participation in public debate should generate a wide range of ideas, and encouraging a breadth of ideas should foster widespread participation.

The "dynamic" part of dynamic diversity, the underlying reason for wanting as many people as possible to engage in public debate about as many ideas as possible, posits free speech as an engine of political and social change. "Those

11. Leading discussions of plural justifications for constitutional speech protections include THOMAS I. EMERSON, TOWARD A GENERAL THEORY OF THE FIRST AMENDMENT (1967); FREDERICK SCHAUER, FREE SPEECH: A PHILOSOPHICAL ENQUIRY (1982).

12. ALEXANDER MEIKLEJOHN, POLITICAL FREEDOM: THE CONSTITUTIONAL POWERS OF THE PEOPLE 26–27 (1960).

13. *Id.* at 26.

14. *See* Spencer Overton, *The Participation Interest*, 100 GEO. L.J. 1259 (2012).

15. *See* Spencer Overton, *Matching Political Contributions*, 96 MINN. L. REV. 1694, 1696, 1706–07 (2012).

who won our independence," wrote Justice Louis Brandeis, "were not cowards. They did not fear political change. They did not exalt order at the cost of liberty."[16] Justice Brandeis reminds us that the vitality of any culture depends on continuous revision of social and political norms, practices, and institutions. If we stop questioning the status quo, we calcify. Change is not an absolute good; societies need stable institutions. In the United States, legal structures both foundational, such as our constitutional divisions of government power, and evolved, such as our two-party system, perpetuate stable institutions, for better and worse. Public discussion is the primary medium for challenging stable institutions and testing new ideas, the space where dynamism finds the oxygen to challenge stability. First Amendment law, on the dynamic diversity model, should help to provide that oxygen.

Dynamic diversity does not hold that the First Amendment should protect only speech that pursues change. Rather, dynamic diversity calls on First Amendment law to recognize the special value of speech for enabling change and, accordingly, to prioritize free speech claims that promote diversity of ideas and participants in public discussion. Any pursuit of political or social change requires ideas and debates about what we should do differently. Action toward change can't happen without speech. At the same time, speech is relatively safe. It lets us hedge our bets at the margin where change challenges stability.[17] First Amendment law protects our right to advocate the violent overthrow of the government, but nothing in our law (not even the Second Amendment, despite what you sometimes hear) lets us take up arms against the government. When a speaker urges action, we can think about the speaker's program and decide whether we should act on it. Even as speech lays the foundation for change, we often decide not to build on that foundation for good reasons that only the distance between speech and action lets us grasp.

*Dissent* lies at the heart of dynamic diversity. Dissent affects not just political but social relationships. It includes artistic, philosophical, and scientific expression that challenges and changes how we think or what we know.[18] Today's social dissent may become tomorrow's political dissent, as the LGBT rights movement's evolution over the past half-century well illustrates. Dynamic diversity places dissent at the core of First Amendment concern not just because of dissent's distinctive value but also because of its distinctive vulnerability. Powerful actors both inside and outside government resist change because change tends to reallocate power. Government may want to suppress certain speech that aids in the search for truth, or enhances personal

16. Whitney v. California, 274 U.S. 357, 377 (1927) (Brandeis, J., concurring).

17. For an influential discussion of how constitutional speech protection modulates the balance between stability and change, see EMERSON, *supra* note 11, at 11–14.

18. For a rich discussion of dissent as a free speech paradigm, see STEVEN H. SHIFFRIN, DISSENT, INJUSTICE, AND THE MEANINGS OF AMERICA (1999).

autonomy, or implicates matters about which the government lacks competence. Government, though, has no *systematic* reason to oppose any of those goals. In contrast, government always has reasons to suppress dissent.

Dynamic diversity clashes elementally with all three major components of managed speech. First, authorizing powerful institutions to manage public debate makes no sense on the dynamic diversity model. Speech managers keep public debate orderly. They channel debate toward preservation of the social and political status quo. The idea value of dynamic diversity, in contrast, seeks a public debate that challenges the status quo by introducing the widest possible range of ideas into the discussion. On the dynamic diversity model, public debate should upend settled expectations and complicate established ways of thinking, exactly the expectations and ways of thinking that speech managers serve to perpetuate. Speech managers can dominate the arenas of speech they manage, limiting the space available to other speakers. That dominance undercuts the participation value of dynamic diversity, which seeks to open public debate to the widest possible range of speakers. Speech managers impose organization and hierarchy in order to constrain public discussion. Under dynamic diversity, only the organization and hierarchy necessary for a vigorous exchange of ideas should structure public debate.

Second, just as dynamic diversity rejects the managed speech tendency to empower speech managers, it rejects the managed speech tendency to scorn outsider speakers. Managed speech treats outsider speakers as useless at best and dangerous at worst. Outsider speakers, however, promote both key values of dynamic diversity. Contributions to public debate by outsider speakers axiomatically advance the participation value. Outsider speakers also tend to advance dynamic diversity's idea value by bringing the perspectives that make them outsiders into public discussion. Those perspectives may include subordination within hierarchies, as in the cases of students or prisoners; identities of race, sex, or sexual orientation; economic marginality; and commitment to nonconforming political, religious, or conscientious values. Outsider speakers tend to favor social or political change. That tendency makes outsider speakers anathema to managed speech, which mistrusts speakers who challenge existing institutions and power arrangements. It makes them paladins of dynamic diversity.

The opposing views of managed speech and dynamic diversity about speech managers and outsider speakers prefigure their final, deepest opposition, about the balance that constitutional speech protections should strike between stability and change. Managed speech prioritizes maintaining social and political stability over fostering change. Dynamic diversity prioritizes fostering change over maintaining stability. Dynamic diversity doesn't seek to level every established belief or institution any more than managed speech aims to prevent every bit of change at all costs. The margin at which the two models diverge, however, is where the Court inscribes most

First Amendment doctrine. For managed speech, the First Amendment should provide meaningful expressive freedom while protecting society from disruption. For dynamic diversity, disruption defines much of expressive freedom's value.

## PRIVATE SPEECH, GOVERNMENT PRESERVES, AND THE ELECTORAL PROCESS

This book divides the Roberts Court's free speech decisions into three subject matter categories: (1) government efforts to restrict privately enabled speech; (2) speech regulations in settings government controls as institutional overseer, landowner, or patron, which I call *government preserves;* and (3) regulations of speech in the electoral process, mainly but not only campaign finance regulations.[19] Each of those categories describes a distinctive set of opportunities for free expression and a distinctive set of challenges posed by government action or inaction.

Part I of this book discusses cases about government regulations of private speech, speech that happens without any direct government support. In Chapter 1, we'll see governments push for excluding particular categories of speech from First Amendment protection. In two prominent decisions, the Roberts Court has emphatically refused to expand categorical exclusions. Free speech advocates have hailed that result. A closer look at the decisions, however, reveals that they matter only marginally as precedent and, more importantly, that their analytic focus on tradition enables the Court to deny First Amendment protection in several other cases. Chapter 2 turns to the more common First Amendment technique of balancing speech interests against government regulatory interests. The Roberts Court has reached divergent outcomes in two major decisions on the First Amendment rights of political dissenters. Virulently anti-LGBT protesters won the right to protest near military funerals. On the other hand, peace activists were denied the right to teach foreign terrorist groups about nonviolent conflict resolution. The peace activists' loss, with its sweeping deference to the government's national security concerns, reaches further and matters more than the funeral protesters' win. A striking contrast to the Court's lack of concern for serious political dissent emerges in a decision that invokes the First Amendment to protect commercial data mining. Part I shows how the Roberts Court protects the autonomy of certain private speakers while letting the government restrict speakers who threaten the political or social status quo.

19. This structure owes a debt to Robert Post's division of expressive activity into social domains of democracy, community, and management. *See* ROBERT C. POST, CONSTITUTIONAL DOMAINS: DEMOCRACY, COMMUNITY, MANAGEMENT (1995).

Part II examines the government's heightened power to regulate speech in government preserves. Chapter 3 considers the speech rights of prisoners, students, and government workers. The Supreme Court has long taken a very narrow view of these institutional subjects' First Amendment rights. The Roberts Court has further weakened speech protections in government institutions, deferring almost completely to the government's managerial authority. Chapter 4 discusses government properties, which First Amendment law calls "public forums," that offer underfunded speakers opportunities to reach audiences. The Roberts Court has limited those opportunities by holding that the government may effectively commandeer certain public forums to express its own ideas or values. A recent decision that strikes down restrictions on antiabortion activists might portend a more speech-protective public forum doctrine, but the Court's reasoning may limit that decision's impact on future cases. Chapter 5 discusses disputes about conditions the government places on subsidies it provides for speech. One of the Roberts Court's two conditional subsidy decisions upholds a rule that government-funded universities must let the military conduct job interviews on campus. In contrast, the other funding decision strikes down a funding condition on agencies that provide social services overseas. That decision, however, mainly mitigates a speech-restrictive element of the public forum cases. The government preserve decisions overwhelmingly defer to the government's managerial authority and reject First Amendment claims from speakers who need government resources.

Part III arrives at the most contentious area of free speech law in the Roberts Court era: the electoral process. Chapter 6 pauses at the edge of the storm to discuss electoral process cases about matters other than campaign finance. In particular, the Roberts Court has followed an important trend from the Rehnquist years by using First Amendment law to strengthen the electoral dominance of the two major political parties. Chapter 7 examines the Roberts Court's most notorious, controversial decision: *Citizens United v. Federal Election Commission*, which strikes down long-standing bans on election spending by corporations and unions. It then examines a potentially more important decision that strikes down federal limits on how much donors may contribute to campaigns. These two decisions give corporations and wealthy donors preferred positions in electoral debates. Chapter 8 discusses another group of Roberts Court campaign finance decisions, which somewhat paradoxically restrict electoral money. These decisions strike down government efforts to increase the resources available for underfinanced candidates and stifle public employee unions' efforts to use mandatory dues payments for political purposes. Only one, very narrow decision actually upholds a government restriction on electoral money. The electoral speech decisions let wealthy, powerful institutions and individuals, who share a strong interest in maintaining existing political distributions of wealth and power, dominate electoral debates, crowding out lesser-funded speakers who might challenge those existing distributions.

Chapter 9, the book's stand-alone closing statement, gathers the strands of critical analysis from the earlier chapters into a focused critique of the Roberts Court's First Amendment. Managed speech emerges from the decisions as a coherent approach to free speech problems. This Court empowers stable, responsible institutions, including both government entities and market actors, to manage public discussion by restricting its participants and content, dominating the discussion, or structuring the terms of the discussion. The decisions shun outsider speakers, social and political dissenters who pose a serious threat of destabilizing dominant norms and institutions, while ignoring inequities in speakers' opportunities to reach audiences. Above all, the Roberts Court's First Amendment embodies a deep commitment to preserving social and political stability. Managed speech fits into a conservative intellectual tradition that extends from Edmund Burke's conception of liberty bounded by dominant institutions and norms to Robert Bork's call for First Amendment protection only of established political processes.

The book closes by briefly proposing how a new Supreme Court, in the nearer or further future, might follow dynamic diversity to improve upon the Roberts Court's First Amendment. In broad terms, I urge the next Court to focus its First Amendment concern on social and political dissenters and other outsider speakers, embrace and promote the creative and constructive capacity of speech to foster social and political change, and squarely confront conflicts between expressive interests that arise in First Amendment disputes. More specifically, I contend that a new Court should place greater emphasis on First Amendment concerns of the contemporary mass media, including revitalization of press freedoms and structural protection of public access to information; review electoral regulations based on whether they advance or reduce opportunities for participation and robust electoral debate; and revitalize the public forum while proactively broadening access to expressive resources.

The Roberts Court has made far-reaching contributions to First Amendment law. Viewing this Court's free speech jurisprudence through the lens of managed speech captures much of what makes those contributions distinctive and important. The Roberts Court's managed speech approach to the First Amendment, in my view, has done much more harm than good. Using First Amendment law to promote social and political stability dampens and restrains public discussion. Understanding managed speech can help us push the Court to do better. Dynamic diversity offers a template for moving First Amendment law in a more engaged, inclusive direction and fostering the noisy public discussion our democracy needs.

# PART ONE

# Private Speech

When most of us consider why we care about constitutional protection for speech, we envision censorship of private expression. The First Amendment bars the government from seizing copies of *Fifty Shades of Grey* from bookstores, banning an art gallery from mounting a Robert Mapplethorpe retrospective, or breaking up an anarchist meeting in your basement. These scenarios all share the same basic structure: speakers, using their own resources, express ideas the government doesn't like; the government wants to restrict the speech; the First Amendment blocks the restriction. The Roberts Court has made its strongest speech-protective decisions in cases such as these, and some free speech advocates have highly praised those decisions. This first part of the book discusses and analyzes the Roberts Court's decisions about regulations of private speech. Those decisions, I will argue, deserve some of their renown. Closer examination, however, reveals that, for every stand the Roberts Court takes to protect private speech, it hands down a more important decision that restricts private speech or that has the effect of muting public debate. The Roberts Court cares about protecting private speech from government regulation, but only within the carefully controlled limits of managed speech.

Chapter 1 deals with legal doctrines that completely exclude certain categories of speech from First Amendment protection. The excluded categories include obscenity, some defamatory speech, and true threats. The federal and California governments argued for expanding that list by adding depictions of extreme violence: animal torture videos in *United States v. Stevens* and bloody video games in *Brown v. Entertainment Merchants*. The Roberts Court refused. These speech-protective categorical decisions, however, carry limited precedential weight. Worse, they actually undermine speech protection by tying categorical exclusions to the Court's account of what our law has traditionally let governments regulate. That tradition-bound approach has led the Court to reinforce or fortify nonprotection for using copyrighted material in *Golan v. Holder*, pandering non-existent child pornography in

*United States v. Williams,* and casting legislative votes in *Nevada Commission on Ethics v. Carrigan.* The Court's most recent categorical speech decision, *United States v. Alvarez,* potentially advances expressive freedom by refusing to exclude false statements of fact categorically from First Amendment protection. The justices, however, could not agree on a rationale for *Alvarez.* The categorical speech cases, celebrated by the Roberts Court's enthusiasts, provide only limited, very mixed benefits for expressive freedom.

Chapter 2 shifts from cases that primarily deal with speech categories to cases that primarily balance speakers' interests against the government's reasons for regulating speech. The Roberts Court has decided two major cases about government efforts to restrict private political dissent, with sharply divergent results. *Snyder v. Phelps* invokes the First Amendment to protect an antigay religious group, which stages vicious protests at the funerals of U.S. soldiers killed in action, against a lawsuit for intentional infliction of emotional distress. *Holder v. Humanitarian Law Project,* in contrast, upholds a federal law that bars advising foreign terrorist groups about peaceful conflict resolution. These two cases suggest that the Roberts Court will protect political dissent against blatant government overreaching when the stakes are low but won't protect dissent that seriously threatens social or political stability. The Court's antipathy to serious political dissent diverges sharply from its patronage of commercial speech. *Sorrell v. IMS Health* extends the First Amendment to protect a company's commercial mining of medical data. That decision views speech narrowly as an economic commodity, and it also benefits only a powerful group of market actors whom the government may have valid reasons for regulating. The final balancing decision, *Reed v. Town of Gilbert,* broadly reaffirms the Court's commitment to protecting private speech from government restriction, but its reasoning risks either fading into triviality or sliding into unworkability.

The Roberts Court has shielded some private speech from government suppression. These first two chapters, however, show that the overall record of these decisions for speech protection is mixed. This Court has cast First Amendment law in the mold of managed speech: selectively empowering government actors and responsible institutions to manage public discussion, marginalizing the expressive interests of dissenters and outsider speakers, and promoting social and political stability. My preferred model for First Amendment law, dynamic diversity, would lead to different results in some of these cases: *Golan, IMS Health,* and, most importantly, *Humanitarian Law Project.* More broadly, dynamic diversity counsels departure from the Roberts Court's First Amendment analysis. The Supreme Court shouldn't constrain free speech doctrine in chains of tradition; rather, it should shape the doctrine to promote broad, inclusive public debate. The Court shouldn't privilege the expressive rights of powerful commercial actors; rather, it should prioritize protection for creative energy and political dissent.

# CHAPTER 1

# The Marrow of Tradition

## *Categorical Exclusions from First Amendment Protection*

Some of the Roberts Court's most distinctive First Amendment decisions deal with categorical exclusions of speech from First Amendment protection. Categorical exclusions define the scope of what the First Amendment protects. The Roberts Court has shown a greater appetite than any Court in four decades for defining those boundaries. The categorical speech decisions often serve as exhibit A for commentators who praise the Roberts Court as strongly speech protective.[1] This chapter, however, will show that the Court's record even in the categorical field is mixed, with actual and potential limits on expressive freedom hidden just below the speech-protective surface.

The Roberts Court has announced a new touchstone for deciding whether to exclude a speech category from First Amendment protection: *tradition.* The Court's tradition-bound analysis has led to speech-protective results in several important cases. That same analysis, however, has let the Court deny protection to other sorts of speech, leaving the government with managerial power over important areas of public discussion. Emphasizing tradition in legal analysis necessarily reinforces whatever institutions and arrangements

1. One commentator spotlights the categorical decisions in crediting the Roberts Court with "a new kind of First Amendment absolutism." *See* Ronald K.L. Collins, *Exceptional Freedom: The Roberts Court, the First Amendment, and the New Absolutism*, 76 ALB. L. REV. 409, 426 (2013).

the guardian of tradition sees as established and settled. The categorical exclusion cases thus open a window into the Roberts Court's efforts to reconcile expressive freedom with a stable social and political order, the driving goal of managed speech.

To understand how categorical exclusions from First Amendment protection work, we need to reach back to the beginning of First Amendment law. Although the First Amendment entered the Constitution in 1791, the Supreme Court did not think pointedly about free speech rights until after World War I,[2] and it never invoked the First Amendment to strike down a law until 1931.[3] As First Amendment doctrine developed, the Court maintained that some categories of speech were so obviously worthless or harmful, and some attendant speech regulations so commonplace, that courts should leave them alone.

The Court's earliest free speech cases, decided in the shadow of World War I and the Russian Revolution, fixated on how speech could lead to violence. The justices repeatedly upheld criminal convictions of communists, socialists, and anarchists (the great paladins of 1920s First Amendment law) under laws that criminalized advocating violent overthrow of the government.[4] Fears about speech and violence broadened during World War II, as reflected in the pivotal case of *Chaplinsky v. New Hampshire*.[5] *Chaplinsky* involved a member of Jehovah's Witnesses (the great paladins of 1940s First Amendment law) who loudly called a police officer "a God damned racketeer" and "a damned Fascist" on a public street. The state convicted the member of violating a local law that forbade "address[ing] any offensive, derisive, or annoying word to any other person . . . [or] call[ing] him by any offensive or derisive name." In affirming the conviction, Justice Frank Murphy explained:

> There are certain well-defined and narrowly limited classes of speech, the prevention and punishment of which have never been thought to raise any Constitutional problem. These include the lewd and obscene, the profane, the libelous, and the insulting or "fighting" words—those which by their very utterance inflict injury or tend to incite an immediate breach of the peace. It has been well observed that such utterances are no essential part of any exposition of ideas, and are of such slight social value as a step to truth that any benefit that may be derived from them is clearly outweighed by the social interest in order and morality.[6]

2. *See* Schenck v. United States, 249 U.S. 47 (1919).
3. *See* Near v. Minnesota, 283 U.S. 697 (1931).
4. *See* Whitney v. California, 274 U.S. 357 (1927); Gitlow v. New York, 268 U.S. 652 (1925).
5. 315 U.S. 568 (1942).
6. *Id.* at 571–72.

That justification in *Chaplinsky* for letting states ban certain kinds of speech established categorical exclusions as a way to set the boundaries of First Amendment protection.

The categorical approach has fostered important limitations on First Amendment rights, some of which have stood the test of time. We hail *New York Times Co. v. Sullivan*[7] as one of the Court's great speech-protective decisions because it severely limits government officials' power to sue their critics for defamation.[8] But *Sullivan* also effectuates, with an evolutionary leap in nuance, the *Chaplinsky* allowance for restricting "libelous" speech. Expression that defames ordinary people gets only limited First Amendment protection.[9] Similarly, the Court long ago decided, in a series of decisions culminating in *Miller v. California*,[10] that "obscene" speech—another item from the *Chaplinsky* catalog—gets no First Amendment protection. *Miller* lets the government ban as obscenity "patently offensive" sexually explicit speech that "appeals to the prurient interest" and lacks redeeming social value.[11] Other post-*Chaplinsky* doctrines deny First Amendment protection to fraudulent speech, at least in a commercial setting,[12] and to speech that conveys a "true threat."[13] These categorical doctrines still matter. People rely on defamation law to protect their reputations and fraud law to protect their wallets. The *Miller* allowance for banning obscenity still puts people behind bars. The true threat doctrine, although somewhat narrow, is crucial where it's relevant.[14]

As an active method for making First Amendment doctrine, however, the categorical approach has been declining for half a century. The Court long ago whittled the "advocacy of violence" category of unprotected speech down to a much finer category of speech that willfully incites someone to imminent violent action.[15] The Court has similarly reined in *Chaplinsky* itself, holding that the "fighting words" exclusion doesn't cover emotionally charged, deeply offensive statements hurled at an unsuspecting audience but not at a particular

7. 376 U.S. 254 (1964).

8. *Sullivan* allows public officials to recover for defamation only upon a showing of "actual malice," meaning that the defendant knew or acted in reckless disregard of the defamatory statement's falsity. *See id.* at 279–80.

9. *See, e.g., Gertz*, 418 U.S. 323.

10. 413 U.S. 15 (1973).

11. *Id.* at 24 (internal quotation marks and citation omitted).

12. *See* Va. State Bd. of Pharmacy v. Va. Citizens Consumer Council, 425 U.S. 748 (1976).

13. *See* Watts v. United States, 394 U.S. 705, 707 (1969) (per curiam).

14. *See* Virginia v. Black, 538 U.S. 343 (2003) (affirming the constitutionality of a ban on cross burnings that amount to true threats). In the only Roberts Court case about true threats, the justices declined to reach the First Amendment issue. *See* Elonis v. United States, 135 S. Ct. 2001 (2015) (overturning on other grounds a federal criminal conviction for making threats).

15. *See* Brandenburg v. Ohio, 395 U.S. 444 (1969).

person.[16] Only once since the Court handed down *Miller* in 1973 has it announced a new category of unprotected speech, when *New York v. Ferber*[17] in 1982 denied First Amendment protection to child pornography. The *Ferber* Court, however, denied protection only to actual images of actual children engaged in sexual conduct. The First Amendment still protects nonphotographic images and written descriptions of children having sex. Unlike other categories of unprotected speech, the *Ferber* child pornography doctrine directly targets not speech but conduct—sexual exploitation of children—that the government obviously has power to regulate.

All of this musty history matters for our purposes because the Roberts Court has thought harder, and done more, about categorical exclusions from the First Amendment than the Court had during the preceding 35 years. The present Court has declared forcefully that it won't expand categorical exclusions. At the same time, and based on the same mode of analysis, the Court has quietly reaffirmed and even strengthened existing categorical limits on the First Amendment's protection.[18]

## ONE HAND GIVES: RESISTING NEW CATEGORICAL EXCLUSIONS

The Roberts Court has twice rejected the categorical approach as a basis for new restrictions on speech. The categorical approach burst back into prominence in ***United States v. Stevens* (2010).**[19] Robert Stevens, an online video dealer, challenged his criminal conviction for violating a federal law that banned making, selling, or possessing certain depictions of animal cruelty.[20] Stevens himself sold videos of pit bulls fighting and attacking other animals, but Congress had really passed the law to combat "crush videos." Aimed at a particular sexual fetish, crush videos depict women in high heels torturing and killing small animals by crushing them.[21] No one questions the government's

16. *See* Cohen v. California, 403 U.S. 15 (1971). For an effort to rehabilitate *Chaplinsky*, see Kent Greenawalt, *Insults and Epithets: Are They Protected Speech?*, 42 RUTGERS L. REV. 287, 294–300 (1990) (attempting to supplement and strengthen the *Chaplinsky* basis for excluding fighting words from First Amendment protection).

17. 458 U.S. 747 (1982).

18. Doctrines that categorically exclude certain types of speech from First Amendment protection stand apart from cases that, with varying degrees of doctrinal formality, treat special government prerogatives as denying a speaker any legally cognizable interest in certain speech. We'll encounter cases of that sort throughout Part II's discussion of speech in government preserves and in Chapter 8's discussion of public sector labor unions' political speech.

19. 559 U.S. 460 (2010). Roberts (majority) (with Stevens, Scalia, Kennedy, Thomas, Ginsburg, Breyer, Sotomayor); Alito (dissenting).

20. *See* 18 U.S.C. § 48 (2010).

21. *See Stevens*, 559 U.S. at 465–66.

power to criminalize actual animal torture. The law at issue in *Stevens,* though, punished only images. The government lawyers in *Stevens* knew they had a big problem, because the law (probably unwittingly) banned a wide range of images, potentially including videos and magazines about hunting and certain religious rituals. Treating this problem as an opportunity, the government swung for the fences, asking the Court to add "depictions of animal cruelty" to the list of unprotected speech categories. The government argued that the Court simply needed to do what it had done decades earlier in *Chaplinsky:* declare that depictions of animal cruelty, as a category of speech, do more harm than good.

Chief Justice Roberts, writing for an 8-1 majority, rejects as "startling and dangerous" the government's proposed cost-benefit test for unprotected categories of speech.[22] Yes, he concedes, the Court in *Chaplinsky* and other cases described categorical exclusions in the language of cost-benefit analysis.[23] Description, however, differs from justification. In every case of a categorical exclusion, the chief justice explains, *tradition* has justified narrowing the scope of First Amendment protection. Every category of speech to which the Court has denied First Amendment protection was simply a "historic and traditional categor[y] long familiar to the bar"[24] as lacking constitutional protection. The chief justice uses the *Ferber* child pornography decision as his main illustration. Child pornography, according to *Ferber,* was "an integral part" of the underlying, illegal abuse of children.[25] The Court, the chief justice asserts, had long treated speech integrally related to unlawful conduct as a category of unprotected speech. Therefore, tradition justified the *Ferber* exclusion of child pornography from First Amendment protection. In contrast, the chief justice maintains, we have no tradition of punishing depictions of animal cruelty. Any future addition to the list of categorical exclusions from First Amendment protection would have to track some traditional allowance for restricting the speech in question.[26]

With its categorical argument in tatters, the government in *Stevens* could only argue weakly that the law used to convict Stevens was narrowly drawn to bar certain "extreme" material. The statutory language, however, belied that argument, and the Court struck down the law in its entirety under a First Amendment rule called the *overbreadth doctrine.* That doctrine prohibits

22. *Id.* at 470.

23. *See id.*

24. *Id.* at 468 (internal quotation marks and citation omitted).

25. New York v. Ferber, 458 U.S. 747, 761 (1982).

26. *See Stevens,* 559 U.S. at 471–72. Tradition has played a similar role in the Roberts Court's engagement with the First Amendment's establishment clause. *See* Town of Greece v. Galloway, 134 S. Ct. 1811, 1819 (2014) (rejecting an establishment clause challenge to a legislative prayer based on "the tradition long followed in Congress and the state legislatures" of beginning legislative sessions with prayers).

the government from restricting a substantial amount of protected speech even where part of the prohibition might pass First Amendment muster. Chief Justice Roberts emphasizes that even "recreational" speech, like hunting videos, gets First Amendment protection.[27] He mocks the government's backup assurance that the Court should trust the executive branch to prosecute only extreme speech.[28] A narrower law, the chief justice suggests, might survive First Amendment review, but not this law.[29]

Only Justice Alito dissented from the *Stevens* Court's decision, striking what has become his occasional, distinctive pose as the Court's defender of moral justifications for restricting deeply offensive speech. To save the statute from fatal overbreadth, he urges a narrow reading of what it prohibits.[30] We'll see Justice Alito object on similar grounds to the Court's reasoning in the next case and to the Court's results in *United States v. Alvarez* (also discussed in this chapter) and *Snyder v. Phelps* (discussed in Chapter 2).

***Brown v. Entertainment Merchants Association*** **(2011)**[31] revisits some of the themes of *Stevens*, in a more controversial dispute with broader social consequences. The video game industry challenged a California law that banned the sale or rental of "violent video games" to children under 18. The law deliberately tracked the contours of the Court's leading obscenity case, *Miller v. California*, as well as another Supreme Court decision that allows states to restrict children's access to sexually explicit but nonobscene material, such as simple nude images.[32] Mimicking those cases, the California law barred minors from buying or renting any video game that a "reasonable person, considering the game as a whole, would find appeals to a deviant or morbid interest of minors." It relied on "prevailing standards in the community as to what is suitable for minors."[33] The California law, more pointedly than the federal law struck down in *Stevens*, stood for the idea that the First Amendment should not bar the government from restricting violent images under the Constitution just as it can restrict sexual images. As Justice Breyer asks in his dissenting opinion: "What kind of First Amendment would permit the

27. *See Stevens*, 559 U.S. at 478–79.

28. *See id.* at 480 ("[T]he First Amendment ... does not leave us at the mercy of *noblesse oblige*.").

29. *See id.* at 482. Congress almost immediately enacted a new, narrower version of the law. *See* Animal Crush Video Prohibition Act of 2010, Pub. L. No. 111–294, 124 Stat. 3277.

30. *See Stevens*, 559 U.S. at 485–91 (Alito, J., dissenting).

31. 564 U.S. 786 (2011). Scalia (majority) (with Kennedy, Ginsburg, Sotomayor, Kagan); Alito (concurring in the judgment) (with Roberts); Thomas (dissenting); Breyer (dissenting).

32. *See* Ginsberg v. New York, 390 U.S. 629 (1968). The *Ginsberg* allowance for restricting minors' access to a broader range of sexual material than *Miller* leaves unprotected is commonly called the "harmful to minors" or "obscene as to minors" doctrine.

33. CAL. CIV. CODE § 1746(d)(1)(A) (2006).

government to protect children by restricting sales of [an] extremely violent video game *only* when [a] woman—bound, gagged, tortured, and killed—is also topless?"[34]

Our kind of First Amendment, respond seven justices, although only five have their hearts in it. Justice Scalia's opinion for an ideologically diverse majority that includes Justices Kennedy, Ginsburg, Sotomayor, and Kagan was his final opinion in a free speech case. It stands as one of his most eloquent statements on expressive freedom. He first reiterates the *Stevens* Court's premise, which California did not challenge, that the First Amendment protects not just sober political messages but also entertainment.[35] The heart of his opinion rejects California's effort to stretch categorical nonprotection for obscenity into categorical nonprotection for violent images. He grounds his analysis in the same idea that animates *Stevens:* tradition. Justice Scalia long advocated using tradition to shape constitutional rights, including First Amendment freedoms.[36] The constitutional difference between sex and violence, he explains in *Entertainment Merchants,* is that our society has traditionally punished sexually explicit images while giving violent images a pass. Bans on violent content would have to be "part of a long (if heretofore unrecognized) tradition of proscription"[37] to justify the California legislature in restricting violent images simply because they're violent. Justice Scalia dips into the well of tradition a second time to reject California's narrower argument that, even if the First Amendment protects violent images for adults, it shouldn't protect them for children. Noting the body counts of *Grimm's Fairy Tales* and high school reading lists, Justice Scalia finds no "longstanding tradition in this country of specially restricting children's access to depictions of violence."[38]

Justice Scalia emphasizes that children have First Amendment rights. He sets California's law alongside government crusades to "protect" children from "penny dreadfuls" in the 1880s, movies in the early twentieth century, comic books in the 1950s, and song lyrics more recently.[39] All of those efforts, he argues, improperly sought to deny children's right of access to information. Justice Thomas, Justice Scalia's most common ally on the Court, contributes a lengthy, solo dissenting opinion to argue that the generation of people who ratified the Bill of Rights never contemplated extending First Amendment

34. *Entertainment Merchants,* 564 U.S. at 857 (Breyer, J., dissenting).

35. *See id.* at 790.

36. *See* Barnes v. Glen Theatre, Inc., 501 U.S. 560, 573–74 (1991) (Scalia, J., concurring in the judgment) (arguing based on tradition that a ban on nude dancing did not implicate the First Amendment); Michael H. v. Gerald D., 491 U.S. 110, 122–27 (1989) (plurality opinion of Scalia, J.) (using a tradition-based analysis to reject a biological father's substantive due process claim for parental rights).

37. *Entertainment Merchants,* 564 U.S. at 792.

38. *Id.* at 795.

39. *See id.* at 797–98.

rights to children.[40] Here Justice Thomas invokes a tradition of parental control over children to counter Justice Scalia's argument that no tradition supports protecting children from violent images. The clash in *Entertainment Merchants* between these two staunch traditionalist justices suggests that tradition may not provide as secure a grounding for categorical First Amendment analysis as Chief Justice Roberts suggested in *Stevens*.

Lacking a categorical ground for its law, California faced a First Amendment balancing analysis. First Amendment balancing (the focus of Chapter 2) requires the government to show that its ends justify its means. The strength of the required showing varies with the nature of the speech restriction. In *Entertainment Merchants,* California restricted video games based on their content. The cornerstone of First Amendment doctrine is the rule that, in most circumstances, the government may not regulate the content of speech unless it can satisfy a highly stringent balancing test: *strict scrutiny.* That test requires the government to show that its speech restriction is "narrowly tailored" to advance a "compelling interest." Justice Scalia finds the video game law "underinclusive" as to the state's interest in stopping the spread of violence. The law restricted only video games, not other violent entertainment, and it didn't stop adult relatives from giving the games to children.[41] He finds the law "overinclusive" as to the state's interest in helping parents control children, because it stopped children from buying or renting violent games even where their parents didn't mind.[42] Even if the government's interests were compelling (which Justice Scalia doesn't decide but appears to presume), a law can't be "narrowly tailored" if it hits so wide of the mark.

Justice Scalia refuses to let violent video games' vivid, interactive imagery justify their suppression. "[A]ll literature is interactive," he declares; the more interactive, the better. To Justice Scalia, censoring video games because of their immersive qualities amounts to punishing a message for its content and effectiveness, exactly the sort of attack on ideas the First Amendment is supposed to prevent.[43]

This is where Justice Scalia loses Justice Alito (joined by Chief Justice Roberts, the author of *Stevens*). Justice Alito agrees that California's law must go, but not for the majority's reasons. Instead, his separate opinion finds the law's definition of "violent video game" unconstitutionally vague.[44] In First Amendment law, *vagueness* dooms a speech-restrictive law. Vague language has a *chilling effect* on protected speech by failing to give notice about which speakers the First Amendment protects, causing cautious speakers who

40. *See id.* at 821 (Thomas, J., dissenting).
41. *See id.* at 801–02.
42. *See id.* at 804.
43. *Id.* at 798.
44. *See id.* at 805–09 (Alito, J., concurring in the judgment).

fall close to the line to self-censor.[45] Justice Alito endorses Justice Scalia's tradition-based distinction between sexual and violent images, asserting that our society's long history of suppressing obscenity "helped to shape certain generally accepted norms concerning expression related to sex," an experience he says did not extend to violent expression.[46] Justice Alito strongly objects, however, to Justice Scalia's sanguine attitude toward video games' immersive technology. Echoing the moral outrage of his *Stevens* dissent, Justice Alito decries some games' "astounding" level of violence, which leave virtual victims "dismembered, decapitated, disemboweled, set on fire, and chopped into little pieces . . . cry[ing] out in agony and beg[ging] for mercy."[47] He views these violent images' technological sophistication as, literally and legally, a game changer.[48]

*Stevens* and *Entertainment Merchants* make serious contributions to constitutional speech protection. The Court in these two cases rejects aggressive efforts by the federal government and the largest state government to expand categorical limits on the First Amendment's scope. Anyone skeptical of the "slight social value" justification the Court gave for categorical exclusions in *Chaplinsky v. New Hampshire* will applaud the Court's refusal to ride that justification further. Anyone disturbed by wholesale exposure of certain kinds of speech to the government's punitive whims will cheer the Court's decision not to write violent images out of the First Amendment. The Roberts Court, in *Stevens* and *Entertainment Merchants,* sharply distinguishes violent conduct, which the government may regulate, from speech that describes or advocates violence, which it may not. However, we'll shortly encounter two other Roberts Court decisions, *Holder v. Humanitarian Law Project* (Chapter 2) and *Morse v. Frederick* (Chapter 3) that undermine First Amendment protection for advocacy of unlawful conduct.

Beyond securing the First Amendment against categorical erosion, *Stevens* and *Entertainment Merchants* express a broad view of the First Amendment's purpose. In Part III we'll see the Roberts Court emphasize the special importance of political speech for our democratic political system. The centrality of political speech in First Amendment law, however, need not diminish protection for other kinds of speech, even speech as arguably frivolous as hunting videos and violent video games. Justice Scalia may state the point too dramatically when he declares in *Entertainment Merchants* that "it is difficult to

45. *See, e.g.*, Baggett v. Bullitt, 377 U.S. 360 (1964) (striking down a loyalty oath for teachers as unconstitutionally vague).

46. *Entertainment Merchants,* 564 U.S. at 812 (Alito, J., concurring in the judgment).

47. *Id.* at 815 (Alito, J., concurring in the judgment).

48. *See id.* at 814–15 (Alito, J., concurring in the judgment). Justice Breyer shared many of Justice Alito's concerns about the majority's analysis, but he saw no vagueness in the California law, leading him to dissent rather than concur in the judgment. *See id.* at 840 (Breyer, J., dissenting).

distinguish politics from entertainment, and dangerous to try,"[49] but his rejection of that distinction as a legal wedge vindicates a broad view of the First Amendment. Even Alexander Meiklejohn, our most eloquent advocate for the special importance of political speech, acknowledged that we need art, literature, and other non-political inputs to make democracy work.[50]

*Entertainment Merchants* also validates children's First Amendment rights. Among the most important free speech cases of the past 40 years is the Rehnquist Court's 1995 decision in *Reno v. American Civil Liberties Union*,[51] which rebuffed Congress' sweeping attempt to purge "indecency" from the Internet. *Reno* strongly affirmed children's expressive freedom.[52] We'll see the Roberts Court take a narrow view of children's free speech rights at school in Chapter 3's discussion of *Morse v. Frederick*, but *Entertainment Merchants* follows the lead of *Reno*.[53] *Entertainment Merchants* also tracks *Reno* by resisting California's plea, and the urging of Justice Alito and Chief Justice Roberts, to suppress new communications technology. The power of interactive software, Justice Scalia forcefully argues, should intrigue rather than frighten us. In this respect, *Entertainment Merchants* offers the Roberts Court's most expansive thinking about how speech can create meaning and enable change.

## THE GIVING HAND WAVERS: LIMITS OF THE SPEECH-PROTECTIVE CATEGORICAL DECISIONS

On closer examination, however, the First Amendment victories in *Stevens* and *Entertainment Merchants* have questionable significance. As statements about the viability of categorical exclusions, these decisions simply preserve a secure status quo. The Court hasn't found a new category of speech to exclude from First Amendment protection since at least the *Ferber* child pornography

49. *Id.* at 790.

50. *See* ALEXANDER MEIKLEJOHN, POLITICAL FREEDOM: THE CONSTITUTIONAL POWERS OF THE PEOPLE 117 (1960).

51. 521 U.S. 844 (1997).

52. *See id.* at 865–66 (distinguishing Ginsberg v. New York, 390 U.S. 629 (1968)).

53. David Post, on the other hand, argues that *Entertainment Merchants* sets speech protection back by "resurrect[ing] a version of *Ginsberg* . . . that shields some speech from First Amendment scrutiny altogether." David G. Post, *Sex, Lies, and Videogames:* Brown v. Entertainment Merchants Association, 2010–2011 CATO SUP. CT. REV. 27, 56. I think Professor Post slightly overstates both how far the *Ginsberg* "harmful to minors" doctrine had fallen before *Entertainment Merchants* and how seriously *Entertainment Merchants* takes the doctrine. Justice Scalia indulges the notion that the *Ginsberg* "harmful to minors" rule shields some speech restrictions from First Amendment scrutiny, but he then shrugs off the rule's relevance. For a normative criticism of the Court's concern for children's First Amendment rights in *Entertainment Merchants*, see Vikram D. Amar & Alan Brownstein, *The Voracious First Amendment:* Alvarez *and* Knox *in the Context of 2012 and Beyond*, 46 LOY. L.A. L. REV. 491, 533–34 (2013).

case in 1982. The Court strongly undercut the categorical exclusions of fighting words and incitement more than four decades ago. Even in the more robust categorical fields of obscenity and defamation, the Court for the past several decades has only tinkered around the edges of the law. The federal and California governments in *Stevens* and *Entertainment Merchants* forced the categorical issue as to depictions of violence, and many people would endorse their core argument that First Amendment law should let legislatures treat depictions of violence as harshly as depictions of sex. No legal or political trend, however, ever suggested the Court would scrape the rust off its categorical scissors to cut violent depictions out of the First Amendment's protection.

The precise holdings in *Stevens* and *Entertainment Merchants* confirm the decisions' limited impact. The "crush videos" that Congress wanted to suppress in *Stevens* represent, to put the point mildly, a niche market, and the Court conspicuously allowed that a narrower ban on those videos might permissibly kill that market. *Entertainment Merchants* has broader effect, because a lot of people play violent video games, while a lot of other people would love to ban them. Money talks, however, and the financial power of the video game industry diminishes the importance of *Entertainment Merchants* for the kinds of unpopular speakers the government most commonly regulates. Both *Stevens* and *Entertainment Merchants* protect commercial products, with neither the Court nor the speakers themselves as interested as consumers (or critics) in what ideas the products convey. As we delve deeper into the Roberts Court's free speech jurisprudence, we'll frequently see the Court treat speech as an economic commodity and favor the First Amendment interests of wealthier and more powerful speakers.

The Roberts Court's distinctive tradition-bound approach to categorical First Amendment analysis exerts a particular drag on the speech-protective force of *Stevens* and *Entertainment Merchants*. As a practical matter, tradition presents a problem of institutional competence. An authoritative account of tradition requires a thorough, nuanced historical analysis, and judges generally aren't historians. Whereas a historian studies questions about the past in order to understand the past, a judge must decide present disputes. The competing opinions in *Entertainment Merchants* illustrate how that job can cloud historical inquiry. Some judicial history is incomplete: Justice Scalia's assertion that "efforts to convince Congress to restrict comic books [in the 1950s] failed"[54] ignores the fact that those efforts succeeded in gutting comic books' content by forcing the industry to embrace severe self-censorship.[55] Other judicial history reflects the judge's preferred result: Justice Alito's claim that state obscenity bans led to conservative sexual norms, which in turn

54. *Entertainment Merchants*, 564 U.S. at 797.

55. *See generally* DAVID HAJDU, THE TEN-CENT PLAGUE: THE GREAT COMIC BOOK SCARE AND HOW IT CHANGED AMERICA (2008).

justified the Court's exclusion of obscenity from the First Amendment, bootstraps a controversial legal doctrine onto a subjective account of social practice. Moreover, the disagreement between Justice Scalia and Justice Thomas about which tradition should decide the case—permitting violent imagery or denying First Amendment protection to children—suggests that judicial history lacks a firm disciplinary foundation.

At a theoretical level, tradition seems an inapt basis for measuring a First Amendment right. Constitutional rights prevent the political majority from imposing on minorities certain burdens that we as a society deem wrong as a matter of foundational law. They're supposed to secure our deepest principles against our political whims, like Odysseus's binding himself to the mast to resist the sirens' song. If the Supreme Court defines constitutional rights as protecting only what the political majority traditionally hasn't chosen or bothered to restrict, then constitutional rights secure nothing; Odysseus just wanders around the deck. Even if we believed that historical questions had clear answers and that the Court could always find those answers and properly render them as law, reliance on tradition to validate categorical speech exclusions would freeze speech restrictions in place wherever they had traditionally prevailed.

Consider the persistence of the obscenity doctrine. The exclusion of "obscenity" from First Amendment protection has always fit uncomfortably with First Amendment law. Obscenity—extremely explicit sexual imagery—doesn't cause immediate violence as do incitement and fighting words. It doesn't make people fear for their lives or their safety as do true threats. It doesn't destroy reputations as does libel. Whatever flaws the justifications for those other categorical First Amendment exclusions may bear, each at least requires a linkage between speech and some tangible harm.[56] Obscenity, in contrast, requires only that speech be "patently offensive" according to "contemporary community standards."[57] Obscenity doctrine thus lets the government punish whatever speech concerns sex and offends people. We might reasonably expect a fresh judicial offensive against categorical First Amendment exclusions to target a doctrine that lets the government punish speech based on (arguably outmoded) norms of sexual morality. Indeed, a landmark Rehnquist Court decision questions whether the government may even regulate *conduct* for purely moral reasons.[58] The Roberts Court, however,

56. Whether harm should ever justify restricting speech is a difficult question. For the leading argument against permitting harm-grounded speech restrictions, see C. Edwin Baker, *Harm, Liberty, and Free Speech*, 70 S. CAL. L. REV. 979 (1997).

57. Miller v. California, 413 U.S. 15, 24 (1973).

58. *See* Lawrence v. Texas, 539 U.S. 558, 577 (2003) (stating, in the course of striking down legal bans on gay sex, that "the fact that the governing majority in a State has traditionally viewed a particular practice as immoral is not a sufficient reason for upholding a law prohibiting the practice.") (internal quotation marks and citation omitted).

has buttressed the obscenity exclusion. Both *Stevens* and *Entertainment Merchants* favorably contrast the obscenity doctrine with government arguments for excluding depictions of violence. The *Stevens* Court's suggestion that a narrower ban on crush videos might pass First Amendment review also nods toward obscenity, given that crush videos exist to feed a sexual fetish. The Roberts Court's fixation on tradition explains its enthusiasm for the obscenity doctrine. How can we tolerate categorical nonprotection of extreme sexually explicit speech, even as we soundly reject categorical nonprotection of extreme violent speech? Because, in this Court's account, we've traditionally been tough on sex and soft on violence.[59]

The *Stevens* Court's tradition-bound approach to categorical First Amendment analysis stands out for its novelty in an area of First Amendment law that hadn't seen any major conceptual innovation for decades. Chief Justice Roberts claims, as the Court often does when it changes the law, that he's simply describing what the Court has been doing all along. Does that claim hold water? Most of the Court's other major categorical speech decisions—*Chaplinsky, the Brandenburg incitement case, the Virginia Pharmacy commercial speech case, Ferber*—say little or nothing about tradition. Instead, they focus on substantive justifications for excluding certain speech from First Amendment protection. Those decisions more closely track the government's "categorical balancing" argument in *Stevens* than the Court's tradition-bound analysis. *Sullivan* and *Miller* fit better into the chief justice's tradition story, because they accommodate long-standing common law provisions that let the state punish defamation and obscenity. Even those decisions, however, mainly give substantive reasons for the speech exclusions they endorse. *Sullivan,* for instance, didn't just declare that the Anglo-American legal tradition allowed recovery for defamation. Rather, the Court worked through why and how far the First Amendment should limit that allowance.[60] Descriptively, then, the tradition-based approach to categorical First Amendment exclusions appears less established than the chief justice makes it out to be.[61] Strategically, however, that approach enhances the justices' flexibility either to disapprove or—as we'll next observe—approve categorical exclusions.

59. The validity of that account varies, depending on how deeply into the history of Western civilization we dig. *See* Geoffrey R. Stone, *Origins of Obscenity*, 31 N.Y.U. REV. L. & SOC. CHANGE 711 (2007).

60. *See* N.Y. Times Co. v. Sullivan, 376 U.S. 254, 268–80 (1964) (conducting an extensive substantive analysis to arrive at the "actual malice" standard).

61. For an extended critique of the historical basis for the Roberts Court's reliance on tradition to justify categorical exclusions, see Genevieve Lakier, *The Invention of Low-Value Speech*, 128 HARV. L. REV. 2166, 2212–18 (2015).

## THE OTHER HAND TAKES: USING TRADITION TO JUSTIFY CATEGORICAL LIMITS ON SPEECH PROTECTION

More troubling from a First Amendment perspective than the limited speech-protective value of *Stevens* and *Entertainment Merchants* is the tradition-based methodology's capacity to restrict speech. These decisions justify their refusals to exclude violent images categorically from First Amendment protection by claiming that only tradition can support a categorical exclusion. Tradition may anchor free speech law more predictably than the balancing approach the government advocated in *Stevens*. However, tradition carries hazards for expressive freedom. Most obviously, the notion that some speech categories might "have been historically unprotected, but have not yet been specifically identified or discussed as such in our case law"[62] seems ripe for manipulation. Clever judges can manipulate any legal doctrine, but manipulation works better when it's covert. Appealing to "tradition" as received truth obscures the fact that reasonable people disagree both about what traditions exist and about how, and how much, tradition should matter in legal decisions. Categorical speech exclusions, like First Amendment law in general, ultimately depend on substantive values. The most transparent way for the Court to decide categorical exclusion cases would be to talk openly about which values matter and why. By rejecting that substantive analysis in favor of the tradition inquiry, the Roberts Court hides the analytic ball.

In three disparate cases, the Roberts Court has upheld and enhanced important categorical exclusions or limitations on the First Amendment's scope. All three decisions justify their denials of First Amendment protection by asserting that the speech at issue has traditionally been subject to regulation. These cases expose the speech-restrictive underbelly of *Stevens* and *Entertainment Merchants*.

The most consequential of the Roberts Court's speech-restrictive categorical decisions, ***Golan v. Holder* (2012)**,[63] upholds against First Amendment challenge a federal statute that writes an international copyright agreement into U.S. law.[64] The agreement restores copyright protection to certain foreign works that had passed into the public domain, meaning that their copyrights had expired and anyone could use or publish them. Artists and publishers who had been freely using the works challenged the statute, claiming that its new

62. *Stevens*, 559 U.S. at 472.

63. 132 S. Ct. 873 (2012). Ginsburg (majority) (with Roberts, Scalia, Kennedy, Thomas, Sotomayor); Breyer (dissenting) (with Alito).

64. *See* 17 U.S.C. § 104A (1994); Berne Convention for the Protection of Literary and Artistic Works (Sept. 9, 1886), as revised at Stockholm (July 14, 1967), 828 U.N.T.S. 222.

constraint on their uses violated the First Amendment.[65] Justice Ginsburg's majority opinion closely follows the reasoning of another opinion she wrote a decade earlier for the Rehnquist Court, *Eldred v. Ashcroft*.[66] *Eldred,* which rejected a First Amendment challenge to a law that extended the durations of existing copyrights, held that the First Amendment generally doesn't apply to copyright disputes. *Golan* reiterates and intensifies the *Eldred* holding. Justice Ginsburg completely rejects the idea that copyright raises any First Amendment problem. She reasons that two long-standing rules of copyright law suffice to answer any free speech concerns. The first rule says authors may not copyright "ideas" but only "expressions." The second rule says making "fair use" of a protected work, for purposes such as criticism, scholarship, and news reporting, does not violate copyright.[67]

*Golan,* like *Eldred* before it, shrugs off what may be one of the most important free speech concerns for our information-driven society. The Internet's rapid growth has multiplied the amount of information that people can access. Increased access encourages people to use information in new and creative ways.[68] In music, for example, hip-hop producers sample old funk, rock, and soul records to create new sounds; bedroom deejays layer seemingly incongruous songs into ingenious mash-ups; and aspiring pop stars court attention by posting their basement recordings on YouTube. We may have good reasons to place some copyright limits on such practices. Even so, shouldn't the First Amendment, our defense against excessive speech restrictions, have something to say about whether and when copyright law applies too broadly and suppresses or chills too much speech?

*Golan* echoes *Eldred* in saying no. Justice Ginsburg embraces a particular, contested economic theory about copyright: Any amount of copyright protection, no matter how long it lasts, serves the uniquely valuable purpose of giving authors incentives to create. That theory raises serious questions. Even if we accept the premise that authors wouldn't create works absent copyright protection, time-limited protection may well suffice to make creation worthwhile, and the protection could incorporate some limits without destroying the incentive to create. On the other side of the conflict, Justice Ginsburg simply ignores the possibility that enabling derivative uses may add more to public discussion than it takes away. She characterizes the creative process as

65. The *Golan* challengers also argued that Congress lacked the power to enact the statute in the first place. The Court rejected that claim. *See Golan,* 132 S. Ct. at 884–89. Justice Breyer's dissent disputes the Court's congressional power holding in light of the First Amendment interests at stake, but he doesn't reach the distinct First Amendment issue. *See id.* at 907–08 (Breyer, J., dissenting).

66. 537 U.S. 186 (2003).

67. *See Golan,* 132 S. Ct. at 889–91.

68. *See* Jack M. Balkin, *Digital Speech and Democratic Culture: A Theory of Freedom of Expression for the Information Society*, 79 N.Y.U. L. REV. 1 (2004).

an arid economic realm where the market's authority maintains an economically desirable status quo. *Golan*, like *Entertainment Merchants* but much more pointedly, treats speech as an economic commodity.

*Golan* goes further in disregarding the First Amendment than *Eldred* did in one important way: its use of a story about tradition to limit speech protection. *Eldred* stated that "[w]hen . . . Congress has not altered the *traditional contours* of copyright protection, further First Amendment scrutiny is unnecessary."[69] That statement implies that the First Amendment bars Congress from changing the "traditional contours" to the extent they protect speech. The law upheld in *Eldred* extended the lengths of copyrights still in effect when the law was enacted. The law upheld in *Golan*, in contrast, revives copyright protection for works whose copyrights had expired. Reviving expired copyrights certainly looks like an important change in the traditional contours of copyright protection. The *Golan* Court, though, finds this distinction unimportant, treating passage of the affected works into the public domain as a legal aberration that "deprived [authors] of protection" during part of "the normal copyright term."[70] The mere persistence of other "traditional contours of copyright protection," namely the idea-expression dichotomy and the fair use doctrine, makes First Amendment review of copyright protections unnecessary.[71] The Court's reliance on tradition in *Stevens* and *Entertainment Merchants* led it to reaffirm First Amendment protection for depictions of violence. The *Golan* Court's reliance on tradition, in contrast, leads it to reaffirm First Amendment *nonprotection* for use of (re)copyrighted material. Rather than parsing copyright holders' and violators' speech interests, asking whether the idea-expression distinction and the fair use doctrine protect enough speech, or giving a substantive reason for letting Congress remove works from the public domain, *Golan* simply invokes tradition to give Congress a pass.[72]

69. *Eldred*, 537 U.S. at 221 (citations omitted; emphasis added).
70. *See Golan*, 132 S. Ct. at 893.
71. *Id.* at 890 (internal quotation marks and citation omitted).
72. Neil Netanel argues that the Court's balancing of interests in *Eldred* and *Golan* enables meaningful protection for speech interests. *See* Neil W. Netanel, *First Amendment Constraints on Copyright after* Golan v. Holder, 60 UCLA L. Rev. 1082 (2013). Netanel likens copyright to defamation, where the Court has similarly balanced interests and denied some speech First Amendment protection. *See id.* at 1088. He calls on the Court to make more rigorous use of existing doctrinal tools—the idea-expression distinction and the fair use doctrine—to protect speech interests in copyright disputes. *See id.* at 1095–113. A crucial difference between copyright and defamation, however, is that the Court has preserved a major role for the First Amendment in defamation cases. *See* N.Y. Times Co. v. Sullivan, 376 U.S. 254, 280 (1964) (imposing a First Amendment requirement that public officials prove "actual malice" to establish liability); Gertz v. Robert Welch, Inc., 418 U.S. 323, 347, 349 (1974) (discussing the First Amendment bar on strict liability and First Amendment limits on punitive damages). *Eldred* and especially *Golan* write the First Amendment out of the copyright script. The idea-expression distinction and the fair use doctrine, as Netanel acknowledges, aren't constitutional mandates but merely limits Congress has chosen to place on copyright.

*Golan* highlights two closely related conundrums in First Amendment law: the public-private distinction and the problem of conflicting speech interests. The Constitution grants rights only to private actors, and it generally imposes obligations to respect rights only on government actors. Accordingly, the structure of a constitutional rights dispute must pit a private rights holder against a public (government) violator. In reality, however, rights disputes don't always break down along those neat lines.[73] Copyright provides a prime example. Copyright disputes tend to involve conflicts between two different sorts of speech interests. The patents and copyrights clause of the Constitution lets Congress protect intellectual property "[t]o promote the Progress of Science and Useful Arts."[74] Copyright promotes authorship by ensuring authors' ability to profit from their works. The Court has held in other contexts that the government violates the First Amendment when it affirmatively interferes with an author's ability to profit from her work.[75] Thus, copyright laws protect a sort of interest that the First Amendment also protects. On the other hand, unauthorized uses of copyrighted materials always involve speech, and many of those uses have artistic, political, or educational value. Copyright violations may therefore fall squarely within the First Amendment's protective scope.

The presence of serious speech interests on both sides of a dispute would seem to require a nuanced analysis that compares and balances the competing interests. The public-private distinction, however, rejects the idea that both parties in a constitutional dispute can claim constitutionally protected interests. One or the other interest must submerge within the "public" category.[76] In a copyright dispute, the congressionally backed interests of copyright holders might appear the likelier candidate for relegation to "public" limbo. In practice, however, the Supreme Court's copyright decisions emphasize copyright holders' rights while denying First Amendment protection to alleged copyright violators. The public-private distinction lets the Court's tradition-bound categorical analysis in *Golan* secure the interests of copyright holders and nullify a potentially disruptive class of First Amendment claims.

73. I analyze this problem at length in Gregory P. Magarian, *The Jurisprudence of Colliding First Amendment Interests: From the Dead End of Neutrality to the Open Road of Participation Enhancing Review*, 83 NOTRE DAME L. REV. 185 (2007).

74. U.S. CONST. art. I, § 8, cl. 8.

75. *See* United States v. Nat'l Treas. Emps. Union, 513 U.S. 454 (1995) (striking down a sweeping ban on honoraria for federal employees); Simon & Schuster, Inc. v. Members of N.Y. State Crime Victims Bd., 502 U.S. 105 (1991) (striking down a law that garnished profits from criminals' published accounts of their crimes to compensate their victims).

76. *See* Magarian, *supra* note 73, at 190–210; Mark Tushnet, *Introduction: Reflections on the First Amendment and the Information Economy*, 127 HARV. L. REV. 2234, 2253–57 (2014).

***United States v. Williams* (2008),**[77] a case that predates *Stevens* and *Entertainment Merchants,* deals with the least politically controversial category of unprotected speech: child pornography. I've explained that the Court's exclusion of child pornography from First Amendment protection, announced decades ago in *New York v. Ferber,* focuses on the act of exploiting children to produce speech, not on an obscenity-style justification for punishing the speech itself. I've also argued that *Ferber* doesn't support the Roberts Court's claim in *Stevens* and *Entertainment Merchants* that tradition must, and does, explain all categorical First Amendment exclusions. *Williams,* although it doesn't talk explicitly about "tradition," leverages the child pornography exclusion's entrenchment to justify expanding the exclusion. The case also appears to define a new category of unprotected speech.

*Williams* follows up a speech-protective Rehnquist Court child pornography case called *Ashcroft v. Free Speech Coalition.*[78] That case struck down a law that criminalized the possession or sale of simulated child pornography (images created on a computer to look like actual children having sex) and of material that had been pandered as, but in fact was not, child pornography. Such materials, *Free Speech Coalition* straightforwardly explained, do not actually exploit children, and they therefore fall outside the *Ferber* justification for withholding First Amendment protection. Congress wanted to cast a wide criminal net, to catch as many people as possible who actually exploit children. The First Amendment, however, bars the government from criminalizing protected speech, no matter how distasteful, to get at unprotected speech.

*Williams* considered a new law through which Congress sought to regain some of what *Free Speech Coalition* took away. The new law, in essence, makes it a federal crime for me to offer you "child pornography" even when the material I have isn't really child pornography or even if I have no material in hand at all, as long as my offer "reflects the belief, or . . . is intended to cause [you] to believe," that the material really is child pornography.[79] How can the government punish the speech of someone who has no material the First Amendment lets the government restrict? The answer, according to *Williams,* is that the panderer in this scenario *offers* to provide material the First Amendment lets the government restrict. The fact that the person making the offer has no unprotected material makes no difference.

Justice Scalia's majority opinion spends a lot of time hashing out what the words of the statute mean. Justice Stevens, frequently Justice Scalia's adversary, adds a concurring opinion that thoroughly analyzes the legislative

77. 553 U.S. 285 (2008). Scalia (majority) (with Roberts, Stevens, Kennedy, Thomas, Breyer, Alito); Stevens (concurring) (with Breyer); Souter (dissenting) (with Ginsburg).
78. 535 U.S. 234 (2002).
79. *See* 18 U.S.C. § 2252A(a)(3)(B) (2012).

process that led to the statute.[80] These strange bedfellows want to prove that the new law punishes different conduct than the law struck down in *Free Speech Coalition*. Justice Souter doesn't buy it, arguing in dissent that *Williams* undermines *Free Speech Coalition* by letting Congress punish speech the earlier case protected.[81] All nine justices agree that the government properly may punish someone for offering to provide child pornography when the offeror, in fact, has nothing at all in hand. Justice Souter (joined by Justice Ginsburg) argues, out of respect for *Free Speech Coalition*, that the government shouldn't be able to punish someone for offering to provide child pornography when the offeror has something in hand that isn't child pornography. Justice Scalia, however, distinguishes the simulated child pornography of *Free Speech Coalition* from "the collateral speech that introduces such material into the child-pornography distribution network."[82]

Justice Scalia's opinion makes a second categorical claim that excludes another type of speech from First Amendment protection. "Offers to engage in illegal transactions," he declares, "are categorically excluded from First Amendment protection."[83] Justice Scalia frames that statement as a simple recitation of existing law. No prior decision, however, identified "offers to engage in illegal transactions" as an unprotected category of speech. Certainly the government frequently punishes criminal offers without First Amendment scruples. Frederick Schauer identifies criminal solicitation as a category of speech that courts simply haven't conceived of First Amendment law as covering.[84] Besides criminal solicitation, other such "uncovered" categories include violations of antitrust laws, securities regulations, and evidentiary rules.[85] A lack of First Amendment coverage works differently from a categorical exclusion. Categorical exclusions, as we've seen, require the Court to identify the excluded category precisely and to give legislatures firm guidance about which speech does and does not fit within the category. In contrast, legislatures decide whether and how to regulate uncovered speech based on ordinary

80. *See Williams*, 553 U.S. at 307 (Stevens, J., concurring).

81. *See id.* at 310 (Souter, J., dissenting).

82. *Id.* at 293. *Williams* also rejects an argument that the pandering law was unconstitutionally vague. *See id.* at 306.

83. *Id.* at 297. Justice Scalia actually mentions yet a third unprotected category, fraudulent commercial speech, in defending the pandering law's application to knowingly false offers to provide child pornography. *See id.* at 299.

84. *See* Frederick Schauer, *The Boundaries of the First Amendment: A Preliminary Exploration of Constitutional Salience*, 117 HARV. L. REV. 1765, 1770–71 (2004).

85. *See id.* at 1777–84. Professor Schauer describes copyright law, at least prior to the Rehnquist Court's decision in Eldred v. Ashcroft, 537 U.S. 186 (2003), as falling into the "uncovered" category as well. *See* Schauer, *supra* note 84, at 1783. He thinks *Stevens* and *Entertainment Merchants* may encourage new First Amendment challenges to legal restrictions on previously uncovered sorts of speech. *See* Frederick Schauer, *The Politics and Incentives of First Amendment Coverage*, 56 WM. & MARY L. REV. 1613, 1633–34 (2015).

policy criteria, with little if any judicial oversight. Noncoverage often occurs in policy areas where legislatures or administrative agencies have set up strong regulatory systems the public has accepted.[86] *Williams* appears to transform criminal solicitation from a noncovered type of speech into a new categorical exclusion.

That transformation could raise hard questions. May the government punish someone who offers to donate (or sell) her time to organize a political protest, such as a sit-in, that involves trespassing? What about *Brandenburg v. Ohio*? That case sharply limits the government's power to punish you if you urge me to break the law. According to *Brandenburg,* the First Amendment protects me unless and until I incite you to commit an imminent act that I know or expect you will commit, where your act will do great harm. Categorically excluding mere proposals of unlawful transactions seems to reopen a door *Brandenburg* closed. The Court has always let legislatures identify and punish most criminal proposals. Turning that passive noncoverage into an active categorical exclusion may force courts to draw difficult doctrinal lines that legislatures have greater competence to chart.

*Williams* stacks up unprotected speech categories to justify punishing speech that doesn't quite fit any of them. The speech at the heart of the case isn't obscenity. It isn't child pornography, although it refers to child pornography that doesn't really exist. The pandering of non-existent child pornography may be fraudulent, which makes a legally solid basis for prosecution. However, child pornography laws carry different consequences from fraud laws, and anyway some of the speech at issue in *Williams*—cases where a panderer incorrectly believes material is child pornography—isn't fraudulent. Pandering child pornography proposes an "illegal transaction," but the material the speakers propose to hand over isn't really illegal. *Williams* only makes sense on tradition's terms. Even though the decision doesn't talk explicitly about tradition, it shows us how a focus on established practices can weaken speech protection. If we have previously denied First Amendment protection to a category of speech (or three), says *Williams,* then that history can justify continuing to ban the speech, or even expanding the scope of the ban.

The final case in the Roberts Court's restrictive categorical trilogy once again uses a tradition-bound analysis, but it also transcends tradition in ways that anticipate the electoral speech cases discussed in Part III. ***Nevada Commission on Ethics v. Carrigan* (2011)**[87] unanimously upholds a Nevada law that bars a "public officer" from voting on, or advocating about, any matter as

86. *See* Schauer, *supra* note 84, at 1805–07.

87. 564 U.S. 117 (2011). Scalia (majority) (with Roberts, Kennedy, Thomas, Ginsburg, Breyer, Sotomayor, Kagan; with Alito (in part)); Kennedy (concurring); Alito (concurring in part and concurring in the judgment).

to which the official has a conflict of interest.[88] Michael Carrigan, a member of the city council of Sparks, Nevada, challenged the law. He argued that his legislative votes expressed his viewpoints and that the First Amendment should bar the government from forcing him to forgo this form of expression.

Justice Scalia once again writes for the Court. As a "preliminary detail," he brushes aside concerns about the Nevada law's restriction on advocacy. "[E]vidently," Justice Scalia surmises, that restriction meant "advocating [a matter's] passage or failure during the legislative debate." Assuming the restriction on voting passes muster, he explains, the restriction on advocacy by officials barred from voting serves to prevent legislative sessions from becoming "massive town-hall meetings."[89] This eminent judicial textualist[90] confidently presumes that "advocacy" refers only to legislative debates. That presumption looks dubious. The Nevada law applies to all "public officers," not just to legislators. Nonlegislative officers don't ordinarily "advocate" in legislative sessions. Thus, the meaning of "advocacy" in the Nevada law appears to encompass more than just legislative debates, and the law raises serious First Amendment problems that Justice Scalia ignores. Even if Justice Scalia's textual presumption is right, strong First Amendment and legislative process interests support letting legislators debate even about bills on which they can't vote. Conflicted legislators' arguments inform both the public and other legislators as surely as arguments by nonconflicted legislators do. As for Justice Scalia's "town-hall meeting" worry, he gives no reason to think a legislator's advocacy becomes more procedurally cumbersome when the legislator has a conflict than when no conflict appears.

Justice Scalia's *Carrigan* analysis mainly addresses the Nevada law's bar on legislative votes by conflicted legislators. First, in the manner of (though without citing) *Stevens*, Justice Scalia emphasizes that a long national tradition supports the constitutionality of recusal requirements for conflicts of interest. Extensively surveying federal and state legal history as to both judges and legislators, he finds not one case that strikes down an even-handed recusal rule.[91] Second, Justice Scalia argues that legislative votes aren't expressive and therefore aren't protected speech. A legislator's vote, he reasons, is not the legislator's expression at all. Rather, "a legislator's vote is the commitment of his apportioned share of the legislature's power to the passage or defeat of a particular proposal."[92] The legislator has no right to vote, and without a rights-bearing speaker, the First Amendment has nothing to protect. This reasoning

88. Nev. Rev. Stat. § 281A.420 (2013).
89. *Carrigan*, 564 U.S. at 121.
90. *See, e.g.*, Antonin Scalia & Bryan A. Garner, Reading Law: The Interpretation of Legal Texts 15–28 (2012).
91. *See Carrigan*, 564 U.S. at 122–25.
92. *Id.* at 125–26.

invokes the public-private distinction, as in *Golan,* to negate an expressive interest. Only Justice Alito's partial concurrence challenges Justice Scalia's argument that legislative votes aren't expressive. Legislative votes, Justice Alito points out, convey information; therefore, they must be protected speech. In the end, however, he agrees with the tradition-based argument for letting the recusal rule restrict speech.[93]

Few people would contest the *Carrigan* holding that the First Amendment doesn't bar recusal rules for public officials. The Court's reasoning, however, implicates this chapter's concerns about the use of categorical exclusions to justify speech restrictions. Like *Golan* and *Williams, Carrigan* invokes tradition to justify nonprotection of speech. Unlike those decisions, *Carrigan* moves beyond tradition to offer an alternative, substantive reason for the Court's holding: the argument that legislative votes aren't expressive. That argument, however, confirms the Roberts Court's readiness to justify categorical First Amendment exclusions. Justice Scalia likens *Carrigan* to two Rehnquist Court electoral speech cases that rejected First Amendment claims against a restriction on whom a political party could nominate for office[94] and a ban on write-in votes.[95] Taken together, those two decisions and *Carrigan* posit roughly "speech in the course of executing governmental or electoral functions" as a speech category unprotected by the First Amendment. That's a big idea, one that *Carrigan* doesn't thoroughly defend.[96] Beyond the problems discussed above with Justice Scalia's analysis of the Nevada law's advocacy ban, Justice Alito makes a strong case that legislative votes have expressive content. His argument may carry even greater force for party nominations and write-in ballots.

*Carrigan* plunges into contentious debates about how political representation should work. When Justice Scalia posits that only constituents, not legislators, have rights in legislators' votes, he implicitly endorses a particular theory of representative government, under which legislators act as agents for their constituents rather than exercising independent judgment.[97] Justice

93. *See id.* at 132 (Alito, J., concurring in part and concurring in the judgment).

94. *See* Timmons v. Twin Cities Area New Party, 520 U.S. 351 (1997), cited in *Carrigan,* 564 U.S. at 127.

95. *See* Burdick v. Takushi, 504 U.S. 428 (1992), cited in *Carrigan,* 564 U.S. at 127. The Roberts Court's decision in *Washington State Grange v. Washington State Republican Party* (discussed in Chapter 6) echoes the *Burdick* view that electoral ballots aren't expressive.

96. For one thing, that categorical exclusion seems to conflict with the Roberts Court's holding in *Doe v. Reed* (discussed in Chapter 6) that signing a petition for a ballot measure is protected speech. Justices Scalia and Alito clash in *Carrigan* over the depth of the conflict. *Compare Carrigan,* 564 U.S. at 128, *with id.* at 133–34 (Alito, J., concurring in part and concurring in the judgment).

97. *See* John Stuart Mill, Considerations on Representative Government 168–81 (1861) (discussing theories of representation). Deborah Hellman includes *Carrigan* among a group of Supreme Court decisions that she criticizes for

Kennedy endorses Justice Scalia's majority opinion but says he might think differently if *Carrigan* raised a different First Amendment concern: that conflict-of-interest recusal rules discourage the kinds of legitimate associations and relationships that might cause conflicts of interest.[98] The case, though, does present that concern. Carrigan argued that the recusal rule violated his First Amendment interests, and those interests include associations forgone or compromised due to the rule. Justice Kennedy's mistrust of legal barriers against political influence will fuel his pivotal opposition to campaign finance regulations (discussed in Chapters 7 and 8). The *Carrigan* Court's failure to engage Justice Kennedy's concern, or more generally to connect its reasoning to the related problems that arise in the campaign finance cases, almost certainly reflects strategic compromise, because the nearly unanimous *Carrigan* majority splits bitterly in campaign finance cases. That strategic choice, however, deters the *Carrigan* Court from fully thinking through its unstated political premises.

One further case provides, by its inaction, more evidence of the Roberts Court's continuing tolerance for categorical limits on the First Amendment. Almost 40 years ago, the Court in *Federal Communications Commission v. Pacifica Foundation*[99] green-lit the Federal Communications Commission (FCC) to regulate broadcast "indecency" in ways the First Amendment prohibits for other media. That broadcast indecency doctrine, a close cousin to the *Miller v. California* allowance for restrictions on obscenity, has drawn increasingly sharp criticism as electronic media have exploded in the new millennium.[100] ***Federal Communications Commission v. Fox Television Stations, Inc.* (2012)**[101] gave the Court a chance to reconsider the doctrine. *Fox* presented a challenge to a particular FCC policy that bans "fleeting expletives" on pain of potentially massive fines.[102] Writing for a nearly unanimous Court, Justice Kennedy dodges the central question whether the fleeting expletives policy, and by

preferring particular theories of democracy. *See* Deborah Hellman, *Defining Corruption and Constitutionalizing Democracy*, 111 MICH. L. REV. 1385, 1389–90 (2013).

98. *See Carrigan*, 564 U.S. at 129–30 (Kennedy, J., concurring).

99. *See* FCC v. Pacifica Found., 438 U.S. 726 (1978) (upholding FCC authority under 18 U.S.C. § 1464).

100. *See, e.g.*, LEE C. BOLLINGER, UNINHIBITED, ROBUST, AND WIDE-OPEN: A FREE PRESS FOR A NEW CENTURY 126–27 (2010).

101. 132 S. Ct. 2307 (2012) (Fox II). Kennedy (majority) (with Roberts, Scalia, Thomas, Breyer, Alito, Kagan); Ginsburg (concurring in the judgment). Justice Sotomayor recused herself from the case because she had served on a panel of the Second Circuit Court of Appeals that issued a decision in the case.

102. *See In re* Complaints against Various Broad. Licensees Regarding Their Airing of the "Golden Globe Awards" Program, 19 FCC Rcd. 4975, 4976 n.4 (2004). The Roberts Court in an earlier iteration of *Fox* held that the "fleeting expletive" policy satisfied statutory limits on the FCC's authority. *See* FCC v. Fox Television Stations, Inc., 556 U.S. 502 (2009) (Fox I) (finding the rule not "arbitrary" or "capricious" under the Administrative Procedure Act).

extension the FCC's broader regime of indecency regulation under *Pacifica,* violates broadcasters' expressive freedom. He simply holds that the FCC's enforcement of a new, tougher definition of "fleeting expletives," announced after the broadcasts at issue in *Fox,* gave broadcasters inadequate notice of what they could and couldn't air. That holding stems not directly from the First Amendment but from the due process clause of the Fifth Amendment. Justice Ginsburg, concurring in the judgment, urges the Court to find a future occasion for reconsidering *Pacifica.*[103]

## ONCE MORE INTO THE BREACH?

Our tour through the Roberts Court's categorical free speech jurisprudence concludes with the Court's most recent categorical decision. ***United States v. Alvarez* (2012)**[104] revives some of the speech-protective promise of *Stevens* and *Entertainment Merchants.* However, the case reinforces the concerns the speech-restrictive categorical decisions raise about the Roberts Court's tradition-based approach to categorical First Amendment exclusions.

*Alvarez* struck down a federal law called the Stolen Valor Act.[105] Congress passed the law to punish people who claim to have won military honors they never actually won. Some people, such as the defendant in this case, Xavier Alvarez, even lie about having received the Congressional Medal of Honor. These lies naturally offend real recipients of military honors and their comrades and relations. The Stolen Valor Act reveals the tip of a very interesting legal iceberg: Should the First Amendment protect outright lies? The value of lying for the pursuit of truth, democratic self-government, or individual fulfillment through speech is hard to pin down. "Lying," however, is an enormous category that sweeps in much and varied speech. At least some lies, such as telling a burn victim's family that their loved one died without pain, or leaking false information about troop movements to a hostile government, can serve good purposes. Thinking categorically about First Amendment protection for lies gets tricky, as the *Alvarez* opinions bear out.

The government wanted the Court in *Alvarez* to exclude lies, as far as possible, from the First Amendment, extending only enough protection to ensure that laws against lying don't chill truthful speech. The government pointed out that many federal and state laws punish various sorts of lies, including

103. *See Fox II*, 132 S. Ct. at 2321 (Ginsburg, J., concurring in the judgment). Justice Thomas in *Fox I* also urged reconsideration of *Pacifica. See Fox I.*, 556 U.S. at 530–35 (Thomas, J., concurring).

104. 132 S. Ct. 2537 (2012). Kennedy (plurality) (with Roberts, Ginsburg, Sotomayor); Breyer (concurring in the judgment) (with Kagan); Alito (dissenting) (with Scalia, Thomas).

105. *See* 18 U.S.C. § 704 (2006).

perjury, commercial fraud, and impersonating a government official. But Justice Kennedy, writing for the four-justice plurality, portrays each of those laws as targeting a "legally cognizable harm associated with a false statement." The Stolen Valor Act, in contrast, "targets falsity and nothing more."[106] Reiterating the holding of *Stevens* that tradition provides the proper lens for analyzing categorical speech exclusions,[107] Justice Kennedy concedes that "our law and tradition show . . . instances in which the falsity of speech bears upon whether it is protected."[108] He insists, however, that those instances don't support categorically excluding lies from First Amendment protection.[109] Perhaps realizing that no tradition forecloses categorical exclusion of lies either, he ends his categorical analysis with warnings about the dangers of "government authority to compile a list of subjects about which false statements are punishable."[110]

Justice Kennedy makes a sound substantive case that even lies can benefit public debate, noting that "the outrage and contempt" lies inspire "can serve to reawaken and reinforce the public's respect" for valuable ideas or institutions (here military medals and their recipients).[111] Then he delves deeper into free speech theory: "Society has the right and civic duty to engage in open, dynamic, rational discourse."[112] Even if we can't be sure public debate will put lies and other bad speech in their place, the First Amendment compels us to take a leap of faith. With the categorical argument out of the way, Justice Kennedy concludes by ruling that the government's serious interest in protecting the integrity of the military honors system doesn't justify restricting false honors claims. Applying strict First Amendment scrutiny, he finds no real evidence that lies about military honors undermine public perception of the honors system, and he urges counter-speech (in the form of an easily accessible registry of military honor recipients) as a better way of preventing whatever harm the lies might do.[113]

Justice Kennedy's opinion speaks for only four justices. The result in *Alvarez* depends on the additional votes of Justices Breyer and Kagan, who concur only in the Court's judgment, not endorsing any of Justice Kennedy's reasoning. "I do not," begins Justice Breyer's concurring opinion, "rest my conclusion upon a strict categorical analysis."[114] What Justice Breyer means, what his opinion

106. *Alvarez,* 132 S. Ct. at 2545 (plurality opinion).

107. *See id.* at 2544 (plurality opinion) (citing United States v. *Stevens,* 559 U.S. 460, 469 (2010)).

108. *Alvarez,* 132 S. Ct. at 2546 (plurality opinion).

109. In the wake of *Alvarez,* Congress enacted a revised Stolen Valor Act that requires an attempt to gain something of value through fraud. *See* Stolen Valor Act of 2013, Pub. L. 113-12, H.R. 258.

110. *Alvarez,* 132 S. Ct. 2547 (plurality opinion).

111. *Id.* at 2550 (plurality opinion).

112. *Id.* (plurality opinion).

113. *See id.* at 2549–51 (plurality opinion).

114. *Id.* at 2551 (Breyer, J., concurring in part and concurring in the judgment).

is all about, is that the Court should use a more flexible balancing analysis to decide whether the government's interest in protecting the integrity of military honors justifies the Stolen Valor Act.[115] Throughout this book we'll see Justice Breyer advocate a pragmatic balancing approach to First Amendment disputes. His ambivalence about the plurality's categorical analysis prevents *Alvarez* from authoritatively ruling out a categorical exclusion of lies. Justice Breyer proceeds to make a characteristically pragmatic argument about why the First Amendment should block at least the Stolen Valor Act's attempt to punish lies, based on his view that the law burdens speech to an extent disproportionate with the government's interest. He agrees with Justice Kennedy that counter-speech can adequately address the law's concerns.

Justice Alito, dissenting for himself and Justices Scalia and Thomas, would deny First Amendment protection to "false factual statements that inflict real harm and serve no legitimate interest."[116] That phrase stacks the rhetorical deck, and Justice Alito's supporting arguments play some questionable cards. He suggests that the government needs the Stolen Valor Act to prevent fraudulent claims for veterans' benefits,[117] although separate fraud laws take care of that. He justifies the Act as checking lies that "debase the distinctive honor of military awards,"[118] although a landmark Rehnquist Court decision on flag burning rejected a very similar sort of interest as illegitimate for punishing speech.[119] He justifies the Act as helping the military "to foster morale and esprit de corps,"[120] although the Court long ago disavowed an early First Amendment decision that validated a very similar interest as more important than free speech.[121] He insists that a registry of military award recipients won't protect the integrity of the honors system because the Defense Department has said it can't create a full registry,[122] which seems to imply that the "false statements of fact" he wants to let the government ban can't actually be proved false. He further objects to a counter-speech remedy because public discussion of false honor claims might "increase skepticism among

115. *See id.* at 2551–52 (Breyer, J., concurring in part and concurring in the judgment).
116. *Id.* at 2557 (Alito, J., dissenting).
117. *See id.* at 2558–59 (Alito, J., dissenting).
118. *Id.* at 2559 (Alito, J., dissenting).
119. *See* Texas v. Johnson, 491 U.S. 397, 410–21 (1989) (rejecting the American flag's function of symbolizing national unity as a justification for a legal ban on flag burning). Christina Wells assails the Stolen Valor Act for resembling the infamous punishment of seditious libel, which she explains sought "to preserve honor and status roles." Christina E. Wells, *Lies, Honor, and the Government's Good Name: Seditious Libel and the Stolen Valor Act*, 59 UCLA L. Rev. Discourse 136, 148 (2012). Vikram Amar and Alan Brownstein, on the other hand, criticize the result in *Alvarez* for paying insufficient regard to military honor. *See* Amar & Brownstein, *supra* note 53, at 519.
120. *See Alvarez,* 132 S. Ct. at 2559 (Alito, J., dissenting).
121. *See* Schenck v. United States, 249 U.S. 47 (1919) (upholding criminal convictions for distributing leaflets that urged conscripts not to join the military).
122. *Alvarez,* 132 S. Ct. at 2559 (Alito, J., dissenting).

members of the public about the entire awards system,"[123] an argument that seems to mistrust the public's capacity for reasoned debate.

Justice Alito centrally invokes tradition to defend the Stolen Valor Act. He posits "a long tradition of [congressional] efforts to protect our country's system of military honors"[124] as well as a long tradition of judicial holdings that lies have no value worth protecting under the First Amendment.[125] His story about tradition carries at least as much weight as the majority justices' contrary efforts to distinguish different kinds of lies by the supposedly different sorts of damage they do. Like Justice Thomas's dispute with Justice Scalia in *Entertainment Merchants* about children's rights, Justice Alito's dispute with Justice Breyer in *Alvarez* about protection for lies exposes the instability of the Roberts Court's tradition-based approach to categorical First Amendment analysis.

To some extent *Alvarez* resembles *Stevens* and *Entertainment Merchants*. Using a tradition-based analysis, *Alvarez* rejects the government's call to place a category of speech outside the scope of First Amendment protection. The category of lies is broader and more vulnerable to a greater variety of attacks than the category of violent depictions.[126] Letting the government punish lies would risk both mistakes in distinguishing false from true statements and abuses of regulatory power to target unpopular speakers.[127] Those considerations make *Alvarez* potentially far more important than *Stevens* or *Entertainment Merchants*, both of whose doctrinal significance I've questioned. The key word, though, is "potentially." Even though six justices in *Alvarez* signed onto arguments that support First Amendment protection for lies, the lack of a majority opinion makes *Alvarez* less valuable as a legal precedent than any of the other decisions discussed in this chapter. In addition, the opinions in *Alvarez* aren't models of analytic clarity.[128] The case stands as a muddled beginning to what will have to be a longer conversation. The dissenting justices' ability to tell a forceful story about why tradition should defeat the First Amendment claim also reinforces doubts about the reliability of the Roberts Court's tradition-bound categorical analysis for protecting speech.

123. *Id.* at 2560 (Alito, J., dissenting).

124. *Id.* at 2557 (Alito, J., dissenting).

125. *See id.* at 2560–62 (Alito, J., dissenting).

126. To take one recent, prominent example, Seana Shiffrin forcefully opposes First Amendment protection for lies because they undermine communication's morally essential function of enabling people to exchange sincerely held ideas and beliefs, which justifies constitutional speech protection. *See* SEANA VALENTINE SHIFFRIN, SPEECH MATTERS: ON LYING, MORALITY, AND THE LAW (2014).

127. *See* MARK TUSHNET, IN THE BALANCE: LAW AND POLITICS ON THE ROBERTS COURT 221 (2013).

128. *See* Amar & Brownstein, *supra* note 53, at 498–500; Rodney A. Smolla, *Categories, Tiers of Review, and the Roiling Sea of Free Speech Doctrine and Principle: A Methodological Critique of* United States v. Alvarez, 76 ALB. L. REV. 499 (2013).

## CONCLUSION

The Roberts Court's recasting of categorical First Amendment doctrine in the mold of tradition exemplifies the commitment to social and political stability that animates managed speech. *Stevens, Entertainment Merchants,* and *Alvarez* all uphold important speech protections, and they contain some of the Supreme Court's most direct, vigorous rhetoric in recent memory about the value of expressive freedom. However, the Court's other, less heralded categorical speech decisions—*Golan, Williams,* and *Carrigan*—show a speech-restrictive Janus face. The Court's tradition-bound analysis forecloses the creation of new categorical exclusions in *Stevens* and *Entertainment Merchants;* it justifies actual or constructive categorical exclusions in *Williams, Golan,* and *Carrigan;* it yields a split decision in *Alvarez.* Privileging tradition subjects present First Amendment disputes to what a majority of the justices takes as the settled wisdom of history. Tradition represents core conservative values: reverence for the past, enthusiasm for legal restrictions on certain types of socially undesirable behavior, and an overarching preference for stability.

The Roberts Court's categorical speech decisions show how the Court empowers responsible, stable institutions to manage public debate. In this chapter's speech-protective cases, the Court itself maintains managerial control over public discussion by working the levers of tradition to block categorical speech exclusions. In the speech-restrictive decisions, the Court employs categorical exclusions to grant the government managerial control. *Golan* reaffirms and deepens the Court's treatment of copyright as a zone of government management unconstrained by First Amendment concerns. *Williams* similarly, though more narrowly, lets the government define the working contours of unprotected child pornography. In subsequent chapters we'll see the Court empower a range of both government and private authorities to exercise managerial control over public debate.

The categorical speech decisions show the outlines of the Roberts Court's strong tendency to subordinate the expressive interests of dissenters and potentially disruptive speakers to the interests of wealthier, more powerful, more responsible speakers and institutions. Past Supreme Courts, in their most radically speech-protective decisions, invoked the First Amendment to protect the rights of disruptive speakers, from anarchists to Jehovah's Witnesses to civil rights agitators. Those decisions left public discussion up for grabs, with no guarantee that the discussion would lead to a stable or comfortable resolution. In contrast, the Roberts Court's tradition-bound approach to First Amendment categories promotes a safer, more controlled version of expressive freedom. Speakers with financial and political stakes in social stability get substantial expressive autonomy, whereas potentially disruptive speakers rarely enter the First Amendment picture. Most of this chapter's First Amendment winners sell speech for substantial profit: the dealers of videos and video games in *Stevens* and *Entertainment*

*Merchants* and the copyright holders in *Golan*—though not, conspicuously, the false claimant of military honors in *Alvarez*. Lies, the class of speech at issue in *Alvarez*, axiomatically undermine social order. *Alvarez* thus pushes against the stabilizing tendency of the other categorical speech decisions. However, the lack of a majority opinion in *Alvarez* denies the decision any mandate.

Throughout this book I will contrast the Roberts Court's managed speech jurisprudence with my preferred model of constitutional speech protection: dynamic diversity. Dynamic diversity seeks to maximize both the range of ideas and the breadth of participation in public debate. A reorientation of the Court's First Amendment jurisprudence from managed speech to dynamic diversity wouldn't alter the results in most of the categorical exclusion cases. The major exception is *Golan*. Where the Roberts Court denied First Amendment protection to people who wanted to keep using material in the public domain and favored the once and future owners of intellectual property, dynamic diversity would reverse the polarities. Under dynamic diversity, the Supreme Court should use the First Amendment to balance authors' incentives for creation against new users' opportunities to recombine cultural material. Both of those interests matter for ensuring substantively rich, broadly participatory cultural conversations. In *Golan*, the new users sought a very limited advantage, and dynamic diversity would have struck the balance in their favor. Dynamic diversity would also reverse the result in *Williams* in order to avoid strengthening categorical exclusions.

As to the other categorical exclusion cases, dynamic diversity would mainly diverge from managed speech at the level of methodology. The foremost justification for constitutional speech protection under dynamic diversity is that free speech has unique power to spur social and political change. Grounding First Amendment law in tradition—in settled, established order—is at best irrelevant and at worst antithetical to that power. Dynamic diversity would take a functional, substantive approach to categorical First Amendment questions, asking whether excluding a given category of speech from First Amendment protection would promote a diversity of ideas and participants in public debate. In some fields, notably defamation and copyright, dynamic diversity would countenance limited, qualify categorical exclusions to accommodate competing expressive interests. Usually, however, excluding whole categories of speech from First Amendment protection serves only to cramp public debate. Dynamic diversity would therefore converge with the Roberts Court's results in *Stevens* and *Entertainment Merchants*.

The next chapter continues to examine the Roberts Court's decisions about regulations of private speech. We'll move from a primary emphasis on First Amendment categories to the Court's more common practice of balancing speech interests against the government's reasons for restricting speech. The balancing decisions, like the categorical decisions, yield mixed results for expressive freedom and reflect the Roberts Court's managed speech approach to the First Amendment.

# CHAPTER 2

# Fair and Balanced

## *Regulations of Political Dissent and Commercial Profit*

Judicial balancing of speech interests against government regulatory goals has dominated First Amendment law since the 1970s. Courts presume that speech, other than the sorts of categorical exclusions discussed in Chapter 1, gets First Amendment protection. That protection, however, yields if the government can present strong enough reasons for regulating speech.[1] First Amendment balancing entails a basic set of questions: Is the government restricting someone's protected speech? If so, does it have a good enough reason to justify the restriction? Even if it does, is it still respecting speech rights as much as possible? We've already seen the Roberts Court in last chapter's *Stevens, Entertainment Merchants,* and *Alvarez* decisions balance speech against regulation after rejecting the government's categorical arguments for excluding speech from First Amendment protection.

A rigorous version of First Amendment balancing, *strict scrutiny,* applies in most cases where government restricts private speech (speech that does not involve any of the forms of government support discussed in Part II). Under strict scrutiny, if the government is restricting speech because of the speech's content or the speaker's viewpoint, the government can defeat a First

1. The phenomenon of "uncovered" speech, discussed last chapter in connection with the *Williams* decision, marks a blind spot in the presumption of speech protection. For a rich discussion of the relationship between the categorical and balancing aspects of First Amendment law, see Joseph Blocher, *Categoricalism and Balancing in First and Second Amendment Analysis*, 84 N.Y.U. L. Rev. 375 (2009).

Amendment claim only if it can show both that (1) it has a "compelling interest," a reason of the very highest importance, for the speech restriction; and also that (2) the speech restriction is "narrowly tailored" or "the least restrictive means" of pursuing its compelling interest. When strict scrutiny applies, the government almost always loses. I've said that strict scrutiny applies in "most" cases where the government regulates the content or viewpoint of private speech and that the government "almost always" loses under strict scrutiny. This chapter shows important exceptions to both of those norms. We'll see the Court, in a case about the special First Amendment niche of commercial speech, review a content-based speech regulation under a milder standard than strict scrutiny. Much more remarkably, we'll also see the government, in a case that pits free speech against national security, win under strict scrutiny.

Two of the major cases discussed in this chapter, *Snyder v. Phelps* and *Holder v. Humanitarian Law Project,* deal with government restrictions on political dissent. Almost a century ago, Justice Brandeis portrayed "the discovery and spread of political truth" as the paradigm of public debate, which he called "a political duty."[2] A major strand of First Amendment theory, tied most strongly to Alexander Meiklejohn, holds that the main point of constitutional speech protection in a democratic system is to help us govern ourselves.[3] "We the people" need to hear as many different political ideas as possible if democracy is going to work. Political dissent is distinctively vulnerable to government restriction. The government and powerful private interests cling to the status quo because they make the status quo. Political dissent, by its nature, challenges the status quo, often very aggressively. Political dissenters take food off the power structure's table. Political dissent stands at the center of my dynamic diversity model of constitutional speech protection.

The Roberts Court has let the government suppress dissent with a real capacity to destabilize the status quo. This chapter traces a similar narrative arc to that of Chapter 1. It begins, as Chapter 1 did, with one of the Roberts Court's speech-protective high points, the *Snyder* decision. As in Chapter 1, however, close examination diminishes the high point, which gives way to a more important speech-restrictive low point, *Humanitarian Law Project.* Then we'll see a renewed emphasis on speech protection in *Sorrell v. IMS Health, Inc.* That decision, which rejects a state regulation of commercial data mining, commodifies speech just like the Chapter 1 copyright extension decision, *Golan v. Holder.* Finally, *Reed v. Town of Gilbert* reiterates First Amendment law's crucial bar against content-based speech regulations. The breadth of the decision's reasoning, however, makes its meaning and impact uncertain. The contrast between *Snyder* and *Humanitarian Law Project* suggests the Roberts

2. Whitney v. California, 274 U.S. 357, 375 (1927) (Brandeis, J., concurring).
3. *See* ALEXANDER MEIKLEJOHN, POLITICAL FREEDOM: THE CONSTITUTIONAL POWERS OF THE PEOPLE (1960).

Court only protects political dissent that doesn't pose a serious threat to social and political stability. The contrast between *Humanitarian Law Project* and *IMS Health* suggests the Roberts Court prioritizes speech for profit over political dissent. Those priorities fit the template of managed speech.

## DEFENDING THE SPEECH WE HATE

"I disapprove of what you say, but I will defend to the death your right to say it."[4] Those famous words might have been written especially for Fred Phelps and his Westboro Baptist Church. Phelps and the Westboro Baptists passionately hate LGBT people. They travel around the country to protest funerals of service members killed in action, promoting the theory that God kills U.S. soldiers and sailors because the United States doesn't sufficiently persecute gays and lesbians. In the events that gave rise to ***Snyder v. Phelps* (2011)**,[5] Phelps and five other church members traveled to Maryland to protest the funeral of Marine Lance Corporal Matthew Snyder, who was killed in action in Iraq. They carried signs with such messages as "Thank God for Dead Soldiers," "God Hates Fags," "God Hates You," "You're Going to Hell," and "Priests Rape Boys" (the Snyder family is Catholic). After the funeral, Snyder's father, Albert, sued the church members in state court under several tort theories, with "intentional infliction of emotional distress" the pivotal claim. Put simply, Albert Snyder claimed that the Phelps Church's actions at his son's funeral had caused him severe emotional harm. A jury awarded him almost $11 million in damages. On appeal, the Phelps Church argued that the state court violated the church's right to freedom of speech when it let the jury award Snyder damages based on the church's political protest activities.

The First Amendment doesn't always prevent people from recovering damages for injuries they suffer from speech. Most prominently, as I noted last chapter, our law has always allowed a private person to recover damages when someone defames the person's reputation. The Supreme Court's seminal 1964 decision in *New York Times Co. v. Sullivan*,[6] however, puts major First Amendment hurdles in the way of public officials who sue for defamation, based on "a profound national commitment to the principle that debate on public issues should be uninhibited, robust, and wide-open."[7] The Court later extended the *Sullivan* limits to defamation suits by certain "public figures,"

4. Evelyn Beatrice Hall, The Friends of Voltaire 199 (1906).
5. 562 U.S. 443 (2011). Roberts (majority) (with Scalia, Kennedy, Thomas, Ginsburg, Breyer, Sotomayor, Kagan); Breyer (concurring); Alito (dissenting).
6. 376 U.S. 254 (1964).
7. *Id.* at 270. *Sullivan* lets a public official win a defamation case only if he can show the defamatory speaker acted with "actual malice," meaning "with knowledge that it was false or with reckless disregard of whether it was false or not." *Id.* at 280.

non-officials who have achieved prominence or notoriety.[8] In a 1988 case, *Hustler Magazine, Inc. v. Falwell*,[9] the Court followed its defamation precedents in barring the Reverend Jerry Falwell, a public figure, from recovering tort damages for a *Hustler* magazine parody that claimed Falwell had sex with his mother. Falwell had sued *Hustler* for intentional infliction of emotional distress, the same legal claim pressed by Snyder. *Falwell* makes that sort of case very hard for public figures such as Falwell to win. Albert Snyder, though, isn't a public figure. He seemingly should be able to recover damages for his emotional distress without upsetting the First Amendment.

In *Snyder v. Phelps*, Chief Justice Roberts' majority opinion looks behind the holdings of *Sullivan* and *Falwell* to emphasize a deeper principle that defeats Snyder's claim. *Sullivan* puts First Amendment limits on defamation suits by public officials not just because of who those officials are but because of what the speech that defames them is about. If I proclaim that the president of the United States is a lying scoundrel, I'm attacking a man's reputation, but mainly I'm criticizing the president of the United States. Just about any criticism of the president, however implausible or personal, has to count as debate on a public issue, unless we want to risk stifling political dissent. The subject under discussion triggers the First Amendment concern. That's the dimension Chief Justice Roberts emphasizes in *Snyder*: "whether th[e] speech is of public or private concern, as determined by all the circumstances of the case."[10] This "public concern" analysis has long played an important role not just in defamation cases but in other areas of First Amendment law.[11] The chief justice concludes that the Phelps Church was protesting about matters of obvious public concern. Phelps Church members descended on Matthew Snyder's funeral not to berate his mourners personally, but to press the church's views about the political and social status of gays and lesbians, views that also implicate other matters of public concern such as war and patriotism. The jury's finding that the church members' speech was "outrageous" depended on a "highly malleable standard," and therefore could not properly trump the First Amendment's protection for speech on matters of public concern.[12]

Albert Snyder's status as a nonpublic figure doesn't change the chief justice's First Amendment analysis. In curbing public officials' and public figures'

8. *See* Curtis Pub. Co. v. Butts, 388 U.S. 130 (1967).

9. 485 U.S. 46 (1988).

10. *Snyder*, 562 U.S. at 451.

11. *See, e.g.*, Pickering v. Bd. of Educ., 391 U.S. 563 (1968) (public employee speech); Fla. Star v. B.J.F., 491 U.S. 524 (1989) (newspaper's publication of sexual assault victim's name).

12. *Snyder*, 562 U.S. at 458. Chief Justice Roberts also rejects Albert Snyder's distinct tort claim of "intrusion upon seclusion," invoking the First Amendment principle that people who find a public display offensive can cure their distress by averting their eyes. *See id.* at 459–60.

defamation suits, the Court has pointed out that public officials and public figures have greater opportunities than private citizens to defend their reputations through the media. The Court has also noted that public officials and (sometimes) public figures choose to place their reputations in the public's crosshairs.[13] The first of those justifications doesn't apply to emotional distress at all, and the second arguably shouldn't apply as strongly to emotional well-being as to reputation. Those differences between reputation and emotion may explain why the Court used *Snyder*, an emotional distress case, to emphasize the importance for speech injury cases of what the defendant is discussing, as distinct from whom the defendant is attacking. What matters at bottom in both defamation and emotional distress cases is whether the defendant is speaking about a matter of public or private concern. In defamation cases, the plaintiff's public or private status works well as a proxy for that underlying criterion. The emotional distress context, on the other hand, requires courts to look directly at what the speech is about.

The Court's result seems unfair to a nonpublic figure such as Albert Snyder. Why do his grief and pain matter less than robust debate about matters of public concern? He didn't set out to make a public statement; he only wanted to bury his son. That human cost prompted (as in last chapter's *Stevens* case) a forceful solo dissent from Justice Alito. He deplores the idea that such speakers as the Phelps Church "may intentionally inflict severe emotional injury on private persons at a time of intense emotional sensitivity by launching vicious verbal attacks that make no contribution to public debate."[14] Justice Alito spotlights serious concerns that free speech advocates sometimes soft pedal. Speech can, and does, injure people. Ignoring those injuries is unfair to those people, who might include you or me as surely as censored speakers might include you or me.

Chief Justice Roberts's reasoning, though, doesn't ignore the harm the Phelps Church did to Albert Snyder. Instead, the chief justice says that harm "turned on the content and viewpoint of the message conveyed."[15] He explains why our societal interest in having robust debate about matters of public concern must outweigh Snyder's interest in recovering for his injury. If everyone in Snyder's position could make speakers pay for the hurt they caused, then all manner of political statements would become too expensive to utter. Think of arguments that undocumented immigrants should go back where they came from, that society shouldn't spend money on extending elderly people's lives,

13. *See* Gertz v. Robert Welch, Inc., 418 U.S. 323, 344 (1974).

14. *Snyder*, 562 U.S. at 464 (Alito, J., dissenting); *see also* Steven J. Heyman, *To Drink the Cup of Fury: Funeral Picketing, Public Discourse, and the First Amendment*, 45 CONN. L. REV. 101, 151 (2012) (arguing that the Court should freely weigh speech rights against other rights related to "individual personality," including "rights to emotional well-being, dignity, privacy, and religious liberty").

15. *Snyder*, 562 U.S. at 457.

or that all police officers are prone to violence. All of those arguments can cause emotional injuries, but they all have political substance.

Moreover, the boundary that divides innocuous from injurious speech can be hazy. Say I want to argue at a school board meeting that single parents are partly to blame for discipline problems in my school district. I believe reasonable people probably can distinguish my argument from a vulgar protest at a military funeral. Still, my argument might deeply distress some single parents—and that jury awarded Albert Snyder $11 million. Better safe, I might decide, than sorry. The Court calls that a *chilling effect* on speech. *Snyder* reflects the insight that chilling speech can damage public debate as surely as banning speech outright.

Justice Alito offers no substantial response to the majority's concerns about stifling political debate and chilling speech. He makes no serious effort to define "Phelps-type" personal attacks, let alone weed them out of protected speech. He insists that the emotional distress tort encroaches only slightly on free speech,[16] but that's really beside his point, because he doesn't want the First Amendment to protect the Phelps protest or its (undefined) ilk at all. He places crucial reliance on the authority of *Chaplinsky v. New Hampshire,*[17] the prototype categorical exclusion case, whose flaws we saw emerge in Chapter 1. Why can't Justice Alito forge his outrage at the *Snyder* result into a workable legal standard?[18] Robert Post has probed what he calls the paradox of public discourse: vigorous public debate can't work if we don't make basic efforts to keep it civil, but imposing civility rules means suppressing ideas and making public debate less vigorous.[19] Dean Post concludes that, in our legal and political conditions, no answer to the paradox exists. First Amendment law accordingly has a hard time dealing with the harm that speech can do.[20]

*Snyder* relies heavily on the distinction between matters of public and private concern. Our legal system often struggles to untangle the public from the private.[21] I've criticized the Roberts Court for its deployment of the

16. *See id.* at 463–64 (Alito, J., dissenting).

17. 315 U.S. 568 (1942), *cited in Snyder,* 562 U.S. at 465 (Alito, J, dissenting).

18. *See also* Heyman, *supra* note 14, at 143–44 (acknowledging that some complaints about injuries from speech "are merely subjective and exist in the eye of the beholder" but offering only "common sense and experience" as tools for winnowing such trivial claims from the weighty interests he would allow to trump free speech).

19. *See* ROBERT C. POST, CONSTITUTIONAL DOMAINS: DEMOCRACY, COMMUNITY, MANAGEMENT 147–48 (1995).

20. A good example is *Virginia v. Black,* 538 U.S. 343 (2003), which considered a First Amendment challenge to a state law that banned cross burning as a tool of intimidation. A plurality of the Court in that case found the law broadly permissible under the First Amendment's categorical exclusion of "true threats" but rejected the law's way of distinguishing threatening cross burning from merely expressive cross burning.

21. *See* Gregory P. Magarian, *The First Amendment, the Public-Private Distinction, and Nongovernmental Suppression of Wartime Political Debate*, 73 GEO. WASH. L. REV. 101 (2004).

public-private distinction in *Golan v. Holder,* last chapter's copyright extension case. *Golan* used the public-private distinction to avoid a difficult legal and normative problem, the conflict between copyright holders' and new users' expressive interests. *Snyder,* in contrast, uses the public-private distinction to resolve a difficult legal and normative problem, the balance of interests between political protest and an individual's emotional well-being. If we believe First Amendment law should protect political debate and dissent with special vigilance, then the "public concern" analysis in *Snyder* does useful work. The Phelps Church's protest undoubtedly hurt Albert Snyder, but what matters under *Sullivan* is whether a speaker addresses issues the political community has reason to care about.[22] As vile as most people find the Phelps Church's protests, we benefit from knowing that such people and ideas exist. Whether Snyder should have to bear the cost of our edification is a different question.[23] In other situations when we fear a speaker will wound or provoke his audience, taxpayers divide the cost of preventing the harm by paying for police to maintain order.[24] Perhaps states should extend that cost-spreading approach to emotional distress by setting up funds to compensate victims of injurious speech.

*Snyder* reaffirms the principle that the First Amendment protects speech on matters of public concern, and the decision clarifies that principle's central importance for First Amendment limits on tort liability for speech. Like *Stevens* and *Entertainment Merchants* last chapter, however, *Snyder* appears unlikely to have broad impact. The decision doesn't come close to protecting the Phelps Church's right to protest however it wants to at military funerals. Consider what the Phelps Church members actually did at Matthew Snyder's funeral. They told city authorities in advance that they planned to protest. They protested for about 30 minutes. They confined themselves to a 10-foot by 25-foot plot of public property, behind a temporary fence, approximately 1,000 feet from the church where the funeral took place, with several buildings between them and the church.[25] They did not raise their voices or use

22. For an argument that the *Snyder* Court placed too much emphasis on the public concern idea, see Vikram D. Amar & Alan Brownstein, *The Voracious First Amendment:* Alvarez *and* Knox *in the Context of 2012 and Beyond*, 46 LOY. L.A. L. REV. 491, 521–23 (2013).

23. Mark Tushnet objects to the *Snyder* result on this basis. *See* MARK TUSHNET, IN THE BALANCE: LAW AND POLITICS ON THE ROBERTS COURT 232 (2013). For a discussion of whether the victims of harmful speech should bear its costs, see Frederick Schauer, *Uncoupling Free Speech*, 92 COLUM. L. REV. 1321 (1992).

24. *See, e.g.*, Cox v. Louisiana, 379 U.S. 536, 550 (1965) (overturning civil rights marchers' convictions for "disturbing the peace" where police on the scene "could have handled the crowd").

25. The fact that the Phelps protesters spoke from public property connects *Snyder* with the "public forum" cases that I discuss in Chapter 4. That fact, however, played only a minimal role in the *Snyder* Court's analysis, which mainly treated the protest as private speech. *See* Snyder v. Phelps, 562 U.S. 443, 456 n.4 (2011).

profanity. They directed their protest at the public rather than the mourners. The funeral procession passed within 200 to 300 feet of the protest. All Snyder saw were the tops of the protesters' signs; he didn't find out what the signs said until he watched the television news.[26]

Chief Justice Roberts declares that laws restricting protesters from getting too close to funerals, enacted by the federal government and 44 states, raise issues not presented in *Snyder*.[27] He emphasizes that the Phelps Church "addressed matters of public import on public property, in a peaceful manner, in full compliance with the guidance of local officials" and "did not . . . disrupt [the] funeral."[28] Weeks after the funeral, a Phelps Church member made a Web post, "the epic," that attacked the Snyder family in more personal terms. The chief justice, however, holds that Snyder did not make the epic a subject of the dispute the Court was deciding, and he states that Internet posts might raise very different issues than those in *Snyder*.[29] The chief justice sums up: "Our holding today is narrow."[30] Justice Breyer, who joined the Court's opinion, wrote a separate concurrence to emphasize how much the result depended on the particular facts of the case.[31]

If you're a Phelps Church member, or any other sort of political protester, *Snyder* doesn't tell you much about your First Amendment rights. All you know for sure is that, if you protest about wholly, clearly political subject matter and wrap your protest in several layers of tactical restraint (however vicious your message might be), a court won't hold you liable for intentional infliction of emotional distress. Take away any one of those elements and you have a different case. If any aspect of your protest is arguably a matter only of private concern, if you don't warn the police that you plan to protest, if you're loud, if you're profane, if you try to get to a position where the person you're protesting can actually see you, if that person does see you, if you appear to address that person directly, or if you continue your protest on your website, then *Snyder* gives you no security. If you face some direct state restriction on

26. *See id.* at 448–49.

27. *See id.* at 456–57. One can make a strong argument that carefully drawn laws allowing buffer zones around funerals shouldn't violate the First Amendment. Funerals express ideas as surely as protests do. The government may properly allocate expressive space among diverse speakers, as long as the allocation doesn't restrict speech opportunities or disfavor particular speakers or ideas. *See, e.g.*, Cox v. New Hampshire, 312 U.S. 569 (1941) (upholding a nondiscriminatory permit requirement for parades on public streets).

28. *Snyder*, 562 U.S. at 460.

29. *See id.* at 449 n.1. Justice Alito objected in vain that "[t]he protest and the epic are parts of a single course of conduct." *Id.* at 469 n.15 (Alito, J., dissenting).

30. *Id.* at 460. Commentators generally agree. *See* Alan Brownstein & Vikram D. Amar, *Afterthoughts on* Snyder v. Phelps, 2011 Cardozo L. Rev. De Novo 43; Clay Calvert, *Too Narrow of a Holding? How—and Perhaps Why—Chief Justice John Roberts Turned* Snyder v. Phelps *Into an Easy Case*, 64 Okla. L. Rev. 111 (2012).

31. *See Snyder*, 562 U.S. at 461 (Breyer, J., concurring).

your protest rather than a private tort claim, *Snyder* tells you even less. In fact, when Chief Justice Roberts mentions the federal and state laws that keep protesters from getting too close to funerals, he favorably cites several cases that upheld broadly similar speech restrictions.[32]

Another factor in *Snyder* further diminishes the decision's importance. Almost everyone detests the Phelps Church, as strongly as most people despise the child pornography panderer from last chapter's *Williams* case. When you grossly offend everyone who cares about either LGBT rights or the military, you've likely reduced your pool of supporters to your immediate family. Literally, in this case: all the protesters at Matthew Snyder's funeral were blood relations of Fred Phelps. On one hand, the Phelps Church's pariah status makes *Snyder* that much more principled. The Court certainly didn't hold in favor of the church to win friends. On the other hand, vindicating the rights of a dissident group is a lot easier when you're sure no one will ever take the group seriously.[33] Justice Oliver Wendell Holmes Jr., dissenting from one of the Supreme Court's first decisions that denied a First Amendment claim by political protesters, called the antiwar dissidents in that case "puny anonymities" and likened their speech to "the surreptitious publishing of a silly leaflet by an unknown man."[34] Such rhetoric, although strategically useful, implies that the First Amendment shouldn't prevail when a more powerful, prominent, or charismatic political dissident mounts a serious protest that threatens to capture the public's attention and maybe even to persuade people to oppose the status quo. A more stringent test of the Court's speech-protective convictions comes when the government tries to suppress political dissent with a more appealing message.

## SUPPRESSING THE SPEECH WE FEAR

At the height of the McCarthy era in the 1950s, the Supreme Court exposed the speech-restrictive underbelly of Justice Holmes's "puny anonymities" rhetoric. In *Dennis v. United States*,[35] the justices let the federal government punish leaders of the U.S. Communist Party for the crime of conspiring to advocate revolution. The communist leaders in *Dennis* hadn't planned, let alone committed, any acts of violence. They hadn't taken active steps toward revolution. They had simply taught and advocated revolutionary communist

32. *See id.* at 456–57.
33. *See* John D. Inazu, *Factions for the Rest of Us*, 89 WASH. U. L. REV. 1435, 1454 (2012) ("It costs us little to protect deeply offensive but politically irrelevant groups like the Westboro Baptists.").
34. Abrams v. United States, 250 U.S. 616, 628–29 (1919) (Holmes, J., dissenting).
35. 341 U.S. 494 (1951).

dogma.[36] Chief Justice Fred Vinson's plurality opinion in *Dennis* declared that the Court had been wrong in its early First Amendment decisions to deny First Amendment rights to antiwar dissidents, anarchists, and communists.[37] Chief Justice Vinson explained, however, that the Communist Party of the 1950s posed a different, more serious kind of threat than those earlier "unknown men." The majority justices' opinions in *Dennis* radiate fear that the international communist conspiracy would subvert the American way of life. Justice Felix Frankfurter, concurring in the judgment, even argued that the Court should simply defer to Congress whenever free speech clashes with national security.[38]

The Supreme Court eventually repaired the hole that *Dennis* punched through the First Amendment. The 1969 case of *Brandenburg v. Ohio*[39] (noted in Chapter 1) holds that the Amendment fully protects mere advocacy of lawless action, as distinct from actual incitement. *Brandenburg,* however, dealt with a ragtag Ku Klux Klan rally in the middle of a rural field. The Klan certainly had, and has, more support public than the Phelps Church of *Snyder,* and it's done far more damage. Even in 1969, however, the Klan had fallen far from its terroristic peak.[40] The *Brandenburg* Court's opinion portrayed the Klansmen in that case as buffoons. That portrayal evokes the Phelps Church and Justice Holmes's "unknown man" much more than it evokes the fearsome communist conspiracy portrayed in *Dennis*. Although academic opinion now favors First Amendment protection for advocating unlawful action, the question has always defined a fault line in free speech theory. Most notably, conservative legal legend Robert Bork argued forcefully that the First Amendment should protect only appeals for lawful political change, not exhortations to revolution.[41]

The Roberts Court's major decision that responds to suppression of significant political dissent resembles *Dennis* more than *Brandenburg*. A federal statute allows the secretary of state to designate non-U.S. groups as "foreign terrorist organizations."[42] A "foreign terrorist" designation carries various legal consequences. A separate federal statute, the "material support law," lays out one such consequence. Under the material support law, any U.S. citizen who provides "material support or resources" to a designated foreign terrorist organization commits a federal crime.[43] The law defines "material support" to

36. *See id.* at 497–98.

37. *See id.* at 506–08.

38. *See id.* at 517, 525–26 (Frankfurter, J., concurring in the judgment).

39. 395 U.S. 444 (1969).

40. *See* John D. Inazu, Liberty's Refuge: The Forgotten Freedom of Assembly 51 (2012).

41. *See* Robert H. Bork, *Neutral Principles and Some First Amendment Problems*, 47 Ind. L.J. 1 (1971). I discuss the affinity of Bork's theory with the Roberts Court's First Amendment in Chapter 9.

42. *See* 8 U.S.C. § 1189(a)(1), (d)(4) (2004).

43. 18 U.S.C. § 2339B(a)(1) (2015).

include, among other things, "any . . . service, including . . . expert advice or assistance, [or] personnel."[44] The case of ***Holder v. Humanitarian Law Project* (2010)**[45] arose when several U.S. groups and individuals (for simplicity, I'll just refer to the Humanitarian Law Project, the lead plaintiff) wanted to provide humanitarian and political support to two designated foreign terrorist organizations: the Kurdistan Workers' Party (PKK), which seeks to create a Kurdish state in Turkey, and the Liberation Tigers of Tamil Eelam (LTTE), which seeks to create a Tamil state in Sri Lanka. Both organizations pursue their goals through a combination of violent attacks, political appeals, and humanitarian projects. The Humanitarian Law Project wanted to train the two groups in peaceful conflict resolution, help them negotiate peace agreements, teach them how to petition international bodies for humanitarian aid, and advocate politically for their goals. Concerned that the material support law might criminalize some or all of those activities, the group went to court, seeking a judgment that using the law to stop or punish them would violate the First Amendment.

Chief Justice Roberts, the author of *Snyder,* wrote the majority opinion in *Humanitarian Law Project* as well. His opinion begins by resolving some important secondary issues. First, the Humanitarian Law Project argued that the Court could read the material support law to bar only activities the actor specifically intends to advance a foreign organization's terrorist agenda. That reading would reduce the material support law to a ban on terrorist conspiracies, which would present no problem for the First Amendment (or the Humanitarian Law Project). The chief justice rejects that narrowing interpretation, holding that the material support law requires only knowledge of an organization's terrorist status.[46] Later, however, he adopts a different narrowing interpretation, which he calls a simple matter of "ordinary meaning." The material support law, he declares, only covers activities "coordinated" with a terrorist organization, not "independent" activities.[47] Second, the Humanitarian

44. 18 U.S.C. § 2339A(b)(1) (2009).

45. 561 U.S. 1 (2010). Roberts (majority) (with Stevens, Scalia, Kennedy, Thomas, Alito); Breyer (dissenting) (with Ginsburg, Sotomayor).

46. *See id.* at 16–18. In this respect, *Humanitarian Law Project* represses speech even more aggressively than *Dennis* did. The *Dennis* Court held that the law under which the government convicted the Communist Party leaders required the government to show that they specifically intended for their advocacy to bring about violent revolution. *See Dennis,* 341 U.S. at 499–500 (plurality opinion). Justice Breyer, dissenting in *Humanitarian Law Project,* advocates something close to a "specific intent" construction of the material support law. *See Humanitarian Law Project,* 561 U.S. at 55–60 (Breyer, J., dissenting).

47. *See Humanitarian Law Project,* 561 U.S. at 23–24. This distinction between independent and coordinated activity also plays an important role in campaign finance law (discussed in Chapters 7 and 8). *See* FEC v. Colo. Republican Fed. Campaign Comm., 533 U.S. 431 (2001) (upholding federal limits on political parties' campaign spending coordinated with candidates).

Law Project argued that key terms in the material support law were unconstitutionally vague. The chief justice, however, finds that the Humanitarian Law Project's proposed activities clearly fit within the words of the law.[48]

The government argued that the Humanitarian Law Project's proposed activities weren't "speech" at all but rather "expressive conduct," actions that just happened to convey a message. The Court applies a more lenient standard of review to restrictions on expressive conduct than to restrictions on pure speech.[49] The government in *Humanitarian Law Project* wanted the benefit of that lenient standard. No, says Chief Justice Roberts; this is a pure speech case.[50] To win, therefore, the government needed to satisfy strict scrutiny. In almost any free speech case, a court's choice to apply strict scrutiny is all the good news the speaker needs. In a nearly unprecedented result, however, the government in *Humanitarian Law Project* prevailed under strict scrutiny.[51]

Recall that, to satisfy strict scrutiny, the government must first show a "compelling interest" for its speech restriction. That showing was easy for the government to make in *Humanitarian Law Project:* The interest in combating terrorism is, in Chief Justice Roberts' words, "an urgent objective of the highest order."[52] The second prong of the strict scrutiny test seemed to present a steeper challenge. The government must show that the challenged speech restriction is "narrowly tailored" to accomplish its compelling interest, which means the government could achieve its compelling interest only by suppressing speech. In *Humanitarian Law Project,* the government had to show that, to fight terrorism effectively, it absolutely needed to bar the Humanitarian Law Project from saying what the group wanted to say to the PKK and the LTTE. The Humanitarian Law Project maintained that the government couldn't possibly make that showing. How can teaching terrorist groups to use peaceful rather than violent strategies hurt the fight against terrorism?

Let me count the ways, answers Chief Justice Roberts. First, he frames the case by portraying all designated terrorist groups as essentially violent and their

48. *See Humanitarian Law Project,* 561 U.S. at 18–25. All nine justices agreed that the law was not unconstitutionally vague. *See id.* at 40 (Breyer, J., dissenting).

49. *See* United States v. O'Brien, 391 U.S. 367 (1968). Chapter 4 discusses the *O'Brien* standard in more detail, in connection with the Roberts Court's public forum decisions.

50. *See Humanitarian Law Project,* 561 U.S. at 27.

51. The government has beaten free speech claims under strict scrutiny in three other Supreme Court cases, but all three come with big asterisks. *Burson v. Freeman,* 504 U.S. 191 (1992), (plurality opinion) upheld a Tennessee law that barred political activities within 100 feet of polling places, but only a plurality of the justices thought strict scrutiny applied in that case. Similarly, a plurality of the Roberts Court has held that a state law regulating electoral fundraising by judges satisfied strict scrutiny in *Williams-Yulee v. Florida Bar* (discussed in Chapter 8). *Austin v. Mich. Chamber of Commerce,* 494 U.S. 652 (1990), upheld under strict scrutiny a state law that banned corporate and union expenditures in election campaigns, but the Roberts Court overruled *Austin* in *Citizens United v. FEC* (discussed in Chapter 7).

52. *Humanitarian Law Project,* 561 U.S. at 28.

resources as fully fungible. "Material support" of the sort the Humanitarian Law Project planned "is a valuable resource [that] frees up other resources within the organization that may be put to violent ends."[53] Any conceivably useful input to a terrorist organization, including training in peaceful conflict resolution, will cash out as terrorist violence. Second, because terrorist groups are incorrigibly violent, "working in coordination with or at the command of the PKK and LTTE serves to legitimize and further their terrorist means."[54] You can't help a terrorist group become less terroristic; you can only help the group *appear* less terroristic, and that appearance promotes terrorism by legitimizing the group. Third, for U.S. groups to provide material aid to terrorist organizations "furthers terrorism by straining the United States' relationships with its allies and undermining cooperative efforts between nations to prevent terrorist attacks."[55]

Critical analysis puts considerable pressure on all three of those central planks in Chief Justice Roberts's reasoning. The idea that political advocacy is "fungible" with terrorist violence presents both empirical and normative problems. Empirically, as Justice Breyer contends in his dissent, the fungibility argument seems implausible, and the Court offers no support for it.[56] Normatively, the Court's description of speech as a fungible economic commodity resonates with *Golan v. Holder,* last chapter's copyright extension case. Here, as there and (we'll see) elsewhere, the Roberts Court treats speech as a vehicle not for exploring ideas but for exchanging value in transactions that have predictable, even inevitable economic consequences. As in *Golan,* the economic account of speech in *Humanitarian Law Project* casts doubt on expression's constructive or transformative capacity. Teaching terrorists to be more peaceful, the chief justice tells us, can't actually make them more peaceful. Terrorism just vacuums up any ideas it encounters and spits them back out as bombs. Why, though, should we limit that premise to terrorists? If speech can't actually transform the way anyone thinks or acts, then why should we grant speech strong constitutional protection at all?

The Court's holding that the government may restrict speech to prevent terrorist organizations from gaining legitimacy raises even deeper First Amendment concerns. As Justice Breyer emphasizes, the Humanitarian Law Project's planned activities amount to speech with a political message.[57] By citing legitimation of terrorism as a dangerous effect that justifies suppressing the speech, the Court lets Congress identify and censor "bad" political ideas. "If there is any fixed star in our constitutional constellation," Justice Robert Jackson famously declared, "it is that no official, high or petty, can prescribe what shall be orthodox in politics, nationalism, religion, or other

53. *Id.* at 30.
54. *Id.*
55. *Id.* at 32.
56. *See id.* at 47–48 (Breyer, J., dissenting).
57. *See id.* at 42–43 (Breyer, J., dissenting).

matters of opinion."[58] *Humanitarian Law Project,* though, holds that the government may punish speech that could cause us to think better of groups the government labels as terrorists. A related problem with the "legitimation" rationale is that preventing legitimation, as opposed to combating it with counterarguments, requires shutting down speech before the speech reaches an audience. The Court has long treated restraints on speech prior to publication as obviously unconstitutional censorship.[59] In addition, the legitimation argument's premise—that terrorist-legitimating speech can change public opinion—belies the Court's claim that peace-promoting speech can't change terrorists' violent nature. Chief Justice Roberts appears to credit terrorists with greater strength of will than the U.S. public.

Beyond those normative problems with the "legitimation" argument, the Court's distinction between coordinated and independent speech that legitimates terrorism feels slippery. As Justice Breyer points out, nothing logically distinguishes coordinated and independent acts of legitimation. In fact, he explains, independent speech will presumably do more to legitimate terrorist organizations than coordinated speech will, because independent advocacy carries greater credibility than concerted action.[60] Chief Justice Roberts responds that Congress (helped, he might have noted, by his own narrow interpretation of the material support law) drew a line between coordinated and independent material aid.[61] Under strict scrutiny, however, legislative fiat can't substitute for a logical fit between means and ends. Recall *Entertainment Merchants* (Chapter 1), in which the Court held that letting parents buy their children violent video games defeated the purpose of barring children from buying the games themselves. In the same way, the opportunity to aid terrorist groups independently would seem to defeat the purpose of banning only coordinated material aid. Moreover, the distinction between coordinated and independent activity artificially segregates the First Amendment rights of speech and assembly. *Humanitarian Law Project* emphasizes both that the material aid statute doesn't bar independent advocacy and that it doesn't bar anyone from joining terrorist organizations.[62] What the Court allows the statute to bar, though, is combining speech with assembly. First Amendment law has a name for that combination: *expressive association,* which the Court has long treated as a distinctively important form of expressive activity.[63]

58. W. Va. State Bd. of Educ. v. Barnette, 319 U.S. 624, 642 (1943).
59. *See, e.g.*, Near v. Minnesota, 283 U.S. 697 (1931).
60. *See Humanitarian Law Project,* 561 U.S. at 52 (Breyer, J., dissenting).
61. *See id.* at 31–32.
62. *See id.* at 39–40.
63. Lower courts have applied *Humanitarian Law Project* in ways that seriously undermine expressive association. *See* Ashutosh Bhagwat, *Terrorism and Associations*, 63 Emory L.J. 581, 591–611 (2014).

The holding of *Humanitarian Law Project* that Congress may suppress speech in order to maintain friendly relations with foreign allies raises further difficulties. One of the most familiar principles in free speech theory is that the government can't enforce a "heckler's veto." That is, the government may not censor or restrict a speaker because the audience doesn't like the speaker or the speaker's ideas.[64] *Snyder v. Phelps* strongly affirms that principle. How, then, can Chief Justice Roberts in *Humanitarian Law Project* cite foreign governments' potential objections to the speech of political dissenters as a constitutionally valid reason for squelching that speech? He offers an example: "The Republic of Turkey . . . would react sharply to Americans furnishing material support"—in the form of speech—"to foreign groups like the PKK."[65] Several years ago, I spoke at a meeting of the Armenian Bar Association in Philadelphia. The keynote speaker was the Armenian-Turkish journalist Hrant Dink. The Turkish government had convicted Dink of violating a law that bars acknowledging the Armenian genocide, an acknowledgment that Turkey views as a grave affront to its national dignity. Not surprisingly, our meeting's attendees applauded Dink's actions, and the program amounted to one long act of coordinated advocacy for genocide recognition and free speech.[66] *Humanitarian Law Project* strongly suggests Congress could have banned that meeting. Chief Justice Roberts might respond that Hrant Dink wasn't a terrorist. The chief justice's opinion for the Court, however, would let Congress assess the Armenian Bar Association's support for Dink "from Turkey's perspective,"[67] a perspective that might well equate Kurdish nationalist terrorists with Armenian genocide apostates.

The *Humanitarian Law Project* majority defers almost completely to the will of Congress and the executive branch. Where "weighty interests of national security and foreign affairs are concerned," Chief Justice Roberts intones, "the lack of competence on the part of the courts is marked, and respect for the Government's conclusions is appropriate." As to terrorism in particular, "information can be difficult to obtain and the impact of certain conduct difficult to assess," making demands for "hard proof" of the need to suppress speech unreasonable.[68] The chief justice trusts Congress' self-restraint to protect free speech rights,[69] exactly the sort of faith he refused to indulge in *Stevens,* last

64. *See, e.g.*, Forsyth Cty. v. Nationalist Movement, 505 U.S. 123 (1992) (striking down a permit system that required demonstrators to pay different costs for police to protect their gatherings depending on audience hostilities).

65. *Humanitarian Law Project,* 561 U.S. at 33.

66. Dink pointedly declared during the discussion that he opposed a French law banning genocide denial as firmly as the Turkish law banning genocide recognition. Four months after our meeting, back home in Istanbul, he was assassinated. *See Turkish Court Sees Conspiracy in Journalist's Death* (Reuters), N.Y. TIMES, May 15, 2013, at A9.

67. *Humanitarian Law Project,* 561 U.S. at 33.

68. *Id.* at 34 (internal quotation marks and citations omitted).

69. *See id.* at 35 ("We also find it significant that Congress has been conscious of its own responsibility to consider how its actions may implicate constitutional concerns.").

chapter's animal cruelty case. To the suggestion that the Humanitarian Law Project's efforts might conceivably do some good, Chief Justice Roberts replies: "Congress and the Executive . . . have concluded that we live in a different world."[70] Four decades before *Humanitarian Law Project,* the Supreme Court in *New York Times Co. v. United States*[71] refused President Richard Nixon's plea to block publication of the Pentagon Papers, a compilation of classified documents about the then-ongoing Vietnam War. The Nixon administration argued that, when the executive branch thinks free speech poses an unacceptable threat to national security, the Court should get out of the way. The Court's rejection of that argument opened a door, politically and ethically if not legally, for revelations such as former government contractor Edward Snowden's 2013 leak of National Security Administration documents that exposed widespread government surveillance of U.S. citizens.[72] *Humanitarian Law Project* closes that door and gives the Nixon administration's demand for deference a belated victory.

*Humanitarian Law Project* closely parallels *Dennis,* the communist advocacy case from the 1950s. The Court proceeds from a formally strong, speech-protective mode of First Amendment analysis. However, the Court views the dispute as involving an existential threat to national security whose special characteristics nullify ordinary free speech principles. The Court thus refuses to enforce the First Amendment against the government's judgment. *Brandenburg v. Ohio,* the Klan rally case, tacitly overruled *Dennis. Humanitarian Law Project,* in turn, appears to defy the central thrust of *Brandenburg:* that the government may only under very narrow, precisely defined conditions punish speech that the government believes threatens public order.[73] The "material supporters" of *Humanitarian Law Project,* like the communists of *Dennis,* aggressively challenge an important part of their era's dominant national security consensus. We'll see in Part III that the Roberts Court treats campaign finance laws as dire threats to core political speech. In contrast, just like the *Dennis* Court couldn't conceive of the U.S. Communist Party's Marxist-Leninist ideas as legitimate political discourse, Chief Justice Roberts practically mocks the Humanitarian Law Project's plea that the material support law restricts political speech.[74] For a Court focused on maintaining political stability and

70. *Id.* at 38.

71. 403 U.S. 713 (1971).

72. *See* Canadian Journalists for Free Expression, Snowden Archive, http://www.cjfe.org/snowden (last visited April 19, 2016).

73. The pressures of the "war on terror" strained *Brandenburg* even before *Humanitarian Law Project. See* Thomas Healy, Brandenburg *in a Time of Terror*, 84 Notre Dame L. Rev. 655 (2009).

74. *See Humanitarian Law Project,* 561 U.S. at 25–26. On the tension between *Humanitarian Law Project* and the Roberts Court's campaign finance decisions, see Aziz Z. Huq, *Preserving Political Speech from Ourselves and Others*, 112 Colum. L. Rev. Sidebar 16 (2012).

preserving order, forceful dissent from the government's national security policies doesn't register as political speech. It registers as a threat.

*Humanitarian Law Project* reveals a Roberts Court that considers itself not bound—perhaps not even authorized—to enforce the First Amendment when the government asserts national security interests to justify suppressing speech. Indeed, the Court's conservative majority later held 5-4 that it lacked jurisdiction to hear another important First Amendment case about national security.[75] Given our government's ongoing and open-ended "war on terror," this extreme deference to the government on national security marks one of the Roberts Court's most important contributions to First Amendment law. *Humanitarian Law Project* casts expressive association with foreign people and groups in our increasingly global culture as something to fear rather than celebrate.[76] An influential constitutional law professor, the University of Chicago's Eric Posner, has advocated criminalizing even the accessing of websites that "glorify, express support for, or provide encouragement for" the Islamic State terrorist group, in order to "protect people . . . from being infected by the ISIS virus by propagandists."[77] *Humanitarian Law Project* might not fully justify such a law, but the decision provides the intellectual raw material for Posner's speech-restrictive reasoning.

Chief Justice Roberts denies any implication in *Humanitarian Law Project* "that any future applications of the material-support statute to speech or advocacy [or] any other statute relating to speech and terrorism would satisfy the First Amendment."[78] As we've seen, however, the chief justice based his majority opinion on broad principles: the fungibility of speech and violence, the propriety of suppressing speech to control the public's political views, and the necessity of suppressing speech to avoid offending U.S. allies. David Cole, who argued the Humanitarian Law Project's case before the Supreme Court, has tried to minimize the decision's importance as precedent. He cites three factors that Chief Justice Roberts claims to limit the decision: the government had a national security interest, the speakers sought to coordinate their

75. When Congress passed a law that let the government surveil U.S. citizens' communications with foreign nationals the government had linked to terrorism, a coalition of human rights, labor, media, and legal groups challenged the law's constitutionality. The Court, in an opinion by Justice Thomas, held that the coalition lacked legal standing under Article III to pursue their case, because their fears of surveillance were too speculative to satisfy the requirement of a concrete injury. *See* Clapper v. Amnesty Int'l USA, 133 S. Ct. 1138 (2013).

76. *See* Timothy Zick, *The First Amendment in Trans-Border Perspective: Toward a More Cosmopolitan Orientation*, 52 B.C. L. Rev. 941 (2011).

77. Eric Posner, *ISIS Gives Us No Choice but to Consider Limits on Speech*, Slate (Dec. 15, 2015), http://www.slate.com/articles/news_and_politics/view_from_chicago/2015/12/isis_s_online_radicalization_efforts_present_an_unprecedented_danger.single.html (last visited Jan. 6, 2016).

78. *Humanitarian Law Project,* 561 U.S. at 39.

speech with terrorist groups, and the terrorist groups were foreign rather than domestic.[79] My Armenian Bar Association story, however, illustrates how even mild political dissent about international issues may involve coordination with foreign nationals and trigger zealous national security objections. The chief justice also makes no promise that the Court will require all three limiting factors to intersect before it extends the decision to justify future bans on expression.

The speech-restrictive decision in *Humanitarian Law Project* matters a lot more than the speech-protective decision in *Snyder v. Phelps*. *Snyder* held quite narrowly that a court may not make protesters, engaged in a very orderly (though uncivil) protest about an obviously political topic, liable for intentional infliction of emotional distress. *Humanitarian Law Project* reveals the strict limits of the First Amendment protection *Snyder* grants to political dissent. Where dissent doesn't just make rude noise but threatens the ordered structures of national security, the Roberts Court lets the government define the boundaries of acceptable expression. In the name of social and political stability, this Court effectively grants the government managerial control over public discussion.

## PRIORITIZING SPEECH FOR PROFIT

The failure of *Humanitarian Law Project* to protect serious political dissent contrasts sharply with another Roberts Court decision that balances private speech interests against government regulatory priorities. ***Sorrell v. IMS Health, Inc.* (2011)**[80] deals not with political activism but with commercial sales practices. Pharmaceutical drugs make more money for their manufacturers during the limited time when patents protect the drugs from generic competitors. To get doctors to prescribe particular drugs, especially the more expensive patented ones, manufacturers send representatives to doctors' offices to talk up their products. Medical industry jargon calls these sales visits "detailing." Like any sales pitch, detailing works a lot better if the detailers know their audience. They want to know what drugs the doctors they visit have prescribed in the past. That's where pharmacies and data miners enter the picture. Federal law requires pharmacies to keep records of the prescriptions they fill. Pharmacies, and sometimes health insurance companies, sell data miners information about which doctors prescribe which drugs ("prescriber-identifying information"). The data miners create reports

79. *See* David Cole, *The First Amendment's Borders: The Place of* Holder v. Humanitarian Law Project *in First Amendment Doctrine*, 6 HARV. L. & POL'Y REV. 147 (2012).

80. 564 U.S. 552 (2011). Kennedy (majority) (with Roberts, Scalia, Thomas, Alito, Sotomayor); Breyer (dissenting) (with Ginsburg, Kagan).

on which drugs particular doctors prescribe, and they sell those reports to drug makers, whose detailers use the reports to shape their sales pitches to the doctors. Detailers might persuade doctors to prescribe consumers the best, least expensive drugs. Then again, they might persuade doctors to prescribe drugs that cost more money than generic alternatives or don't best fit patients' medical needs. Detailers, after all, don't work for consumers. They work for drug makers, who want to maximize profits.

Vermont was one of several states that didn't like detailing's downside for consumers. State regulators worried that detailing, greased by prescriber-identifying information, was eroding medical privacy and driving up drug prices. Accordingly, the state passed a statute, the Prescription Confidentiality Law,[81] that barred pharmacies and insurers from selling prescriber-identifying information, barred pharmacies and insurers from letting prescriber-identifying information be used for marketing, and barred drug makers and detailers from using prescriber-identifying information for marketing (with all these restrictions waivable if a doctor consented). The law made clear that its restrictions did not apply to uses other than marketing, such as healthcare research, education, and law enforcement. Not surprisingly, the various players in the detailing game—the pharmacies and insurers who sell prescriber-identifying information in the first place; the data miners who buy, analyze, and resell the information; and the drug makers who use the information for detailing—disliked the law intensely. Several of them challenged it as a violation of their First Amendment rights. The Roberts Court in *IMS Health* sustained the challenge and struck down the Vermont law.

Two background legal doctrines help situate the *IMS Health* decision. The first concerns not the First Amendment but the Court's general approach to government regulations of business. At the turn of the last century, as the industrial revolution hummed along, states had begun to put limits on various employment practices: minimum wage and maximum hour mandates, allowances for union organizing, workplace safety rules, and so on. In a series of decisions, the Supreme Court struck down a significant number of such state laws. The Court proclaimed that the Constitution's Fourteenth Amendment, which broadly states that "[n]o state shall . . . deprive any person of life, liberty, or property, without due process of law,"[82] barred states from interfering with the rights of employers and workers to contract freely about working conditions. The key decision in *Lochner v. New York*,[83] which struck down a law that limited the hours bakeries could make their employers work, gives this period of constitutional bars on business regulations its name: the *Lochner* era. The era ended with a thud. During the Great Depression, most people

81. Vt. Stat. Ann., tit. 18, § 4631 (2007).
82. U.S. Const. amend. XIV.
83. 198 U.S. 45 (1905).

realized that forbidding state regulations of business had contributed to the economic collapse. The Supreme Court, in its most abrupt and one of its most important reversals of course, repudiated *Lochner.* The Court admitted that it had made two huge mistakes. First, it shouldn't have used a constitutional provision as vague as the due process clause to block the people's representatives from making public policy. Second, it shouldn't have scuttled government efforts to regulate business in the public interest.[84] Since then, conservatives and liberals alike have condemned "Lochnerism" as the archetype of judicial overreaching.[85]

The other legal doctrine that informs *IMS Health* is the Supreme Court's special approach to "commercial speech" under the First Amendment. For decades the justices assumed that commercial advertising got no First Amendment protection at all.[86] In 1976, however, they changed course. *Virginia State Board of Pharmacy v. Virginia Citizens Consumer Council, Inc.*[87] acknowledged that commercial speech, defined as speech that "does no more than propose a commercial transaction," provides socially valuable information.[88] At the same time, the Court recognized that the government sometimes has valid reasons for regulating commercial speech.[89] The justices therefore put commercial speech in a unique First Amendment category. It gets constitutional protection, unlike obscenity or fighting words, but it doesn't get full protection. In *Central Hudson Gas & Electric Corporation v. Public Service Commission of New York,*[90] the Court announced that it would review commercial speech regulations under an "intermediate scrutiny" standard (the sort of flexible standard Justice Breyer advocated in his *Alvarez* concurrence).[91] Under the doctrine of *Virginia Pharmacy* and *Central Hudson,* the Court has struck down

84. *See* Nebbia v. New York, 291 U.S. 502 (1934).

85. *See, e.g.*, ROBERT BORK, THE TEMPTING OF AMERICA (1997); CASS SUNSTEIN, THE PARTIAL CONSTITUTION (1998). The occasional dissenter keeps the debate alive. *See* DAVID BERNSTEIN, REHABILITATING *LOCHNER:* DEFENDING INDIVIDUAL RIGHTS AGAINST PROGRESSIVE REFORM (2012).

86. *See, e.g.*, Valentine v. Chrestensen, 316 U.S. 52 (1942).

87. 425 U.S. 748 (1976).

88. *See id.* at 762–65.

89. *See id.* at 770–72.

90. 447 U.S. 557 (1980).

91. The *Central Hudson* test states:

> For commercial speech to [get any First Amendment protection], it at least must concern lawful activity and not be misleading. Next, we ask whether the asserted governmental interest is substantial. If both inquiries yield positive answers, we must determine whether the regulation directly advances the governmental interest asserted, and whether it is not more extensive than is necessary to serve that interest.

*Id.* at 566.

commercial speech regulations that sought to influence consumers through enforced ignorance.[92]

The *Lochner* era and the commercial speech doctrine converge because First Amendment limits on commercial speech regulations might seem to resurrect *Lochner*. When the Court strikes down a commercial speech regulation, it bars the government from regulating business, just as *Lochner* did. First Amendment protection for commercial speech, however, differs from *Lochner* in several important ways. The First Amendment protects something particular—speech—whereas the broad language of the due process clause let the *Lochner* Court bar any business regulation it didn't like. The *Central Hudson* intermediate scrutiny standard, by giving government regulators some leeway, further limits the range of regulations the Court may strike down. Most importantly, at least some First Amendment checks on commercial speech regulation advance the public interest by ensuring consumers' access to commercial information. *IMS Health* presents the important question whether the public interest justifies states in regulating drug detailing or, instead, compels the Court to protect detailing.

Justice Kennedy's opinion for the Court holds that Vermont's law impermissibly discriminated against detailing.[93] He firmly rejects Vermont's argument that its law regulated only business conduct and not speech. Business regulations may incidentally restrict speech without violating the First Amendment, as when a fair hiring law forbids employer from posting "whites only" signs. Vermont's law, however, used the messages and identities of certain speakers—detailers—as the basis for its restrictions.[94] Justice Kennedy accepts for the sake of argument that all the law regulates is commercial speech.[95] Even so, Vermont loses. The state offered two sets of justifications for the law. First, the law protected the privacy and integrity of the doctor-patient relationship. It kept records private, insulated doctors from hard sell tactics, and prevented interference with doctors' decisions about which drugs to prescribe. Justice Kennedy rejects these privacy justifications because the law's exceptions allow people other than detailers, such as academic researchers, to get and use prescriber-identifying information. He rejects the undue influence argument as anathema to free speech: "If pharmaceutical marketing affects treatment decisions, it does so because doctors find it persuasive."[96] Second, Vermont argued that the law, by making detailing less effective, lowered medical costs and promoted public health. Justice Kennedy allows that the state's desire to make medical care less expensive and more effective "may

92. *See, e.g.*, 44 Liquormart, Inc. v. Rhode Island, 517 U.S. 484 (1996) (striking down a ban on alcohol price advertising).
93. *See* Sorrell v. IMS Health, Inc., 564 U.S. 552, 563–64 (2011).
94. *See id.* at 566–67.
95. *See id.* at 571.
96. *Id.* at 576.

be proper." Pursuing that desire by hampering speech, however, is not. Only "free and uninhibited speech" may resolve the "debate" about which drugs doctors should prescribe.[97]

Justice Kennedy hedges his analysis on two important points. First, *IMS Health* harbored a separate First Amendment issue with potential to overshadow the commercial speech question: whether buying and selling data flows such as prescriber-identifying information should get First Amendment protection.[98] Justice Kennedy implies that data flows themselves amount to speech.[99] The Vermont law's supposed discrimination against detailers, however, lets him resolve the case without squarely deciding whether and to what extent the First Amendment protects trade in data flows.[100] Second, Justice Kennedy does not make clear whether the Vermont law discriminates only against the *content* of certain speech or more narrowly against a particular *viewpoint*. If he means to say the law singles out only content, he has a problem: the commercial speech doctrine, unlike ordinary First Amendment law, permits greater regulation of commercial speech because of its content. If he means to say the law singles out a viewpoint, something even the commercial speech doctrine prohibits, he has a different problem: drug makers' desire to maximize profit from patented drugs seems hard to construe as a point of view. By mostly avoiding the term "viewpoint-based restrictions" but repeatedly accusing Vermont of making "*speaker-based* restrictions," which isn't a term of art in First Amendment law, Justice Kennedy tries to weave a path between these two pitfalls.[101]

Justice Breyer's *Sorrell* dissent views the Vermont law through a completely different lens from the majority. He sees the law's "effect on expression" as "inextricably related to a lawful government effort to regulate a commercial enterprise."[102] Invoking the First Amendment to micromanage government

97. *Id.* at 578.

98. *Compare, e.g.*, Ashutosh Bhagwat, Sorrell v. IMS Health: *Details, Detailing, and the Death of Privacy*, 36 Vt. L. Rev. 855 (2012) (contending that courts probably will, but generally should not, treat data flows as protected speech) *with* Jane Bambauer, *Is Data Speech?*, 66 Stan. L. Rev. 57 (2014) (arguing that courts generally should treat data flows as protected speech).

99. *See IMS Health*, 564 U.S. at 570.

100. For an extended discussion, see Neil Richards, Intellectual Privacy 79–84 (2015).

101. *IMS Health*, 564 U.S. at 563 (emphasis added). Only once does Justice Kennedy directly accuse Vermont of "aim[ing] at a particular viewpoint," *id.* at 565, but that statement qualifies a claim that the law merely discriminates based on viewpoint "in its practical operation." *Id.* (internal quotation marks and citation omitted). At another point Justice Kennedy similarly calls the law "content-based and, *in practice*, viewpoint-discriminatory." *Id.* at 571 (emphasis added). These semantics matter, because the Court generally does not treat laws that suppress certain viewpoints only in practice, rather than on purpose, as discriminating impermissibly based on viewpoint. *See, e.g.*, United States v. O'Brien, 391 U.S. 367 (1968).

102. *IMS Health*, 564 U.S. at 581 (Breyer, J., dissenting).

regulations of commerce, he charges, replicates the mistake of *Lochner*.[103] The fact that the law affects a particular sort of speech—detailing—makes no legal difference for Justice Breyer, because all commercial regulations target particular commercial conduct. In any event, the prescriber-identifying information at issue only exists because government regulations require it. By further regulating the information's use, Vermont merely seeks to control government resources.[104] Even if the Vermont law did regulate speech, Justice Breyer contends, it should easily pass *Central Hudson* review. The law imposes only minor burdens on commercial speech.[105] The state has substantial, speech-neutral interests in protecting public health and privacy. Justice Breyer chides the majority for imagining (even) less speech-restrictive ways Vermont could have pursued those interests, rather than deferring to Vermont's reasonable policy decision to restrain detailing.[106]

For a detailer to talk with a doctor about a drug's attributes is plainly speech. Formally, Justice Breyer's call for deference to Vermont's policy judgment about detailing echoes Chief Justice Roberts's call for deference in *Humanitarian Law Project*. A great many business regulations restrict speech—think of corporate disclosure requirements, or limits on employers' freedom to discourage union organizing—and we can't just wish those regulations out of First Amendment arguments by pretending they regulate only conduct or commerce.[107] *Virginia Pharmacy*, however, set forth an animating principle for First Amendment protection of commercial speech: consumers should have all available information for making commercial decisions.[108] That focus on consumer information keeps commercial speech protection from crossing into *Lochner* territory. *IMS Health* isn't about open-market communication between businesses and consumers. Rather, it's about closed-door communication between drug makers and doctors. Vermont's law did not stop any information from reaching consumers. Yes, detailing is speech, but it isn't a sort of speech the Court has ever before shielded from government regulations designed to protect public health.[109] What's new and important about

103. Justice Breyer twice invokes *Lochner* to attack the majority. *See id.* at 591–92, 602–03 (Breyer, J., dissenting).

104. *See id.* at 587–88 (Breyer, J., dissenting). The majority forcefully disputes this argument. *See id.* at 568–69.

105. Justice Breyer derides Justice Kennedy's claim that the law discriminates against detailing, noting that no evidence supports the majority's suggestion that Vermont would use the law to "counter-detail" inexpensive generic drugs. *See id.* at 594–95 (Breyer, J., dissenting).

106. *See id.* at 596–99 (Breyer, J., dissenting).

107. *See* Ernest A. Young, Sorrell v. IMS Health *and the End of the Constitutional Double Standard*, 36 Vt. L. Rev. 903 (2012).

108. *See* Va. State Bd. of Pharmacy v. Va. Citizens Consumer Council, Inc., 425 U.S. 748, 769–70 (1976).

109. *See* Tamara R. Piety, *"A Necessary Cost of Freedom"? The Incoherence of* Sorrell v. IMS, 64 Ala. L. Rev. 1 (2012).

*IMS Health* is that the Court, for the first time, has struck down a commercial speech regulation solely to protect businesses' ability to maximize profits. That shift takes the treatment of speech as an economic commodity, visible both in Chapter 1's copyright extension case *Golan v. Holder* and in the "fungibility" reasoning of *Humanitarian Law Project*, to a new level. It could portend a future move to protect commercial speech broadly and strictly, without regard to consumers' informational interests.

Vermont restrained detailing largely to advance medical privacy. The Court dismisses that interest as a mere pretext for censorship: the state couldn't possibly care about privacy, Justice Kennedy insists, because it allowed researchers and educators to access prescriber-identifying data. Vermont, however, decided that a chain of profit-minded sellers, resellers, and marketers would take less care to preserve medical privacy than researchers and educators.[110] Certainly privacy concerns can lead to improper speech restrictions. *Snyder v. Phelps* stands for the principle that not even the intimacy of a family's grief should justify barring political protests. Recall, however, the *Snyder* Court's suggestion that states properly may keep funeral protesters outside reasonably drawn "buffer zones." If we don't grant funerals some measure of privacy, the protesters' message will simply drown out the mourners' message. In this sense, privacy needn't be the enemy of speech; rather, privacy in an important sense is a precondition for speech.[111] *IMS Health* only indirectly implicated consumers' privacy, because the data in the case explicitly identified only doctors, not patients. Still, the Court's dismissal of Vermont's privacy argument on grounds of anti-commercial discrimination could justify subordinating privacy interests to commercial profit motives in future cases.

Vermont also wanted to stop what we might call the "medical-data complex" of drug makers, pharmacies, data miners, and ultimately doctors from exploiting consumers' information deficit to extract more of their money. The Vermont legislature found that discussion about which drugs doctors should prescribe "is frequently one-sided in that brand-name companies invest in expensive pharmaceutical marketing campaigns to doctors."[112] Detailing, by circulating information above consumers' heads, denies people the power to participate autonomously in discussions about their medical care. Even if good policy reasons justified that denial, why should the First Amendment shield it against a state's contrary policy judgment? Notwithstanding Justice Kennedy's pronouncement that "in the fields of medicine and public health . . . information can save lives,"[113] *IMS Health* appears to save nothing but drug makers' profits.

110. *See* Tushnet, *supra* note 23, at 230.
111. *See* Richards, *supra* note 100.
112. 2007 Vt. Acts & Resolves 80, § 1(4).
113. Sorrell v. IMS Health, Inc., 564 U.S. 552, 566 (2011).

The Roberts Court's only other commercial speech decision, ***Milavetz, Gallop & Milavetz v. United States* (2010)**,[114] upholds two narrow speech restrictions in the federal Bankruptcy Code. Justice Sotomayor wrote the majority opinion, her first free speech opinion after replacing Justice Souter on the Court and one of the few she has written to date. The decision first rejects overbreadth and vagueness challenges to a bankruptcy law that bars debt relief agencies from advising their clients to incur more debt prior to a bankruptcy filing.[115] The Court then employs a lenient standard of review, which lets the government compel disclosure of commercial information to avoid misleading consumers,[116] to uphold a second bankruptcy law that makes debt relief agencies state in their advertisements that they are, in fact, debt relief agencies.[117] *Milavetz* sits at an intersection of *Alvarez* (Chapter 1) and *IMS Health:* it makes clear that the First Amendment does not protect commercial lies. In reaching that conclusion, the decision breaks no new ground. The Court's commercial speech doctrine has always denied First Amendment protection to false and misleading advertisements.[118] In addition, the justices usually show little patience when members of their own profession try to hide shifty business practices behind the First Amendment.[119]

## SIGNS AND SIGNIFIERS

The Roberts Court's most recent decision that balances protected speech against government regulation, ***Reed v. Town of Gilbert* (2015)**,[120] is so simple that it's confounding. *Reed* strikes down a municipal rule that governs the

114. 559 U.S. 229 (2010). Sotomayor (majority) (with Roberts, Stevens, Kennedy, Ginsburg, Breyer, Alito; with Scalia, Thomas (in part)); Scalia (concurring in part and concurring in the judgment); Thomas (concurring in part and concurring in the judgment). Justice Thomas wrote separately to argue, as he has elsewhere, that commercial speech should get full First Amendment protection. *See id.* at 255 (Thomas, J., concurring in part and concurring in the judgment). Justice Scalia wrote separately to scold then-newly arrived Justice Sotomayor for a single footnote in her opinion that violates his rule against using legislative history materials to interpret statutes. *See id.* at 253 (Scalia, J., concurring in part and concurring in the judgment).

115. *See id.* at 239–48 (discussing 11 U.S.C. § 526(a)(4) (2010)).

116. *See Milavetz,* 559 U.S. at 249–50 (citing Zauderer v. Office of Disciplinary Counsel, 471 U.S. 626 (1985)).

117. *See Milavetz,* 559 U.S. at 248–53 (discussing 11 U.S.C. § 528 (2008)).

118. *See, e.g., Va. State Bd. of Pharmacy,* 425 U.S. at 771–72.

119. *See, e.g., Zauderer,* 471 U.S. at 650–53 (upholding disciplinary action against a lawyer who made misleading claims about a contingent fee arrangement). In Chapter 8 we'll encounter a campaign finance decision, *Williams-Yulee v. Florida Bar,* that takes a similar hard line on ethics for the legal profession.

120. 135 S. Ct. 2218 (2015). Thomas (majority) (with Roberts, Scalia, Kennedy, Alito, Sotomayor); Alito (concurring) (with Kennedy, Sotomayor); Breyer (concurring in the judgment); Kagan (concurring in the judgment) (with Ginsburg, Breyer).

size, number, and location of outdoor signs. Gilbert, Arizona, like many municipalities, had a sign rule that distinguished among signs based on what the signs announced or advertised. "Ideological signs" could be up to 20 square feet in size and displayed anywhere in town without time limits. "Political signs," designed to influence elections, could only be 16 square feet on residential property (larger in some other settings) and displayed only 60 days before and 15 days after an election. "Temporary directional signs related to a qualifying event"—meant to guide people to an event or meeting—could only be six square feet, with no more than four signs posted at once on a single property, and displayed only for 12 hours before and one hour after the event. The Good News Community Church, a small Christian group that had no church building, placed signs around Gilbert inviting people to the various, irregular places where the group held services. The town enforced its sign law stringently against the church. The church challenged the law, claiming that Gilbert violated the church's First Amendment rights by regulating "temporary directional signs" more harshly than other kinds of signs.

Justice Thomas's majority opinion restates and enforces the most familiar rule of First Amendment speech doctrine: when the government regulates speech based on the speech's content, the Court subjects the regulation to strict scrutiny. Justice Thomas explains that Gilbert's law, by making differential rules for signs with different messages, facially discriminated based on content. One need only read the law to see the discrimination. Gilbert's assertion that the town held no animus against temporary directional messages doesn't matter, nor does the fact that the law didn't discriminate against specific viewpoints.[121] In the strict scrutiny analysis, Gilbert claimed that it distinguished among categories of signs to promote traffic safety and the town's aesthetic appeal. Justice Thomas assumes, without deciding, that both of those interests rise to the "compelling" level, but he finds the law insufficiently tailored to satisfy strict scrutiny. Many kinds of signs, he explains, could cause traffic problems or dampen aesthetic appeal, and nothing about the Gilbert law's content distinctions tracks either interest.[122]

Nothing in Justice Thomas's opinion seems at all remarkable. Why, then, did six justices see the need to express caveats of varying intensity? At one level, the hubbub simply reflects the practical importance of sign regulations. Signs appear all over, nearly all governments regulate them, and the *Gilbert* Court's firm adherence to content neutrality may undermine many of those regulations. Justice Thomas promises that "[o]ur decision today will not prevent governments from enacting effective sign laws." He points out that governments may still pursue safety and aesthetic interests by regulating signs' "size, building materials, lighting, moving parts, and portability"; by broadly

121. *See id.* at 2227–30.
122. *See id.* at 2231–32.

restricting signs on public property; and by carefully tailoring preferences for warning, directional, and identification signs in ways that satisfy strict scrutiny.[123] Justice Alito, concurring for himself and Justices Kennedy and Sotomayor, adds an uncommonly direct (and, for regulators, no doubt very welcome) laundry list of permissible, content-neutral bases on which governments may regulate signs, including (among others) placement on public as opposed to private property, commercial as opposed to residential signs, and total numbers of signs per mile of roadway. Justice Alito also underscores the government's broad latitude to post signs that express its own messages (flashing the theme of "government speech" that will figure prominently in several cases in Part II).[124]

At a deeper level, the tensions in *Gilbert* reflect long-standing debates about both the coherence[125] and the desirability[126] of a strict content neutrality requirement. Justice Kagan, concurring in the Court's result but not its reasoning for a more skeptical trio that includes Justices Ginsburg and Breyer, contends that demanding strict content neutrality raises both analytic and normative problems. Analytically, Justice Kagan picks apart Justice Alito's assertion that regulators may safely impose time limits on signs that advertise one-time events. Such a regulation, she notes, distinguishes speech based on subject matter and therefore violates the majority's rule against content discrimination.[127] Even figuring out what counts as content neutrality can present a major problem. (We'll see the Court wrestle with that same problem in the context of antiabortion clinic activism in Chapter 4.) Normatively, Justice Kagan warns that cities will either have to repeal laws that favor helpful street and residential signs or else learn to live with signs run amok. The likely travails of regulating signs under the majority's strict requirement of content neutrality, she predicts, may force the Court to sit as "a veritable Supreme

123. *Id.* at 2232.

124. *See id.* at 2233–34 (Alito, J., concurring).

125. *Compare, e.g.*, Leslie Kendrick, *Content Discrimination Revisited*, 98 VA. L. REV. 231 (2012) (defending content neutrality's coherence by likening the doctrine to equal protection doctrine's prohibition on suspect classifications) *with* Erwin Chemerinsky, *Content Neutrality as a Central Problem of Freedom of Speech: Problems in the Supreme Court's Application*, 74 S. CAL. L. REV. 49 (2001) (arguing that the Supreme Court has failed to develop and apply the content neutrality principle in sufficiently coherent ways).

126. *Compare, e.g.*, Seth P. Kreimer, *Good Enough for Government Work: Two Cheers for Content Neutrality*, 16 U. PA. J. CONST. L. 1261, 1303 (2014) (arguing that content neutrality serves better than viewpoint neutrality or inquiries into proportionality to "minimize interferences with free speech that reflect and establish pernicious habits of censorship") *with* Ashutosh Bhagwat, Reed v. Town of Gilbert: *Signs of (Dis)Content?*, 9. N.Y.U. J. LAW & LIBERTY 359, 367–69 (2016) (criticizing strict content neutrality as an irrational constraint on government's power to allocate scarce spatial resources).

127. *See Gilbert*, 135 S. Ct. at 2237 n.* (Kagan, J., concurring in the judgment).

Board of Sign Review."[128] That Supreme Board, she implies, may lack the courage of the Supreme Court's content neutrality convictions.

Justice Kagan and Justice Breyer, who contributes his own solo concurrence in the judgment, contend that the strong presumption against content-based regulations has both laudable uses and appropriate limits. Justice Breyer attacks the workability and internal coherence of a strict content neutrality requirement. We've seen, especially in considering the child pornography pandering case *United States v. Williams* (Chapter 1), the persistence of tacit limitations on the First Amendment's coverage. Justice Breyer invokes those limitations to indict the *Gilbert* majority's insistence on strict content neutrality. Securities disclosure rules, labeling requirements for consumer products, doctor-patient confidentiality mandates—all of these and more, he suggests, would need to satisfy strict scrutiny or else fall under the majority's approach.[129] The Court could save such laws, as Justice Thomas suggests it might save carefully crafted content-based sign laws, by "watering down" strict scrutiny, but that would hamper First Amendment law's ability to combat more pernicious speech restrictions.[130]

Although Justices Kagan and Breyer rebuke Gilbert's discriminatory sign law, both maintain that many common, content-based sign restrictions, such as allowing illumination of home address numbers but not of other residential signs, raise no serious First Amendment issues. Justice Kagan would mandate content neutrality only where content-discriminatory laws either evince viewpoint discrimination or remove important ideas from public discussion.[131] The *Gilbert* sign law, she says, fails "even the laugh test."[132] Justice Breyer, following his approach from *IMS Health* and last chapter's military honors case *Alvarez,* would strike down the law because it "works harm to First Amendment interests that is disproportionate in light of the relevant regulatory objectives."[133]

Many sign disputes present questions about the availability of government property for sign placements. Although *Gilbert* arose as a general challenge to a sign regulation, the case points toward concerns distinctive to speech on government property. Those concerns, which also lay in the

128. *Id.* at 2239 (Kagan, J., concurring in the judgment).

129. *See id.* at 2234–35 (Breyer, J., concurring in the judgment). Justice Breyer takes the opportunity in *Gilbert* to reiterate his criticism of *IMS Health* as incorrectly decided and unduly rigid. *See id.* at 2235 (Breyer, J., concurring in the judgment).

130. *Id.* (Breyer, J., concurring in the judgment); *see also id.* at 2237 (Kagan, J., concurring in the judgment). Justice Thomas's hint about a more flexible approach to strict scrutiny resonates with the Roberts Court's striking rejections of First Amendment challenges under apparent strict scrutiny in both *Humanitarian Law Project* and *Williams-Yulee v. Florida Bar* (discussed in Chapter 8).

131. *See Gilbert,* 135 S. Ct. at 2237 (Kagan, J., concurring in the judgment).

132. *Id.* at 2239 (Kagan, J., concurring in the judgment).

133. *Id.* at 2235–36 (Breyer, J., concurring in the judgment).

background of *Snyder v. Phelps*, will take center stage in Chapter 4's discussion of the public forum doctrine. Government property, as a source of expressive opportunities, holds special importance for marginal and underfinanced speakers, who tend to lack private expressive resources. Both Justice Thomas's majority opinion in *Gilbert* and Justice Alito's concurrence emphasize the government's power to restrict signs on its own property. Even as Justice Thomas acknowledges the special value of signs as an expressive medium for underfinanced speakers,[134] he favorably cites a past decision that disregarded a seemingly neutral law's disparate impact on socially marginal speakers and ideas.[135] In contrast, although Justice Breyer's and Justice Kagan's rejections of strict content neutrality might seem less speech-protective than the *Gilbert* majority, their opinions expressly advocate opening public discussion to marginal and underfinanced speakers. Justice Breyer singles out public forum cases as a distinctly appropriate context for applying a presumption that content-based speech restrictions violate the First Amendment.[136] Justice Kagan urges applying content analysis instrumentally, "to preserve an uninhibited marketplace of ideas in which truth will ultimately prevail."[137] In Chapter 4 we'll see the Roberts Court—led by its liberal wing—weaken the public forum as a source of expressive opportunities. Justices Breyer and Kagan in *Gilbert* express some sympathy in the other direction.

*Gilbert* should aid challengers to other sign ordinances that replicate Gilbert's blunt content discrimination. The decision's broader impact is hard to predict. We might read the case as a mundane recitation of First Amendment boilerplate in the workaday context of sign laws, a reminder of the Court's content neutrality principle that doesn't disturb the many established exceptions and hedges. On the other hand, the case may represent a bold new commitment to ferreting out content discrimination wherever it occurs. Elements of Justice Thomas's analysis, such as the statement that laws "defining regulated speech by its function or purpose"[138] impermissibly discriminate against the content of speech, could harden into a more stringent mode of review for future cases. In that event, Justices Breyer and Kagan's practical concerns might loom large, as judges confronted both the analytic problems of identifying content discrimination and the fraught choice between striking down innocuous content-based regulations and weakening strict scrutiny.

134. *See id.* at 2225.
135. *See id.* at 2228–29 (discussing Ward v. Rock Against Racism, 491 U.S. 781 (1989)).
136. *See Gilbert*, 135 S. Ct. at 2234 (Breyer, J., concurring in the judgment).
137. *See id.* at 2237 (Kagan, J., concurring in the judgment) (internal quotation marks omitted).
138. *Id.* at 2227.

## CONCLUSION

The balancing cases discussed in this chapter, taken together, fuel the managed speech account of the Roberts Court's First Amendment. *Snyder* reinforces the First Amendment's vital protection for speech about matters of public concern. *Gilbert* likewise speaks in strongly speech-protective terms about content neutrality. Those two decisions, despite their uncertain impact, seem committed to about promoting broad, inclusive public discussion. However, the two other major cases discussed in this chapter belie that commitment. Chief Justice Roberts's opinion in *Humanitarian Law Project* delivers what may be the Supreme Court's strongest blow against First Amendment protection for political dissent since the *Dennis* communist advocacy decision 65 years ago. Where *Snyder* declares the importance of open public debate, *Humanitarian Law Project* passively defers to federal officials who condemn dissent as a threat to national security. Congress, the chief justice tells us, may presume that pacifist advice to terrorists will inevitably advance their violent methods, may ban speech that "legitimates" terrorism, and may suppress domestic political expression to avoid offending foreign allies. *Humanitarian Law Project* epitomizes managed speech. It empowers a responsible institution, here the government, to manage public debate; it disregards and even denigrates the expressive interests of political dissenters who threaten to disrupt established power structures; and it strongly prioritizes the preservation of social and political order.

*Sorrell v. IMS Health,* like *Snyder* and unlike *Humanitarian Law Project,* sustains a First Amendment claim. *IMS Health,* though, substantially diverges from *Snyder.* Whereas the Court in *Snyder* invokes the First Amendment to protect public debate, *IMS Health* has nothing to do with public discussion or public information. Instead, the decision commodifies speech to protect the narrow interest of a specific group of commercial actors, an interest directed solely toward commercial profit. By shielding drug detailing from government regulation, the Court empowers commercial actors to decide which drugs become available, without consumers' knowledge or input. Like last chapter's copyright case *Golan v. Holder, IMS Health* follows a rigid public-private distinction to ignore a collision between opposed expressive interests. Both decisions portray more economically powerful speakers as censorship's victims and dismiss less economically powerful speakers as censorship's undeserving constituents. Just as *Golan* and *Humanitarian Law Project* let the government manage public discussion, deciding whether and how information may flow, *IMS Health* lets a class of commercial actors do so.

These first two chapters show the primacy of economic power in the Roberts Court's First Amendment. The Supreme Court during the *Lochner* era used constitutional law to replace legislative ordering of social and economic affairs with ordering by economic market forces. The Roberts Court, likewise, appears to conceive of public discussion as an economic sphere that powerful market actors can and should manage.[139] All of this Court's private speech decisions that touch commercial matters, whether the decisions protect speech (*Stevens, Entertainment Merchants, IMS Health*) or restrict it (*Golan*), validate the market's authority to decide the value of different kinds of speech. Meanwhile, the Roberts Court's most notable case about political dissent, *Humanitarian Law Project*, insulates the economic and political status quo from serious disruption. The other political dissent cases give trivial distractions a pass. Xavier Alvarez, the Phelps Church, and the Good News Community Church posed no serious threat to established order, and the Court validated their free speech rights in decisions that work minimal changes in established law. In contrast, the Humanitarian Law Project threatened national security, the very cornerstone of established order, and the Court rejected its First Amendment claim. Under the Roberts Court's First Amendment, anchors of economic order win, while threats to political order lose.

A shift in the Court's First Amendment orientation from managed speech to dynamic diversity would change more results in this chapter's cases than in last chapter's. Dynamic diversity would validate *Snyder* while focusing more attention on the conflict between the expressive interests of military funeral mourners and the Phelps Church. Likewise, a dynamic diversity opinion in *Gilbert* would firmly reject Gilbert's sign ordinance while considering whether some forms of government content regulation might promote, rather than retard, robust public discussion. A dynamic diversity take on *Humanitarian Law Project*, however, would completely scrap the Roberts Court's decision. The humanitarian groups in that case are paladins of dynamic diversity's ambitions to maximize the range of ideas and participants in public discussion. Those groups sought to challenge the government's authority over national security, a magnet for uncritical public consensus and obedience. The government may properly use a range of powers to discourage and punish violent conduct, but dynamic diversity extols the democratic value of protecting even, especially, the most disturbing, potentially destabilizing speech. As for *IMS Health*, dynamic diversity recognizes no positive basis for protecting data

139. A thorough empirical analysis of Supreme Court business cases finds that the Roberts Court generally favors business positions more than earlier Courts. *See* Lee Epstein et al., *How Business Fares in the Supreme Court*, 97 MINN. L. REV. 1431 (2013). Likewise, a comparison of Roberts Court First Amendment decisions to contemporaneous lower court decisions, focusing on the predominant First Amendment meme of content neutrality, finds that commercial interests and wealthy individuals fare much better in the Roberts Court, while less powerful speakers fare much worse. *See* Kreimer, *supra* note 126, at 1277–302. For a commentary on Roberts Court First Amendment decisions that favor property interests, see Julie E. Cohen, *The Zombie First Amendment*, 56 WM. & MARY L. REV. 1119 (2015).

mining against selective state regulation in the commercial sphere. Dynamic diversity generally calls for aggressive judicial enforcement of the First Amendment, but sometimes no good reason justifies intervention.

Three hallmarks of managed speech emerge from these first two chapters: empowering stable, responsible institutions to manage speech, disfavoring marginal or disruptive speakers, and ensuring that First Amendment law preserves, rather than threatens, social and political stability. These three elements permeate the Roberts Court's free speech jurisprudence. The next three chapters, which deal with speech that uses various sorts of government resources to reach its audience, will sharpen our view of managed speech in action.

# PART TWO

# Speech in Government Preserves

A lot of speech uses government resources. State and local governments operate public school systems and universities, where students, teachers, professors, and administrators constantly engage in expressive activity. The federal and state governments rank among the largest employers in many places, and government employees have special knowledge and motives to speak out about government abuses. Governments operate prisons and military bases, places where people living under severe restrictions often want to express themselves and where outsiders often want to protest government policies. Governments own all sorts of property: real property, which includes parks, sidewalks, and office buildings; and intangible property, which includes participatory programs, websites, and public broadcast media. Governments also provide substantial funding for domestic and international relief work, medical and scientific studies, and the arts. Political advocates, researchers, and creators use government resources to reach audiences. The Internet has somewhat diminished the importance of government resources for speech, and suburbanization and privatization had somewhat diminished it before that. What's left still makes up a major bounty of expressive resources, especially crucial for speakers who don't have the wealth of, say, the video game or prescription drug industries, whose self-powered speech we saw the Court protect in Part I.

Government institutions, property, and funding, which I'll collectively call *government preserves,* raise a special kind of First Amendment problem. When speech disputes arise in government preserves, the government isn't acting in its unique regulatory role, as in Part I. Instead, it's acting more like a private institutional manager, property owner, or philanthropist. On one hand, the government should have greater power to regulate its own resources than it has to regulate purely private conduct. That increased power must include some power to regulate speech, because speech can interfere with government operations or undercut the public's uses of government resources for other purposes. On the other hand, speech doesn't lose its constitutional value when it uses government resources. Government can make an important contribution to public discussion by helping underfunded speakers reach audiences. The Roberts Court's decisions about speech in government preserves, discussed in the next three chapters, aggressively promote all three central elements of managed speech: empowering institutional speech managers, disregarding marginal and disruptive speakers, and maintaining social and political stability.

Chapter 3 deals with speech disputes in government-run institutions: prisons, schools, and government offices. In each of these settings, the Roberts Court has sharply diminished expressive freedom. Prisoners' status among the most despised groups in society raises acute concerns about government restrictions on their speech. In the most important prison speech case in almost two decades, *Beard v. Banks,* the Court defers almost completely to prison officials' denial of prisoners' access to expressive material. Adolescents' experience of expressive freedom plays a crucial role in their development as people and as citizens. In the most important student speech case in almost two decades, *Morse v. Frederick,* the Court strengthens school officials' power to punish students' speech, even speech that happens off campus. Government employees know more than anyone else about government wrongdoing. In the most important public employee speech case in over a decade, *Garcetti v. Ceballos,* the Court squelches a government lawyer's effort to address alleged wrongdoing in his own office. In each of these decisions, the Roberts Court treats the speech of government institutional subjects as a threat to public order. In each case the Court lets government use its power as an institutional manager to maintain order by suppressing speech.

Chapter 4 deals with speech on public property. First Amendment doctrine uses a set of rules called the public forum doctrine to frame these sorts of disputes. The Roberts Court has decided four public forum cases. The first, *Pleasant Grove City v. Summum,* asks whether public parks' availability for private speech requires the government to find space in a park for any large monument a private group might decide to donate. The Court unsurprisingly says no, but it justifies that result by holding that a donated monument placed in a park becomes the government's own speech. What may look like government suppression of private speech can dodge the First Amendment altogether if the government is not really regulating other speakers but rather channeling its own speech through them. The government claims to act just like a private speaker, able to express its own ideas and exclude others. The second public forum case, *Walker v. Texas Division, Sons of Confederate Veterans,* largely follows *Summum* in the different context of specialty license plates. These cases, like the decisions about institutional subjects in Chapter 3, aggressively validate the government's managerial authority.

*Christian Legal Society v. Martinez* considers whether the public forum doctrine bars a public law school from making a school-sponsored student group admit members the group doesn't want. The Court says no. That result fortifies universities' distinctive role in promoting discussion and interaction among people with different viewpoints, but it also compounds the government speech decisions' weakening of public access to government expressive resources. The latest public forum decision, *McCullen v. Coakley*, strikes down a "buffer zone" that a state had imposed to protect patients and workers at clinics that provide abortion services. While recognizing the legitimacy of the state's goal, *McCullen* delivers the Court's strongest, most skeptical analysis in many years of government efforts to restrict speech on government property. *McCullen* seems to counter the speech-restrictive elements of the other public forum cases. Chief Justice Roberts's majority opinion, however, follows logic that could leave abortion opponents in a privileged First Amendment position and other political activists out in the cold.

Finally, Chapter 5 discusses two cases in which the federal government tried to restrict speech as a condition of government funding. The government gives out money for all sorts of reasons. Usually the government may freely attach strings to its largesse. Strings that tie off speech or assembly, however, present a First Amendment problem. The Roberts Court's first subsidized speech decision, *Rumsfeld v. Forum for Academic and Institutional Rights (FAIR)*, unanimously upholds a rule that requires universities that get government funds (nearly all public and private universities) to let government agencies interview students on campus for jobs. The other subsidized speech case, *Agency for International Development v. Alliance for Open Society International*, stands alongside *McCullen* as the only other major Roberts Court decision to strike down a speech restriction in a government preserve. *Open Society* rejects the government's command that groups it funds to do relief work in the developing world, some of which try to help sex workers, must declare opposition to prostitution. I'll contend that *Open Society* serves mainly to keep the government speech genie inside the bottle *Summum* opened.

The Roberts Court's government preserve decisions expand government control over a wide range of speech. The decisions let the government-as-manager suppress speech with a potency that we saw the Court in Part I at least sometimes deny to the government-as-regulator. The Court strengthens government authority in the institutional settings of prisons, schools, and government offices. It uses the government speech doctrine to deny First Amendment protection in expressive property the law has long treated as open to diverse speakers and views. It sends mixed messages about the freedom to speak in public forums and the freedom to use government funds for speech. The Roberts Court's government preserve decisions, more starkly than any other group of cases, show this Court's commitment to managed speech. These decisions are anathema to my alternative model for constitutional speech protection, dynamic diversity. Whereas dynamic diversity opposed the reasoning more than the results of the private speech decisions in Part I, a dynamic diversity analysis would counsel opposite results in most of the government preserve cases. Government support for expressive activity strongly benefits dynamic diversity's core goals of maximizing the range of ideas and participants in public discussion. Accordingly, dynamic diversity consistently and strongly favors institutional subjects, speakers in public forums, and government-subsidized speakers when the government tries to restrict their expression.

# CHAPTER 3

# My House, My Rules

## *Strengthening Government Managers' Control over Institutional Speech*

In Part I, we saw the government use its regulatory authority to limit speech. The Court, although not striking down every speech-restrictive regulation, strongly criticized regulatory limits on speech. Often, however, the government doesn't act in its unique regulatory role. Instead, it does things that analogous private actors, to some extent, also do. Chapters 4 and 5 will discuss two of those quasi-private government functions: owning property and giving out money.

This chapter deals with another quasi-private government function: managing institutions. The government manages numerous prisons, schools, and workplaces.[1] (When I talk about schools in this chapter, I mean primary and secondary schools. Colleges and universities, because most of their students are adults, present different First Amendment problems, examples of which we'll encounter in Chapters 4 and 5.) The government, unlike a private actor, must obey the Constitution's commands not to violate rights, including the

1. Military bases have also spawned institutionally distinctive First Amendment decisions. *See, e.g.*, Greer v. Spock, 424 U.S. 828 (1976) (upholding regulations that banned certain political activity at Fort Dix). The Roberts Court has not confronted a First Amendment case arising from a military base, although the Court unanimously rejected a political protester's claim that a military base expelled him in violation of a federal statute. *See* United States v. Apel, 134 S. Ct. 1144 (2014). First Amendment cases about military bases that deal with the rights of outside speakers rather than institutional subjects fit with the public forum cases discussed in Chapter 4 rather than the institutional speech cases discussed in this chapter.

First Amendment.[2] Therefore, the government should have weaker authority in managing institutions than private actors have. At the same time, the special nature of government authority cuts in the other direction. The government, unlike a private actor, runs institutions for the benefit of the public. Therefore, the government should have stronger authority in managing institutions than private actors have.

This is a paradox, and it presents a challenge for courts. Judges and justices have to respect the First Amendment rights of prisoners, students, and public employees while also avoiding undue interference with the government's service to the people. The Supreme Court for decades has struck that balance mostly in the government's favor. No student or prisoner has won a major free speech case in the Supreme Court since the 1960s. Public employees lose more cases than they win. The Court doesn't subject restrictions on the speech of prisoners, students, and public employees to the rigorous strict scrutiny review that we saw in private speech cases. Instead, each of these institutional settings has generated its own special form of First Amendment analysis, weighted toward the government.

The long history of Supreme Court deference to government institutional managers in free speech cases might have seemed to leave the Roberts Court little room to diminish expressive freedom further in government institutions. Early in Chief Justice Roberts's tenure, however, the Court considered three major cases that deal with speech suppression by prison wardens, high school principals, and government employers. Against the odds, the justices managed to make First Amendment law in all of these areas even less speech protective than it was before. These decisions grant sweeping latitude to government institutional managers, blithely disregard institutional subjects' expressive interests, and fixate unblinkingly on the stable functioning of prisons, schools, and government offices. Even more firmly and consistently than the private speech decisions discussed in Part I, the institutional speech decisions implement the tenets of managed speech.

## UP THE RIVER WITH NOTHING TO READ

***Beard v. Banks* (2006)**[3] involved a challenge by state prisoners to a ban on their access to certain reading materials. Pennsylvania's prison system includes a section called the Long-Term Segregation Unit (LTSU). The LTSU

2. The Supreme Court occasionally has sustained constitutional claims against private actors that get power from the government. *See, e.g.*, Marsh v. Alabama, 326 U.S. 501 (1946).

3. 548 U.S. 521 (2006). Breyer (plurality) (with Roberts, Kennedy, Souter); Thomas (concurring in the judgment) (with Scalia); Stevens (dissenting) (with Ginsburg), Ginsburg (dissenting). Justice Alito recused himself from the case because he had

houses the worst of the system's worst, the state's 40 or so most violent, resistant inmates. The LTSU has two levels. Level 1 houses the less extreme prisoners, whereas level 2 houses the hardest cases. Prison officials impose stronger restrictions on LTSU-2 inmates than on anyone else. In *Beard,* Pennsylvania prison officials forbade LTSU-2 inmates from receiving newspapers, magazines, or personal photographs. Most free speech cases deal with restrictions on what people may say or write, but the Supreme Court has made clear that the First Amendment also protects our rights to get, have, and read expressive materials.[4] That theme, recall, arose in the video game case, *Entertainment Merchants* (Chapter 1), when Justice Scalia emphasized that children's First Amendment rights undercut a state ban on selling them violent video games. In *Beard,* a LTSU-2 prisoner argued that barring his access to newspapers, magazines, and personal photographs violated his First Amendment right to receive information.

The Court upheld the restriction. Justice Breyer's plurality opinion[5] begins by setting out the legal framework. Past Court decisions say that regulations on prisoner speech present no First Amendment problem as long as a regulation is "reasonably related to valid corrections goals [and] not an exaggerated response to those objectives."[6] This is the language of *rational basis review,* the softest standard of constitutional review in the Court's analytic toolbox. The government wins almost every rational basis case, and *Beard* follows that form. Pennsylvania officials offered several reasons for keeping newspapers, magazines, and personal photographs from LTSU-2 inmates. Justice Breyer finds that one reason suffices: "the need to motivate better behavior on the part of particularly difficult prisoners."[7] According to the state, withholding newspapers, magazines, and personal photos was a strategy for getting LTSU-2 prisoners to behave better. Justice Breyer finds that story reasonable on its own terms.[8] The plurality defers almost completely to the state, requiring no evidence that the challenged regulation actually improves prisoner behavior. Indeed, Justice Breyer scolds the Court of Appeals from whose

served on the panel of the Third Circuit Court of Appeals that issued the decision the Supreme Court reviewed.

4. *See, e.g.*, Lamont v. Postmaster General, 381 U.S. 301 (1965) (striking down a federal law that required postal customers to file an affirmative request before the Post Office would deliver "communist propaganda").

5. Although Justice Breyer's opinion only speaks for a plurality of the Court, prison officials nationwide may safely impose regulations as harsh as the plurality permits. Justice Thomas's concurrence in the judgment, which provides his and Justice Scalia's decisive votes, goes even further than the plurality opinion, arguing that prisoners have no rights at all beyond the Eighth Amendment's bar on "cruel and unusual punishments." *See Beard,* 548 U.S. at 537–38 (Thomas, J., concurring in the judgment).

6. Turner v. Safley, 482 U.S. 78, 93 (1987).

7. *Beard,* 548 U.S. at 530 (plurality opinion).

8. *See id.* at 533 (plurality opinion).

adverse decision the state petitioned the Supreme Court for not taking the state's word on crucial issues in the case.[9] In contrast, he insists that the prisoner who challenged the rule did not show enough facts in his favor to avoid a judgment against him at this stage in the lawsuit.[10] Justice Breyer makes no special First Amendment inquiry; in fact, he finds this dispute functionally identical to an earlier case that didn't even deal with First Amendment rights.[11]

Justice Stevens, dissenting, approaches the case from a fundamentally different perspective. He begins by positing "our society['s] unmistakable commitment to apply the rule of law in an evenhanded manner to all persons, even those who flagrantly violate their social and legal obligations."[12] He agrees with the plurality that the Court should use the "reasonably related" test to decide the case. Unlike the plurality, however, he thinks that standard permits, even requires, searching judicial inquiry into the state's reasons for suppressing prisoners' access to information. Justice Stevens first considers and rejects an argument the state made but the plurality ignores: that withholding newspapers, magazines, and personal photos from LTSU-2 prisoners improves prison security.[13] He then considers the decisive argument that barring LTSU-2 inmates' access to newspapers, magazines, and personal photographs helps prison authorities control the inmates' behavior.[14] He rejects that argument for three reasons. First, the state hasn't shown that withholding newspapers, magazines, and personal photos actually does much to improve how hardened prisoners behave. Most other states and the federal prison system, he notes, don't use this approach. Second, the plurality's reasoning lets states restrict prisoners' rights however they please in order to compel whatever behavior they want. Third, and gravest, trying to control isolated prisoners' behavior by denying them important expressive materials "comes perilously close to a state-sponsored effort at mind control."[15]

To Justice Stevens's criticisms of *Beard* we can add an additional legal concern. The case that sets out the "reasonable relation" test for restrictions on prisoners' speech requires that a prison rule, to be considered "reasonable," must be "content neutral."[16] (Recall the justices' debate about the proper

9. *See id.* at 535 (plurality opinion).
10. *See id.* at 527–30, 534–35 (plurality opinion).
11. *See id.* at 533 (plurality opinion) (citing Overton v. Bazzetta, 539 U.S. 126, 134 (2003), a case about prisoners' right to family visitation).
12. *Beard*, 548 U.S. at 542 (Stevens, J., dissenting).
13. *See id.* at 543–46 (Stevens, J., dissenting).
14. *See id.* at 546–52 (Stevens, J., dissenting).
15. *Id.* at 552 (Stevens, J., dissenting). Justice Ginsburg, besides joining Justice Stevens's dissent, wrote separately to chastise the plurality for too quickly closing off the prisoner's opportunity to gather and present facts in support of his claim. *See id.* at 553 (Ginsburg, J., dissenting).
16. *See* Turner v. Safley, 482 U.S. 78, 93 (1987).

reach of a content neutrality requirement in the Chapter 2 municipal sign case, *Gilbert.*) The regulation in *Beard* bans LTSU-2 inmates from getting magazines, newspapers, and personal photographs, but it lets them get "legal and personal correspondence, religious and legal materials, [and] two library books." That's a straightforward content distinction, and the *Beard* plurality doesn't even ask Pennsylvania to justify it.

The opinions in *Beard* don't disagree about fine points, or even coarse chunks, of First Amendment doctrine. This is a case about first principles: How far should First Amendment law go to protect one of society's most despised groups? The plurality doesn't answer Justice Stevens's substantive objections because the plurality justices don't believe the Court has any business asking substantive questions about prison speech restrictions. *Beard,* more pointedly than any past Supreme Court decision, defers to prison authorities in defining prisoners' First Amendment rights. The Court's analysis echoes its extraordinary deference in the case about material aid to terrorist groups, *Humanitarian Law Project* (Chapter 2). In *Beard,* though, the government is playing a different sort of role. It isn't regulating the behavior of ordinary citizens, such as the human rights groups in *Humanitarian Law Project.* Rather, it's managing behavior in an institution it runs. In this setting, the Roberts Court casually, almost reflexively, defers to the government manager's authority. *Beard* gives prison authorities a green light to block prisoners' access to expressive materials in whatever ways prison authorities think, or claim, the deprivation will help make prisoners behave better. It reduces expressive freedom to a bargaining chip.

## "WE DON'T NEED NO THOUGHT CONTROL"

Public schools share at least two important descriptive characteristics with prisons.[17] First, the government in both prisons and schools exercises managerial power over people whose presence in those institutions subjects them to special forms of government authority. Second, courts in First Amendment cases give government managers in both settings very similar sorts of deference and legal latitude.

The Supreme Court under Chief Justice Earl Warren, in the Vietnam War-era decision *Tinker v. Des Moines Independent Community School District,*[18] established the legal principle that public school students do not "shed their constitutional rights to freedom of speech or expression at the schoolhouse

17. Aaron Caplan properly warns against drawing careless prescriptive analogies between these two very different sorts of institutions. *See* Aaron H. Caplan, *Freedom of Speech in School and Prison,* 85 WASH. L. REV. 71 (2010).
18. 393 U.S. 503 (1969).

gate."[19] *Tinker* upheld grade school students' right to wear black armbands at school to protest the war. The Court held that schools may punish students' speech only when the speech threatens "materially and substantially [to] disrupt the work and discipline of the school."[20] That test still nominally applies in student speech cases. However, the 45-year-old holding in *Tinker* marks the peak of the Court's commitment to students' free speech rights. Since then, the Court has let a grade school punish a student for using sexual double entendres during a speech in a student election campaign,[21] and it has let a high school censor articles about pregnancy and divorce in a student newspaper.[22] In the student election case, the school's managerial interest in protecting younger students from sexual content trumped the student speaker's First Amendment interest in promoting his candidate. In the school newspaper case, the school's managerial interest in maintaining control of the newspaper as a curricular offering trumped student editors' and writers' First Amendment interest in reporting on how teenagers grappled with hard problems. As in prisons, the Supreme Court in school speech cases has long favored institutional managers' interest in suppressing speech over institutional subjects' interest in speaking and receiving information.

The early Roberts Court case ***Morse v. Frederick* (2007),**[23] decided a year after *Beard,* seemed to present a stronger First Amendment claim than those earlier student speech cases. In 2002, the Olympic torch passed through Juneau, Alaska. High school principal Deborah Morse decided to let students gather outside their school building to watch the torch relay. Across the street from the school, as the torch and news cameras approached, a group of friends, most of them students at the high school, unfurled a 14-foot banner that read "BONG HiTS 4 JESUS." Morse crossed the street and ordered the group to remove the banner. One student, senior Joseph Frederick, refused. Morse confiscated the banner and suspended Frederick. Frederick challenged his punishment on First Amendment grounds. The facts in *Morse* differ from those in the earlier student election and student newspaper cases in two significant ways. First, the speech in those earlier cases happened on school grounds. Frederick, in contrast, spoke off school premises. That distinction would seem to weaken the school's interest in maintaining tight control over students' behavior. Second, the student speakers in the earlier cases made coherent statements that school officials could plausibly cast as undermining order or threatening harm. Frederick's banner, in contrast, looked like colorful

19. *Id.* at 506.

20. *Id.* at 513.

21. *See* Bethel Sch. Dist. No. 403 v. Fraser, 478 U.S. 675 (1986).

22. *See* Hazelwood Sch. Dist. v. Kuhlmeier, 484 U.S. 260 (1988).

23. 551 U.S. 393 (2007). Roberts (majority) (with Scalia, Kennedy, Thomas, Alito); Thomas (concurring); Breyer (concurring in the judgment); Stevens (dissenting) (with Souter, Ginsburg).

gibberish. That distinction would seem to foreclose any solid basis for school officials to punish the speech.

The Court, however, rejected Frederick's First Amendment claim. Chief Justice Roberts, writing for a five-justice majority, first disposes of Frederick's argument that the school shouldn't be able to punish him for off-campus conduct. Principal Morse, the chief justice explains, let her students watch the torch relay during school hours, with teachers supervising them. The event was therefore an official school activity.[24] That analysis seems fair enough as to the students who stepped out of their classrooms and stood in front of the school building. Frederick and his cohorts, however, present a different problem. The opinion describes Frederick as having been late to school on the day of the torch relay.[25] From this, one can fairly infer that he never set foot on school grounds that day before unfurling his banner. Leaving aside any appropriate penalties for tardiness or truancy, Frederick appears to have removed his display of the banner from school jurisdiction. Perhaps he avoided the school building for exactly that purpose. Chief Justice Roberts emphasizes that most students who stood in front of the school building could easily see and read Frederick's banner.[26] That, however, seems like a tenuous basis for expanding school authorities' control over the speech of people who spend some of their time, but not all of it, as the school's students. May a school really punish a student for any effect the student's speech has on other students, whenever and wherever it happens?

Principal Morse argued that she believed Frederick's banner advocated illegal drug use, contrary to school policy, and that she therefore properly suspended Frederick under the "materially and substantially disrupt" test from *Tinker.* Chief Justice Roberts first defers to Morse's interpretation of the banner. While acknowledging that the banner was "cryptic," the chief justice pronounces Morse's reading "reasonable."[27] That's a major extension of the earlier student speech cases' deference to schools. To let school officials decide how much and what sort of control over student speech the school's educational function demands is one thing. To let school officials decide, in the first instance, what students' words actually mean is something very different. The chief justice proceeds to mock Frederick's story that his banner was just nonsense,[28] stressing the banner's "undeniable reference to illegal drugs" and rejecting out of hand the possibility that the banner might have had political meaning.[29]

24. *See id.* at 400–01.
25. *See id.* at 397.
26. *See id.* at 401.
27. *Id.*
28. *See id.* at 402 (referring to this explanation as "[t]he best Frederick can come up with").
29. *Id.* at 402–03.

How, then, does the *Tinker* "materially and substantially disrupt" test apply to Frederick's banner? It doesn't. Instead, Chief Justice Roberts treats this case much like the categorical exclusion decisions we considered in Chapter 1. Because Frederick's banner advocated (on Morse's reading) illegal drug use in a manner visible to other students, Morse could punish Frederick to protect those students from his pernicious message. Frederick, in the chief justice's view, didn't merely disturb the school's functioning in a way that limits him to the spare First Amendment protection of *Tinker*. Rather, he threatened school policy in a way that gets no First Amendment protection at all. The chief justice, while claiming that earlier cases already rendered the *Tinker* test optional,[30] doesn't make clear what legal standard does apply to Frederick's banner. Given how much leeway even the *Tinker* test grants school authorities, the Court's rejection of that test as too speech protective for *Morse* strongly suggests that no student, outside perhaps the structure of a school-sponsored political debate on drug policy, could ever get First Amendment protection for a statement that advocated illegal drug use. Moreover, the chief justice's reasoning bears no logical limitation to advocacy of illegal drug use. He licenses what Justice Stevens condemns in dissent as "stark viewpoint discrimination"[31] against an unknowable range of advocacy.

Justice Alito, joined by Justice Kennedy, contributes a concurring opinion in *Morse* that tempers some of the majority opinion's more sweeping implications. Justice Alito spotlights and rejects an ambitious argument floated by Morse (and the federal government, which supported Morse in the case): that school officials should have power to punish any speech that interferes with a school's "educational mission." He points out that adopting that test would let schools define their educational missions in viewpoint-based terms and suppress such opposing viewpoints as the antiwar message in*Tinker.*[32] Justice Alito's opinion, in the context of his strong advocacy elsewhere for religious believers' rights,[33] suggests a concern for religious parents who have to send their children to public schools.[34] Perhaps the "Jesus"

30. *See id.* at 404–06.

31. *Id.* at 437 (Stevens, J., dissenting). At the other end of the Court, Justice Thomas writes separately to argue that public school students have no First Amendment rights. *See id.* at 410 (Thomas, J., concurring). Justice Breyer opts out of the First Amendment debate altogether, maintaining that the legal principle of "qualified immunity" should dispose of some of Frederick's suit against Morse and that speech-neutral reasons can justify Morse's suspension of Frederick. *See id.* at 425 (Breyer, J., concurring in the judgment). The chief justice doesn't buy Justice Breyer's dodge. *See id.* at 400 n.1.

32. *See id.* at 423 (Alito, J., concurring).

33. *See, e.g.*, Burwell v. Hobby Lobby Stores, Inc., 134 S. Ct. 2751 (2014) (interpreting a federal statute to exempt corporations from regulations that offend their asserted religious beliefs) (opinion for the Court by Justice Alito).

34. *See Morse*, 551 U.S. at 424 (Alito, J., concurring) ("Most parents, realistically, have no choice but to send their children to a public school and little ability to influence what occurs in the school."). Conservative Christian advocates featured prominently

in Frederick's banner caught Justice Alito's attention as much as the "bong hits." Justice Alito also affirms that schools exercise government power, not just some abstract simulation of private power.[35] Even so, he fully endorses the majority opinion. Advocacy of illegal drug use, he argues, does more than express a viewpoint. It threatens students' safety. He likens speech that advocates drug use to speech that incites violence.[36] Like the majority, he disregards the Court's long-standing distinction between advocacy and incitement.[37]

*Morse* exemplifies two important tendencies in the Roberts Court's First Amendment jurisprudence. First, the majority justices' opinions echo both *Humanitarian Law Project* and *Golan v. Holder* (the copyright extension case discussed in Chapter 1) by denying the complex, critical, potentially constructive nature of outsider speech and instead branding such speech as a threat to social order. "BONG HiTS 4 JESUS," as Justice Stevens argues in dissent, provides a blank slate for ascribing meaning.[38] Nothing in the facts of the case provides any context for reading the banner as advocating illegal drug use. A reasonable person—even a high school student—could read the banner as a raspberry in the face of Olympic pomp; as a mockery of Christianity, or for that matter a celebration of Jesus Christ as a nonconformist who defied the legal and social norms of his day; or simply as description rather than advocacy of drug use. Frederick claimed he just wanted to turn the TV cameras his way, to court attention and provoke some kind of response. That sort of prank against reason has a long history, reaching from dada and situationism to yippies and punk rockers.[39] In any event, we've seen that the First Amendment protects speech not just for the speaker's sake but also for the sake of the larger community that may benefit from hearing what she has to say. Everyone gets to decide what, if anything, "BONG HiTS 4 JESUS" means and what we think of the message.

Second, the Roberts Court in *Morse* as in *Beard* treats government suppression of speech not as a presumptive constitutional violation but as a prerogative of institutional authority. In school as in prison, the Court accords government institutional managers a high degree of deference. Principal

among the groups who submitted briefs that urged the Court to sustain Frederick's First Amendment claim. *See id.* at 395 n.*. In fact, the *Morse* majority took its reasoning directly from a brief submitted by the Liberty Legal Institute. *See* Emily G. Waldman, *A Post-*Morse *Framework for Students' Potentially Hurtful Speech (Religious and Otherwise)*, 37 J.L. & EDUC. 463, 485–87 (2008).

35. *See Morse*, 551 U.S. at 424 (Alito, J., concurring).

36. *See id.* at 424–25 (Alito, J., concurring).

37. *See* Brandenburg v. Ohio, 395 U.S. 444 (1969); Whitney v. California, 274 U.S. 357 (1927) (Brandeis, J., concurring).

38. *See id.* at 439–42 (Stevens, J., dissenting).

39. *See* GREIL MARCUS, LIPSTICK TRACES: A SECRET HISTORY OF THE TWENTIETH CENTURY (1990).

Morse doesn't just get to assert the challenges of running her institution. She also gets to decide what her institutional subjects' speech means, how and why their speech does and doesn't matter, and how the speech will impact her institution. *Morse,* in fact, gives students even less First Amendment protection than *Beard* gives prisoners. Recall that in the prison setting, as in the school setting, earlier Supreme Court decisions balanced the speech of institutional subjects against the institutional manager's interest in maintaining the institution's function. The balancing approach didn't provide prisoners much speech protection, but the First Amendment exerted some pull against institutional power. In *Beard,* all the justices agreed that the established balancing test applied; the majority just applied it in an extremely permissive way. In *Morse,* on the other hand, the Court denies that the *Tinker* "materially and substantially disrupt" test for student speech even comes into play. The Court strongly privileges the institution's power to control its subjects' speech over the subjects' expressive autonomy.

*Morse* continues a line of Supreme Court decisions that provide only limited, idiosyncratic guidance about how the First Amendment applies to speech in public schools.[40] Lower courts have disagreed about how much and what sorts of speech *Morse* removes from the First Amendment's protection.[41] Even so, *Morse* resonates with the Court's long-standing tendency to let school officials run their institutions with minimal if any First Amendment constraints. School officials can credibly read *Morse,* even with Justice Alito's caveats, as another link in the chain formed by the earlier student election and student newspaper cases, further emboldening schools to limit students' expressive rights.

Before proceeding to the final case in the Roberts Court's major institutional trilogy, we need to linger for a moment at school. In ***Tennessee Secondary School Athletic Association v. Brentwood Academy* (2007),**[42] a private high school challenged an interscholastic sports authority's punishment of the school for aggressive recruitment of middle school athletes. The Court held that, when a private school voluntarily joins a state athletic association, it subjects itself to the association's reasonable limits on expressive freedom, including "hard sell" recruiting tactics. On the

40. *See* Frederick Schauer, *Abandoning the Guidance Function:* Morse v. Frederick, 2007 SUP. CT. REV. 205.

41. *Compare, e.g.*, Ponce v. Socorro Indep. Sch. Dist., 508 F.3d 765, 770 (5th Cir. 2007) (holding that *Morse* supersedes *Tinker* for speech that school officials believe advocates a violent act) *with* Noxoll v. Indian Prairie Sch. Dist., 523 F.3d 668, 672–73 (7th Cir. 2008) (treating *Morse* as allowing school officials only to bar advocacy of illegal drug use).

42. 551 U.S. 291 (2007). Stevens (majority (in part), plurality (in part)) (with Souter, Ginsburg, Breyer; with Roberts, Scalia, Kennedy, Alito (in part)); Kennedy (concurring in part and concurring in the judgment) (with Roberts, Scalia, Alito); Thomas (concurring in the judgment).

surface *Brentwood* resembles *Morse:* the Court lets a state institution restrict a speaker's efforts to influence the behavior of a vulnerable audience. Brentwood Academy, however, was a more resourceful and sophisticated speaker than Joseph Frederick, and the restriction on Brentwood's speech arose from an established institutional rule rather than an institutional manager's ad hoc discretion.[43] Justice Stevens's opinion never indulges the idea, so prominent in the Roberts Court's major institutional speech cases, that a government institution enjoys a quasi-private prerogative to suppress speech. Instead, he focuses on the institution's specific function, the precise threat the speech posed to that function, and the speaker's capacity to deliver on the threat.[44]

## FREE ENOUGH FOR GOVERNMENT WORK

Government workplaces bring even closer to the surface than schools or prisons the basic paradox of institutional speech disputes. Government employees work for the people. We therefore have a direct interest in government workplaces' effectiveness and integrity. How, then, should constitutional law reconcile government employees' expressive rights with the people's interest in functional government? If courts fully embrace the private employment analogy, they can simply ignore employees' free speech interests. In general, private employers can fire their employees for any reason, including objection to employees' speech. The government, however, has an ever-present obligation to respect constitutional rights, which private employers don't share. In addition, we can reasonably question how much benefit the people get from allowing government employers to suppress employees' expression. Speech seems unlikely to threaten the functions of workplaces as much as the functions of schools or, especially, prisons.[45] On the other side of the ledger, government employees generally know more than the rest of us about how our government may be serving us badly.

43. Perhaps courts should much more readily defer to government institutional managers in First Amendment cases when an institution maintains a formal speech policy. *See* Gia B. Lee, *First Amendment Enforcement in Government Institutions and Programs*, 56 UCLA L. Rev. 1691, 1745–74 (2009). In my view, the presence of a formal speech policy is necessary but not sufficient to justify deference.

44. The Court's five conservative justices concurred in the judgment to emphasize that the athletic association could properly restrict Brentwood's speech only because membership in the association was voluntary rather than compulsory. *See Brentwood Academy*, 551 U.S. at 304 (Kennedy, J., concurring in part and concurring in the judgment); *id.* at 306 (Thomas, J., concurring in the judgment).

45. *See* Scott A. Moss, *Students and Workers and Prisoners—Oh My! A Cautionary Note about Excessive Institutional Tailoring of First Amendment Doctrine*, 54 UCLA L. Rev. 1635, 1669 (2007) (setting out a typology of the risks that uncontrolled speech presents for different government institutions).

Another decision from the rights-protective Warren Court in the 1960s, *Pickering v. Board of Education*,[46] held that public employees should enjoy moderate First Amendment protection when they speak as citizens about matters of public concern. Later cases make clear that when an employee speaks not about a matter of public concern but rather about a matter of purely private interest, the First Amendment provides no protection against job-related consequences.[47] If the Court finds that a government employer has disciplined an employee for speaking as a citizen about a matter of public concern, it must then determine whether the employer's interest in maintaining government efficiency outweighs the employee's expressive interest.[48] Like the similar balancing tests for prisoners' and students' speech, the public employee speech test provides much less than the full measure of First Amendment protection. Two practical factors, however, distinguish the Supreme Court's record on public employee speech from its records on prisons and public schools. First, the Court over the years has decided more public employee speech cases than prisoner speech cases and student speech cases combined. Second, employees have occasionally prevailed in important cases, although the government has won more and bigger victories.[49]

The Roberts Court made its major statement about public employee speech in ***Garcetti v. Ceballos* (2006)**.[50] Richard Ceballos was a lawyer who supervised prosecutors in the office of Los Angeles County District Attorney Gil Garcetti. In early 2000, a lawyer for a criminal defendant approached Ceballos about defects in a search warrant used to gather key evidence against the defendant. The defense lawyer claimed the affidavit the sheriff's department had used to get the warrant misrepresented key facts. Ceballos investigated the claim and concluded that the affidavit was indeed faulty. He wrote his superiors a memo that described the problem and urged them to dismiss the prosecution. The higher-ups, after a tense meeting with Ceballos and sheriff's department employees, went ahead with the prosecution. The defense moved to exclude evidence acquired pursuant to the allegedly defective warrant. At a hearing on that motion, the defense called Ceballos to testify, and he explained why he thought the affidavit was faulty. The trial judge rejected the defense motion. In the wake of these events, Ceballos's superiors gave him worse assignments

46. 391 U.S. 563 (1968).

47. *See, e.g.*, Connick v. Myers, 461 U.S. 138 (1983).

48. *See* Pickering, 391 U.S. at 572–73.

49. *See, e.g.*, United States v. Nat'l Treasury Emps. Union, 513 U.S. 454 (1995) (striking down a federal ban on rank-and-file government employees' receipt of honoraria for speaking or writing).

50. 547 U.S. 410 (2006). Kennedy (majority) (with Roberts, Scalia, Alito, Thomas); Stevens (dissenting); Souter (dissenting) (with Stevens, Ginsburg); Breyer (dissenting).

and denied him a promotion. Ceballos claimed these actions retaliated against his criticism of the affidavit. The Supreme Court had to decide whether such retaliation violated the First Amendment.

The case broke down 5-4 along the Court's conservative-liberal fault line. Justice Kennedy wrote for the conservative majority, rejecting Ceballos's claim. The opinion begins by ascribing to past cases a sharp distinction between employees who speak as employees and employees who speak as citizens.[51] Ceballos's speech unquestionably dealt with a matter of public concern: the probity of a criminal prosecution. Therefore, the government could only avoid a *Pickering* First Amendment analysis if Ceballos spoke as an employee rather than a citizen and if that distinction made a decisive legal difference. Justice Kennedy zeroes in on a factor that distinguishes *Garcetti* from earlier public employee speech cases: here, the employee delivered the speech at issue in the course of his job duties. Ceballos, Justice Kennedy explains, was just doing his job when he wrote his memo that criticized the affidavit and recommended dropping the prosecutions. If and when his superiors retaliated against him based on the content of the memo, they were simply exercising proper supervisory authority. What matters, Justice Kennedy stresses, is not that Ceballos spoke in his workplace rather than in a public setting, or that he spoke about his work rather than about something else. What matters is that Ceballos spoke "pursuant to [his] official duties."[52]

The majority proceeds to hold that, when a government employer disciplines an employee based on speech in the course of the employee's official duties, the First Amendment never comes into play. The employee doesn't get even the limited benefit of the *Pickering* employee speech balancing test, because course-of-duty speech always amounts to speech made as an employee rather than speech made as a citizen. To examine course-of-duty speech disputes under the balancing test, Justice Kennedy insists, would improperly "displace[] managerial discretion by judicial supervision."[53] As in *Morse*, where the Court categorically denied speech that advocates illegal drug use the benefit of the student speech balancing test, the Court in *Garcetti* cuts another institutional subject's First Amendment claim off at its knees.

Trying to explain why speech in the course of an employee's duties differs from other speech, Justice Kennedy describes course-of-duty speech as "what the employer itself has commissioned or created."[54] That move gestures toward a recent innovation in First Amendment law called the *government speech doctrine*. The Court has held that, if the government enlists a private person or group to speak on the government's behalf, the speech gets no First

51. *See id.* at 417–20.
52. *Id.* at 421.
53. *Id.* at 423.
54. *Id.* at 422.

Amendment protection, because the government itself is speaking.[55] In that scenario, the speaker becomes the government—or, more precisely, a low-level government functionary. The government speech doctrine has great potency, because it turns seemingly autonomous, private speech into mere government action. It's a magic trick that makes First Amendment rights disappear. We'll see the government speech doctrine in action next chapter. The doctrine doesn't fit *Garcetti,* because someone in Ceballos's position exercises independent judgment, rather than just parroting a government policy.[56] Justice Kennedy's nod toward government speech, though, underscores his determination to avoid First Amendment analysis.

Justice Souter's dissenting opinion in *Garcetti,* joined by Justices Stevens and Ginsburg, sharply contests the majority's view that all speech in the course of a public employee's job duties should lose First Amendment protection. Among other concerns, Justice Souter posits that the Court's decision may inspire public employers to expand job descriptions as a way of increasing their control over employees' speech.[57] In his view, any speech made "with a citizen's interest" should count as citizen rather than employee speech for First Amendment purposes.[58] That formulation short-circuits the majority's basis for setting course-of-duty speech apart from other employee speech and outside the First Amendment's scope. Justice Souter argues, in fact, that course-of-duty speech may matter more than other speech for First Amendment purposes. From the people's perspective, course-of-duty speech may have the greatest impact on whether and how the employee advances the public's interest in government effectiveness, responsiveness, and integrity. From the employee's standpoint, course-of-duty speech may reflect the employee's deep commitment to public service.[59] Justice Souter acknowledges that speech in the course of an employee's duties may pose a greater threat than other employee speech to government operations. He agrees that the government should have substantial power to prevent disruptions from course-of-duty speech. He maintains, however, that the *Pickering* balancing test can properly weigh the competing factors and "make adjustments that serve all of the values at stake."[60] In his view, the First Amendment should

55. In characterizing government employees' course-of-duty speech as the government's creation, Justice Kennedy cites a passage in *Rosenberger v. Rector & Visitors of Univ. of Va.*, 515 U.S. 819, 833 (1995), that discusses and tries to explain the then-emergent government speech doctrine.

56. *See Garcetti,* 547 U.S. at 436–38 (Souter, J., dissenting).

57. *See id.* at 431 n.2 (Souter, J., dissenting). Justice Kennedy brushes off Justice Souter's concern as formalistic and states that the scope of a government employee's job duties is a practical question. *See id.* at 424. Justice Souter responds that the government can manipulate a practical inquiry as well as a formal job description.

58. *Id.* at 428 (Souter, J., dissenting).

59. *See id.* at 430–33 (Souter, J., dissenting).

60. *Id.* at 434 (Souter, J., dissenting).

protect speech in the course of a public employee's duties when the employee "speaks on a matter of unusual importance and satisfies high standards of responsibility in the way he does it."[61]

Justice Breyer, as in his *Beard* plurality opinion and his *Snyder* concurrence from last chapter, stakes out a position between his colleagues' poles. He seems more in tune with the majority's underlying concerns, criticizing Justice Souter's approach for inviting too much judicial oversight of government operations.[62] The absolutist character of the majority's holding, however, troubles Justice Breyer. He views Ceballos's case as an exceptional one, warranting First Amendment protection, for two reasons. First, Ceballos was not merely an employee but a professional, and his course-of-duty speech therefore had to satisfy canons of professional conduct. Second, the Constitution requires prosecuting attorneys such as Ceballos to discover and share with the defense evidence in the government's possession that may substantially help the defendant. These professional and constitutional mandates, in Justice Breyer's view, supported Ceballos's memo and testimony, and the District Attorney's Office had little if any legitimate basis for countermanding them.[63]

Defenders of *Garcetti* coalesce around a principle of what one has called "managerial prerogative."[64] Government managers, they argue, need to be able to evaluate their employees' work. Managers must have power to discipline or even fire employees if speech required for their work is substandard or plain wrong. If judges used the First Amendment to substitute their own employee evaluations for those of managers, government efficiency would suffer, undermining the same public interest the First Amendment is supposed to protect.[65] Can managerial prerogative justify the *Garcetti* Court's exclusion of all course-of-duty speech from First Amendment protection? The public's interest in course-of-duty speech cases cuts both ways, in favor of government managers' control of the institutions they manage but also in favor of public employees' freedom to tell us what the government is doing. The balancing test the Court has long used in public employee speech disputes weighs those competing aspects of the public interest. It lets courts distinguish legitimate from illegitimate reasons for punishing course-of-duty speech. Accepting the *Garcetti* Court's wholesale scrapping of judicial balancing in course-of-duty speech cases requires negating the First Amendment side of the balance and accepting all managerial decisions about course-of-duty speech as categorically valid.

61. *Id.* at 435 (Souter, J., dissenting).
62. *See id.* at 447–49 (Breyer, J., dissenting).
63. *See id.* at 446–47 (Breyer, J., dissenting).
64. Lawrence Rosenthal, *The Emerging First Amendment Law of Managerial Prerogative*, 77 FORDHAM L. REV. 33 (2008).
65. *See id.* at 44–52.

Four distinct but related stories try to explain how managerial prerogative can remove course-of-duty speech entirely from First Amendment protection.[66] Each of these stories reflects a repeating motif in the Roberts Court's First Amendment jurisprudence: (1) use of categorical reasoning to exclude speech from First Amendment protection, (2) manipulation of the public-private distinction to negate expressive interests, (3) strong deference to government authority, and (4) association (if not outright equation) of private speech with government speech.

First, consider the "no First Amendment interest" story. Public employees' speech in the course of their job duties, this story emphasizes, doesn't generally reach the public at all. Instead, it's usually confined within the government workplace. Therefore, it can't have any First Amendment weight. Course-of-duty speech may improve internal government efficiency, but "government efficiency is not a First Amendment value."[67] The "no First Amendment interest" story plays a variation on the speech-restrictive uses of categorical reasoning we saw in Chapter 1. This story neglects a crucial way that public employee speech can advance the public interest. Vincent Blasi posits that a major function of free speech is to check government abuses.[68] Usually we think of this "checking function" as happening through public debate. On the conventional view, public employees can only perform the checking function when they speak to the public.[69] However, public employees can also perform the checking function within the government workplace. If a government lawyer tries to persuade his superiors not to break the law, he's checking a government abuse, and thus serving the public interest, whether or not the broader public learns about the abuse or the lawyer's attempt to stop it. A government employee can speak "as a citizen, on a matter of public concern" not only by speaking *to* the public but also by speaking *for* the public. Of course, the employee may be mistaken, incompetent, or skewed by an ulterior motive, but the *Pickering* balance serves to ferret out those problems. Commentators have also criticized the "no First Amendment interest" story's core distinction between citizen and employee as artificial and hostile to political dissent.[70]

66. My analysis here concentrates on the public's interest in government employees' speech. Employees' own interests in speaking present an additional, distinct source of First Amendment concern. *See* Cynthia Estlund, *Harmonizing Work and Citizenship: A Due Process Solution to a First Amendment Problem*, 2006 SUP. CT. REV. 115, 150–51.

67. Kermit Roosevelt III, *Not as Bad as You Think: Why* Garcetti v. Ceballos *Makes Sense*, 14 U. PA. J. CONST. L. 631, 650 (2012); *see also* Rosenthal, *supra* note 64, at 38.

68. *See* Vincent Blasi, *The Checking Value in First Amendment Theory*, 2 LAW & SOC. INQUIRY 521 (1977).

69. *See* Roosevelt, *supra* note 67, at 649–50.

70. *See* Caroline M. Corbin, *Mixed Speech: When Speech Is Both Private and Governmental*, 83 N.Y.U. L. REV. 605, 670 (2008); Orly Lobel, *Citizenship, Organizational Citizenship, and the Laws of Overlapping Obligations*, 97 CAL. L. REV. 433 (2009).

The second story analogizes government employment to private employment. A workplace is a workplace, says this "private analogy" story. Private employees don't get to mouth off and escape their bosses' wrath, least of all in their course-of-duty speech, and public employees shouldn't get to do so either.[71] We've already seen versions of the private analogy story fuel the Court's reasoning in the prisoner and student speech cases. The problem with this story is that, although the public has no First Amendment interest in private sector employees' speech, we have a strong First Amendment interest in government employees' speech.[72] The *Garcetti* distinction between speaking as a citizen and speaking as an employee resonates with the copyright case *Golan v. Holder* (Chapter 1) by manipulating the public-private line more aggressively than any past public employee speech case. The private becomes public: the Court treats Ceballos's seemingly autonomous speech as belonging to his government employer.[73] At the same time, the public becomes private: the Court treats the subject of Ceballos's speech, alleged misconduct by government officials, as the sort of internal matter that an employer may choose to disregard.[74]

The third attempted justification for excluding public employees' course-of-duty speech from First Amendment protection is the "judicial restraint" story. The Court in *Garcetti,* as in all the other decisions we've seen in this chapter, defaults to a position of judicial noninterference, deferring almost completely to government officials. The *Garcetti* Court and its defenders maintain that the government will do better than courts in balancing government efficiency interests against free speech interests. The Constitution, however, doesn't let the government subordinate free speech to its own goals. Justice Kennedy in *Garcetti* reassures us that "a powerful network of . . .

71. *See* Garcetti v. Ceballos, 547 U.S. 410, 436–38 (2006); Roosevelt, *supra* note 67, at 637.

72. Perhaps the Court should recognize a First Amendment interest in private employees' speech about matters of public concern. For my own qualified argument along these lines, see Gregory P. Magarian, *The First Amendment, The Public-Private Distinction, and Nongovernmental Suppression of Wartime Political Debate*, 73 Geo. Wash. L. Rev. 101, 150–72 (2004).

73. Pauline Kim thoroughly debunks the private employment analogy from the standpoint of employment law. *See* Pauline T. Kim, *Market Norms and Constitutional Values in the Government Workplace*, 94 N.C. L. Rev. 601, 631–47 (2016); *see also* Estlund, *supra* note 66, at 144–49; Adam Shinar, *Public Employee Speech and the Privatization of the First Amendment*, 46 Conn. L. Rev. 1 (2013).

74. The Court has wrestled with the limits of government-private analogies in other areas of constitutional law. *See* South-Central Timber Dev. Inc. v. Wunnicke, 467 U.S. 82 (1984) (finding limits on the "market participant exception" to the commerce clause's prohibition of states' regulating interstate economic matters); Hudgens v. NLRB, 424 U.S. 507 (1976) (rejecting an argument that, because a private shopping center had some functional equivalence to a municipal shopping district, the shopping center was a "state actor" subject to constitutional rules).

whistle-blower protection laws and labor codes" will protect employees who call out government wrongdoing.[75] But not every jurisdiction has such protections, and even strong labor and whistle-blower laws don't obviate the First Amendment's primacy for protecting speech. The *Garcetti* Court warns that giving course-of-duty speech the benefit of the *Pickering* balancing test would subject the government to overly burdensome litigation. A decision in Ceballos's favor certainly would have enabled some bogus lawsuits. The crucial question, though, is whether the public benefit from the valid lawsuits *Garcetti* just as certainly prevented would outweigh the cost in the other direction.[76] A simple presumption against judicial review sheds no light on that question.

Finally, consider the "work product" story. If course-of-duty speech is effectively a form of property that the employee creates for the government manager's benefit, then a broad range of public employee speech arguably needs and deserves no First Amendment protection.[77] Seventh Circuit Court of Appeals judge Frank Easterbrook has cited *Garcetti* to support a holding that everything a public school teacher says in the classroom is her "stock in trade, the commodity she sells to her employer in exchange for a salary."[78] The crucial question is how much course-of-duty speech the work product story accurately describes. Helen Norton advocates a strict approach to granting public employers ownership of their employees' speech. She urges courts, as a check on the government speech doctrine in general and on *Garcetti* in particular, to treat course-of-duty expression as government speech only when (1) the government expressly claimed the speech as its own when it authorized the speech, and (2) the audience understands the speech as government speech.[79] Aggressive defenders of *Garcetti* claim that treating all course-of-duty speech as work product would promote government accountability, by ensuring that managers answer for their employees' statements.[80] Professor Norton flips that script, pointing out that distinguishing employees' autonomous speech from their work product better promotes government

75. *Garcetti,* 547 U.S. at 425.

76. Cynthia Estlund seeks a middle course by proposing an understanding, based on "First Amendment policy," that public employment contracts include a procedural due process right to an administrative hearing, not judicial review, before employees can face reprisals for "course of duty" speech, and perhaps other speech, on matters of public concern. Estlund, *supra* note 66, at 156.

77. *See* Roosevelt, *supra* note 67, at 648 (offering both a narrow version and a preferred broad version of this approach); Rosenthal, *supra* note 64, at 49.

78. Mayer v. Monroe Cty. Cmty. Sch. Corp., 474 F.3d 477, 479 (7th Cir. 2007). Other lower courts have similarly read *Garcetti* to permit broad restrictions on public employees' speech. For a compendium of early post-*Garcetti* decisions, see Helen Norton, *Constraining Public Employee Speech: Government's Control of Its Workers' Speech to Protect Its Own Expression*, 59 Duke L.J. 1, 13–16 (2009).

79. *See* Norton, *supra* note 78.

80. *See* Rosenthal, *supra* note 64, at 38.

accountability by ensuring that people actually know when the government is and isn't speaking.[81]

In the wake of *Garcetti*, the Roberts Court decided two further, narrower public employee speech cases.[82]

***Lane v. Franks* (2014)**[83] walks *Garcetti* back, but only a bit. The issue in *Lane* was whether First Amendment protection for public employee speech extends to an employee's sworn testimony, compelled by subpoena, that is not part of the employee's job duties. Lower courts in the case, relying on *Garcetti*, had held that the First Amendment didn't protect a mid-level supervisor's testimony at the corruption trial of a state legislator about why the supervisor had fired the legislator from a state job. The Supreme Court unanimously reversed. Justice Sotomayor's opinion chastises the lower courts for reading *Garcetti* too broadly. *Garcetti* only denies First Amendment protection to course-of-duty speech; it says nothing about off-duty speech that conveys information learned on the job. That sort of speech sits at the core of First Amendment protection for public employees, because we want public employees to report government abuses.[84] As Justice Sotomayor recognizes, the lower courts' approach in *Lane* runs counter to the Court's entire corpus of pre-*Garcetti* public employee speech decisions.[85] They only took that approach because *Garcetti* invited courts to exclude a large, imprecisely defined swath of public employee speech that "owes its existence to a public employee's professional responsibilities"[86] from First Amendment protection. *Lane* gives public employees a welcome assurance that they may testify about their work without fear of retaliation. However, had the Court not carved out course-of-duty speech in *Garcetti* as a First Amendment-free zone, the *Lane* issue never would have come up.

In ***Borough of Duryea v. Guarnieri* (2011)**,[87] a public employee alleged that his employer had retaliated against him for filing a union grievance and a subsequent lawsuit. He got his case to the Supreme Court via a novel strategy of calling his grievance and lawsuit not "speech" but rather "petition[s]

81. *See* Norton, *supra* note 78, at 30–32; *see also* Kim, *supra* note 73, at 640–45.

82. After Justice Scalia's death, the Court issued a mixed constitutional and statutory decision that allows an employee to challenge an adverse employment action that the employer took out of a mistaken belief that the employee had engaged in certain expressive activity. *See* Heffernan v. City of Paterson, 136 S. Ct. 1412 (2016).

83. 134 S. Ct. 2369 (2014). Sotomayor (majority) (with Roberts, Scalia, Kennedy, Thomas, Ginsburg, Breyer, Alito, Kagan); Thomas (concurring) (with Scalia, Alito).

84. *See id.* at 2378–80.

85. *See id.*

86. Garcetti v. Ceballos, 547 U.S. 410, 421 (2006).

87. 564 U.S. 379 (2011). Kennedy (majority) (with Roberts, Ginsburg, Breyer, Alito, Sotomayor, Kagan); Thomas (concurring in the judgment); Scalia (concurring in the judgment in part, dissenting in part).

[to] the Government for [] redress of grievances."[88] The petition clause, which sits alongside the speech, assembly, and press clauses in the First Amendment, rarely gets the modern Court's attention, mainly because the speech clause over time has absorbed most legal disputes about political protest.[89] Writing for a nearly unanimous Court in *Guarnieri*, Justice Kennedy held that the same First Amendment rules that govern public employee speech also govern public employee petitions, and in particular that public employee petitions must address "matters of public concern" in order to get First Amendment protection.[90] Justice Scalia, concurring in the judgment in part and dissenting in part, calls the majority's analysis both too speech protective and not speech protective enough. On one hand, he doubts the premise, stated by the majority but not contested in the case, that lawsuits and administrative grievances count as "petitions" at all.[91] On the other hand, he insists that petitions historically addressed both public and private matters, making the "public concern" requirement that applies to public employee speech disputes excessive for petition disputes.[92] He would extend First Amendment protection to any petition that an employee addresses to the government in its capacity as sovereign, rather than its capacity as employer.[93]

Although both *Lane* and *Guarnieri* largely ratify the legal status quo, they present a sharp contrast in rhetoric. Justice Sotomayor in *Lane* starts her legal analysis with a thorough account of the First Amendment interests, especially public interests, that animate the Court's public employee speech jurisprudence. Her opinion emphasizes the value of public employees' speech. In contrast, Justice Kennedy in *Guarnieri* echoes his *Garcetti* opinion by heavily stressing government employers' efficiency interests and the danger that employee grievances, particularly lawsuits, will disrupt efficiency. He denies that the public has a general interest in fair and efficient resolution of public employees' grievances. The justices' difference in emphasis mirrors their dueling priorities and positions from *Garcetti.*

88. U.S. Const. amend. I.

89. Ronald Krotoszynski forcefully advocates taking the petition clause more seriously as an independent source of expressive freedom. *See* Ronald J. Krotoszynski, Jr., Reclaiming the Petition Clause: Seditious Libel, "Offensive" Protest, and the Right to Petition the Government for a Redress of Grievances (2012).

90. *See Guarnieri*, 564 U.S. at 387–90.

91. *See id.* at 401–04 (Scalia, J., concurring in the judgment in part and dissenting in part).

92. *See id.* at 404–07 (Scalia, J., concurring in the judgment in part and dissenting in part).

93. *See id.* at 407–08 (Scalia, J., concurring in the judgment in part and dissenting in part). Justice Thomas, writing separately, agrees with Justice Scalia that the "public concern" requirement shouldn't apply to petitions, but he would still subject even public employees' "sovereign petitions" to the *Pickering* balancing test. *See id.* at 399–401 (Thomas, J., concurring in the judgment).

## CONCLUSION

This chapter began with a paradox. The Court should give prisoners, students, and public employees an edge in First Amendment disputes with the government, because those institutional subjects have constitutional rights. At the same time, though, the Court should give the government an edge, because the government manages institutions for the public's benefit. The Court has long balanced those competing interests in the government's favor. In this chapter we've seen the Roberts Court double down on limiting institutional subjects' First Amendment rights. The Court's major public institutional speech decisions display the three central motifs of managed speech: empowering institutional authorities to manage speech, here by deferring almost completely to the government's reasons for suppressing speech; denying First Amendment protection to marginal, dissenting speakers, here by discounting institutional subjects' speech interests; and orienting legal analysis toward the stable functioning of government institutions.

The institutional speech decisions give the government managerial control over institutional subjects' speech. In Chapter 2 we saw the Court defer completely to Congress in *Holder v. Humanitarian Law Project,* the case about "material support" for terrorist groups. The cases discussed in this chapter involve less weighty policy concerns and more pedestrian government functions, but they give the government the same sort of latitude. The Court lets a prison warden, a school principal, and a district attorney assess the importance of the speech at issue, declare how severely the speech threatens the institution's functioning, and choose the means of suppressing the speech. These decisions grant government institutional authorities the same managerial prerogatives as private institutional authorities. The Court claims incompetence to second-guess the institutional expertise of government managers. Federal judges, however, get their training in schools, administer the criminal justice system, and are themselves government employers and employees.[94] More importantly, the Court insists that institutional managers need tight control over their subjects' speech to protect their institutions' stable functioning.

The institutional speech decisions treat institutional subjects' speech as a threat to social and political stability. In *Beard,* the Court lets prison authorities use speech as a tool of punishment and control. Prisoners' access to newspapers, magazines, and personal photographs becomes currency that prison officials can exchange for prisoners' good behavior. In *Morse,* the Court reads a high school student's cryptic epigram "BONG HiTS 4 JESUS" as encouraging other students to use illegal drugs and accordingly allows school authorities

94. Moss, *supra* note 45, at 1667.

to punish the student. *Garcetti* lets a government employer suppress an employee's substantive criticism of the employer's practices in order to maintain public trust and protect working relationships within the government. To the extent the institutional subjects' speech challenges government power, most obviously in *Garcetti,* that political goal doesn't strengthen but rather undermines the institutional subjects' First Amendment claim. In *Morse* and *Garcetti* the Court removes institutional subjects' speech entirely from First Amendment protection, avoiding even the weak balancing tests that usually protect the speech rights of students and public employees.

Dynamic diversity, my alternative First Amendment model to managed speech, would upend the results and reasoning in this chapter's major cases. Prisoners, students, and public employees all bring important insights and viewpoints to public debates. Society generally prefers to forget about prisoners, but they can testify to the terms and conditions of incarceration for which the political community bears collective responsibility. Students represent the political community's future, and youth confers as distinct a perspective on public issues as experience. Public employees often have deeper insights than anyone into the government's workings and failings. At the margin this chapter's cases occupy, where the government tries to press its managerial authority beyond normal boundaries, dynamic diversity compels, at a minimum, serious judicial review of institutional subjects' First Amendment claims. In these particular cases, dynamic diversity would counsel decisions for the speech claimants. Prisoners shouldn't lose access to basic sources of information as a matter of disciplinary leverage. Students, especially off school grounds, shouldn't have to self-censor any message an administrator might interpret as objectionable or improper. Public employees shouldn't face discipline for making conscientious efforts to discourage their superiors from breaking the law. The reasonable First Amendment protections the Roberts Court denied in these cases would advance dynamic diversity by allowing these institutional subjects to bring their valuable knowledge and ideas into public discussion.

Besides public institutions, the government can claim special authority to control speech in two other contexts. The government owns physical and intangible property that people use for speech. The government also funds various kinds of speech. The next two chapters deal with those two sorts of government preserves. Most of the cases will proceed along the Roberts Court's dominant track, subordinating disruptive speech to managerial control in the name of social and political stability.

# CHAPTER 4

# Speakers, Cornered

## *Weakening the Public Forum*

Governments, state and federal, use their property to provide numerous services, from transportation to beautification, education to administration. Government property has great value for speakers without independent means to reach large audiences. If you want to promote an unpopular or obscure political cause, and you can't afford to design an effective website or buy TV time, you can organize a street rally, post notices on utility poles, or stage a concert in a park. Some government property houses institutions such as prisons, high schools, and offices. Last chapter we saw the Roberts Court deal with First Amendment claims that arise from those institutions' subjects. This chapter deals with disputes that arise when the government tries to restrict ordinary people from speaking on or with government property. The paradigm setting for this kind of expression is real property—land and physical structures—but the government also owns and maintains more abstract sorts of property, such as institutional sponsorship and opportunities to participate in government programs. The Internet and shifts of commerce from public to private spaces have pulled some speech away from government property.[1] However, the durability of physical space as a medium for human interaction ensures the continuing importance of government property for First Amendment law.

The Supreme Court decides First Amendment cases that arise from real property and its analogs under a special set of rules called the *public forum*

1. *See, e.g.*, Jack M. Balkin, *Old-School/New-School Speech Regulation*, 127 HARV. L. REV. 2296, 2301–06 (2014).

*doctrine*. This doctrine seeks to mediate the same basic dilemma we saw in the last chapter's institutional speech cases. Government holds and maintains property for the public's use and enjoyment. We need streets and sidewalks to move around. We enjoy the beauty and utility of parks and other green areas. Libraries and museums, airports and train stations, public auditoriums and arenas all help us manage and enjoy our lives. The importance of those benefits suggests that government should have greater power to restrict activity, including speech, on property it owns. On the other hand, the distinctive importance of government property for speakers, especially speakers with limited resources, makes government property crucial for inclusive, wide-ranging public discussion and debate. A venerable example is Speakers' Corner in London's Hyde Park, where anyone can speak and many passersby will hear. Given the expressive value of government property, governments arguably shouldn't have any greater power to regulate speech on government property than on private property.

In attempting to reconcile these competing interests, the public forum doctrine starts with the insight that some government property, in the mold of Speaker's Corner, has long been available for expressive activity. That sort of property, including sidewalks, streets, and parks, is the quintessential *traditional public forum*.[2] The government may not restrict the content or viewpoint of speech in a public forum unless it can satisfy the same strict scrutiny the Court applies to content-based restrictions on private speech (as we saw in Part I). The government, however, gets to maintain and manage its property, even when that property is a public forum. Accordingly, the public forum doctrine gives government significant leeway in regulating the *time, place, or manner* of speech in a public forum.[3] The government may not stop you from urging people on a public sidewalk to vote Republican, but it may stop you from blasting "Vote Republican!" from a sound truck in a residential neighborhood at 2 am. When the government in a public forum regulates only the time, place, or manner of speech, not the speech's content, the Court subjects the regulation only to a species of "intermediate scrutiny" called the *O'Brien* test.[4] That test, which broadly resembles the *Central Hudson* test we saw for commercial speech in Chapter 2 and the balancing tests for speech in schools and government workplaces we saw in Chapter 3, tends in practice to favor the government.[5]

2. *See* Hague v. Comm. for Indus. Org., 307 U.S. 496, 515–16 (1939) ("[S]treets and parks . . . have immemorially been held in trust for the use of the public and, time out of mind, have been used for purposes of assembly, communicating thoughts between citizens, and discussing public questions.").

3. *See* Cox v. New Hampshire, 312 U.S. 569, 576 (1941).

4. *See* United States v. O'Brien, 391 U.S. 367 (1968).

5. *See* Ward v. Rock Against Racism, 491 U.S. 781 (1989); Clark v. Cmty. for Creative Non-Violence, 468 U.S. 288 (1984); Members of City Council v. Taxpayers for Vincent, 466 U.S. 789 (1984) (all upholding speech restrictions under the "time, place, or manner" balancing test).

Beyond the traditional public forum, the government may choose to designate other property as a public forum. Doing so usually creates a *limited public forum,* designed for speech on particular subjects or for particular purposes.[6] In a limited public forum, the government may use reasonable means to maintain the forum's purpose, as long as it doesn't discriminate against particular viewpoints. However, the government triggers strict scrutiny if it tries to limit the content or viewpoint of speech that satisfies the forum's purpose. Most other government property—neither traditionally established nor designated as a public forum—falls into the category of the *nonpublic forum.* In a nonpublic forum, the government may freely restrict the content of speech. Even there, however, the government may not restrict some viewpoints and favor others.

The public forum doctrine has a mixed record for promoting broad-based public debate. The doctrine has formalized an arrangement that lets governments, not just for the public benefit but also for self-interested managerial ends, restrict speech on government property, notably public political protests. The Supreme Court, especially since 1970, has usually favored governments over speakers in public forum disputes. Although public forum speakers have found greater success in lower courts,[7] many important lower court decisions follow the Supreme Court's generally speech-restrictive lead. A federal court of appeals, for example, notoriously approved Boston's shunting of protestors at the 2004 Democratic National Convention to a fenced-in "designated demonstration zone" outside convention delegates' sight and hearing.[8] Legal scholars have long criticized the public forum doctrine as insufficiently speech-protective.[9] Those criticisms persist today.[10]

At the same time, the doctrine embodies First Amendment law's strongest acknowledgment that if we want effective public debate, we need a broad distribution of opportunities for speakers to reach audiences. For the most part, First Amendment law takes private speech as it comes, curbing government's

6. *See, e.g.*, Rosenberger v. Rector & Visitors of Univ. of Va., 515 U.S. 819, 829 (1995) (university student activities fund).

7. *See* Seth P. Kreimer, *Good Enough for Government Work: Two Cheers for Content Neutrality*, 16 U. PA. J. CONST. L. 1261, 1291–95 (2014).

8. *See* Bl(a)ck Tea Soc'y v. City of Boston, 378 F.3d 8 (1st Cir. 2004).

9. Leading examples include ROBERT C. POST, CONSTITUTIONAL DOMAINS: DEMOCRACY, COMMUNITY, MANAGEMENT 199–267 (1995); Daniel A. Farber & John E. Nowak, *The Misleading Nature of Public Forum Analysis: Content and Context in First Amendment Adjudication*, 70 VA. L. REV. 1219 (1984); Kenneth Karst, *Public Enterprise and the Public Forum: A Comment on* Southeastern Promotions, Ltd. v. Conrad, 37 OHIO ST. L.J. 247 (1976).

10. *See, e.g.*, JOHN D. INAZU, CONFIDENT PLURALISM: SURVIVING AND THRIVING THROUGH DEEP DIFFERENCE 50–65 (2016); TIMOTHY ZICK, SPEECH OUT OF DOORS: PRESERVING FIRST AMENDMENT LIBERTIES IN PUBLIC PLACES 167–71 (2009); Tabatha Abu El-Haj, *All Assemble: Order and Disorder in Law, Politics, and Culture*, 16 U. PA. J. CONST. L. 949, 1024–30 (2014).

power to restrict speakers who have their own expressive resources. Some court decisions and academic commentators, however, contend that the First Amendment, properly understood, guarantees not just protection against government restrictions but also some measure of fairness in distributions of expressive resources.[11] The Supreme Court in the late 1960s took distribution of expressive access seriously. The Warren Court let Congress, over broadcast networks' First Amendment objections, make broadcasters present a diverse range of content and ideas,[12] and the Court even gave speakers conditional access to private property generally open to the public.[13] Within a few years, though, the Court under Chief Justice Warren Burger reversed or scaled back those distributive access decisions.[14] The public forum doctrine, at least in theory, remains the primary legal vehicle for distributing expressive access to marginal or underfunded speakers.

The Roberts Court has decided four cases that focus on the public forum doctrine. The decisions, like last chapter's institutional speech decisions, largely apply the tenets of managed speech. The Court's liberal wing[15] has influenced the public forum decisions more than any other area of the Roberts Court's free speech jurisprudence, prevailing in three of them by 5-4 votes. That alignment might cause us to expect a divergence from the Roberts Court's usual First Amendment mode. The public forum decisions, however, advance managed speech by resisting calls to distribute expressive access. Two of the decisions negate free speech arguments entirely, holding that seemingly private speech in a public forum is actually government speech outside the First Amendment's scope. Another decision defers to university administrators in rejecting a religious student group's claim that the First Amendment protects its right to restrict its membership on moral grounds. Both of those techniques subordinate marginal, potentially disruptive viewpoints to government control, protecting the stable functioning of government institutions and programs. The final public forum decision marks an important departure, sustaining antiabortion street activists' challenge to a legal "buffer zone" that barred their speech near abortion clinics. That decision takes the dangers of

11. *See, e.g.*, Jerome A. Barron, *Access to the Press—A New First Amendment Right*, 80 HARV. L. REV. 1641 (1967); Owen M. Fiss, *Free Speech and Social Structure*, 71 IOWA L. REV. 1405 (1986); Kenneth Karst, *Equality as a Central Principle in the First Amendment*, 43 U. CHI. L. REV. 20 (1975).

12. *See* Red Lion Broad. Co. v. FCC, 395 U.S. 367 (1969).

13. *See* Amalgamated Food Emps. Union v. Logan Valley Plaza, Inc., 391 U.S. 308 (1968).

14. *See* Hudgens v. NLRB, 424 U.S. 507 (1976) (overruling *Logan Valley Plaza*); Miami Herald Pub. Co. v. Tornillo, 418 U.S. 241 (1974) (largely contradicting the reasoning of *Red Lion Broadcasting*).

15. Justices Ginsburg, Breyer, Sotomayor, and Kagan made up the Court's "liberal wing" as of 2016. Justices Sotomayor and Kagan replaced Justices Souter and Stevens, both of whom had also belonged to the liberal group.

"time, place, or manner" rules more seriously than the Court has in decades. Some of the decision's rhetoric, however, suggests the Court's newfound vigilance may apply only in narrow circumstances, leaving in place the Court's general skepticism of public forum claims.

## GOVERNMENT SPEECH, SET IN STONE

Summum is a small religious sect founded in 1975 and based in Salt Lake City. In 2003, Summum came up with a clever way to get its largely unknown beliefs before a broad audience. Pioneer Park in Pleasant Grove City, Utah, like many parks, houses several permanent monuments. Among those monuments is a depiction of the Ten Commandments, which the Fraternal Order of Eagles donated to the city decades ago. Summum offered the city a similar monument for placement in the park that would depict Summum's Seven Aphorisms.[16] Pleasant Grove City, the sect reasoned, had let certain groups donate monuments for a public park, a classic public forum. The public forum doctrine prohibits discrimination against speech in public forums based on its content or viewpoint. Therefore, the First Amendment should compel the city to accept the Seven Aphorisms monument and place it in Pioneer Park. Pleasant Grove City, however, rejected the monument. The city told Summum that it only accepted monuments that directly related to the city's history or that groups with "longstanding ties to the Pleasant Grove community" donated. Summum sued Pleasant Grove City under the First Amendment.

In ***Pleasant Grove City v. Summum* (2009)**,[17] the Roberts Court unanimously rejected Summum's claim. Justice Alito, writing for the majority, duly acknowledges that Pioneer Park is a traditional public forum. He holds, however, that "a permanent monument in a public park is not a form of expression to which forum analysis applies."[18] Justice Alito draws two distinctions between monuments and other sorts of expression common in public forums, such as parades, distributions of literature, and speeches. First, monuments are permanent, whereas all those other forms of speech are transient.[19] Second, governments exercise judgment, "selective receptivity," in deciding which donated monuments to accept and reject.[20] The first distinction, for Justice

16. "The principles of knowing Creation are seven; those who know these possess the Magic Key to whose touch all locked doors open to Creation," http://www.summum.us/philosophy/principles.shtml (last visited Apr. 3, 2015). Limited space and an aversion to cheap irony foreclose memorializing the seven aphorisms in their entirety here.

17. 555 U.S. 460 (2009). Alito (majority) with Roberts, Stevens, Scalia, Kennedy, Thomas, Ginsburg, Breyer; Stevens (concurring) with Ginsburg; Scalia (concurring) with Thomas; Breyer (concurring); Souter (concurring in the judgment).

18. *Id.* at 464.

19. *See id.* at 478–79.

20. *Id.* at 471.

Alito, demands a way out of the ordinary public forum paradigm. The First Amendment can't possibly make governments accept any and all permanent monuments that anyone might want to place in a public park.[21] The second distinction provides the way out. Justice Alito declares Pleasant Grove City's acceptance and placement of monuments to be not a regulation of private speech but an instance of *government speech.* When a government accepts a donated monument, the government supplants the donor as the entity whose voice and viewpoint animates the monument's message. The disappearance of the private speaker from this scenario eliminates any First Amendment interest. In contrast, Justice Alito sees a strong interest on the government's side. He treats the government just like a private property owner.[22] People who see monuments on private or government property, he reasons, ascribe the monuments' messages to the property owner. A city, like the owner of a shopping mall or a stadium, must therefore get to control which views people ascribe to it.[23]

The "recently minted government speech doctrine,"[24] which made a cameo appearance in the public employee speech case *Garcetti* (Chapter 3), takes center stage in *Summum.* Speech by government actors complicates the speaker-regulator distinction in First Amendment law.[25] Two decades ago, in narrowly upholding a challenge to a federal family planning rule that barred certain doctors who receive federal money from advising their patients about abortion services, the Court under Chief Justice Rehnquist seemed to indulge the startling idea that the government sometimes may discriminate against a speaker's viewpoint.[26] The Court later explained that the bar on abortion counseling had not, in fact, suppressed any private speaker. The government, instead, had simply paid doctors to speak the government's message.[27] The Rehnquist Court later used the government speech doctrine to reject beef producers' First Amendment attack on a law that made them support a government-run beef advertising campaign.[28]

In an effort to avoid the government speech doctrine, Summum argued that governments should have to embrace monuments' messages formally in order to have courts treat the monuments as government speech. In response, Justice Alito delivers a rich, even postmodern account of how monuments and other speech mean different things to different people and change

21. *See id.* at 479–80.
22. *See id.* at 470–71.
23. *Id.* at 473.
24. *Id.* at 481 (Stevens, J., concurring).
25. *See* Mark G. Yudof, When Government Speaks: Politics, Law, and Government Expression in America (1983).
26. *See* Rust v. Sullivan, 500 U.S. 173 (1991).
27. *See* Rosenberger v. Rector & Visitors of Univ. of Va., 515 U.S. 819, 833 (1995).
28. *See* Johanns v. Livestock Mktg. Ass'n, 544 U.S. 550 (2005).

in meaning over time.[29] This allocation stands alongside Justice Scalia's celebration of video games' interactivity in *Entertainment Merchants* (Chapter 1) as one of the Roberts Court's most vivid statements about free expression's complexity and value. It contrasts sharply with the Court's reductive dismissal of speakers' messages in contexts such as the material aid to terrorists case, *Humanitarian Law Project* (Chapter 2) and in the "BONG HiTS 4 JESUS" case, *Morse v. Frederick* (Chapter 3). Justice Alito, however, appears to have climbed out on this limb solely to save Pleasant Grove City from having to own up to its convictions.[30] If the city had to embrace the message of Pioneer Park's Ten Commandments monument, the Court's government speech analysis would run into a serious problem under the First Amendment's establishment clause,[31] which bars the government from adopting religious beliefs.[32] Justice Alito's apparent celebration of semiotic nuance really just bleaches the Ten Commandments monument of religious meaning.[33]

Several justices contributed concurring opinions in *Summum* that endorse the majority's government speech holding while hedging its implications. Justices Stevens and Ginsburg, frequent skeptics of government speech arguments, embrace this one based on a belief that it doesn't expand the government speech doctrine at all.[34] Justice Breyer tries to recast the Court's government speech holding as his favored sort of nuanced balancing analysis, one that does "not [employ] a rigid category."[35] Justice Souter alone declined to join the majority opinion, filing a concurrence that marked his last free speech opinion before he retired in June 2009. Even Justice Souter agrees that Pleasant Grove City should prevail under the government speech doctrine,

29. *See Summum*, 555 U.S. at 474–78.

30. Scholars have sharply criticized the *Summum* Court for treating the government as a speaker without requiring it to embrace any message. *See* Randall P. Bezanson, *The Manner of Government Speech*, 87 DEN. U. L. REV. 809, 812–15 (2010); Steven G. Gey, *Why Should the First Amendment Protect Government Speech When the Government Has Nothing to Say?*, 95 IOWA L. REV. 1259, 1312–13 (2010); Helen Norton & Danielle Keats Citron, *Government Speech 2.0*, 87 DENV. U. L. REV. 899, 916–17 (2010).

31. "Congress shall make no law respecting an establishment of religion . . . ." U.S. CONST. amend. I.

32. *See, e.g.*, McCreary Cty. v. Am. Civil Liberties Union, 545 U.S. 844 (2005) (holding that a Ten Commandments display in a county courthouse had a religious purpose and thus violated the establishment clause). Justice Scalia added a concurring opinion in *Summum* solely to proclaim the irrelevance of the establishment clause for the case. *See Summum*, 555 U.S. at 482 (Scalia, J., concurring).

33. *See* Douglas Laycock, *Government Sponsored Religious Displays: Transparent Rationalizations and Expedient Post-modernism*, 61 CASE W. RES. L. REV. 1211, 1244–49 (2011) (criticizing the *Summum* Court for downplaying the Ten Commandments' religious significance).

34. *See Summum*, 555 U.S. at 481 (Stevens, J., concurring).

35. *Id.* at 484 (Breyer, J., concurring). Note how Justice Breyer's semantic resistance to categorical reasoning in *Summum* resonates with his similar approach in the Stolen Valor Act case, *Alvarez* (Chapter 1).

but he refuses to concede that monuments are always or nearly always government speech. Rather, he would "go slow in setting [the government speech doctrine's] bounds."[36] All three concurring opinions signal some caution about invoking the government speech doctrine in future cases. (I'll argue in the next chapter that the Court, in a more recent decision about subsidized speech, has taken that caution at least somewhat to heart.)

Justice Alito in *Summum* raises a serious concern that making governments dump into public parks whatever monuments any person or group drops off at city hall might very well drown parks in monuments.[37] Notwithstanding that concern, *Summum* weakens the public forum both in the Court's treatment of speakers and in its treatment of government.

As to speakers, the Court's labeling of Pleasant Grove's monument regime as "government speech" rather than government regulation removes the dispute from the First Amendment's coverage. The decision therefore resembles both the cases from Chapter 1 in which the Court embraced or strengthened categorical exclusions from First Amendment protection and the cases from Chapter 3 about speech by students (*Morse*) and public employees (*Garcetti*). In all those instances, the Roberts Court found ways to remove apparent First Amendment disputes from the First Amendment's purview. In *Summum* the justices similarly insist that Pleasant Grove's selection and placement of monuments in Pioneer Park burdens no private speech.[38] However, if a city can fill a park with massive, permanent statements of the government's views, the park may lose its character as a public forum.[39] Justice Alito acknowledges that "monuments . . . monopolize the use of the land on which they stand and interfere permanently with other uses of public space,"[40] but he ignores how the Court's government speech holding strengthens that monopoly. As critics of *Summum* have warned, the government may claim the power to suppress dissident ideas on the ground that those ideas can't coexist harmoniously or coherently with the government's preferred message.[41] In fact, a federal

36. *Summum*, 555 U.S. at 485 (Souter, J., concurring in the judgment). Justice Souter expresses particular concern about the difficulty of reconciling the government speech approach to *Summum* with the establishment clause. *See id.* at 485–87.

37. *See id.* at 479–80.

38. *See id.* at 474; *see also id.* at 481–82 (Stevens, J., concurring).

39. For a rich development of this critique of *Summum*, see Timothy Zick, Summum, *The Vocality of Public Places, and the Public Forum*, 2010 BYU L. REV. 2203, 2225–33.

40. *Summum*, 555 U.S. at 479.

41. Erwin Chemerinsky posits, for example, that after *Summum* a city could embrace a pro-war demonstration as the government's own message to justify banning an anti-war demonstration. *See* Erwin Chemerinsky, *Not a Free Speech Court*, 53 ARIZ. L. REV. 723, 731–32 (2011); *see also* RANDALL P. BEZANSON, TOO MUCH FREE SPEECH? 101–02 (2012); Joseph Blocher, *Viewpoint Neutrality and Government Speech*, 52 B.C. L. REV. 695 (2011); Helen Norton, *Imaginary Threats to Government's Expressive Interests*, 61 CASE W. RES. L. REV. 1265 (2011).

appellate court has cited *Summum* to justify the Secret Service in excluding peaceful dissenters from a presidential speech, a decision the Roberts Court declined to review.[42]

Even short of such literal crowding out, the *Summum* Court's rigid application of the government speech doctrine chills public forum speech. Imagine a small Southern town whose leaders indulge nostalgia for antebellum society. They foreswear the "village tyranny" of actively barring or punishing people with opposing views,[43] but they lard the town park with statues of Confederate "heroes" and "happy" slaves. If you wanted to use the park for a rally to protest excessive force by police against people of color, would you worry about government reprisals? Would you feel comfortable mounting any sort of protest, celebration, or discussion under those shadows? Huge slabs of stone emphatically signal which subjects and viewpoints governments will tolerate. As the *Summum* Court points out, governments' arguments for their policies and actions contribute to public debate. Even so, shouldn't First Amendment principles place some limits on government dominance of the debate? Some scholars argue that democratic norms or constitutional principles should foreclose the government from expressing illiberal or excessively partisan values[44] or even compel the government to express liberal democratic values.[45] Even if we don't go that far, government advocacy that discourages other speakers, soaks up too much oxygen from public discussion, or heavily skews debates about the government's own actions still presents a First Amendment problem.

*Summum* embodies the Roberts Court's practice of denying First Amendment protection to the speakers who need it most: the marginal, the outnumbered, the underfinanced. We've seen similar antipathy to marginal speakers in the copyright extension case *Golan v. Holder* (Chapter 1), the material aid to terrorists case *Humanitarian Law Project* (Chapter 2), and all the institutional speech cases discussed in Chapter 3. In the public forum setting, that antipathy reinforces the Supreme Court's long-standing disregard for underfunded speakers' access to expressive opportunities. The Summum sect may have interesting things to teach us. Alternatively—or additionally—Summum may be a band of fanatics whose aphorisms reveal an odious, dangerous belief system. Either way, drawing Summum's members into public discussion would enhance the discussion. The Court, though, pushes Summum and its ideas back to the social margins.

42. *See* Weise v. Casper, 593 F.3d 1163 (10th Cir.), *cert. denied,* 562 U.S. 976 (2010).
43. *See* Kreimer, *supra* note 7, at 1279–81 (discussing the power of "village tyrants" to restrict speech).
44. *See* Nelson Tebbe, *Government Nonendorsement*, 98 MINN. L. REV. 648 (2013).
45. *See* COREY BRETTSCHNEIDER, WHEN THE STATE SPEAKS, WHAT SHOULD IT SAY? HOW DEMOCRACIES CAN PROTECT EXPRESSION AND PROMOTE EQUALITY (2012).

As to government, the *Summum* Court echoes the institutional speech decisions discussed in Chapter 3 by treating government activity, in this case ownership and maintenance of property, as if it were private activity. The Court long ago established that private landowners may exclude unwanted speakers.[46] We have no "private forum doctrine." The public forum doctrine, then, embodies the principle that the government isn't just another private landowner. Governments' claims of dominion over property rest entirely on the people's interest in the property. The public forum doctrine defines the government's obligation to take the people's interest in speech seriously by providing substantial expressive opportunities.[47] *Summum,* by subordinating the people's expressive interest to the city's interest in "presenting the image of the city that it wishes to project,"[48] denies the very essence of the public forum. Public forums are supposed to help people criticize and counterbalance power, especially government power. They aren't supposed to help government co-opt public debate by casting its propaganda in granite. As for the concern that people will inevitably ascribe the meanings of park monuments to government, the long, well-recognized history of diverse speech in public parks should foreclose any danger of mistaken attribution.

The *Summum* Court's equation of government activity with private activity lets select private speakers use the cloak of "government speech" to gain improper advantage over other private speakers. *Summum* shields against First Amendment objections a process in which a private speaker, such as the Fraternal Order of Eagles, donates a monument, which the government may then claim as its own while excluding competing monuments. What if the donor exercises leverage over the government to get its monument accepted and placed? Administrative lawyers worry about "regulatory capture," when a regulated entity or industry effectively dictates the content of the regulations that supposedly bind it.[49] If a monument donor effectively captures a city government, it can use government power to advance its ideas and suppress competing ones. When we consider *Citizens United* and the Roberts Court's other campaign finance decisions (in Chapters 7 and 8), we'll see the Court insist repeatedly that the First Amendment absolutely forbids the government to diminish one speaker's expressive rights in order to enhance another speaker's expressive rights. *Summum,* though, empowers the government to give a favored speaker preferential treatment.

46. *See, e.g.*, Hudgens v. NLRB, 424 U.S. 507 (1976). The Court has also held, though, that legislatures may require certain landowners, such as owners of shopping centers, to tolerate some unwanted expressive activity. *See* PruneYard Shopping Ctr. v. Robins, 447 U.S. 74 (1980).

47. *See* Zick, *supra* note 39, at 2210–12.

48. *Summum*, 555 U.S. at 473.

49. *See, e.g.*, Ian Ayres & John Braithwaite, *Tripartism: Regulatory Capture and Empowerment*, 16 LAW & SOC. INQUIRY 435 (1991).

The *Summum* Court might have avoided its erosion of the public forum in a variety of ways. The Court could require municipalities to run proposed monuments through a citizen review process, in which people and groups with different viewpoints could express their support, opposition, or concerns. Alternatively, the Court could require municipalities to rotate placement of monuments in parks, thus alleviating the problem of scarce space that pushed the monument problem outside the public forum doctrine in *Summum*. More broadly, the Court could bar the government from crowding speakers out of the public forum unless it provides them with a substitute forum.[50] Administering any of these proposals would require judicial assertiveness and creativity, because the proposals all challenge familiar understandings of how monuments function. *Summum,* in avoiding that challenge, echoes the Roberts Court's preoccupation with tradition in the categorical speech exclusion cases (discussed in Chapter 1). *Summum* privileges above all other priorities in the public forum the government's traditional prerogative to place permanent monuments. That privileging ignores public forum speech's own deep roots in our history. The Court built the public forum doctrine on the premise that parks, streets, and sidewalks have been open for speech "immemorially . . . time out of mind." We even call those sorts of property *traditional* public forums. *Summum* dodged a conflict between two venerable practices: opening public parks to expressive activity and filling those parks with government-selected monuments.

The Court's most recent public forum case follows *Summum,* but it doesn't match the *Summum* Court's consensus. Instead, the case displays a pattern we'll see in all the remaining public forum decisions and almost nowhere else in the Roberts Court's free speech canon: the Court's four liberals, with a different conservative ally in each case, prevail by 5-4 margins.

Texas, like many states, makes specialty license plate designs available to vehicle owners. One way the state generates specialty plates is by allowing nonprofit groups to submit designs to the state Department of Motor Vehicle Board. State law gives the Board broad discretion to approve or reject specialty plate applications, although the Board usually approves them. Some 350 specialty plates, celebrating everything from sports teams to civic groups to school alumni pride, appear on Texas roads. The Board oversees the final design of each specialty plate, and the state owns all the designs it approves and uses. In 2009, the Texas Sons of Confederate Veterans submitted to the Board a specialty plate design that incorporates two images of the Confederate battle flag. The Board invited public comments on the design. Many Texans objected based on the flag's racism. In 2011 the Board denied the Sons of Confederate Veterans' application. The Board expressed concern that the

50. *See* Blocher, *supra* note 41, at 764–67.

Confederate plates would present a distinctive safety hazard, but it also cited the flag's offensiveness to many people as a reason for denying the application. The Board thus plainly rejected the application based on disapproval of viewpoints associated with the Confederate flag. The First Amendment, as we've seen, forbids viewpoint discrimination against protected speech. The Sons of Confederate Veterans therefore claimed the denial violated their First Amendment rights.

In ***Walker v. Texas Division, Sons of Confederate Veterans* (2015)**,[51] a bare Supreme Court majority rejected the Sons of Confederate Veterans' claim by holding that Texas's specialty license plates are government speech. Justice Breyer's majority opinion relies almost completely on the precedential weight of *Summum*. As with the *Summum* park monuments, he argues, states have long used license plates to communicate their messages; Texas maintains its license plates for its own expressive purposes; and, even though private speakers initially generate many plate designs, the government ultimately controls which plates reach the road.[52] Justice Breyer especially elaborates on the second of those similarities. License plates, he contends, "are, essentially, government IDs." The state emblazons "Texas" across the top of every plate, issues all the plates, requires all vehicles to display them, and owns every plate design. People who pay to display specialty plates, Justice Breyer argues, presumably want the association with the state; otherwise, they could just display bumper stickers.[53] He concedes that, unlike the monuments in *Summum*, license plates are not permanent public displays and aren't subject to resource scarcity. He maintains, however, that those factors mattered for justifying the result in *Summum* only because the government property at issue there was a park, a traditional public forum.[54] To the Sons of Confederate Veterans' argument that the specialty plates are a limited public forum, Justice Breyer responds that designated and limited public forums only arise when the government intentionally opens property for autonomous public expression. Texas's policies and practices around its specialty license plates, along with the discontinuity between the plates and other government properties the Court has labeled as public forums, show that the state didn't intend to open the plates as a public forum.[55]

The decisive fifth vote for the liberal justices' position in *Walker* came from a highly unlikely source: Justice Thomas, who almost never stands alone against his other conservative colleagues. Justice Thomas didn't contribute a separate concurring opinion, and nothing in Justice Breyer's opinion seems to resonate

51. 135 S. Ct. 2239 (2015). Breyer (majority) (with Thomas, Ginsburg, Sotomayor, Kagan); Alito (dissent) (with Roberts, Scalia, Kennedy).
52. *See id.* at 2248–49.
53. *See id.* at 2249.
54. *See id.* at 2249–50.
55. *See id.* at 2250–52.

with Justice Thomas's judicial philosophy. However, Justice Thomas on a few occasions has taken stands against egregious expressions of racism. His dissent in *Virginia v. Black*,[56] a Rehnquist Court case about cross burnings, notably deconstructs racist symbolism. Distaste for our society's most historically freighted racist talisman seems the likeliest explanation for Justice Thomas's surprising vote in *Walker*.

No less an authority on *Summum* than that decision's author, Justice Alito, wrote the *Walker* dissent for the Court's other conservatives. The majority, Justice Alito charges, "passes off private speech as government speech" and "establishes a precedent that threatens private speech that government finds displeasing."[57] He poses a test: If you sat by a Texas roadside and watched cars whiz by, seeing specialty plates that proclaimed "Rather Be Golfing" and celebrated the University of Notre Dame, would you really believe Texas was extolling those subjects over, say, bowling and the University of Southern California? Of course you wouldn't. Governments, Justice Alito argues, speak in order to promote their governing agendas, but obviously Texas doesn't mean to promote anything with specialty license plates. The state simply wants to raise revenue by charging for the plates.[58] Texas, he insists, has converted the space on its specialty license plates not taken up by state-mandated information into "little mobile billboards." If we let the state ban messages it doesn't like from these little mobile billboards, then the state could do the same thing if it sold space on "big, stationary billboards," and that must violate the First Amendment.[59]

Justice Alito then attacks the majority's specific reliance on *Summum*. Governments, he argues, have not historically used license plates to communicate as they have used public monuments. Texas's practice over two decades of allowing private entities to submit specialty plate designs "crossed the line" between government and private speech. The specialty license plate program, he argues, hasn't reflected the "selective receptivity" that characterized the monument approval process in *Summum*. The state just wants to make as much money as possible from specialty plates. Justice Alito calls the majority's suggestion that people who get specialty plates desire the association with the state "dangerous," because many private speakers would welcome government approval of their messages. Finally, he emphasizes the lack in the specialty license plate context of the "scarce space" problem that characterized the monument problem in *Summum*. States, he insists, have a lot of license plate space, and Texas has simply chosen to sell that space to private speakers. Selling the space creates a limited public forum, and Texas violated

56. 538 U.S. 343, 388 (2003) (Thomas, J., dissenting).
57. *Walker*, 135 S. Ct. at 2254 (Alito, J., dissenting).
58. *See id.* at 2255–56 (Alito, J., dissenting).
59. *Id.* at 2256 (Alito, J., dissenting).

the First Amendment when it made viewpoint a condition of access to that forum.[60]

How well Texas's specialty license plate program fits the *Summum* template is a close question. As Justice Alito argues, images and slogans on license plates don't present the problem of physical permanence in scarce space that drove the *Summum* Court's result. Governments don't rely on license plates to convey important ideas in the way they often rely on monuments. On the other hand, specialty license plates don't have to matter as much or speak with the same weight and nuance as public monuments to count as government speech. The Court has applied the government speech label to federally funded medical counseling[61] and collective agricultural advertising.[62] License plates, more than those media, exist as zones of government control. Texas creates and issues license plates for a purely regulatory purpose, makes them available for privately conceived messages only as an adjunct to that purpose, and maintains control over which plates ultimately appear. The risk that people will ascribe a speaker's message to the government, which Justice Alito took very seriously in the dubious context of *Summum,* seems more salient for specialty license plates, small spaces that contain little more than private speech, a number, and the state's name.[63] Justice Alito warns that treating specialty plates as government speech sets a dangerous precedent, but the alarm sounds brittle. License plates, in their relationship to state power and in how they convey meaning, don't strongly resemble any other sort of government property where people express ideas. They seem to matter a lot less than parks for public discussion.

Despite these forceful elements in Texas's argument, *Walker* reinforces the speech-restrictive logic of *Summum* by again refusing to call government property where people express ideas a public forum. As in *Summum,* the *Walker* Court's reliance on the government speech doctrine lets the government deny a valuable expressive resource to viewpoints the government opposes. The historical moment of *Walker* vividly illustrates the stakes of the public forum doctrine for speakers with unpopular views. In a remarkable confluence of events, the Court handed down *Walker* the day after a white supremacist gunman murdered nine congregants at Charleston, South Carolina's Emanuel A.M.E. Church. Photos quickly emerged of the killer posing with the Confederate battle flag. Within a week, many southern Republicans had joined a longtime chorus of voices on the Left in calling the flag a racist symbol and urging states

60. *See id.* at 2258–62 (Alito, J., dissenting). Justice Alito also argues vigorously that Texas rejected the Confederate plate design because of its viewpoint, a point the majority doesn't dispute. *See id.* at 2262–63 (Alito, J., dissenting).

61. *See* Rust v. Sullivan, 500 U.S. 173 (1991).

62. *See* Johanns v. Livestock Mktg. Ass'n., 544 U.S. 550 (2005).

63. For a critique of the ascription argument in *Walker,* see Mary-Rose Papandrea, *The Government Brand*, 110 Nw. U. L. Rev. 1195 (2016).

to remove it from official settings.[64] The Court's decision in *Walker* suppresses an image that events following the Charleston massacre proved to carry an increasingly unpopular political message.

The Roberts Court's two remaining public forum cases, like *Summum*, deal with religious speech, but not speech as exotic as the seven aphorisms of Summum. Instead, these cases arose on the front lines of the culture war, where religious speech runs into questions of LGBT identity and abortion rights.

## GOD, GAYS, AND GROUPS

The Christian Legal Society (CLS) is a nationwide organization of theologically conservative Christian lawyers and law students. CLS requires its officers and members to abide by a set of religiously grounded principles, including the belief that only couples in opposite-sex marriages should have sex. Accordingly, CLS bars from membership anyone who engages in "unrepentant homosexual conduct" (and for that matter unrepentant, nonmarital straight sex). In 2004 CLS sought to establish a chapter at the Hastings College of Law, a school in the University of California system. Like most public colleges and universities, Hastings provides recognition and resources for a diverse range of registered student organizations (RSOs). Hastings maintains a "take all comers" policy for RSOs. Under that policy, RSOs must accept for membership any student, subject only to exclusions for certain forms of misconduct (such as missing mandatory group meetings). Hastings rejected CLS's application for RSO status because CLS's membership restrictions would have violated the all-comers policy. CLS sued Hastings, claiming that the denial of RSO status denied the group's First Amendment rights of speech and expressive association.

In ***Christian Legal Society v. Martinez* (2010)**,[65] a bitterly divided Roberts Court rejected CLS's claim. CLS raised what it presented as two distinct grounds for First Amendment relief. First, CLS made a public forum argument. The parties agreed that the RSO program was a limited public forum.[66] Recall that the government (here, Hastings) may impose reasonable, viewpoint-neutral speech restrictions to preserve a limited forum's purpose. CLS claimed that Hastings violated the First Amendment by discriminating against CLS's theologically conservative viewpoint. Second, CLS claimed that Hastings had

64. *See* Frances Robles et al., *Governor Joins the Call to Take Down Rebel Flag*, N.Y. TIMES (June 22, 2015) at A1.

65. 561 U.S. 661 (2010). Ginsburg (majority) (with Stevens, Kennedy, Breyer, Sotomayor); Stevens (concurring); Kennedy (concurring); Alito (dissenting) (with Roberts, Scalia, Thomas).

66. *See id.* at 679 n.12.

violated CLS's separate First Amendment freedom of expressive association. The Supreme Court has held that the First Amendment gives groups a right to exclude members they don't want to admit.[67] CLS argued that Hastings' all-comers policy denied CLS that right.

Justice Ginsburg's majority opinion in *Christian Legal Society,* joined by the Court's other liberals and Justice Kennedy, holds that CLS's limited public forum claim subsumes its expressive association claim.[68] The public forum doctrine, Justice Ginsburg reasons, acknowledges the government's greater control over its own property than over private space. Assembling on government property subjects people to that greater control, just like speaking on government property does. Justice Alito, dissenting for the Court's other conservatives, likens *Christian Legal Society* to *Healey v. James,*[69] a Vietnam-era case in which the Supreme Court invoked the freedom of association to make a Connecticut state college recognize a chapter of Students for a Democratic Society. Justice Alito argues that the denial of recognition in *Healey* imposed the same sort of burden as Hastings's denial of recognition to CLS. The majority, he maintains, wrongly does exactly what the *Healey* Court refused to do: defer to educational administrators' judgment about sound education policy, notwithstanding First Amendment concerns.[70] Justice Ginsburg, however, emphasizes a pivotal distinction: the college in *Healey,* like other universities in similar past cases, discriminated against the student group's viewpoint.[71] Viewpoint discrimination dooms any speech regulation.

For the majority, the fact that the all-comers policy applies equally to all student groups shows that Hastings didn't discriminate against CLS's viewpoint. How can a policy that covers everyone discriminate against anyone? CLS, though, argued that, even if the all-comers policy was neutral on its face, it had the effect of discriminating against nonmainstream views such as CLS's theological conservatism. Rejecting that argument, Justice Ginsburg points out that a finding of viewpoint discrimination requires discriminatory intent. Differential impact on particular speakers isn't enough.[72] Justice

67. *See, e.g.*, Boy Scouts of Am. v. Dale, 530 U.S. 640 (2000) (recognizing a First Amendment right of the Boy Scouts to exclude a gay scoutmaster).

68. *See Christian Legal Soc'y,* 561 U.S. at 678–83. Scholars have criticized the majority for treating expressive association like speech under the public forum doctrine. *See* John D. Inazu, Liberty's Refuge: The Forgotten Freedom of Assembly 147–49 (2012); Ashutosh Bhagwat, *Associations and Forums: Situating* CLS v. Martinez, 38 Hastings Const. L.Q. 543, 560–66 (2011).

69. 408 U.S. 169 (1972).

70. *See Christian Legal Soc'y,* 561 U.S. at 718–21 (Alito, J. dissenting).

71. *See id.* at 683–85 & n.15. Justice Kennedy, the author of one of those past cases, presses the viewpoint distinction in his concurring opinion. *See id.* at 703–04 (Kennedy, J., concurring) (contrasting *Christian Legal Society* with *Rosenberger v. Rector & Visitors of Univ. of Va.*, 515 U.S. 819 (1995)).

72. *See Christian Legal Soc'y,* 561 U.S. at 694–96; *see also id.* at 700 (Stevens, J., concurring).

Alito doesn't contest the majority's impact-intent distinction. Instead, he argues that the Court should judge Hastings not on the all-comers policy but rather on an earlier non-discrimination policy, which he claims discriminated against religious associations by barring them from excluding nonbelievers and those engaged in sexually immoral behavior.[73] Whatever its merit, that bait-and-switch argument doesn't address the substance of the Court's First Amendment holding.[74] Justice Alito argues further that even the all-comers policy discriminates based on viewpoint because, he insists, Hastings adopted it as a pretext for attacking conservative Christians.[75] His legal premise here is solid—discriminatory pretext is a form of discriminatory intent—but the majority dismisses his evidence of Hastings's illicit motive as flimsy and contrived.[76]

Once the majority finds Hastings's all-comers policy viewpoint neutral, *Christian Legal Society* comes down to the question of whether the policy was a reasonable way to maintain the RSO limited public forum for its intended purpose of supporting student organizations. Justice Ginsburg views the RSO program as an extension of Hastings's educational mission and a product of the school's "license to choose among pedagogical approaches."[77] She therefore approaches the reasonableness question "[w]ith appropriate regard for school administrators' judgment"[78]—in other words, with sweeping deference. She identifies four reasonable grounds for the all-comers policy: ensuring that all students have access to Hastings's educational benefits, simplifying administration of Hastings's broader non-discrimination policy, encouraging interaction among students with diverse perspectives while developing skills for resolving differences, and conveying the school's determination not to support discrimination that Californians oppose.[79] The all-comers policy looks even more reasonable, she maintains, when one considers that it doesn't hurt CLS much. Even without official recognition and access to certain resources, CLS can still speak effectively to the Hastings community.[80] In response, Justice Alito claims that Hastings's purpose in creating the forum was simply to help students form and participate in groups with a diverse range of viewpoints. None of the four grounds on which the majority pronounces the all-comers policy reasonable, he argues, actually serves that broad purpose.[81] In

73. *See id.* at 722–27 (Alito, J. dissenting).
74. Justice Stevens's concurring opinion maintains that, even had Hastings applied the non-discrimination policy rather than the all-comers policy, the result in the case should not change. *See id.* at 698–703 (Stevens, J., concurring).
75. *See id.* at 735–39 (Alito, J. dissenting).
76. *See id.* at 697–98 & n.29.
77. *Id.* at 686.
78. *Id.* at 687.
79. *See id.* at 687–90.
80. *See id.* at 690–91.
81. *See id.* at 728–35 (Alito, J., dissenting).

effect, Justice Alito says the all-comers policy can't be a reasonable way of maintaining the limits on the forum's purpose because the forum, on its own terms, has no effective limits.

The majority might have transcended the limitations of conventional public forum analysis by framing the case in instrumental terms, as a dispute about how—not whether—universities may promote expressive freedom. On an instrumental view of constitutional speech protection, First Amendment law should optimize what Thomas Emerson called a "system of free expression"[82] to advance whatever instrumental goal(s) justify expressive freedom. My dynamic diversity model of constitutional speech protection calls for an instrumental First Amendment analysis to increase the range of ideas and participants in public discussion. Optimizing a system of free expression always entails restraining government interference in public debate. Depending on the instrumental goal(s), however, certain government regulations may actually contribute to an optimal system.[83] In any event, government plays too broad a role in society to avoid all interference with speech. In designing a system of free expression, we need to ask not whether government action will influence public debate but how it should do so.[84]

Hastings's all-comers policy dictates what I'll call an *integrationist* approach to free expression in the realm of official student organizations. The Christian Legal Society, in contrast, demanded what Justice Alito calls a "pluralis[t]" approach.[85] Under an integrationist approach, many or all settings in which public discussion occurs admit people of many or all viewpoints. Contentious debate occurs *within* those various settings. Under a pluralist approach, many or all settings in which public debate occurs comprise people with narrower ranges of views. Contentious debate occurs *between and among* those various settings. Integration, because it empowers larger institutions, risks marginalizing idiosyncratic speakers. On the other hand, pluralism may favor more powerful groups at the expense of less powerful individual speakers and may reduce intergroup discussions to numbing recitations of first principles.[86] Higher education challenges students to think outside their preconceptions. If an integrationist approach to student organizations promotes dialogue among students with different viewpoints, *Christian Legal Society* substantially advances the system of free expression. On the other hand, integration may homogenize groups across a campus or

82. *See* THOMAS I. EMERSON, TOWARD A GENERAL THEORY OF THE FIRST AMENDMENT (1966).

83. *See* OWEN M. FISS, THE IRONY OF FREE SPEECH (1996); CASS R. SUNSTEIN, DEMOCRACY AND THE PROBLEM OF FREE SPEECH (1993).

84. *See* SUNSTEIN, *supra* note 83, at 35–38.

85. *Christian Legal Soc'y,* 561 U.S. at 734 (Alito, J., dissenting).

86. *See* Cass R. Sunstein, *Deliberative Trouble? Why Groups Go to Extremes*, 110 YALE L.J. 71 (2000).

even discourage group formation. If pluralism enables groups with different views to form distinctive identities and then engage meaningfully with one another, *Christian Legal Society* impedes the system of free expression.[87]

An instrumental analysis in *Christian Legal Society* would require the Court to consider who should decide how a school's support for student groups can best advance expressive freedom. One might complain, as I have in discussing other Roberts Court decisions, that the Court in *Christian Legal Society* granted public law school administrators the prerogatives of private law school administrators, mistakenly waiving the First Amendment in the name of a questionable equivalence between government and private actors. I don't think that complaint holds water for *Christian Legal Society* if we view the case as presenting a choice between integrationist and pluralist approaches to fostering public discussion. In the prison, primary education, and public employment settings discussed in Chapter 3, the Court deferred to government choices of institutional efficiency over institutional subjects' speech interests. In contrast, Hastings's preference for integration over pluralism is a choice between First Amendment models, not a choice of some other government priority over expressive freedom. Moreover, public higher education administrators, unlike most government officials, are in the business of promoting expression.[88] Scholars have argued that courts should consider the special expressive character of certain institutions, including the media, libraries, and universities, when reviewing those institutions' speech-related decisions.[89] The Supreme Court has sometimes followed that advice.[90] That institution-specific, speech-regarding justification for deference has salience for *Christian Legal Society*.

Rather than engaging the integration-pluralism dynamic, however, the opinions in *Christian Legal Society* wedge the case into the public forum mold. The majority likely decided the case correctly under present public forum law, given two of that law's important features. First, the "reasonableness" standard that applies to limited public forums usually inspires only the most

87. *See* Nelson Tebbe, *Associations and the Constitution: Four Questions about Four Freedoms*, 92 N.C. L. Rev. 917, 933–36 (2014) (using sorting theory to argue that, for a society to get the benefits of grouping similar people together, it must determine the optimal level of social organization at which that grouping should occur).

88. Educators' special commitment and competence to promote speech can distinguish deference here from situations where the Court avoids weighing competing First Amendment interests by simply deferring to legislative or executive authority. *See* Gregory P. Magarian, *The Jurisprudence of Colliding First Amendment Interests: From the Dead End of Neutrality to the Open Road of Participation Enhancing Review*, 83 Notre Dame L. Rev. 185 (2007).

89. *See* Paul Horwitz, First Amendment Institutions (2013); Frederick Schauer, *Towards an Institutional First Amendment*, 89 Minn. L. Rev. 1256 (2005).

90. *See, e.g.*, Ark. Educ. Television Comm'n v. Forbes, 523 U.S. 666 (1998) (giving public broadcasters nearly the same discretion to exclude speech that private broadcasters enjoy, because broadcasters distinctively promote speech).

lenient, perfunctory brand of judicial review. Second, and closely related, the Court tends to defer strongly to government managers of public forums when it balances speakers' First Amendment interests against the managers' countervailing non-speech interests.[91] The *Christian Legal Society* majority rides both of those features of public forum law to their logical, speech-restrictive conclusion. As to lenient review, Justice Ginsburg's second and fourth justifications for the all-comers policy subordinate First Amendment interests to, respectively, administrative convenience and popular will.[92] As to strong deference, she treats the Hastings College of Law very much like we saw the Court in Chapter 3 treat prisons, schools, and public workplaces: as a zone of managerial control. Deferring to school authorities simply because they have authority differs greatly from deferring based on university administrators' commitment and competence to promote free speech.

In dissent, Justice Alito might have launched a frontal assault on the reflexive deference that characterizes conventional public forum analysis. He might also have pushed back against the majority's insistence that a government action's disproportionate impact on marginal speakers or ideas, as opposed to the government's discriminatory intent, has no relevance for a First Amendment challenge. After all, the requirement of content neutrality in the public forum derives substantially from the principle that speakers with different ideas and agendas should have the same access to public expressive spaces.[93] Justice Alito's avoidance of those deeper arguments against the majority shows that the dissenters in *Christian Legal Society* have no greater desire than the majority to challenge conventional public forum law's ingrained managerial compromises.

*Christian Legal Society* joins *Summum* and *Walker* in diminishing the public forum. The Court lets government managers constrain what might have been more contentious, dynamic public debate. The constraint shows especially vividly in Justice Kennedy's praise for law schools' inculcation of "rational . . . respectful . . . [and] professional" expressive modes in students.[94] Those qualities, of course, can improve the tone of public discussion. However, they can also narrow its content and blunt its ultimate impact on social institutions. *Christian Legal Society* follows the managed speech script by fortifying managerial control over speech in the name of social stability.

91. *See supra* cases cited note 5.

92. Perhaps norms against identity-based discrimination should inform the social context that grounds the public forum doctrine. They never have, though, and Justice Ginsburg doesn't argue in *Christian Legal Society* that they should.

93. *See* Police Dep't of Chi. v. Mosley, 408 U.S. 92 (1972) (striking down a city ordinance that banned picketing around schools but exempted labor picketing). For an argument on behalf of a "strong" version of content neutrality that would consider effects as well as intent, see Kreimer, *supra* note 7, at 1316–28.

94. Christian Legal Soc'y v. Martinez, 561 U.S. 661, 705 (2010) (Kennedy, J., concurring).

## WILL THE BUFFER BE UNBROKEN?

If you pass by a clinic that provides abortion services, you'll likely encounter antiabortion activists. Some of those activists harass, intimidate, and threaten clinic workers and patients. The intensity of opinions about abortion sometimes generates crowds of antiabortion protesters, together with their pro-choice adversaries, big enough to impede sidewalk and street traffic. States take varied approaches to these problems. The Rehnquist Court in *Hill v. Colorado*,[95] by a 5-4 vote, upheld against a First Amendment challenge a "floating buffer zone" law. That law barred anyone outside an abortion clinic from coming within eight feet of another person, without that person's consent, for the purpose of "protest, education, or counseling."[96] Critics have long charged that *Hill,* by validating such a precisely targeted speech restriction, licensed blatant discrimination against antiabortion views.

In 2007 Massachusetts enacted a "fixed buffer zone" law. This law made it a crime simply to stand within a 35-foot radius of any facility (other than a hospital) that provides abortion services. The law exempted people entering or leaving the facility, law enforcement or other municipal employees doing their jobs, people passing by on their way to and from somewhere else, and, most important, "employees or agents of [the facility] acting within the scope of their employment."[97] A group of Massachusetts antiabortion activists led by Eleanor McCullen challenged the law. McCullen describes herself as a "sidewalk counselor." She approaches women who are walking toward family planning clinics and tries to persuade them not to get abortions by speaking to them and giving them literature. She seeks to gain women's trust by addressing them in a nonthreatening manner. The fixed buffer zone law, by forcing McCullen to operate from a distance, made her strategy harder to execute.

***McCullen v. Coakley* (2014)**[98] declares Massachusetts's fixed buffer zone law unconstitutional. The decision deals with two distinct legal issues. Everyone agreed that the sidewalks in *McCullen,* like the park in *Summum,* are quintessential, traditional public forums and that the Massachusetts law restricted enough speech to bring the First Amendment into play. The first issue in the case was whether the Massachusetts law was "content based" or "content neutral." If the Massachusetts law discriminated against the content or viewpoint of speech, then the Court would subject the law to strict scrutiny. On the

95. 530 U.S. 703 (2000).

96. In two other cases the Rehnquist Court partially upheld and partially rejected court injunctions against antiabortion clinic activists. *See* Schenck v. Pro-Choice Action Network, 519 U.S. 357 (1997); Madsen v. Women's Health Ctr., 512 U.S. 753 (1994).

97. MASS. GEN. LAWS ch. 266, § 120E 1/2 (2012).

98. 134 S. Ct. 2518 (2014). Roberts (majority) (with Ginsburg, Breyer, Sotomayor, Kagan); Scalia (concurring in the judgment) (with Kennedy, Thomas); Alito (concurring in the judgment).

other hand, if the law was unrelated to the content or viewpoint of speech—if it was content neutral—then the Court would apply the much more lenient *O'Brien* intermediate scrutiny test. Because the *McCullen* Court found the law content neutral, the second issue in the case was whether Massachusetts tailored its law sufficiently to satisfy *O'Brien.* A content-neutral law that inadvertently burdens speech survives *O'Brien* review as long as it doesn't "burden substantially more speech than is necessary to further the government's legitimate interests."[99]

Chief Justice Roberts wrote the majority opinion in *McCullen,* joined by the Court's four liberal justices (Ginsburg, Breyer, Sotomayor, and Kagan). The majority finds Massachusetts's fixed buffer zone law content neutral because the law advanced the non-speech-related goals of public safety, clinic access, and avoiding sidewalk congestion.[100] Reaching that holding required dealing with two problematic features of the law.

First, the law singled out the areas around abortion clinics for regulation. Speech around abortion clinics tends to concern abortion. Therefore, the law limited speech about abortion disproportionately. That sounds like content-based discrimination. As Chief Justice Roberts points out, however, states may properly target legislation at the actual problems that confront them. Because abortion clinics present distinctive safety, access, and traffic concerns, states may impose rules to address those concerns without applying the same rules to banks or grocery stores.[101] Justice Scalia, in a characteristically sharp, caustic concurrence in the judgment (joined by Justices Kennedy and Thomas), asks whether the Court would treat targeted restrictions on the sidewalks around a political convention, a civil rights march, or the IRS building as content-neutral.[102] It's an odd question, because one can easily imagine content neutral reasons for imposing special restrictions in those locales, if they fostered the same kinds of disturbances Massachusetts identified at abortion clinics. One can also imagine governments, in response to Justice Scalia's suspicion, throwing up their hands and addressing narrow concerns about particular locales by broadly restricting speech everywhere. The chief justice's admonition that "legislatures should be encouraged to choose [policies] that restrict[] less speech, not more"[103] captures a big problem with Justice Scalia's argument.

99. Ward v. Rock Against Racism, 491 U.S. 781, 799 (1989).

100. For an analysis of the conceptual difficulties the content regulation issue presented in *McCullen,* see Leslie Kendrick, *Nonsense on Sidewalks: Content Discrimination in* McCullen v. Coakley, 2014 SUP. CT. REV. 215.

101. *See McCullen,* 134 S. Ct. at 2530–32. The Supreme Court axiomatically treats "place" regulations as content neutral. *See* Kendrick, *supra* note 100, at 228.

102. *See McCullen,* 134 S. Ct. at 2543 (Scalia, J., concurring in the judgment).

103. *Id.* at 2532.

Justice Scalia cites several pieces of indirect evidence to show that Massachusetts's law discriminated against both the content and viewpoint of antiabortion speech.[104] To begin, he contests Chief Justice Roberts's dismissal of the law's disproportionate effect on abortion-related speech. Justice Scalia, like Justice Alito in *Christian Legal Society,* doesn't argue that the First Amendment protects against disparate impacts on speech. Rather, he argues that the presence of disparate impact proves the government's malicious intent to discriminate against views it opposes. As in *Christian Legal Society,* though, the majority refuses to credit a thinly supported assertion that the government lied about its motives. Justice Scalia makes a related argument that the Massachusetts fixed buffer zone law must have targeted antiabortion speech because it replaced an earlier law that had the same discriminatory motives as the statute the Court upheld in *Hill.* That argument has two logical problems: it depends on the belief that *Hill* was wrong (a belief that, as Justice Scalia points out, the *McCullen* majority suggests but does not declare), and it ascribes the (asserted) defect of an old law to a new one. Finally, Justice Scalia argues that the fixed buffer zone law must have targeted antiabortion speakers, because it sweepingly protected all clinics at all times, not just particular clinics when the record showed problems had occurred (really just Boston on Saturdays). Here Chief Justice Roberts credits Justice Scalia's premise, but he thinks the law's overbreadth goes to the tailoring issue (more on that in a moment), not the content neutrality issue.[105]

The second basis for McCullen's claim that the Massachusetts law discriminated against the content and/or viewpoint of antiabortion speech was more technical but potentially more forceful. Recall that the law exempted clinic employees and agents acting within the scope of their employment. Aha!, exclaim Justice Scalia and Justice Alito (who wrote his own solo concurrence in the judgment on this point). Surely clinic workers, acting in the scope of their employment, tell approaching potential patients that abortion is safe and beneficial, that the clinic does its work well, and that antiabortion activists are crazy or wrong. Therefore, the employee-agent exemption in the Massachusetts law favors the clinics' viewpoint and discriminates against the antiabortion activists' viewpoint.[106] Here Chief Justice Roberts treads very carefully. The record in the case did not show that any Massachusetts clinic authorized its employees to advocate pro-choice views to patients in the buffer zone. If clinic employees or agents nonetheless did so, that would violate the law, not indict the law's motive.[107] Justice Scalia responds that the

104. *See id.* at 2543–46 (Scalia, J., concurring in the judgment).
105. *See id.* at 2532.
106. *See id.* at 2546–48 (Scalia, J., concurring in the judgment); *see also id.* at 2549–50 (Alito, J., concurring in the judgment).
107. *See id.* at 2532–34.

scope of a clinic worker's or agent's employment necessarily includes advocacy in favor of the clinic's work. Chief Justice Roberts, however, maintains that Massachusetts properly could, and did, enact its law based on its best understanding of how clinics actually operate. Justice Scalia points out that, even if no clinic worker actually spoke out of turn, the constitutionality of a speech restriction shouldn't depend on whether opposing speakers choose to exercise their own, unrestricted capacity to speak. But a state can fix this problem simply by interpreting its law not to permit the sort of gamesmanship that worries Justice Scalia. Massachusetts in fact issued just such an interpretation of the fixed buffer zone law after McCullen filed her lawsuit.[108]

By finding that the Massachusetts fixed buffer zone law didn't discriminate against the content (let alone the viewpoint) of speech, the majority gave the government the benefit of the forgiving *O'Brien* test to resolve the tailoring issue. Past Supreme Courts applied that test in decision after decision to hold that governments had sufficiently tailored all manner of speech restrictions to deal with content-neutral regulatory concerns.[109] *McCullen,* in its decisive holding, breaks that pattern. Chief Justice Roberts concludes that the Massachusetts law, even though content neutral, burdened much more speech than necessary to achieve its permissible goals of preserving public safety, ensuring clinic access, and avoiding sidewalk congestion.[110] Noting that no other state has a fixed buffer zone law (though several municipalities do), the chief justice surveys alternative, less speech-restrictive methods that other jurisdictions have used to address clinic problems. He finds that Massachusetts didn't look hard enough at such alternatives. Dodging an attack by Justice Scalia, the chief justice makes clear that his reference to alternative methods of regulating abortion protests does not entail any judgment about the constitutionality of those alternatives.[111] (This same hedging of bets plays an important role in the chief justice's key campaign finance opinion in *McCutcheon v. Federal election Commission*, discussed in Chapter 7.) Everyone on the Court appears to agree with the substance of the chief justice's *O'Brien* analysis, though the four concurring justices decline to join even that portion of the majority opinion, in order to avoid what Justice Scalia derides as "an apparent but specious unanimity."[112]

In striking down the Massachusetts law, Chief Justice Roberts strongly emphasizes Eleanor McCullen's status as a "counselor." He goes out of his way to contrast "protesters" unfavorably with "counselors." He points out that past Court decisions have shown special solicitude for "normal conversation and

108. After McCullen filed her lawsuit, the Massachusetts attorney general issued an interpretive letter that had exactly this effect. *See id.* at 2534 n.3.

109. *See supra* cases cited note 5.

110. *See McCullen,* 134 S. Ct. at 2534–40.

111. *See id.* at 2538 n.8.

112. *Id.* at 2548 (Scalia, J., concurring in the judgment).

leafleting" as bedrock methods of public communication. To Massachusetts's argument that its buffer zone law left numerous forms of protest available, Chief Justice Roberts responds that McCullen and her colleagues "are not protestors." He continues: "They seek not merely to express their opposition to abortion, but to inform women of various alternatives and to provide help in pursuing them." He takes pains to distinguish McCullen's "quiet conversations" from the unruly riot of protesters, including "vociferous opponents of abortion," who were not part of the case.[113]

*McCullen* could become the Roberts Court's most important speech-protective decision from the standpoint of dynamic diversity. If the Court is serious about looking hard at the breadth of regulations that restrict public speech, the tailoring analysis of *McCullen* could go far toward invigorating the public forum doctrine as an engine of broad access to expressive opportunities. At least one federal district court has invoked *McCullen* to bar prosecutions of left-wing political protesters.[114] The ideologically diverse range of street protests against powerful institutions and gatherings could all benefit from the more skeptical, searching version of the *O'Brien* test the Roberts Court models in *McCullen*.

Good reasons, however, counsel caution in predicting that *McCullen* will revitalize speech protection in the public forum. First of all, where did this newfound enthusiasm for a meaningful tailoring analysis come from? The Supreme Court hasn't struck down a statute under the *O'Brien* tailoring requirement in the public forum context in more than three decades.[115] Major doctrinal shifts in the Supreme Court usually build on some legal trend or progression, visible at least with hindsight. Nothing like that is evident here. The Supreme Court has shown a strong, long-standing tendency to defer to the government in "time, place, or manner" cases. If *McCullen* really represented a paradigm shift, we would expect the majority opinion to give us a thorough, general critique of the old tendency and defense of the new direction. It gives us no such thing.

What the opinion says confirms the doubts raised by what it doesn't say. When Chief Justice Roberts extols the virtues of one-on-one "counseling" and leafleting, he seems to advocate strong protection for inexpensive, and thus broadly accessible, means of communication. The chief justice thus appears to push back against the stabilizing tendency I've described in other Roberts Court First Amendment decisions. But his explicit exclusion of "protesters"

113. *Id.* at 2536–37.

114. *See* Rebecca Martinez, *Judge's Order Could Lead to Dismissal of Cases against Moral Monday Protesters*, WUNC (Aug. 5, 2014), http://wunc.org/post/judges-order-could-lead-dismissal-cases-against-moral-monday-protesters (last visited Aug. 30, 2016) (discussing Judge Joyce Hamilton's reliance on *McCullen* to dismiss several cases against North Carolina protesters).

115. *See* United States v. Grace, 461 U.S. 171 (1983).

from the opinion's speech-protective rationale casts his analysis in an exclusive rather than inclusive light. If counseling gets First Amendment protection that protesting doesn't, then *McCullen* holds little if any promise for most political activists. Self-styled counseling in the public forum is an activity distinctive if not unique to the antiabortion movement. In his concurrence in the judgment, Justice Scalia accuses the Court's content neutrality analysis of indulging special First Amendment exceptions that burden only antiabortion speakers.[116] The Court's tailoring analysis suggests just the opposite. This may be a case that ends up benefiting few if any speakers other than a subset of avid abortion opponents.[117]

The *McCullen* "counselor" meme resonates with principles of managed speech. McCullen's advice to prospective abortion patients makes for a rare species of counseling. Normally counseling is something people seek out, not something others press upon them. The most familiar exceptions to that norm arise in institutional settings such as prisons, schools, and treatment facilities. We saw in Chapter 3, and again in this chapter's account of *Summum,* that the Roberts Court tends to grant institutional managers wide latitude in First Amendment cases. That deference to managers reflects a commitment to maintaining social and political stability. To the extent *McCullen* creates special, narrow protection for "counselors" while discounting "protesters," it likewise promotes stability. Counselors such as McCullen, Chief Justice Roberts suggests, deserve exceptional speech protection because they're reserved, orderly, and responsible—much like school principals and prison wardens.

## CONCLUSION

As with the institutional speech cases discussed in Chapter 3, the Roberts Court's four public forum decisions affirm and accelerate a speech-restrictive approach that reaches back decades. Also like the institutional speech cases, the public forum decisions display the Roberts Court's distinctive adherence to managed speech. One way to evaluate public forum cases is to consider which free speech claimants win and lose. Losers in the Roberts Court include a fringe religious group in *Summum,* a marginal civic group in *Walker,* a politically controversial student group in *Christian Legal Society,* and—implicitly—all manner of disruptive political protesters in *McCullen.* The only public forum winners in

116. *See McCullen,* 134 S. Ct. at 2541 (Scalia, J., concurring in the judgment).

117. A unanimous Roberts Court gave an unsurprising victory to another antiabortion activist without reaching any First Amendment issue, overturning a lower court's curious holding that the activist's success in his lawsuit did not make him a "prevailing party" eligible for a statutory award of attorney's fees. *See* Lefemine v. Wideman, 133 S. Ct. 9 (2012).

the Roberts Court have been the antiabortion "sidewalk counselors" in *McCullen,* who engage an effectively captive audience in low-key (albeit fraught) conversations. That strategy won't work for most speakers who want to use public forums. The Roberts Court's public forum decisions take a broad range of analytic approaches. Justice Alito in *Summum* and Justice Breyer in *Walker* desert public forum analysis for the more hospitable government speech doctrine. Justice Ginsburg in *Christian Legal Society* sticks to a conventional, deferential public forum analysis. Chief Justice Roberts in *McCullen* gives free speech advocates a narrow, qualified victory. All of these approaches grant the government substantial power to manage the substance of speech in the public forum while shielding the government from charges of viewpoint discrimination.

The public forum decisions show the Roberts Court promoting managed speech across ideological lines. *Summum* was unanimous, although the Court's liberals expressed faint concerns in concurrences. The liberals controlled *Walker* and *Christian Legal Society,* with most of the conservatives in dissent. In *McCullen,* Chief Justice Roberts led the liberal wing along a circuitous path to reach a result that all nine justices at least tacitly endorsed. The conservative justices express some First Amendment passion in dissents and concurrences, but their arguments focus more on the cases' particular circumstances than on any deeper deficiencies in First Amendment law. One could fairly ask whether their arguments offer any benefit for speakers who aren't conservative Christians. Not one opinion in any of these cases offers a penetrating critique of current public forum law. Instead, the cases mainly show us a full array of justices content to preserve a speech-restrictive public forum doctrine.

The public forum decisions promote managerial control of public discussion. The government speech doctrine in *Summum* and *Walker* fully substitutes government control for expressive freedom. Both decisions let administrative managers run expressive media. The Court's deference to government institutional managers in *Christian Legal Society* brings that case into line with last chapter's institutional speech decisions, which let government managers broadly restrict the expressive freedom of institutional subjects. *McCullen,* like the drug detailing case *IMS Health* (Chapter 2), expands the managerial concept into the private sphere, privileging what the Court portrays as a distinctively responsible, valuable class of speakers. Like the institutional speech decisions in Chapter 3, the public forum decisions depict an opposition between distribution of expressive opportunities and maintenance of social stability. Distributing expressive opportunities opens public debates to marginal, often dissident speakers who challenge prevailing political and economic arrangements. In contrast, letting managers restrict or direct discussion, in the public forum as in government institutions, promotes more orderly, less contentious public debate.

As with the categorical First Amendment cases discussed in Chapter 1, a shift from managed speech to dynamic diversity would revise the reasoning in the Roberts Court's public forum cases more than the results. *McCullen* approaches dynamic diversity's First Amendment ideal more closely than any Roberts Court decision we've seen so far save the video game case *Entertainment Merchants* (Chapter 1) and the funeral protest case *Snyder v. Phelps* (Chapter 2). Crucially, though, a managed speech analysis in *McCullen* would eschew Chief Justice Roberts's preference for "counsellors," instead promoting greater consideration for speech interests in all "time, place, or manner" cases. *Christian Legal Society* would present a challenge for dynamic diversity. A dynamic diversity analysis would avoid the reflexive deference to institutional authority that marks Justice Ginsburg's opinion. It would also reverse the Court's disregard for the distributive effects of government regulations in limited public forums. Whether a rule disproportionately mutes particular viewpoints should matter for public forum analysis. The hard questions would be whether the Court should trust university administrators to make policy decisions about how best to promote free speech and, if not, whether an integrationist or pluralist approach to support for student groups would better advance dynamic diversity's goals of maximizing the ideas and participants in public discussion.

The government speech doctrine represents a potent, volatile threat to dynamic diversity's project of broadening public debate. The Supreme Court should use that doctrine as sparingly as a builder uses explosives. A dynamic diversity analysis in *Summum* would reach the same result the Roberts Court did, out of practical necessity: for the public forum doctrine to treat permanent monuments such as rallies or parades would almost literally petrify our public parks. However, the importance dynamic diversity places on distribution of expressive opportunities would leave *Summum* a public forum case. The dynamic diversity analysis would grapple with the paradox of allocating permanent parcels in a presumptively open, shared expressive space. Dynamic diversity would respond to that paradox by charging municipalities to develop content-neutral criteria for choosing monuments and methods for incorporating public input in monument decisions. The logic of the government speech doctrine fits *Walker* better than *Summum*. License plates serve a precise government function, they carry the state's name and project the state's authority, and they have only marginal importance for public debate. Even so, a designer license plate program creates cheap expressive opportunities of particular value to marginal, dissenting speakers. Dynamic diversity would reject viewpoint-based constraints on those opportunities.

The final chapter in this second part of the book examines how the Roberts Court has handled the remaining question about First Amendment law in government preserves: What kinds of conditions may the government impose on direct subsidies for speech?

# CHAPTER 5

# There's Always a Catch

## *Speech-Restrictive Conditions on Government Funding*

The final sort of government preserve in which free speech disputes arise, after Chapter 3's government institutions and Chapter 4's government property, is government money. The Constitution's spending clause allows the federal government to pursue its policy goals by spending funds.[1] Often the government funds speech, or activities that include speech, in fields ranging from the arts to education to medical research. To ensure that such speech subsidies achieve their policy purposes, the government sometimes attaches speech-restrictive conditions to subsidies. Those conditions can raise serious First Amendment concerns. For example, in the 1990s the federal government tried to bar lawyers whom it funded to represent poor clients from constitutionally challenging laws that disadvantaged their clients.[2] Does the government, when it funds speech, get to suspend the ordinary First Amendment bar against telling speakers what they can't say?

Cases about speech-restrictive conditions on government funding share the basic dynamic of the institutional speech and public forum cases. The government provides a resource that helps a speaker reach an audience; the speaker wants to speak freely; the government wants to maintain control over its resource. But government decisions to fund speech, unlike the government's maintenance of public property, entail conscious exercises of political

1. U.S. CONST. art. I, § 8, cl. 1; *see also* South Dakota v. Dole, 483 U.S. 203 (1987).
2. *See* Legal Serv. Corp. v. Velasquez, 531 U.S. 533 (2001).

discretion. Defenders of government prerogatives, such as Justices Scalia and Thomas, thus take a harder line on subsidies than on public forums. At the other extreme, one can argue (though no current justice does) that private speech the government opts to subsidize should get the same First Amendment protection the Court, at least in theory, gives speech in public forums. The Court's subsidized speech decisions have charted a middle course, letting the government attach strings to some speech subsidies but not others, based on a multifactor analysis.[3] Subsidy schemes that violate the First Amendment fit into a broader constitutional principle that bars the government from using its spending power to impose unconstitutional conditions.[4]

The Roberts Court has decided two subsidized speech cases, both with majority opinions by Chief Justice Roberts. The decisions present a stark contrast. The first, from the earliest days of the Roberts Court, anticipated other decisions we've seen in which this Court has placed apparent free speech problems entirely outside the First Amendment's scope. In the familiar managed speech mode, the Court subordinates political dissent to government managerial control and protects the stable functioning of government programs. The second subsidized speech case, which arose more recently, yields one of the Roberts Court's most speech-protective decisions, emphatically striking down a condition on a speech subsidy. However, I'll contend that we can best understand that decision as designed to rein in the speech-restrictive implications of this Court's own government speech adventurism, discussed in Chapter 4.

## ALL'S FAIR IN WAR (NEVER MIND LOVE)

When John Roberts took over as chief justice in 2005, the U.S. military services still enforced a "don't ask, don't tell" policy against gay and lesbian service members. The issue of "gays in the military" formed a major fault line

3. *Compare* Regan v. Taxation With Representation, 461 U.S. 540 (1983) (letting Congress ban tax-exempt charities from lobbying because the charities could segregate their lobbying and tax-funded activities) *and* Rust v. Sullivan, 500 U.S. 173 (1991) (letting the government bar certain federally funded doctors and clinics from advising patients about abortion, ultimately because the funded activity was government speech) *with* FCC v. League of Women Voters, 468 U.S. 364 (1984) (striking down a ban on advertising by federally funded broadcasters because the broadcasters couldn't segregate their editorializing and government-funded activities) *and Velasquez*, 531 U.S. 533 (striking down a ban on constitutional challenges to laws by federally funded lawyers because the ban discriminated based on the viewpoint of speech).

4. *See* Kathleen M. Sullivan, *Unconstitutional Conditions*, 102 HARV. L. REV. 1415 (1989). Applying that principle, the Roberts Court struck down a part of the Affordable Care Act that rescinded states' Medicaid funding if they refused to extend Medicaid coverage. That condition, the Court held, unconstitutionally undermined states' autonomy. *See* Nat'l Fed'n of Indep. Bus. v. Sebelius, 132 S. Ct. 2566, 2601–07 (2012) (plurality opinion).

in the culture wars.[5] Like many such fault lines, this one ran right under the nation's colleges and universities. Beginning in the 1970s, many law schools found a way to express and dramatize their opposition to the military's antigay discrimination. Legal employers descend on law campuses every fall to interview promising students. Prominent among the interviewers are government employers, including the uniformed attorneys of the military services. Large numbers of law schools, citing the military's discriminatory policies, barred military employers from their on-campus recruiting processes. The government was not amused. In 1996 Congress passed the Solomon Amendment, which required universities to give military recruiters the same access to students on campus that other employers enjoyed, or else lose access to substantial federal funds.[6] Most law schools and their parent universities depend substantially on government support. The Solomon Amendment effectively forced law schools to swallow their scruples about LGBT rights and welcome military employers back to campus.

The law schools, not surprisingly, brought a lawsuit. A coalition of law schools called the Forum for Academic and Institutional Rights (FAIR) challenged the Solomon Amendment as an unconstitutional condition that violated their First Amendment rights to both free speech and expressive association. As to free speech, FAIR contended the Solomon Amendment forced universities and law schools either to risk losing crucial federal funding or to betray their principled opposition to the armed services' antigay discrimination. As to expressive association, FAIR's argument roughly parallels the argument we saw a group with very different substantive commitments make in *Christian Legal Society v. Martinez* (Chapter 4). Just as the Christian Legal Society claimed a First Amendment right not to associate with sexually active gays and lesbians, the FAIR schools claimed a First Amendment right not to associate with employers who discriminated against gays and lesbians.

In ***Rumsfeld v. Forum for Academic and Institutional Rights*** **(2006)**[7] Chief Justice Roberts wrote for a unanimous Court in rejecting FAIR's First Amendment claims. The unanimity—unusual in any First Amendment case, let alone such an ideologically fraught one—may reflect collegial deference to a then-newly installed chief justice in one of his first major opinions on the Court, his first opinion in a free speech case. It may also exemplify the

5. *See* DON'T ASK, DON'T TELL: DEBATING THE GAY BAN IN THE MILITARY (Aaron Belkin & Geoffrey Bateman eds., 2003).

6. *See* 10 U.S.C. § 983 (2013). The amendment originally required simple access to campus for military recruiters but was later amended to require the same degree of access afforded to any other employer.

7. 547 U.S. 47 (2006). Roberts (majority) (with Stevens, Scalia, Kennedy, Souter, Thomas, Ginsburg, Breyer). Justice Alito did not join the Court until after it had heard oral argument in *FAIR*.

Court's frequent distaste for lawyers as First Amendment litigants (compare the *Milavetz* lawyer advertising case in Chapter 2 and the *Williams-Yulee* campaign finance decision in Chapter 8). Or perhaps *FAIR* was just an easy case; Chief Justice Roberts's opinion certainly makes it sound that way.

The chief justice first rejects an interpretation of the Solomon Amendment that might have avoided or at least minimized the First Amendment problem. Some law professors argued that universities could satisfy the amendment by barring from campus all employers who discriminated against gays and lesbians, not just military employers. No, the chief justice holds: the Solomon Amendment bars universities from giving any employer better access to campus than military recruiters.[8] He proceeds to frame the case as one in which the government deserves special deference, because the Solomon Amendment deals with military matters.[9] *FAIR* thus models the national security-based deference we've seen the Court grant the government in the later "material support for terrorists" case, *Holder v. Humanitarian Law Project* (Chapter 2). Even one who embraces *Humanitarian Law Project* might doubt how strongly the government's interest in conveniently recruiting lawyers advances national security.[10] The chief justice, however, declares that the Court may not second-guess the government about the Solomon Amendment's importance or efficacy.[11]

Chief Justice Roberts then disposes of FAIR's First Amendment claims. As we've seen the Roberts Court do in restrictive categorical speech cases such as *Golan v. Holder* (Chapter 1), in the student and public employee speech cases *Morse v. Frederick* and *Garcetti v. Ceballos* (both Chapter 3), and in the public forum cases *Summum* and *Walker* (both Chapter 4), the *FAIR* Court holds that the case presents no First Amendment issue at all. The Solomon Amendment, the chief justice declares, in no meaningful sense restricts speech. FAIR argued that the amendment improperly required universities to say things they didn't want to say. When law schools admit recruiters to campus, they often help the recruiters by sending emails to students or posting notices on the recruiters' behalf. The First Amendment provides strong protections against "compelled speech" when the government forces people to speak against their conscientious views.[12] In Chief Justice Roberts's view, however, the Solomon Amendment mostly regulates conduct. It "compels" at worst only trivial speech, especially given that the schools provide the same sort of support for other employers

8. *See id.* at 56–58.

9. *See id.* at 58.

10. No evidence appears to show that the Solomon Amendment improved the military's ability to recruit lawyers. *See* Dale Carpenter, *Unanimously Wrong*, 2006 CATO SUP. CT. REV. 217, 246.

11. *See FAIR*, 547 U.S. at 67–68.

12. *See, e.g.*, W. Va. State Bd. of Educ. v. Barnette, 319 U.S. 624 (1943) (striking down a school's requirement that all students must salute the flag and recite the Pledge of Allegiance).

who recruit on campus.[13] The government, he says, simply could have ordered law schools that receive federal funds to host and support military recruiters.[14]

FAIR argued relatedly that the Solomon Amendment violated the First Amendment by requiring law schools to host or sponsor the message of a speaker—the military—to which they objected. The chief justice rejects this "compelled sponsorship" claim because, he says, hosting the military's objectionable message in no way hampers the schools' ability to express their own views, including their opposition to military discrimination, and in no way implies that they support the military's practices.[15] Finally, the Court considered whether the Solomon Amendment directly restricted the schools' expression. Decades ago, *United States v. O'Brien*[16] established limited First Amendment protection for conduct that expresses ideas. We've seen the Court apply the *O'Brien* test, which mandates intermediate scrutiny for content-neutral speech regulations, in the *McCullen* abortion clinic decision (Chapter 4). The chief justice in *FAIR* explains that the schools' conduct of excluding military recruiters isn't expressive, because the exclusion only conveys a message if the schools explain its meaning. The exclusion itself lacked any expressive content.[17]

Chief Justice Roberts concludes by finding that, just as the Solomon Amendment did nothing to undermine the law schools' speech, it also did nothing to undermine their freedom of expressive association. FAIR maintained that its member schools couldn't effectively express their opposition to antigay discrimination if they were forced to associate with an institution, the military, that blatantly discriminated against gays and lesbians. The chief justice, relying on past decisions that barred the government from interfering with groups' membership decisions, holds that association with the military neither forces the schools to accept members they don't want nor discourages members they do want.[18] The chief justice closes his opinion with an apparent slap at the liberal academic establishment, scolding the law schools for "stretch[ing]," "overstat[ing]," and "exaggerating" their expressive interests and the First Amendment's reach.[19]

Despite the absence in *FAIR* of concurring opinions (or perhaps because of that absence; free speech theory tells us that dissent breeds stronger reasoning[20]), the Court's First Amendment analysis raises serious doctrinal questions. Chief Justice Roberts rejects the law schools' compelled speech claim largely because the schools voluntarily provided other employers the same

13. *See FAIR*, 547 U.S. at 61–62.
14. *See id.* at 59–60.
15. *See id.* at 63–65.
16. 391 U.S. 367 (1968).
17. *See FAIR*, 547 U.S. at 65–68.
18. *See id.* at 68–70.
19. *Id.* at 70.
20. *See generally* CASS R. SUNSTEIN, WHY SOCIETIES NEED DISSENT (2005).

kind of speech support (emails, notices) that they didn't want to provide the military. But one's choice to speak on behalf of people whose ideas one embraces shouldn't dictate whether one must speak on behalf of people whose ideas one abhors. The chief justice rejects the schools' compelled sponsorship claim because, he says, forcing the schools to host an objectionable speaker doesn't prevent them from criticizing that speaker. In the key precedent he cites, however, the Court held that the First Amendment barred a city from making organizers of a St. Patrick's Day parade include a float whose message they opposed—as it happens, a pro-LGBT float.[21] Couldn't those parade organizers, by the logic of *FAIR*, have defused their First Amendment claim simply by adding an anti-LGBT float to their parade? The Court's dismissal of the schools' concern that obeying the amendment would make people think the schools supported the military's policies[22] strikes another questionable note, especially given how seriously we've seen the Court take that same concern from a city government in the park monument case *Summum*.

The chief justice holds that the schools' conduct in excluding military recruiters wasn't expressive, because the conduct required speech to explain it. But that's just as true for the foundational exemplar of expressive conduct from the *O'Brien* case itself: young men's burning of their draft cards during the Vietnam War.[23] No one would have understood that conduct as expressing opposition to the war without the (loud) verbal explanations that accompanied it. The First Amendment expressive conduct doctrine protects conduct that expresses ideas, in addition to words that may accompany the conduct, because the conduct adds content beyond what speech expresses. Political flag burning provides a vivid example.[24] Finally, the chief justice rejects FAIR's expressive association claim because the Solomon Amendment didn't damage law schools' ability to choose their membership. The trouble with that reasoning is that law schools—unlike the NAACP and the Boy Scouts, which brought earlier, successful expressive association claims[25]—aren't membership organizations. The Court's focus on membership as a factor in expressive association implies a narrowing of expressive association doctrine.[26]

21. *See* Hurley v. Irish-Am. Gay, Lesbian & Bisexual Group, 515 U.S. 557 (1995) (discussed in *FAIR*, 547 U.S. at 63–64).

22. *See FAIR*, 547 U.S. at 64–65.

23. *See* United States v. O'Brien, 391 U.S. 367 (1968).

24. *See* Texas v. Johnson, 491 U.S. 397 (1989) (striking down a state ban on expressive flag burning); John H. Ely, *Flag Desecration: A Case Study in the Roles of Categorization and Balancing in First Amendment Analysis*, 88 Harv. L. Rev. 1482 (1975).

25. *Cf.* Boy Scouts v. Dale, 530 U.S. 640 (2000); NAACP v. Alabama, 357 U.S. 449 (1958).

26. *See* Carpenter, *supra* note 10, at 250–52; Erwin Chemerinsky, *Why the Supreme Court Was Wrong about the Solomon Amendment*, 1 Duke J. Const. L. & Pub. Pol'y 259, 275–76 (2006).

The *FAIR* decision strongly reinforces the Roberts Court's commitment to managed speech. Like many of this Court's free speech decisions, including most of the other government preserve cases, the Court lets a powerful institution exert managerial control in order to prevent speech from undermining social and political stability. The distinctive contribution of *FAIR* is to show how speech subsidies can function as a means of managing public discussion.[27] In *FAIR* as in *Humanitarian Law Project*, the speech manager in question is the ultimate guardian of order—the military—and the Court frames the stability interest in the grave terms of national security. The *FAIR* Court doesn't merely reject the First Amendment claim but frames the case in a way that makes the First Amendment wholly irrelevant.[28] The *FAIR* opinion also anticipates *Summum* and *Walker* by showing greater concern for government speech, the military recruiters' communication with law students, than for private speech.[29] Finally, *FAIR* mirrors numerous Roberts Court decisions, from *Humanitarian Law Project* to *Walker*, in marginalizing a kind of speech—here, activism in support of LGBT rights—that aims to destabilize settled institutional arrangements and promote social change.

## RUNNING TO STAND STILL

The Roberts Court's other decision about a speech condition on government funding contrasts sharply with *FAIR*. The decision deals with the government's transnational fight against HIV and AIDS. In 2003 Congress enacted a law that funds nongovernmental organizations (NGOs) to help combat the spread of HIV and AIDS. The law requires that every recipient organization "have a policy opposing prostitution and sex trafficking."[30] The government viewed eradicating prostitution as a necessary battle in the war against HIV and AIDS, and it wanted to fund only NGOs willing to endorse that battle. Two NGOs that receive funds under the law, Alliance for Open Society International and

27. In *Ysursa v. Pocatello Education Association*, discussed in Chapter 8, we'll see the Roberts Court classify a state government program as a subsidy in order to negate speakers' First Amendment interest in the aid the program provided for their speech.

28. The Court's holding that FAIR's activity lacked expressive character foreclosed a potentially important question about the public-private distinction: How could the public law schools in the FAIR coalition state a First Amendment claim at all? *Cf.* United States v. Am. Library Ass'n, 539 U.S. 194, 211–12 (2003) (plurality opinion) (declining to reach the question whether public libraries may state a First Amendment claim). For an argument that ascribing expressive associational interests to government employers such as public law schools would conflict with the expressive rights of government employees, see Paul M. Secunda, *The Solomon Amendment, Expressive Associations, and Public Employment*, 54 UCLA L. Rev. 1767 (2007).

29. *See* Rumsfeld v. Forum for Acad. & Inst. Rights, 547 U.S. 47, 61 n.4 (2006).

30. United States Leadership Against HIV/AIDS, Tuberculosis, and Malaria Act, 22 U.S.C. § 7631(f) (2008).

Pathfinder International, challenged this "policy requirement" as a violation of their First Amendment rights. These organizations work on the ground in several countries to discourage unsafe sex and other practices that can transmit HIV. They argued that the policy requirement forced them either to forgo funding under the law or to embrace the government's anti-prostitution viewpoint. The groups in no way advocate prostitution or human trafficking, but their mission makes working with prostitutes a practical imperative. They feared that if they had to declare opposition to prostitution, prostitutes would stop listening to them. The NGOs also worried that some host governments would object to the anti-prostitution posture.

As in *FAIR*, Chief Justice Roberts wrote the majority opinion in ***Agency for International Development v. Alliance for Open Society International*** **(2013)**.[31] This time, however, he and a 6-2 majority ruled against the government, striking down the policy requirement as a violation of the NGOs' First Amendment right against compelled speech. The chief justice distinguishes *Open Society* from *FAIR* by emphasizing that the First Amendment here, unlike in *FAIR*, would have barred the government from simply ordering NGOs to embrace the government's anti-prostitution policy.[32] Finding a live First Amendment interest required Chief Justice Roberts in *Open Society* to do what he avoided in *FAIR:* analyze the relationship between the First Amendment interest and the government's use of a funding condition to subvert that interest.

The chief justice begins his analysis by noting that, "as a general matter," a funding recipient's recourse when the government imposes on funding "a condition [that] may affect the recipient's exercise of its First Amendment rights" is simply "to decline the funds." That general rule applies whenever a funding condition simply "specif[ies] the activities Congress wants to subsidize." In contrast, speech conditions violate the First Amendment when they "seek to leverage funding to regulate speech outside the contours of the program itself."[33] Two kinds of speech conditions, the chief justice explains, fit the former, constitutionally safe category: those in which the recipient can maintain a "dual structure," with one part of its operations speaking freely and the other part obeying the government's speech condition; and those in which "Congress . . . selectively fund[s] certain programs to address an issue of public concern, without funding alternative ways of addressing the same problem."[34] The Court in past cases has discussed the first kind of permissible condition in terms of a recipient's capacity to "segregate" government-funded

31. 133 S. Ct. 2321 (2013). Roberts (majority) (with Kennedy, Ginsburg, Breyer, Alito, Sotomayor); Scalia (dissenting) (with Thomas). Justice Kagan did not participate in *Open Society*, presumably because she had worked on the case as U.S. Solicitor General before ascending to the Supreme Court.

32. *See id.* at 2327.

33. *Id.* at 2328.

34. *Id.* at 2329.

(and conditioned) activities from activities that use nongovernment funds. The second kind of permissible condition embodies the difference between private speech and what the Court has treated as government speech.

The government speech doctrine, which we encountered last chapter in *Summum* and *Walker*, plays a distinctive role in conditional funding cases. Past Supreme Court decisions have recognized that the government can operate in either of two different modes when it funds speech. In the more familiar mode, the government wants to promote the speaker's message. The government operates as a *patron*. Sometimes, however, the government wants the speaker to promote the government's message. In this other mode, the government in effect pays a private speaker to act as a surrogate. The government operates not as a patron but as a *speaker*. The Court lets the government in speaker mode do something that might seem beyond the constitutional pale: impose viewpoint-based conditions on speech subsidies. When a private speaker speaks as the government's surrogate, the private speaker has no First Amendment rights. The effective speaker is the government itself.[35]

The chief justice explains that the policy requirement in *Open Society* impermissibly dictated funding recipients' speech outside the scope of the government's policy. For one thing, a different section of the AIDS funding law bars recipients from using federal funds to promote prostitution. Therefore, the chief justice reasons, the policy requirement must be trying to control NGOs' speech beyond what the government funds.[36] The government tried to justify the policy requirement as a mere "selection criterion," a way of making sure funding recipients share the government's priorities. Chief Justice Roberts, though, points out that the policy requirement continues to control recipients after the government selects them for funding. The government speech doctrine might justify that continuous control. The chief justice, without ever using the words "government speech," rejects that justification. "This case," he explains, "is about compelling a grant recipient to *adopt a particular belief* as a condition of funding."[37] That's the heart of the *Open Society* opinion. The Court won't let Congress, under cover (implicitly) of the government speech doctrine, force an autonomous, private speaker to change the beliefs that define its identity. Chief Justice Roberts accuses the government of trying to make NGOs "pledge allegiance" to the government's views.[38]

The government tried to soften the policy requirement's impact, before *Open Society* reached the Supreme Court, by establishing "affiliate

35. *See, e.g.*, Rust v. Sullivan, 500 U.S. 173 (1991) (upholding a condition on a federal family planning subsidy that barred subsidized doctors and clinicians from discussing abortion with their patients).

36. *See Open Society*, 133 S. Ct. at 2330.

37. *Id.* (emphasis added).

38. *Id.* at 2332.

guidelines" that allowed recipients to segregate their government funded, anti-prostitution activities from their independently funded, prostitution-neutral activities.[39] If an NGO can maintain its identity simply by segregating its functions, the government argued, who cares if the government co-opts one segregated piece? Chief Justice Roberts, however, concludes that the *Open Society* NGOs can't really segregate their activities in a way that secures their First Amendment interest. If an NGO creates an affiliate that condemns prostitution in order to get government funding, he explains, the main NGO can purport to remain neutral about prostitution "only at the price of evident hypocrisy." Beyond that hypocrisy problem, the policy requirement fails First Amendment muster because, even if the NGO segregates its functions, "the arrangement does not afford a means for the *recipient* [the government-funded branch of the NGO] to express *its* beliefs."[40] That last point is important, because it suggests that a funding recipient's ability to segregate its activities will no longer save a funding condition that compels any part of the funded entity to speak in the government's voice.

The government also asked the Court to uphold the policy requirement because, without the requirement, NGOs could use government money to free up funds from other sources to promote prostitution and sex trafficking. This "offsetting funds" argument suffers from at least two logical defects. First, the government's affiliate guidelines, discussed above, would have allowed the NGOs to do exactly what this argument warns against: abide by the government's funding rules while using private funds to say whatever the NGO wanted. Second, the NGOs' apparent practice prior to the policy requirement, and their position in challenging it, was to remain neutral about prostitution. They never sought to promote prostitution. The offsetting funds argument thus demanded a cure for which there was no disease. Chief Justice Roberts, though, doesn't seize on either of those logical failings to defuse the government's offsetting funds argument. Instead, he points to a third problem: that the offsetting funds argument incorrectly "assumes that federal funding will simply supplant private funding, rather than pay for new programs or expand existing ones."[41] The chief justice, in other words, rejects the government's premise that the NGOs' government and nongovernment funds were fungible. His optimism here about the dynamic possibilities of speech clashes with his pessimistic assumption in *Humanitarian Law Project* that terrorist groups would convert any "material support," including conflict resolution counseling, into fuel for mayhem. The difference, the chief justice maintains, is that the record in *Humanitarian Law Project* "indicated that support for [designated terrorist] organizations' nonviolent operations was funneled

39. *See* 45 C.F.R. § 89.3 (2011).
40. *Open Society*, 133 S. Ct. at 2331.
41. *Id.*

to support their violent activities."[42] That's a bold gloss on the *Humanitarian Law Project* facts.

Justice Scalia's *Open Society* dissent reflects his posture, throughout his career, as the Court's strongest advocate for letting the government demand First Amendment concessions as a price of funding. "The First Amendment," he declares, "does not mandate a viewpoint-neutral government."[43] Justice Scalia embraces the government's explanation of the policy requirement as simply a criterion for selecting which groups to fund, and he has no problem with the government's ongoing control over NGOs' speech.[44] In essence, he views NGOs' government-funded expression as government speech—though he, like the majority, never uses that term. Framing the funding condition as effectively a vehicle for government speech obviates the majority's core concern that the policy requirement coerced the NGOs to speak. On Justice Scalia's account, the NGOs stopped speaking for themselves as soon as they accepted conditional government funding.

Justice Scalia presses further on several fronts. He suggests that the First Amendment wouldn't bar the government from imposing a speech condition on funding even if the condition didn't advance the policy goal behind the funding.[45] He concedes that the *Open Society* NGOs showed no interest in promoting prostitution, but he nonetheless insists that the Court should always assume funding recipients might use government funds to free up private funds for undermining the government's policy agenda.[46] He insists that a funding recipient's ability to segregate its government-funded activities from other activities shouldn't affect the constitutionality of funding conditions.[47] Finally, he portrays ideological conditions on government benefits as grounded in constitutional tradition.[48] Precedent, though, appears to undercut those last two points. The Court's decisions about funding conditions routinely emphasize the importance of a recipient's ability to segregate government and private funds.[49] The Court has also found ideological conditions

42. *Id.*
43. *Id.* at 2332 (Scalia, J., dissenting).
44. *See id.* at 2332–33 (Scalia, J., dissenting).
45. *See id.* at 2333 (Scalia, J., dissenting).
46. *See id.* at 2333–34 (Scalia, J., dissenting).
47. *See id.* at 2334 (Scalia, J., dissenting).
48. *See id.* at 2335 (Scalia, J., dissenting).
49. *See* Rust v. Sullivan, 500 U.S. 173, 197 (1991) (citing segregability of subsidized and nonsubsidized activities in upholding a speech condition); FCC v. League of Women Voters, 468 U.S. 364, 400 (1984) (emphasizing nonsegregability of subsidized and nonsubsidized activities in striking down a speech condition); Regan v. Taxation With Representation, 461 U.S. 540, 544 (1983) (upholding a speech condition based in part on the recipient's capacity to segregate its nonsubsidized activities); *see also Regan*, 461 U.S. at 552–54 (Blackmun, J., concurring) (emphasizing the importance of segregability for First Amendment analysis of speech conditions).

on government benefits unconstitutional, not only in the funding and loyalty oath contexts but also for government employment[50] and contracting.[51]

*Open Society* might complicate the managed speech account of the Roberts Court's First Amendment jurisprudence. The Court rejects a government effort to assert institutional control over an important policy debate. It allows a group of modestly funded speakers with perspectives outside the social and political mainstream to speak their consciences in a way that genuinely pushes back against a strong policy consensus. In considering the Roberts Court's other strongly speech-protective decisions, I've contended either that the Court's methodology enabled speech restrictions in other cases (the categorical decisions in Chapter 1), that its holding was too narrow to have a major impact (*Snyder v. Phelps,* Chapter 2), that its speech-protective priorities were misplaced (*Sorrell v. IMS Health,* Chapter 2), or that its reasoning threatened to undermine its speech-protective holding (*McCullen v. Coakley,* Chapter 4). *Open Society* suffers from none of those shortcomings.

*Open Society* arguably undercuts four different speech-restrictive decisions of the Roberts Court: *FAIR,* because *Open Society* rejects a government effort to compel expressive activity in exchange for a speech subsidy; *Humanitarian Law Project,* because *Open Society* rebuffs the government's effort to control speakers' expression in a sensitive overseas setting; and *Summum* and *Walker,* because *Open Society* cuts against the government speech doctrine.

The first two conflicts don't amount to much, because Chief Justice Roberts portrays the stakes in *Open Society* as both higher for the speakers and lower for the government than in either *FAIR* or *Humanitarian Law Project.* On the speakers' side of the balance, *FAIR* reduces the law schools' expressive interest to nothing, whereas *Humanitarian Law Project* largely dismisses the expressive burden the government's "material support" law imposed on the activist groups. *Open Society,* in contrast, portrays the NGOs' interest in avoiding compelled speech as both more important in the abstract and more threatened by the challenged law. On the government's side of the balance, *Open Society* treats the government's anti-prostitution policy as less pressing than both the government's military recruitment policies as portrayed in *FAIR* and the government's antiterrorism policies as portrayed in *Humanitarian Law Project.* The chief justice's premises in *Open Society* about the speakers' and government's interests leave the decisions in *FAIR* and *Humanitarian Law Project* (both of which, remember, he also wrote) undisturbed.

50. *See* Elrod v. Burns, 427 U.S. 347 (1976) (holding that political loyalty requirements for government employees generally violate the First Amendment).

51. *See* O'Hare Truck Serv., Inc. v. City of Northlake, 518 U.S. 312 (1996) (holding that political loyalty requirements for government contractors generally violate the First Amendment).

The government speech dimension of *Open Society* is the one that substantially explains the decision. The government speech doctrine achieved great momentum in the early years of the Roberts Court, when *Summum* boldly extended the doctrine into the public forum. (*Walker* followed *Open Society* chronologically and relies on *Summum*.) I've argued that the government speech doctrine, by subjecting seemingly private speech to government control, strongly advances managed speech. Even so, the government speech doctrine is a volatile, potent force whose implications remain uncertain. Earlier Courts have handled the doctrine with at least intermittent caution. Most notably, the Rehnquist Court rejected an attempt by the federal government to characterize federally funded lawyers' representation of indigent clients as government speech.[52] *Summum*, and the Court's nod toward the government speech doctrine in the public employee speech case *Garcetti* (Chapter 3), suggested that the Roberts Court might continue to expand the doctrine aggressively. *Open Society* gave the Court an opportunity to do so. The Court, however, declined to move more expressive activity into the government speech column. Instead, Chief Justice Roberts—keeper of the Court's institutional capital—steered away from the government speech vortex.

*Open Society* is the first case to enforce the First Amendment's prohibition on compelled speech against a conditional speech subsidy. That combination of elements has caused some leading legal scholars to praise the decision as a speech-protective landmark.[53] Chief Justice Roberts's opinion, however, makes no suggestion that compelled speech is qualitatively worse than, or even materially distinct from, the compelled silence at issue in the earlier conditional subsidy cases. With no such distinction, *Open Society* just adds another link to the Supreme Court's ambivalent chain of subsidized speech decisions. First Amendment law in this area remains what it long has been: a fact-bound doctrinal obstacle course where First Amendment challengers and the government probably will keep trading wins and losses. Likewise, the government speech doctrine remains what it somewhat more recently has become: an under-theorized black hole that may, at any time, swallow up another chunk of First Amendment protection but whose gravitational pull the Court maintains some commitment to resisting.

*Open Society* in no way calls the holding of *Summum* into question. Rather, Chief Justice Roberts's refusal to let the words "government speech" escape his keyboard hedges the Court's bets. The chief justice tells us only that the *Open*

52. *See* Legal Servs. Corp. v. Velasquez, 531 U.S. 533, 541–45 (2001) (refusing to extend the government speech doctrine to government-funded lawyers' representation of clients). On the other hand, the Rehnquist Court treated federally funded doctors' advice to pregnant women as government speech. *See* Rust v. Sullivan, 500 U.S. 173 (1991).

53. *See* Laurence Tribe & Joshua Matz, Uncertain Justice: The Roberts Court and the Constitution 259–64 (2014).

*Society* policy requirement extended the government's control over speech too far and coerced the NGOs too much. If *Open Society* runs away from the most aggressive implications of the Roberts Court's government speech decisions, it's only running to stand still.

## CONCLUSION

*Rumsfeld v. FAIR* firmly rejects a First Amendment claim from subsidized speakers. *Agency for International Development v. Alliance for Open Society International* strongly affirms another such claim. The foundations of *FAIR* appear sturdier and more deeply grounded. Like several other Roberts Court decisions we've encountered, *FAIR* makes a point of denying the very basis for a First Amendment claim. The decision considers and narrowly construes several prominent First Amendment doctrines—compelled speech, compelled sponsorship, and expressive association—in ways that could reverberate outside the confines of subsidized speech. In contrast, a divided Court in *Open Society* acted to restrain (not revise) the Roberts Court's own government speech cases. The decision's conceptual basis appears underdeveloped.[54] A future Court may uncover elements of the *Open Society* Court's reasoning that point toward more speech-protective avenues in government preserves. For now, though, *FAIR* provides stronger support for shrugging off future challenges to speech conditions than *Open Society* provides for sustaining them.

From the standpoint of dynamic diversity, these two decisions could hardly present a sharper contrast. Dynamic diversity would compel reversal of *FAIR*. The Court's view that a coalition of law schools formed for the express purpose of opposing a controversial government policy had no expressive interest in whether its members had to promote that policy seems brusque at best and hostile at worst. Dynamic diversity would respect both the weight of FAIR's substantive position and the importance of letting its members express that position through their operational decisions. On the other side of the balance, dynamic diversity would assess the government's national security interest in stifling expression with the same wariness as in the "material support for terrorists" decision, *Holder v. Humanitarian Law Project* (Chapter 2). Given the de minimis impact of the law schools' actions on national security, a dynamic diversity analysis would find for the law schools as easily as a unanimous Court found for the government. On the other hand, *Open Society*

54. Joseph Blocher criticizes the majority's pivotal distinction between conditions that operate inside and outside the funding program, and he argues that no alternative principle fully justifies the decision. *See* Joseph Blocher, *New Problems for Subsidized Speech*, 56 WM. & MARY L. REV. 1083 (2015); *see also* Charles W. "Rocky" Rhodes, *Speech, Subsidies, and Traditions:* AID v. AOSI *and the First Amendment*, 2013 CATO SUP. CT. REV. 363, 380–91 (urging the Court to fill the analytic gap in *Open Society* by using tradition to distinguish between permissible and impermissible funding conditions).

joins *Entertainment Merchants* (Chapter 1), *Snyder v. Phelps* (Chapter 2), and *McCullen v. Coakley* (Chapter 4) in the pantheon of Roberts Court free speech decisions that advance dynamic diversity. *Open Society* would benefit from greater analytic clarity, but reconciling freedom with control in subsidy cases is a hard problem. Dynamic diversity would posit that maximizing the range of ideas and participants in public debates requires strong protection even for government-subsidized speakers. That position, however, would tee up a different problem: how to persuade a government with minimal leverage over speech it subsidizes that it should keep subsidizing speech.

*FAIR* flows smoothly into the larger speech-restrictive current of the Roberts Court's government preserve decisions. More even than the private speech cases discussed in Part I, the government preserve decisions show managed speech ascendant. Each case presents a conflict between the government—the prototype of managerial authority—and a speaker that lacks independent expressive means. Thus, although the government preserve cases don't expand the roster of winning corporate and establishment free speech claimants from Part I, they swell the ranks of marginal and dissident losers: the *Beard v. Banks* prisoners, failed whistle-blower Richard Ceballos, and banner-waving student Frederick Morse (all Chapter 3); the Summum sect, the Sons of Confederate Veterans in *Walker,* and the Christian Legal Society (all Chapter 4); and the FAIR coalition of law schools. The Roberts Court's government preserve decisions display the three core, interconnected architectural elements of managed speech: empowerment of strong, responsible institutions, here government entities, to manage the scope and content of public debate; hostility toward the speech interests of political dissenters and other outsider speakers who pose a risk of destabilizing the status quo; and a commitment to protecting social and political stability from speech that might challenge settled arrangements of social and political power.

The government preserve decisions use several different methods to establish managerial control over speech while marginalizing dissenting and outsider speakers. Several of these cases flatten the public-private distinction, treating government officials very much like private managers of institutions, property, and money. In the most extreme instances, the government speech doctrine inverts the public-private dichotomy. *Summum* and *Walker* let government managers convert apparently private speech into the government's own expression. That conversion eliminates both the private claimant and the putative government violator from the conventional structure of a constitutional rights dispute. The government speech trope hangs in the background of *FAIR,* where the Court expresses great concern about the government's ability to communicate with potential military lawyers even as it dismisses the law schools' free speech interest. *Open Society* pointedly refuses to stretch the government speech doctrine further, but it doesn't pare back the earlier government speech decisions.

Other government preserve cases use a variation on the categorical methodology of Chapter 1 to negate free speech claims against government managers. In *Morse v. Frederick* (Chapter 3) the Court excludes advocacy of illegal drug use from even the lenient constitutional review that ordinarily applies to speech restrictions in schools. In *Garcetti v. Ceballos* (also Chapter 3) the Court similarly disqualifies government employees' "course of duty" expression from the balancing test that usually governs public employee speech cases. In *FAIR* the Court places law schools' communications and relationships with on-campus interviewers outside the scope of both the First Amendment's speech and expressive association protections. The remaining decisions, while going through the motions of First Amendment analysis, defer to government managers with a force matched among the private speech cases only by *Humanitarian Law Project*. *Beard* subordinates federal prisoners' expressive interests to a credulous account of prison officials' disciplinary needs. *Christian Legal Society v. Martinez* (Chapter 4) privileges higher education administrators' managerial will over students' aspirations to a structure of diverse intellectual engagement. To the extent such decisions as *Morse, Garcetti,* and *FAIR* gesture toward the possibility of First Amendment review, they express a similar deference to the government defendants' claimed interest in managerial efficiency.

The deep theme that unites the government preserve decisions across the three chapters in Part II, and ties them to the most important private speech decisions from Part I, is the Roberts Court's dogged defense of social and political stability. In government preserve decision after decision, the Roberts Court beats back First Amendment threats to the stable continuity of government operations. The Court prevents prisoner, student, and employee speakers from destabilizing government institutions of Chapter 3; it bars or defuses public forum claims that threaten the government's dispositions of property in Chapter 4; and it negates a claim in *FAIR* that would loosen the government's control over its funds. *Garcetti* and *Summum* both erase First Amendment claims in what seem like archetypal settings for the operation of First Amendment law: a whistle-blower's effort to correct government wrongdoing and the open forum of a public park. In both cases, the Court subordinates outsider speakers' expressive interests to what the justices see as a higher principle of social and political stability.

The first two parts of this book have shown how the Roberts Court's free speech decisions about regulations of private speech and speech in government preserves develop the managed speech mode of First Amendment jurisprudence. What's left is the largest group of Roberts Court First Amendment decisions, all focused on the conceptually narrow but hard-fought terrain of the electoral process. The next three chapters turn to that most complex and contentious precinct of the Roberts Court's First Amendment.

## PART THREE

# Speech in the Electoral Process

The Roberts Court has spent far more time on regulations of money in politics than on any other First Amendment problem. *Citizens United v. Federal Election Commission* is this Court's most famous and controversial decision, and it's only the beginning. No prior Court has decided so many important campaign finance cases in such a short period of time, and no Court has delivered such a consistent, emphatic series of campaign finance holdings. Justice Sandra Day O'Connor's replacement by Samuel Alito, almost simultaneous with John Roberts's installation as chief justice, created a solid majority for using the First Amendment to strike down most campaign finance regulations. Justice Kennedy is no swing vote on this issue. He has long called as loudly as anyone on the Court for First Amendment checks on campaign finance laws. The Roberts Court's conservative majority has delivered an almost unbroken series of decisions that raise First Amendment protection of political money to a historic peak. Those decisions have split the Court down its middle. All have come with substantial controversy, and nearly all have come on 5-4 votes.

One reason I treat the campaign finance decisions separately in this last part of the book is their sheer volume. A more important reason is that the justices, academic commentators, and the public disagree, at a very basic level, about what sort of First Amendment cases these are. For strong supporters of the Roberts Court's approach, campaign finance regulations are government censorship. Accordingly, the campaign finance decisions are ordinary private speech cases that should fit unobtrusively in Part I. More measured skeptics of campaign finance regulation would agree that this discussion belongs in Part I, but they would isolate the campaign finance decisions, applying a more lenient balancing test to campaign finance regulations. In contrast, some opponents of the Roberts Court's decisions would argue that campaign finance disputes belong in Part II, because they view elections as a species of government preserve, in which the distinctive purposes of electoral debate should inform the First Amendment's application. The strongest opponents of the Roberts Court's approach would contend that campaign finance doesn't belong in this book at all. They would hew to Justice Stevens's declaration that "[m]oney is property; it is not speech."[1]

The Roberts Court's strengthening of First Amendment protection for electoral money carries a powerful impact for public political debate. People disagree sharply, again, about how to assess that impact. Supporters of the Roberts Court's campaign finance decisions insist that a free flow of political money advances expressive freedom by letting electoral speakers say what they want to say. In contrast, some opponents of these decisions charge the Court with applying the First Amendment too aggressively and wrongly second-guessing legislative judgments about how to run elections. Other opponents go further, arguing that campaign finance regulations actually advance First Amendment values by allowing more participants and ideas into electoral debates.

The three defining elements of managed speech pervade the Roberts Court's electoral speech decisions. First, the decisions empower what the Court perceives as stable, reliable managers for electoral debate. In contrast to the government preserve decisions in Part II, the speech managers here are private rather than government actors. *Citizens United* and this Court's other attacks on campaign finance regulations reject government regulation in favor of control by corporations and wealthy individuals. The electoral speech decisions also enhance the managerial power of the major political parties. Second, the electoral speech decisions disregard the expressive interests of dissenters and outsider speakers. Increasing the importance of money in politics dampens the voices of people who lack money, the same speakers who gain little from the Roberts Court's private speech decisions and who lose heavily in its government preserve decisions. The Court also denies First Amendment relief to an insurgent candidate who challenges the major parties' nominating structures. Third, the electoral speech decisions serve managed speech's ultimate goal of promoting social and political stability. The Roberts Court portrays corporations, wealthy individuals, and the major parties as established, responsible actors in a political system that exists to satisfy the most powerful interest groups. By virtue of their social and economic primacy, all these private speech managers have a strong interest in shaping a debate that validates existing social and economic power structures.

Chapter 6 begins the discussion of electoral speech regulations by canvassing the handful of Roberts Court decisions about free speech in the electoral process that don't concern campaign finance. *New York State Board of Elections v. Lopez Torres* rejects a First Amendment claim that New York's system for

1. Nixon v. Shrink Mo. Gov't PAC, 528 U.S. 377, 398 (2000) (Stevens, J., concurring).

selecting parties' judicial nominees, which makes judicial candidates go through party nominating conventions, violates candidates' right to participate in elections. *Washington State Grange v. Washington State Republican Party* upholds Washington's nonpartisan primary system, which places the top candidates to emerge from a nonpartisan primary on the general election ballot, labeled with their party preferences, although the majority signals that the parties may well have a claim once the state implements the system. These decisions about political parties show an important continuity with Rehnquist Court decisions that used First Amendment law to maintain political stability by strengthening the major parties. Finally, *Doe v. Reed* holds that the First Amendment does not categorically bar states from publicizing the names of people who sign initiative and referendum petitions. That decision dodges a clash between two different expressive interests: petition signatories' interest in avoiding reprisals for their political activity, and the electorate's interest in information about who supports ballot measures.

Chapter 7 examines the Roberts Court's most important, sweeping campaign finance decisions, focusing on the two blockbusters: *Citizens United* and *McCutcheon v. Federal Election Commission*. Both decisions substantially increase the role money can play in elections. The Supreme Court's cornerstone 1976 campaign finance decision, *Buckley v. Valeo*, cleaved the campaign finance universe. The government could almost never regulate expenditures by campaigns and candidates, but the government got substantial latitude to regulate contributions to campaigns and candidates. The Roberts Court's decision in *Randall v. Sorrell* marks the first time the Supreme Court ever struck down a state's contribution limits under the lenient *Buckley* analysis. *Citizens United* expands the *Buckley* prohibition on expenditure regulations, striking down restrictions on corporate and union expenditures that *Buckley* itself left untouched. *McCutcheon*, though less notorious than *Citizens United*, could prove more important. The *McCutcheon* Court upends the *Buckley* settlement by striking down a substantial piece of the federal law that limits how much donors may contribute to congressional campaigns. The Court's opinion contains reasoning that could justify striking down all contribution limits. *McCutcheon* also fortifies the major political parties as managers of electoral debate.

Chapter 8 assesses the remaining Roberts Court decisions about money and politics. Like the Chapter 7 decisions, almost all the decisions in Chapter 8 strike down campaign finance regulations. However, in sharp contrast to the Chapter 7 decisions, the Chapter 8 decisions all *reduce* the role of money in elections. *Davis v. Federal Election Commission* strikes down a federal law that increased the amounts of campaign contributions that a candidate could raise when facing an opponent who used substantial personal wealth to campaign. Similarly, *Arizona Free Enterprise Club's Freedom PAC v. Bennett* strikes down a state law that increased the public funds available to candidates whose privately funded opponents amassed large campaign war chests. Both of those decisions foil government efforts to enhance voter information. Another set of decisions restricts unions' ability to raise and spend money for electoral advocacy. The most significant cases in this group, *Knox v. SEIU, Local 1000* and *Harris v. Quinn,* restrict public employee labor unions' ability to spend nonmembers' "agency fees" for political purposes, based on the nonmembers' First Amendment right not to fund union political activities they don't support. The labor speech cases diminish unions' managerial power, but the Court makes clear that it views unions as destabilizing rather than stabilizing institutions. Finally, *Williams-Yulee v. Florida Bar* stands out as the sole Roberts Court decision to uphold a direct government restriction on the flow of money into politics. The case, however, deals only with a narrow, ethically charged ban on personal solicitation by candidates for state judgeships.

The Roberts Court's electoral speech decisions aggressively advance managed speech. *Citizens United* and *McCutcheon* free wealthy and powerful actors to inject more money into the electoral process, whereas the Chapter 8 decisions constrain the ability of the government and labor unions to counter the influence of wealth and power. The Roberts Court's campaign finance decisions reject both government regulation of electoral debate and broadly dispersed opportunities for participation. Instead, the decisions amplify the voices of wealthy, powerful speakers who have strong interests in maintaining social and political stability. My dynamic diversity approach to First Amendment law would reach opposite results in most of the electoral speech cases. For dynamic diversity, broad participation and a wide range of issues should characterize electoral debates. The Roberts Court's major contribution to the law of free speech in elections, supercharging the influence of private money, actively undermines dynamic diversity's goals by enhancing the voices of a small group of speakers with a narrow range of policy preferences. Likewise, the Roberts Court's solicitude for the major political parties encourages marginalization of political dissenters, speakers whose expressive interests lie at the core of dynamic diversity.

# CHAPTER 6

# Of Parties and Petitions

## *Regulations of Election Procedures*

The Roberts Court, as the next two chapters will show at length, has spent the vast majority of its energy in the electoral field on regulations of money in politics. The First Amendment, however, also protects the basic right to speak in the course of election campaigns; the associational rights of political groups, notably political parties; and various individual interests in electoral participation. The Rehnquist Court decided a large, varied group of electoral speech cases. The Roberts Court, in contrast, has addressed nonfinancial election regulations in only three First Amendment cases.[1] All three decisions deny election-related First Amendment claims, although they deal with very different sorts of free speech interests. These cases provide useful insights, outside the campaign finance crucible, about how this Court views electoral speech.

Two of the Roberts Court's nonfinance electoral speech cases deal with the interests of the major political parties. Sometimes the major parties invoke the First Amendment to challenge government regulations as undermining the parties' associational rights. In other cases, voters or would-be candidates invoke the First Amendment to challenge government actions that elevate the parties' interests over individuals' expressive rights. The Rehnquist Court strongly vindicated the major parties' First Amendment claims while giving the back of its hand to First Amendment litigants who challenged the parties'

1. An additional Roberts Court decision tacitly acknowledged a likely First Amendment problem with an election regulation, holding unanimously that challengers to a state law that criminalized certain false electoral statements had legal standing under Article III to pursue their claim before the state actually enforced the law against them. *See* Susan B. Anthony List v. Dreihaus, 134 S. Ct. 2334 (2014).

prerogatives. Those parallel lines of decisions gave the major parties substantial control over electoral debates and processes for the manifest purpose of maintaining the parties' stabilizing influence in our electoral system, at a heavy cost to dissenting voices and political dynamism. More directly than any other line of First Amendment cases, the Rehnquist Court's decisions about political parties prefigure the Roberts Court's managed speech paradigm.[2]

The Roberts Court has rejected one First Amendment claim that sought to curb the major political parties' autonomy and another claim that sought to enhance it. Both decisions, however, show strong regard for the parties' constitutional prerogatives. The Court rejects an insurgent candidate's challenge to a restrictive state nomination process. In contrast, the Court gently rebuffs a First Amendment claim by the parties, finding merit in their arguments but signaling that they brought the claim too early and framed it too broadly. The first decision extends the Rehnquist Court's patronage of the major parties, whereas the second does nothing to undermine it. The Roberts Court treats the major political parties as responsible managers of electoral debate, while disfavoring First Amendment claims that challenge the parties' autonomy. The Court's other nonfinance electoral speech decision declines to balance competing First Amendment interests in participatory autonomy and public information.

## IT'S MY PARTY (AND I'LL NOMINATE WHOM I WANT TO)

Political scientists widely view the two major U.S. political parties as stabilizing forces in electoral politics.[3] The dominance of two large parties requires voters to form broad electoral coalitions. That arrangement tends, for better or worse, to mute or marginalize a broad range of political ideas outside the mainstream of public opinion (though it can also enable party elites to advance their pet policies without strong public support). In the terms I used for discussing *Christian Legal Society v. Martinez* (Chapter 4), our two-party system embodies an integrationist, as opposed to pluralist, structure of electoral competition. The two major parties present a perennially vexing problem for the public-private distinction, because they simultaneously exist as associations of private citizens and structures of government power. That duality complicates the application to the parties of constitutional law, including First Amendment law.[4] The major parties strive to maintain both the prerogatives of power and the protections of constitutional rights.

2. *See* Gregory P. Magarian, *Regulating Political Parties under a "Public Rights" First Amendment*, 44 Wm. & Mary L. Rev. 1939 (2003).
3. *See, e.g.*, E. E. Schattschneider, Party Government (1959).
4. *See, e.g.*, Smith v. Allwright, 321 U.S. 649 (1944) (rejecting a dominant political party's claim that its primary election was a private function and that it could therefore exclude African-American voters from the primary).

Candidate selection procedures have spawned some of the most contentious First Amendment battles between government regulators and political parties. In theory parties may select their nominees for elective offices through whatever processes they choose. The states, however, design election ballots and set ballot access requirements, tasks that effectively allow them to regulate party nomination procedures. In the wake of the progressive era a century ago, for example, many states made parties choose their nominees through direct primary elections rather than insider "smoke-filled room" meetings.[5] The Supreme Court under Chief Justice William Rehnquist invalidated several candidate selection laws as violations of political parties' First Amendment right of association. The Rehnquist Court struck down Connecticut's bar on independent voters' participation in party primaries;[6] California's bar on parties' endorsing candidates in primaries,[7] and California's "blanket primary," in which any voter on primary election day could vote for any array of candidates regardless of party.[8] Only in narrow circumstances did the Rehnquist Court ever reject the major parties' First Amendment claims.[9]

At the same time, the Rehnquist Court rejected First Amendment challenges to election laws that favor the major parties. In the primary election setting, the Rehnquist Court upheld Oklahoma's limitation of primary voting to party members and registered Independents.[10] In the general election setting, the Court upheld Minnesota's prohibition on minor parties' co-nomination of major party candidates[11] and Arkansas's effective closure of televised candidate debates to major-party candidates.[12] The Rehnquist Court explicitly validated the major political parties' stabilizing function in the U.S. political process, holding that states may "favor the traditional two-party system [to] temper the *destabilizing effects* of party splintering and excessive factionalism."[13]

The Rehnquist Court's First Amendment decisions about political parties form a blueprint for the Roberts Court's managed speech paradigm. The Roberts Court has decided two First Amendment cases about political parties'

5. *See* Eric Lawrence *et al.*, *The Adoption of Direct Primaries in the United States*, 19 PARTY POLITICS 3 (2013).

6. *See* Tashjian v. Republican Party of Connecticut, 479 U.S. 208 (1986).

7. *See* Eu v. San Francisco Cty. Democratic Cent. Comm., 489 U.S. 214 (1989).

8. *See* Cal. Democratic Party v. Jones, 530 U.S. 567 (2000).

9. *See* Colo. Republican Fed. Campaign Comm. v. FEC, 533 U.S. 431 (2001) (holding that, although parties could freely make campaign expenditures if not coordinated with their candidates, the government could regulate coordinated party expenditures as contributions from the party to the candidate); Morse v. Republican Party of Virginia, 517 U.S. 186 (1996) (plurality opinion) (subjecting a party's entry fee for its state convention to the Voting Rights Act's preclearance requirement).

10. *See* Clingman v. Beaver, 544 U.S. 581 (2005).

11. *See* Timmons v. Twin Cities Area New Party, 520 U.S. 351 (1997).

12. *See* Ark. Educ. Television Comm'n v. Forbes, 523 U.S. 666 (1998).

13. *Timmons*, 520 U.S. at 367 (emphasis added).

prerogatives. One rejects an outsider's First Amendment claim against a party's legal autonomy. The second rejects parties' challenge to a state regulation, but with caveats that respect the parties' interest. These cases show that the Roberts Court has maintained the Rehnquist Court's commitment to protecting the major political parties' autonomy.

In ***New York State Board of Elections v. Lopez Torres* (2008),**[14] the Roberts Court unanimously rejected a First Amendment challenge to New York's system for choosing parties' judicial nominees. Under state election laws, any party that received at least 50,000 votes in the last gubernatorial election must choose its nominees for state trial judgeships through a vote of delegates at a party convention. Party members elect the convention delegates from state assembly districts in a "delegate primary." Anyone who wants to run for a party delegate position must submit a petition signed, during a designated 37-day period, by 500 registered party members who live in the assembly district or by 5 percent of all registered party members in the district, whichever is less. A nominee selected through the party convention process gets a spot on the general election ballot. Alternatively, a candidate may gain access to the ballot as an independent or minor party representative by submitting a petition signed by 3,500 or 4,000 voters in the judicial district (the number varies by district size) or 5 percent of the number of voters in that district in the last gubernatorial election, whichever is less.[15]

Margarita Lopez Torres was a Democratic county judge. She had failed three times to win her party's nomination for a state trial judgeship because, she charged, party leaders had blackballed her for refusing to hire employees based on their party loyalty. She and several other unsuccessful candidates sued the state, claiming that the nomination system violated voters' and prospective candidates' First Amendment right of expressive association. The U.S. Court of Appeals for the Second Circuit held that the First Amendment requires states to give voters and candidates a realistic opportunity to participate in a party's nominating process. New York's law denied that opportunity, the lower court explained, because the nomination system required candidates to get an onerous number of petition signatures and supportive delegates, because party machines could control delegates, and because one or the other major party dominated each of the state's judicial districts. Concerns about the vitality and integrity of New York's party-driven candidate selection system may have informed the Court of Appeals' decision.[16]

14. 552 U.S. 196 (2008). Scalia (majority) (with Roberts, Stevens, Souter, Thomas, Ginsburg, Breyer, Alito); Stevens (concurring) (with Souter); Kennedy (concurring in the judgment) (with Breyer in part).

15. *See id.* at 199–201.

16. *See* James A. Gardner, *New York's Judicial Selection Process Is Fine—It's the Party System That Needs Fixing*, NYSBAJ (Sept. 2007) at 42 (criticizing failings in New York's

Justice Scalia begins his opinion for a unanimous Supreme Court by describing the nature and limits of political parties' First Amendment rights and declaring that Lopez Torres can't rely on the parties' rights.[17] That declaration makes sense on its surface, because the law Lopez-Torres challenged imposes a requirement on the major parties, not on Lopez Torres. Justice Scalia's framework, however, subverts the essence of Lopez Torres's complaint: that the major parties use the state-mandated nomination system—which members of the major parties enacted as legislators—to suppress electoral competition. Justice Scalia uses the public-private distinction to cast the major parties as innocent bystanders to Lopez Torres's irrational assault on a law that doesn't affect her. We've seen the Court in the park monument case *Summum* and the license plate case *Walker* (both Chapter 4) use the government speech doctrine to invert the power relationships that defined those disputes. Justice Scalia's framing of *Lopez Torres* works a similar inversion. It suggests that the Roberts Court, like the Rehnquist Court before it, cares deeply about the major political parties' rights but very little about the rights of political insurgents who challenge the parties' prerogatives.

Having framed Lopez Torres's claim as incoherent, Justice Scalia not surprisingly proceeds to find it meritless. Voters have a right to vote in primary elections, he explains, but candidates have no right to run in parties' nomination processes (here the state conventions). Even if candidates had such a right, New York's petition requirement for lining up supportive convention delegates would be reasonable. What really troubles Lopez Torres, says Justice Scalia, is that she keeps losing the nominating contest, and the party's anointed candidates keep winning. Her problem is "not [] the state law, but [] the voters' (and their elected delegates') preference for the choices of the party leadership."[18] She's just a sore loser. That story, however, ignores a premise of Lopez Torres's challenge: that the results of state conventions don't accurately reflect voters' will.

Justice Scalia makes a striking commentary on the wisdom, as distinct from the legality, of conventions as structures for nominating candidates. He concedes somewhat grudgingly that states may, within the bounds of parties' First Amendment rights, subject parties to nominating procedures designed to help insurgent candidates. The First Amendment, however, does not compel states to give candidates a "fair shot" at nomination. What even amounts to a "fair shot," he says, is a question courts must defer to legislatures—but then

party structure for causing problems in the state's judicial candidate selection system); Lawrence N. Gray, *Ballot Rigging—How It's Done in New York*, NYSBAJ (May, 2013) at 33–35 (describing high potential for electoral corruption in New York's Supreme Court nomination system).

17. *See Lopez Torres*, 552 U.S. at 202–03.

18. *Id.* at 205.

he weighs in on the legislative question. "[T]here is good reason to believe," he asserts, that the New York legislature prefers the convention system to primaries because a primary system empowers "voters uninformed about judicial qualifications" and "places a high premium upon the ability to raise money." Conventions, moreover, are "a traditional means of choosing party nominees."[19] Beginning with the dogfight video case *Stevens* (Chapter 1), we've seen the Roberts Court use tradition to define, and sometimes limit, First Amendment rights. *Lopez Torres* uses tradition to elevate political parties above "uninformed voters" as managers of electoral debates.

Justice Scalia finally considers Lopez Torres's argument that the lack of partisan competition at the general election stage should compel a First Amendment guarantee of a more competitive nominating process. His reasoning about partisan entrenchment as an electoral structure closely tracks his reasoning about conventions as a nominating structure. Why, he asks, should the general election's competitive prospects affect the constitutional rights of candidates who seek a party's nomination? Lopez Torres's answer must be that, when a single party controls the general election, candidates and voters need competitiveness in the party's nominating process, or else the parties will fully control who holds public office. Justice Scalia, though, portrays single-party entrenchment, like nominating convention outcomes, as an unimpeachable result of true voter preferences. He concedes that states have power to discourage party monopolies, provided of course that they respect parties' associational rights. However, he falls back on Justice Holmes's familiar First Amendment metaphor of the "open marketplace [of] ideas." Government may not interfere with that marketplace, and federal courts may not "*manage the market* by preventing too many buyers from settling upon a single product."[20] That analysis implies that, absent judicial interference, the "market" is perfectly free. In his broader reasoning, however, Justice Scalia appears content if not enthusiastic to let the major political parties dictate the "buyers'" choices.

*Lopez Torres* radiates essential Roberts Court First Amendment themes. The Court treats political association like an economic commodity, mirroring the copyright extension case *Golan v. Holder* (Chapter 1), the "material aid to terrorists" case *Holder v. Humanitarian Law Project,* and the drug detailing case *Sorrell v. IMS Health* (both Chapter 2). The processes by which political association yields outcomes the political parties want may appear public, but they're really private "marketplace" transactions. Power imbalances between private entities with conflicting expressive interests either don't exist or don't matter. In fact, the Court resolves to prevent apparently weaker entities (here political

19. *Id.* at 205–06.

20. *Id.* at 207–08 (emphasis added). The Court quotes Justice Holmes from Abrams v. United States, 250 U.S. 616, 630 (1919) (Holmes, J., dissenting).

insurgents) from invoking governmental (here judicial) power against apparently stronger entities (here the major political parties). As in the material aid to terrorists case *Humanitarian Law Project* (Chapter 2), the Court in *Lopez Torres* flatly dismisses the First Amendment concerns of serious political dissidents. *Lopez Torres* gives the major political parties—responsible stabilizing agents—managerial control over what otherwise might become an unstable sphere of important expressive activity. This is the same sort of control the private speech cases give to powerful or wealthy speakers and the government preserve cases give to government actors.[21] The major parties, with their combination of private and public qualities, resemble both of those other sets of speech managers.

Washington State, generally favors more direct voter participation than New York in parties' selection of nominees. Washington for decades held a blanket primary, which chose the parties' nominees by allowing voters to vote for any candidate of any party for each office on the ballot. The Rehnquist Court in *California Democratic Party v. Jones*[22] struck down blanket primaries as a violation of political parties' freedom of association, effectively scuttling Washington's chosen system. State voters then passed an initiative that set up a nonpartisan primary, with the top two finishers advancing to the general election. The initiative included a potentially important twist: a candidate may choose a "partisan preference," which appears with the candidate's name on the primary ballot. In ***Washington State Grange v. Washington State Republican Party* (2008)**[23] the two major political parties (joined, as usual in challenges to state restrictions on parties' autonomy, by the Libertarian Party) claimed the partisan preference rule violated their freedom of association, by usurping their right to nominate candidates of their choice and by forcing them to associate with candidates they didn't support. For example, Courtney Love could run for governor in the primary, listing her party preference on the ballot as "Republican," and the Republican Party couldn't stop her. Voters might believe the Republican Party endorsed or approved of Love. If she reached the general election, voters might mistakenly perceive her as the Republican Party's nominee. That, in the parties' view, would amount to

21. Justice Kennedy concurred in the judgment, emphasizing that New York's alternative, petitioning mechanism for access to the ballot as an independent or minor party candidate lessens whatever constitutional burden the convention system might impose. He also declares, in a passage Justice Breyer joins, that the rule of law must govern judicial elections. *See Lopez Torres*, 552 U.S. at 209–13 (Kennedy, J., concurring in the judgment). Justice Stevens, who joined the majority opinion, nonetheless added a brief concurrence that tweaks Justice Scalia by insinuating that New York's convention system, although constitutional, is "stupid." *Id.* at 209 (Stevens, J., concurring) (internal quotation marks omitted).

22. 530 U.S. 567 (2000).

23. 552 U.S. 442 (2008). Thomas (majority) (with Roberts, Stevens, Souter, Ginsburg, Breyer, Alito); Roberts (concurring) (with Alito); Scalia (dissenting) (with Kennedy).

the same sort of forced association and forced endorsement that law schools complained about (to no avail) in the military recruiting case, *Rumsfeld v. FAIR* (Chapter 5).

In a quirk that underscores the public-private confusion I've emphasized in First Amendment cases about political parties, the Washington State Grange joined the suit in defense of the law. The Grange is a longstanding fraternal, social, and civic organization that has expanded from its original emphasis on farmers' interests to back a variety of social and political reforms. The Grange proposed and promoted Washington's nonpartisan primary system. The absence from the case name of the state and state officials shows how First Amendment disputes, especially but not only those that involve political parties, sometimes concern conflicts between competing expressive interests rather than simple disputes between a burdened speaker and a censorious government.[24] Here, although the political parties raised their associational interest against the partisan preference rule, the state and the Grange defended the rule on the ground that it gave voters useful information about candidates.

Justice Thomas, writing for a 7-2 majority, rejects the political parties' First Amendment claim. He begins by emphasizing that the parties opted to pursue a "facial challenge" to Washington's new primary system.[25] That means they challenged the whole law, prior to its actual implementation. Sometimes facial challenges can be useful, as when the government and regulated entities agree about how an important law will work. In general, though, the Court sets a high bar for facial challenges in order to avoid premature, under-informed, or unnecessary judicial interventions.[26] If a challenged law has any applications likely to pass constitutional muster, the Court usually will reject the facial challenge, leaving open the possibility of a later challenge to the law "as applied" in concrete circumstances. The political parties in *Washington State Grange* brought a facial challenge because they insisted the partisan preference rule would harm them no matter how the state implemented that rule. The Court had to decide whether the partisan preference rule would cause the parties such inevitable, serious harm that the Court needed to strike down the whole law.

Justice Thomas says no. The rule doesn't interfere with parties' actual nominations of candidates because Washington's primary system doesn't select parties' nominees. Parties remain free to nominate candidates outside the primary system, although the primary determines which candidates appear on the general election ballot. The rule, then, could only hurt the parties by confusing

24. *See* Gregory P. Magarian, *The Jurisprudence of Colliding First Amendment Interests: From the Dead End of Neutrality to the Open Road of Participation Enhancing Review*, 83 Notre Dame L. Rev. 185 (2007).

25. *See Wash. State Grange*, 552 U.S. at 449–51.

26. *See* United States v. Salerno, 481 U.S. 739, 745 (1987) (requiring facial challengers to show "that no set of circumstances exists under which [the challenged statute] would be valid").

voters about the relationships (or lack thereof) between particular parties and candidates. Justice Thomas holds that the parties' voter confusion concerns rest, at this stage, on "sheer speculation."[27] Until the state implemented the rule by designing primary ballots, no one could know whether the rule would really confuse voters. The state might, say, include a disclaimer on the ballot that the candidates' partisan preferences don't reflect endorsements by the parties. Because the rule on its face doesn't seriously harm the parties, the Court applies a lenient standard of review, simply asking whether the state has any important reason for listing party preferences on primary ballots. Washington's interest in informing voters about candidates, the Court holds, easily meets that standard.[28]

Justice Scalia, the Court's staunchest advocate throughout his career for the major parties' interests, dissented in *Washington State Grange*.[29] He maintains that any association a primary ballot makes between a political party and a candidate the party doesn't support hurts the party. Forcing a party to bear an undesired association with a candidate distorts the party's message to voters and impedes the party's growth. Justice Scalia states this argument in economic terms. The partisan preference rule undermines a political party's "trademark, so to speak."[30] The party's "goodwill is hijacked."[31] Justice Scalia's language, as in his *Lopez Torres* majority opinion, sounds the theme of speech as an economic commodity.

As we saw him do in the abortion protest case *McCullen v. Coakley* (Chapter 4), Justice Scalia attacks the state's motives. "It is no mystery what is going on here," he declares. "There is no state interest behind this law except the Washington Legislature's dislike for bright-colors partisanship, and its desire to blunt the ability of political parties with noncentrist views to endorse and advocate their own candidates."[32] That's an intriguing theory, because it ties the parties' First Amendment arguments to the electorate's broader expressive interest in vigorous electoral debate. It also casts the state as an undesirable rival to the parties' familiar role as stabilizers of that debate. "The Washington Legislature," though, didn't enact the challenged primary system. The state's

27. *Wash. State Grange,* 552 U.S. at 452–58.

28. *See id.* at 458.

29. Aside from his work on *Jones* and other electoral speech cases, Justice Scalia fiercely defended political patronage systems against the Rehnquist Court majority's First Amendment scruples. *See, e.g.*, Rutan v. Republican Party of Illinois, 497 U.S. 62, 92 (1990) (Scalia, J., dissenting).

30. *Wash. State Grange,* 552 U.S. at 464 (Scalia, J., dissenting).

31. *Id.* at 466 (Scalia, J., dissenting). Chief Justice Roberts's concurrence reads like an effort to bridge Justice Scalia's conviction that the partisan preference rule will harm the parties and Justice Thomas's insistence that the parties' lawsuit jumped the gun. *See id.* at 459 (Roberts, C.J., concurring). That effort, however, only seems to annoy Justice Scalia further, prompting him to add a section to his dissent for the sole purpose of rebuking the chief justice. *See id.* at 467–69 (Scalia, J., dissenting).

32. *Id.* at 470 (Scalia, J., dissenting).

voters enacted it directly, and Justice Scalia musters no evidence that the voters sought to mire the state in centrism, let alone that they succeeded in doing so. His error of attribution may reflect a failure to engage with Washington voters' desire to foster a more open, participatory electoral system.[33] Justice Scalia likewise fails to substantiate his deeper premise that weakening the major political parties imposes a consensus-based electoral structure.

*Washington State Grange*, in a rare result, rejects a First Amendment challenge by the major political parties to an electoral regulation. Unlike *Lopez Torres,* this decision recognizes the public nature of the candidate selection process. The majority opinion, however, paints with a very fine brush, preserving the Court's solicitude for the major parties' associational freedom. The case only arose because the Rehnquist Court, at the major parties' behest, had invalidated the blanket primary system Washington really wanted to use. Even as Justice Thomas rejects the parties' premature challenge to the new system, he warns Washington that only a carefully designed primary ballot can have any hope of surviving a future as-applied challenge.

The parties' "voter confusion" argument, which the majority takes very seriously, amounts to a demand for managerial power over public debate: let us control what information does and doesn't reach voters, or else they won't understand what they're hearing and they'll make a mess of things.[34] Chief Justice Roberts also sets the dispute in a managerial cast when he declares, consistently with the speech-restrictive decisions discussed in Chapter 4, that election ballots aren't public forums. He supports that view by citing the Rehnquist Court precedent that licensed states to "favor the traditional two-party system" as a way of "temper[ing] the destabilizing effects of party splintering and excessive factionalism."[35] Taken together, *Lopez Torres* and *Washington State Grange* suggest that the Roberts Court prizes the major parties' autonomy as highly as the Rehnquist Court did.

## SIGNED, SEALED, DELIVERED . . . DISCLOSED

The Rehnquist Court's final nonfinance electoral speech case presents a constitutional issue not about candidate elections but about direct democracy. Washington's voters installed the primary election system at issue in

33. *See* Lani Guinier, *Foreword: Demosprudence through Dissent*, 122 Harv. L. Rev. 4, 84 (2008).

34. *See* Christopher Elmendorf, *Refining the Democracy Canon*, 95 Cornell L. Rev. 1051, 1087–88 (2010) (arguing that *Washington State Grange* lets states diminish the value of the "party cue" that advocates of responsible party government see as a benefit of a strong party system).

35. *See Washington State Grange,* 552 U.S. at 461 (Roberts, C.J., concurring) (citing Timmons v. Twin Cities Area New Party, 520 U.S. 351 (1997)).

*Washington State Grange* by an initiative, a direct democracy measure that allows voters to enact new laws. The other major direct democracy device is the referendum, which allows voters to judge laws enacted by the legislature. In 2009 the Washington legislature passed a law, controversial at the time, that extended domestic partnership benefits to same-sex couples. Washington, like most states, makes proponents of an initiative or referendum gather a set number of petition signatures to get their measure on the ballot. A group called Protect Marriage Washington gathered over 137,000 petition signatures for a referendum on the domestic partnership law. Supporters of the domestic partnership law invoked the state's public records law to get copies of the referendum petitions. Referendum proponents and some people who signed the referendum petition sued, arguing that releasing the signers' names would violate their First Amendment rights by enabling supporters of the domestic partnership law to harass them for their political speech.

Past political dissidents have raised the same sort of First Amendment claim as the Washington referendum signers. In the landmark 1958 case of *NAACP v. Alabama,*[36] the Supreme Court under Chief Justice Earl Warren blocked Alabama's demand to get the state NAACP's membership list. The justices, with the McCarthy era a fresh memory and Jim Crow in full force, had little trouble concluding that the state wanted to use the list for political harassment. In contrast, the foundational campaign finance decision *Buckley v. Valeo*[37] rejected a facial challenge to a federal law that makes political campaigns and candidates disclose the names of people who contributed money to them. (Next chapter we'll see the Court in an unheralded part of the *Citizens United* decision reaffirm the *Buckley* holding on disclosure.) However, the *Buckley* Court left open the possibility that it might suspend the disclosure requirement in future cases where the unpopularity of particular candidates or parties gave contributors special reason to fear harassment.[38] A few years after *Buckley,* the Court sustained just such an "as applied" challenge in a case with the self-explanatory name *Brown v. Socialist Workers '74 Campaign Committee.*[39]

In ***Doe v. Reed* (2010),**[40] Washington's referendum petition signers repeated the strategic error of the challengers in *Buckley* and *Washington State Grange.* The signers didn't technically bring a facial challenge, because they only attacked the application of the public records law to petition signatures.

36. 357 U.S. 449 (1958).
37. 424 U.S. 1 (1976).
38. *See id.* at 60–74.
39. 459 U.S. 87 (1982).
40. 561 U.S. 186 (2010). Roberts (majority) (with Kennedy, Ginsburg, Breyer, Alito, Sotomayor); Breyer (concurring); Alito (concurring); Sotomayor (concurring) (with Stevens, Ginsburg); Stevens (concurring in part and concurring in the judgment) (with Breyer); Scalia (concurring in the judgment); Thomas (dissenting).

Really, though, they brought a facial challenge wrapped in an as-applied challenge. Rather than claiming that their opposition to domestic partnership benefits for same-sex couples raised a particular danger of harassment should the state reveal their names, the signers insisted that any and all disclosures of direct democracy petition signatures under the public records law would violate the First Amendment. Chief Justice Roberts rejected that broad argument and refused to block disclosure of the petitions. The Court voted 8-1 for the result, but that vote count masks a divergence in reasoning that yielded six separate opinions by the majority justices, plus a dissent.

Chief Justice Roberts begins his legal analysis by holding that signing a direct democracy petition is, indeed, an expressive act that creates a First Amendment interest. This is where Justice Scalia diverges from the majority. He agrees that the signatories should lose their challenge, but he gets to that result by denying that signing a petition is expressive at all. Instead, tracking his majority opinion in the legislative self-dealing case *Nevada Commission on Ethics v. Carrigan* (Chapter 1), Justice Scalia argues that signing a petition is a legislative act. The chief justice shrugs off Justice Scalia's objection, explaining that signing a direct democracy petition has both expressive and legislative aspects. Having decided that the First Amendment applies to the case, the chief justice points out that releasing signers' names under the public information law wouldn't directly stop anyone from speaking. He emphasizes that the Court gives states latitude to implement election procedures. Accordingly, as in *Washington State Grange,* the state need show only that, as a general matter, some important government interest supports revealing the names of direct democracy petition signers.

Washington posits two interests in disclosure: informing the public about who supports petitions, and preserving the integrity of the electoral process. Disclosure arguably has greater informational value for voters in direct democracy campaigns than in candidate elections, where voters have more useful alternative sources of information.[41] Justice Alito's concurrence and Justice Thomas's dissent, however, deride Washington's public information interest as a thinly veiled excuse for harassment of political dissidents. Perhaps with that objection in mind, Chief Justice Roberts ignores the public information interest and predicates his holding entirely on the state's electoral integrity interest. He accepts the state's argument that opening direct democracy petitions to public scrutiny can provide a valuable backstop for state officials' efforts in ferreting out fraudulent signatures. The chief justice admits the electoral integrity interest might not satisfy the First Amendment if the state sought to expose controversial petition signers, including the opponents of

41. *See, e.g.*, Michael Kang, *Campaign Disclosure in Direct Democracy*, 97 MINN. L. REV. 1700, 1712–19 (2013).

same-sex domestic partnerships here, to the serious dangers of reprisal their views might inspire. Such case-specific risks, however, don't justify the challengers' demand to bar *all* disclosures of petition signatures. The chief justice appears to bring the public information interest back into the case through a side door when he holds that, beyond fraud avoidance, the state's electoral integrity interest "also extends more generally to promoting transparency and accountability in the electoral process."[42]

The flood of concurring and dissenting opinions in *Doe* spills out in two opposite directions. On one side, Justice Alito (concurring) and Justice Thomas (dissenting) want the Court to go further in protecting petition signers' rights. Justice Alito joins the majority opinion, but he urges the Court to make future "as applied" challenges easy for petition signers to win.[43] As in his dissent from *Christian Legal Society*, he seems focused on the particular vulnerability of conservative Christians to persecution by LGBT rights advocates. Lamenting without documenting "[t]he widespread harassment and intimidation suffered by supporters of California's [anti-same-sex marriage] Proposition 8"[44] and asserting that the Washington petition signers had a strong First Amendment claim "both through analogy and through their own experiences,"[45] he validates an "as applied" challenge not before the Court. Expressing special mistrust for the state's interest in informing the public, Justice Alito ominously writes: "[I]t is alleged that [the] express aim [of two groups who wanted to publish the petition signers' names] was to encourage uncomfortable conversations."[46]

Justice Thomas objects on broader grounds and in deeper terms to the majority's result. He, alone among the justices, would rule categorically that the First Amendment should always prevent states from publicizing the names of people who sign direct democracy petitions. He states the problem in systemic terms, emphasizing that the public availability of petition signatures "chills citizen participation in the referendum process."[47]

The other concurrences warn against going further than the majority does to protect petition signers. They reflect a diverse range of concerns. Justices Stevens and Scalia revive their skirmish from a Rehnquist Court case, *McIntyre v. Ohio Elections Commission,*[48] about First Amendment protection

42. *Doe,* 561 U.S. at 198.
43. After the adverse decision in *Doe,* Proposition 8 petition signers brought an as-applied challenge to public disclosure of their names. The trial judge evaluated the challengers' evidence for their fear of reprisals and rejected their claim. *See* ProtectMarriage.com v. Bowen, 830 F. Supp. 2d 914 (E.D. Cal. 2011).
44. *Doe,* 561 U.S. at 205 (Alito, J., concurring).
45. *Id.* at 212 (Alito, J., concurring). No substantial evidence of harassment in direct democracy campaigns has appeared. *See* Kang, *supra* note 41, at 1719–20.
46. *Doe,* 561 U.S. at 208 (Alito, J., concurring) (internal punctuation omitted).
47. *Id.* at 229 (Thomas, J., dissenting).
48. 514 U.S. 334 (1995).

for anonymous political speech. Justice Stevens, who authored the *McIntyre* holding that people have a right to circulate political pamphlets anonymously, distinguishes *McIntyre* from *Doe*. He maintains that revealing petition signers' names burdens First Amendment interests only minimally and indirectly while advancing the state's important interest in avoiding fraud.[49] Justice Scalia, who dissented sharply in *McIntyre*, insists that "harsh criticism, short of unlawful action, is a price our people have traditionally been willing to pay for self-governance."[50] As in his opinions about political parties' First Amendment interests, Justice Scalia in *Doe* shows no concern about election rules' potential to discourage participation in electoral processes.

Justices Sotomayor and Breyer both resist imposing on *Doe* the standard public-private, regulation versus rights structure of constitutional law, but they approach the public-private tension from opposite directions. Justice Sotomayor, echoing (and quoting) some of Justice Scalia's rhetoric, contends that initiative and referendum campaigns are public affairs. Accordingly, she finds that disclosing direct democracy petition signers' names presents a lesser constitutional problem than disclosing what she characterizes as the private matter of campaign contributors' names in *Buckley*.[51] Justice Sotomayor's conception of direct democracy as a public matter leads her, like Justice Stevens and against Justice Alito, to argue that the Court should impose a heavy burden of persuasion on future "as applied" challenges to petition disclosures. In contrast, Justice Breyer, in a brief opinion, frames *Doe* as "implicat[ing] competing constitutionally protected interests." We've seen Justice Breyer advocate an interest-balancing approach to free speech disputes in the violent video game case *Entertainment Merchants*, the "stolen valor" case *Alvarez* (both Chapter 1), and the sign regulation case *Reed v. Town of Gilbert* (Chapter 2). In *Doe* he argues that an interest-balancing approach has special appeal where private rights come into conflict.[52] (Oddly, Justice Breyer joins both the majority opinion and the opinion of Justice Stevens, who declines to join the majority.)

Exactly what First Amendment interest does *Doe* implicate? The Washington petition signers based their First Amendment claim on the fear that, if the government revealed their names, their political opponents would harass and attack them. Those posited attacks, though, would amount to private action, unless the government actively encouraged or participated in them.[53] Constitutional law ordinarily does not require the government to

49. *Doe*, 561 U.S. at 215–19 (Stevens, J., concurring in part and concurring in the judgment).

50. *Id.* at 228 (Scalia, J., concurring in the judgment).

51. *See id.* at 213–15 (Sotomayor, J., concurring).

52. *See id.* at 202 (Breyer, J., concurring).

53. *See* Randall P. Bezanson, Too Much Free Speech? 225–26 (2012); Monica Youn, *The Chilling Effect and the Problem of Private Action*, 66 Vand. L. Rev. 1473, 1477–79 (2013).

protect people from private action that undermines their rights.[54] Perhaps *Doe* implicates the right to anonymous speech announced in the *McIntyre* case. As Justice Stevens contends, however, a right to anonymity seems a poorer fit for formal participation in public political processes than for the pamphleteering of *McIntyre*. Alternatively, the petition signers may have a First Amendment interest in expressive association. As in *Humanitarian Law Project*, the Court in *Doe* may miss an important linkage between association and speech. But does an individual's signing of a petition amount to association, any more than casting a vote does? Whatever sort of speech interest *Doe* presents, the Court holds that the First Amendment applies (at least in theory) to signing a direct democracy petition. How far does that protection reach? Does it cover casting a vote? Participating in a candidate selection caucus? Political processes seem to differ from ordinary public debate, but qualifying that difference could involve a cascade of hard First Amendment questions.

*Doe* at once parallels and diverges from *Washington State Grange*. Both decisions reject First Amendment challenges as overly general and premature. The decisions differ in how they treat the state's interest in informing the public about electoral matters. Once the *Washington State Grange* majority decides to apply lenient scrutiny in evaluating Washington's partisan preference rule, it finds the state's interest in informing the public about candidates' partisan preferences sufficient to justify the rule. In contrast, the *Doe* majority avoids direct reliance on the public information interest. The Court's consideration of the public information interest in *Washington State Grange* exposes the clash between First Amendment interests in that case. The Court's dodging of the public information interest in *Doe* obscures a similar clash. What matters more in fostering a dynamic, broadly participatory democratic political system and public discussion: protecting direct democracy petition signers from the risk of reprisals for their political participation, or fully informing the public about which voters put a measure on the state ballot? The most striking passage in any of the *Doe* opinions is Justice Alito's warning against "uncomfortable conversations." That warning suggests that one justice, at least, wants to advance managed speech by insulating electoral debates from the contention and upheaval that information can fuel.

54. *See, e.g.*, DeShaney v. Winnebago Cty Dep't of Soc. Serv's, 489 U.S. 189 (1989) (holding that a state agency's failure to prevent child abuse did not violate the child's fourteenth amendment right to liberty). In a context very far from *Doe*, I have argued that the Court should extend First Amendment protection to block some private constraints on expressive freedom. *See* Gregory P. Magarian, *The First Amendment, the Public-Private Distinction, and Nongovernmental Suppression of Wartime Political Debate*, 73 GEO. WASH. L. REV. 101 (2004).

## CONCLUSION

The Roberts Court's two First Amendment decisions on political parties reflect the Court's commitment to managed speech. The view of political parties the Rehnquist Court passed down to the Roberts Court licenses the largest, most powerful institutions in U.S. politics to shape and dominate electoral debates. *Lopez Torres,* the most decisive and important of this chapter's three decisions, largely follows the Rehnquist Court's form. Justice Scalia's majority opinion in *Lopez Torres* strongly affirms both the primacy of the major political parties and the Court's antipathy to political dissidents. Likewise, his dissent from the Court's mildest of rebukes to the major parties in *Washington State Grange* casts the parties as dynamic political forces under attack by a scheming centrist orthodoxy. His reasoning subordinates voters' unpredictable political will to the major parties' authority. The *Washington State Grange* majority lags only slightly behind Justice Scalia, fully endorsing the major parties' associational rights as a dominant value in the First Amendment law of elections. The Court tells the parties not that they misplayed their First Amendment hand but merely that they played it prematurely.

*Doe v. Reed* had the potential to complicate the managed speech narrative. The case offered the Court an opportunity to balance the importance of anonymity for inclusive political participation against the importance of knowledge about others' participation for informed political debate. Performing that balance might have advanced our understanding of the competing First Amendment interests that electoral speech disputes often present. The Court, however, avoided that challenging task, instead resting its decision on Washington's interest in electoral integrity. As a result, *Doe* ends up saying little of consequence.

A dynamic diversity analysis would reach the opposite result from the Roberts Court in *Lopez Torres.* Our major party duopoly, whatever its benefits, undermines dynamic diversity by driving voters and candidates into two broad coalitions that tend to marginalize radical and dissenting voices. Lopez Torres's challenge to New York's hegemonic nomination rules sought only a marginal check on the major parties' power (effectuated through the state government) to structure electoral debate and the electoral process. Where managed speech rejects that limited adjustment as an unacceptable incursion on the parties' autonomy, dynamic diversity would view it as a modest step toward curbing the parties' dominance. The result in *Washington State Grange* wouldn't change under dynamic diversity, except that the case never would have arisen. Washington only adopted the nonpartisan primary system the *Washington State Grange* Court tentatively upheld because the Rehnquist Court's *Jones* decision had barred the state from using its preferred blanket partisan primary system. *Jones,* more directly than *Lopez Torres,* advanced the major parties' autonomy at the expense of narrowing electoral debate. The dynamic diversity model would have compelled the opposite result in *Jones*, allowing Washington to keep its blanket primary and foreclosing the narrower *Washington State Grange* dispute.[55]

*Doe v. Reed* poses a challenge for dynamic diversity. The case presents a conflict between First Amendment interests: petition signers' interest in anonymous participation and the public's interest in political information. Each of those interests advances dynamic diversity's goals of broadening the ranges of ideas and participants in electoral debate. Contrary to managed speech, dynamic diversity would acknowledge and confront the conflict. Courts would need to consider empirical data on how Washington's disclosure law affected electoral debate and then to strike the optimal balance between the competing interests. Although *Doe* presents a First Amendment issue for which the judicial branch bears ultimate responsibility, a court in dynamic diversity mode might defer to the state's policy judgment. Before deferring, the Court would need to satisfy itself that the state had thoroughly considered the First Amendment interests at stake.

The next two chapters discuss the Roberts Court's much more consequential campaign finance decisions. We'll see those decisions, in the same managed speech vein as *Lopez Torres*, empower corporations and wealthy individuals to exercise managerial control over electoral debate. The campaign finance decisions link directly to *Lopez Torres* by protecting the major parties' managerial role. The Roberts Court's approach to electoral money promotes the speech of established institutions with strong interests in the social and political status quo while checking the disruptive potential of socially and economically marginal speakers.

55. For an extended critique of Jones, see Magarian, *supra* note 2, at 2011–24.

## CHAPTER 7

# Letting Money into Elections

## Citizens United *and* McCutcheon

Few cases cast as long a shadow over any area of First Amendment law as *Buckley v. Valeo*[1] over the law of campaign finance regulation. That epic 1976 Burger Court decision generally permits government to regulate how much money people may contribute to candidates (contribution limits) and generally forbids government from regulating how much money candidates and others may spend on election campaigns (expenditure limits). This chapter analyzes the Roberts Court's most prominent campaign finance decisions, those that engage the *Buckley* holdings on expenditure limits and contribution limits. First we'll see an early Roberts Court decision, *Randall v. Sorrell,* which began to re-examine both of the central *Buckley* holdings. That case reveals the sharp disagreements that have riven this Court on campaign finance from the beginning. Then we'll dig into the Roberts Court's two key campaign finance decisions, which boldly revise the two core holdings in *Buckley. Citizens United v. Federal Election Commission*, the Court's most notorious First Amendment decision, strikes down the one federal expenditure limit that had survived in the *Buckley* era. *McCutcheon v. Federal Election Commission* strikes down a federal contribution limit, something the Court had never done before.

*Citizens United* and *McCutcheon* impose the norms of managed speech on the First Amendment law of campaign finance. By their unprecedented departures from the *Buckley* holdings on both expenditure limits and contribution limits, these decisions authorize powerful, wealthy actors to shape and direct public discussion around elections. As to expenditures, *Citizens United*

1. 424 U.S. 1 (1976).

lets business corporations spend freely from their general treasuries to advocate for or against candidates. Because of the majority's reasoning, all sorts of moneyed interests may give unlimited funds to so-called super PACs. As to contributions, *McCutcheon* lets wealthy donors maximize their largesse to as many candidates as they wish, a capacity that serves to enhance the major political parties' influence in electoral debates. Both decisions push less wealthy and powerful speakers, likely to dissent from the policy positions of corporations and wealthy donors, toward the margins of a money-driven electoral process. At no other time in our nation's history has First Amendment law so firmly protected the influence of private money in electoral discourse. By enlisting what the Roberts Court majority views as responsible managers for electoral debate and muting the voices of potentially disruptive speakers, the decisions promote the essential managed speech goal of political stability.

## THE *BUCKLEY* EQUILIBRIUM

*Buckley* reviewed a set of sweeping 1974 amendments to the Federal Election Campaign Act (FECA). The amendments responded to the Watergate scandal, much of which related to improprieties in the financing of President Nixon's 1972 re-election campaign. Federal law before Watergate already restricted money in federal elections. The Tillman Act of 1907 bars corporations from making campaign contributions to candidates for federal office. Congress in 1943 extended that bar to labor unions. The Taft-Hartley Act of 1947, crucially for this chapter's story, barred both corporations and unions from spending money "in connection with" any federal election. FECA, enacted in 1971, formalized the ability of corporations and unions to create political action committees (PACs), separate legal entities that raise funds separate from corporate and union general treasuries, to spend in support of federal candidates.

The 1974 FECA amendments expanded both sorts of restrictions the Tillman and Taft-Hartley Acts had imposed on political money. First, Congress imposed broad-based *contribution limits,* restricting how much money any individual, entity, or "political committee" could give to any candidate during any election cycle *(base limits)* and how much money any contributor could give in total to federal candidates during the election cycle *(aggregate limits).* Second, Congress imposed rigorous *expenditure limits,* restricting how much money various actors could spend during federal campaigns. Different expenditure limits applied to candidates and their campaigns, independent spenders (those who spend money in support of a candidate but don't coordinate with the candidate or campaign), and self-financing candidates. The FECA amendments also added to federal law the contribution disclosure requirements I noted last chapter in connection with the petition signature case *Doe v. Reed.*

The *Buckley* majority opinion[2] began by announcing the cornerstone principle of campaign finance law: the use of money in political campaigns is speech protected by the First Amendment.[3] Candidates need money to buy TV time, to rent halls for speeches and rallies, and to print campaign literature. Those and other forms of speech can't happen without money. *Buckley* declared the Court's resolve to protect "the voices of people and interest groups who have money to spend."[4] Moreover, the *Buckley* Court emphasized, campaign money has special constitutional importance, because political speech lies at the core of First Amendment protection. The Supreme Court has never formally placed political speech in a special First Amendment category, but the justices' rhetoric frequently extols the paramount value of political speech.[5] The money a political candidate spends on TV spots, speeches, and online media serves to inform the public about the candidate's views and qualifications. The *Buckley* Court accordingly subjected both the FECA amendments' contribution limits and expenditure limits to First Amendment review.

But not the same review. The *Buckley* majority drew a sharp constitutional distinction between contributions and expenditures.[6] When a contributor gives money to a candidate, the majority acknowledged, the contributor expresses support for the candidate. The amount of the contribution, however, adds little to that expression. Moreover, the contribution only yields political speech when an intervening actor, the candidate, aggregates and spends it. Contributions, therefore, have real but limited First Amendment value. Applying a species of intermediate scrutiny, *Buckley* upheld the contribution limits under an *anti-corruption rationale.* The majority explained that the government has an important interest in "limit[ing] the actuality and appearance of corruption resulting from large individual financial contributions."[7] Carefully drawn contribution limits, like those in the 1974 FECA amendments, can advance the government's interest in avoiding actual and apparent political corruption and not violate the First Amendment. *Buckley* upheld both the base and aggregate federal contribution limits.

In contrast to its lenient review of the contribution limits, the *Buckley* majority held that electoral spending brings information straight to the voters, and restricting expenditures therefore burdens the core First Amendment interest in political communication. Applying strict scrutiny, *Buckley* found the anti-corruption rationale irrelevant for justifying expenditure limits, because

2. Uniquely for such an important and lengthy decision, the Court issued *Buckley* with a per curiam majority opinion, meaning the opinion names no author.

3. *See Buckley,* 424 U.S. at 14–19.

4. *Id.* at 17.

5. *See* Gregory P. Magarian, *Substantive Due Process as a Source of Constitutional Protection for Nonpolitical Speech*, 90 MINN. L. REV. 247, 251–75 (2005).

6. *See Buckley,* 424 U.S. at 19–22.

7. *Id.* at 26.

spending happens apart from the transactions that can cause corruption. The majority then rejected the "governmental interest in equalizing the relative ability of individuals and groups to influence the outcome of elections" as an alternate basis for expenditure limits.[8] In a much-quoted passage, *Buckley* condemned that *equalization rationale*: "[T]he concept that government may restrict the speech of some elements of our society in order to enhance the relative voice of others is wholly foreign to the First Amendment[.]"[9] Finding no salient, constitutionally valid justification for the FECA amendments' expenditure limits, the *Buckley* majority struck down the limits on candidate campaign spending, independent spending, and self-financing.

The *Buckley* distinction between contributions and expenditures, like the judgment of Solomon, satisfies no one. Critics of campaign finance regulation argue that the First Amendment should strongly protect both contributions and expenditures. Advocates of campaign finance regulation contend that government should have substantial power to restrict both contributions and expenditures. *Buckley* also creates a perverse incentive for candidates, forcing them to chase an endless trail of legally limited contributions in order to feed a theoretically infinite opportunity to spend. For sitting legislators, fundraising can crowd out the people's business.[10] Despite widespread disapproval, the Burger and Rehnquist Courts stood by the *Buckley* framework. The Rehnquist Court in its 2000 decision *Nixon v. Shrink Missouri Government PAC*[11] expressly reaffirmed the *Buckley* contribution-expenditure distinction.

## *PUTTING* BUCKLEY *IN PLAY*

One of the Roberts Court's earliest First Amendment decisions shows the Court's immediate unease with the *Buckley* campaign finance framework. ***Randall v. Sorrell* (2006)**[12] involved a challenge to a 1997 Vermont law that mirrored the contribution and expenditure limits in the 1974 FECA amendments. Knowing that its expenditure limits flew directly in the face of *Buckley,*

8. *See id.* at 44–58.
9. *Id.* at 48–49.
10. For a discussion of these varied objections to *Buckley,* see Burt Neuborne, *One Dollar-One Vote: A Preface to Debating Campaign Finance Reform*, 37 WASHBURN L.J. 1 (1997). "[T]he survival of *Buckley* thus far has not been a matter of logic but of the lack of an alternative that commands the support of a majority of the Court." Richard Briffault, WRTL *and* Randall: *The Roberts Court and the Unsettling of Campaign Finance Law*, 68 OHIO ST. L.J. 807, 841 (2007).
11. 528 U.S. 377 (2000).
12. 548 U.S. 230 (2006). Breyer (plurality) (with Roberts; with Alito (in part)); Alito (concurring in part and concurring in the judgment); Kennedy (concurring in the judgment); Thomas (concurring in the judgment) (with Scalia); Stevens (dissenting); Souter (dissenting) (with Ginsburg; with Stevens (in part)).

Vermont asked the Court either to overrule the *Buckley* strict scrutiny standard for expenditure limits or to permit expenditure limits based on the state's compelling interest in shielding candidates from excessive fundraising. Vermont's contribution limits were the lowest in the nation, ranging from $200 per election cycle for state representative candidates to $400 per election cycle for candidates for governor and other statewide offices. The limits applied to contributions not just by individuals but also by political committees and political parties. The challengers—Vermont voters, political parties and committees, and former candidates for office—argued that the law violated even the *Buckley* Court's permissive standard for contribution limits, because the Vermont limits' stringency kept candidates from amassing enough money to communicate their positions to voters.

The Court in *Randall* held that both Vermont's expenditure and contribution limits violated the First Amendment. Justice Breyer delivered the Court's judgment, but only Chief Justice Roberts joined his opinion in full, and only Justice Alito joined it in part. In striking down the expenditure limits, Justice Breyer relies squarely on the precedential weight of *Buckley*. He refuses to overrule the *Buckley* bar on expenditure limits, citing stare decisis, the doctrine of judicial respect for precedent.[13] (We'll see later Roberts Court campaign finance decisions depart significantly from stare decisis.) Justice Breyer also rejects Vermont's plea that the *Buckley* Court had not considered, as a justification for expenditure limits, the government's interest in reducing the amount of time candidates must spend raising funds. The section of the lengthy *Buckley* opinion that upheld the FECA amendments' public election financing provisions mentioned the problem of time spent fundraising and noted that the Court of Appeals decision and Supreme Court briefs in *Buckley* had also discussed it. "[I]t is highly unlikely," Justice Breyer writes, "that fuller consideration of this time protection rationale would have changed *Buckley*'s result."[14]

The *Randall* plurality's fealty to *Buckley* might have made Vermont's contribution limits appear as safe as the state's expenditure limits were doomed. The Supreme Court since *Buckley* had upheld every contribution limit it encountered. *Buckley,* however, described one circumstance in which a contribution limit might violate the First Amendment: "[C]ontribution restrictions could have a severe impact on political dialogue if the limitations prevented candidates and political committees from amassing the resources necessary

13. *See id.* at 242–44 (plurality opinion). Justice Alito departs from Justice Breyer's opinion only in maintaining that Vermont did not ask the Court to overrule *Buckley* on expenditure limits. Justice Alito therefore argues that the plurality should not have decided that issue. *See id.* at 263–64 (Alito, J., concurring in part and concurring in the judgment).

14. *Id.* at 245 (plurality opinion).

for effective advocacy."[15] The *Randall* challengers argued that Vermont's limits ran afoul of that proviso. The problem for their argument was that *Buckley* offered no concrete measure of "necessary resources" or for that matter "effective advocacy."

We've seen Justice Breyer, from the military honors case *Alvarez* (Chapter 1) to the sign regulation case *Reed v. Town of Gilbert* (Chapter 4) to last chapter's petition signature case *Doe v. Reed,* advocate a flexible, interest-balancing approach to First Amendment analysis. He takes that same approach in striking down Vermont's contribution limits. Finding no path of least resistance for assessing "how low is too low," Justice Breyer sees "no alternative to the exercise of independent judicial judgment[.]"[16] The severity of Vermont's contribution limits, he writes, makes them suspect: Vermont set its limits lower than the federal limits upheld in *Buckley,* lower than the state limits the Rehnquist Court upheld in *Shrink Missouri Government PAC,* lower than any other state's limits. Justice Breyer finds the limits ultimately "not closely drawn," and thus invalid, because evidence in the record suggests the limits will preclude effective advocacy. Most important, he concludes the limits will prevent challengers from mounting effective challenges in races that might otherwise be competitive.[17] That conclusion implies that Vermont imposed strict contribution limits for the impermissible purpose of stacking the electoral deck in incumbents' favor.

Justice Breyer expresses particular concern about the contribution limits' effect on the major political parties. The Vermont law, he warns, "threatens harm to a particularly important political right, the right to associate in a political party."[18] Letting the state impose strict contribution limits on the major parties would severely diminish a crucial source of funds for candidates. The limits inhibit not just direct party contributions to candidates but also coordinated party spending on candidates' behalf, stunting the parties' ability to influence elections. The limits also block parties from aggregating small contributions to affect competitive races, a constraint which in turn discourages donors from contributing to the parties. Justice Breyer's concern in *Randall* for the major political parties' associational rights resonates with the decisions from last chapter, particularly the *Lopez Torres* case about nominating procedures, that continue the Rehnquist Court's solicitude for the parties' interests. We'll shortly see the linkage between contribution limits and the parties play a central role in the Court's unprecedented assault on contribution limits in *McCutcheon.*

15. Buckley v. Valeo, 424 U.S. 1, 21 (1976).
16. *Randall,* 548 U.S. at 249 (plurality opinion).
17. *Id.* at 253–56 (plurality opinion). Justice Breyer's opinion places greater emphasis than other Supreme Court campaign finance decisions on how political money affects competitive elections. *See* Briffault, *supra* note 10, at 829–37.
18. *Randall,* 548 U.S. at 256 (plurality opinion).

The concurring and dissenting opinions in *Randall* display a full spectrum of views on *Buckley* and campaign finance. Justice Thomas, joined by Justice Scalia, concurred in the judgment. He cheers the plurality's decision to strike down both Vermont's contribution and expenditure limits. However, he strongly criticizes the *Buckley* distinction between contribution limits and expenditure limits. For Justice Thomas, expenditures have just as much First Amendment value as contributions, and he would therefore overrule the *Buckley* allowance for contribution limits. "*Buckley*," he concludes, "provides no consistent protection to the core of the First Amendment, and it must be overruled."[19] Justice Kennedy also concurred in the judgment. His brief, somewhat cryptic opinion hints that he might join Justices Thomas and Scalia in overruling the *Buckley* allowance for contribution limits. He reprises his dissent from *Shrink Missouri Government PAC*, a decision he accuses of having subjected contribution limits to "unduly lenient review." He echoes Justice Breyer's theme that "political parties have been denied basic First Amendment rights." He does not, however, set forth a clear basis for his vote to strike down Vermont's contribution limits. "Viewed within the legal universe we have ratified and helped create," he intones, "the result the plurality reaches is correct; given my own skepticism regarding that system and its operation, however, it seems to me appropriate to concur only in the judgment."[20]

Justice Souter's dissent, joined by Justice Ginsburg, takes strong issue with Justice Breyer on the relatively narrow question whether Vermont's contribution limits satisfy *Buckley* and takes cautious issue on the potentially more explosive question of Vermont's expenditure limits. The portion of Justice Souter's opinion on contribution limits, which Justice Stevens joins as well, chides Justice Breyer for second-guessing the Vermont legislature about the level at which campaign contributions can fund effective electoral advocacy. Justice Souter especially emphasizes the absence of evidence that the legislature imposed the contribution limits to protect incumbents.[21] As to Vermont's expenditure limits, Justice Souter calls the conclusion that the restrictions contradict *Buckley* "at least premature."[22] He takes Vermont's interest in reducing candidates' fundraising time very seriously. *Buckley*, he stresses, did not weigh the time protection interest as a basis for the FECA expenditure limits specifically. Justice Souter makes clear, however, that he means "not . . . to overrule *Buckley* but to apply *Buckley*'s framework[.]"[23]

Justice Stevens, who joined the Supreme Court just after *Buckley*, completes what he calls the *Randall* "cacophony."[24] He contends, in diametric opposition

19. *Id.* at 273 (Thomas, J., concurring in the judgment).
20. *Id.* at 264–65 (Kennedy, J., concurring in the judgment).
21. *See id.* at 287 (Souter, J., dissenting).
22. *Id.* at 281 (Souter, J., dissenting).
23. *Id.* at 283 (Souter, J., dissenting).
24. *Id.* at 280 (Stevens, J., dissenting).

to Justice Thomas and going further than Justice Souter, that the Court should overrule the *Buckley* bar on expenditure limits. Invoking concepts from the public forum doctrine (Chapter 4), Justice Stevens calls expenditure limits "far more akin to time, place, and manner restrictions than to restrictions on the content of speech."[25] The Court, he maintains, has adhered more faithfully to the permissive *Buckley* holding on contributions than to the restrictive holding on expenditures. Justice Stevens would readily validate expenditure limits under the anti-corruption rationale as well as the equalization rationale, and also to prevent wealth from distorting the electoral process. However, he views Vermont's "interest in freeing candidates from the fundraising straitjacket" as "even more compelling."[26] Echoing Justice White's dissent in *Buckley,* Justice Stevens would uphold expenditure limits "so long as the purposes they serve are legitimate and sufficiently substantial."[27] Under that permissive standard, he would validate Vermont's expenditure limits as well as its contribution limits.

The justices' splintered positions in *Randall* make this decision the canary in the Roberts Court's campaign finance coal mine. The liberal Justice Breyer's willingness to write an anti-regulatory lead opinion, which surprised commentators at the time,[28] looks in retrospect like a hopeful quest for what turned out to be non-existent common ground. The Roberts Court has made good on the portents of *Randall,* moving First Amendment law on both expenditures and contributions in a more restrictive direction.

## *CITIZENS UNITED:* DO CORPORATIONS DREAM OF PROFIT-MAXIMIZING SHEEP?

To understand the epic *Citizens United* decision, we first need to consider two post-*Buckley* legal developments, as well as a precursor decision to *Citizens United.*

*Legal Development 1:* Austin v. Michigan Chamber of Commerce. Following *Buckley,* the Supreme Court struck down most expenditure limits it encountered. Notably, the Burger Court in *First National Bank of Boston v. Bellotti*[29] affirmed the right of corporations to spend money in state initiative and referendum campaigns, and the Rehnquist Court in *Federal Election Commission v. Massachusetts Citizens for Life (MCFL)*[30] affirmed the right of ideological

25. *Id.* at 277 (Stevens, J., dissenting).
26. *Id.* at 278 (Stevens, J., dissenting).
27. *Id.* at 277 (Stevens, J., dissenting) (quoting *Buckley,* 424 U.S. at 264 (White, J., dissenting)).
28. *See* Lillian R. BeVier, *Full of Surprises—and More to Come:* Randall v. Sorrell, *The First Amendment, and Campaign Finance Regulation*, 2006 Sup. Ct. Rev. 173, 186–91; Briffault, *supra* note 10, at 827–28.
29. 435 U.S. 765 (1978).
30. 479 U.S. 238 (1986).

nonprofit groups to spend in candidate elections. In *Austin v. Michigan Chamber of Commerce*,[31] however, the Rehnquist Court upheld a Michigan law that barred corporations from spending general treasury funds to support state electoral candidates. The *Austin* majority, in an opinion by Justice Thurgood Marshall, applied strict scrutiny, as *Buckley* requires for expenditure limits. Justice Marshall, however, found that Michigan had narrowly tailored its law to serve a compelling interest in fighting "the corrosive and distorting effects of immense aggregations of wealth that are accumulated with the help of the corporate form and that have little or no correlation to the public's support for the corporation's political ideas."[32] This *anti-distortion rationale* sought to prevent economic wealth, gained through the economic market with the help of corporate law, from overwhelming electoral politics. The disconnect between institutional wealth and public support distinguished the business corporations of *Austin* from the ideological nonprofits of *MCFL*. The *Austin* majority noted that Michigan corporations could still spend in elections by creating political action committees to raise money separate from general treasury funds. Both Justice Scalia and Justice Kennedy dissented vigorously.

Depending on one's perspective, *Austin* either betrayed or fulfilled the *Buckley* mandate on expenditure limits. The argument for betrayal is that *Buckley* subjected expenditure limits to strict scrutiny and struck down a seemingly comprehensive package of federal expenditure limits. In that light, no expenditure limit should survive rigorous judicial review. The argument for fulfillment is that, three decades before *Buckley*, Congress in the Taft-Hartley Act had enacted a close equivalent to the Michigan law upheld in *Austin*, barring corporations and unions from spending money from their general treasuries "in connection with" federal elections. Neither *Buckley* nor any other case had questioned the Taft-Hartley restrictions, even as the Court struck down other expenditure limits. In that light, *Buckley* appeared to accommodate the federal corporate and union spending limits and their state equivalents.

*Legal Development 2: McCain-Feingold.* The *Buckley* Court, at the outset of its expenditure limits analysis, held that the 1974 FECA expenditure limits would be unconstitutionally vague unless the Court read them as applying only to political messages that explicitly contained statements such as "Vote for candidate X" or "Vote against candidate Y." That caveat, which became known as the "magic words" rule, ensured that political spenders could advocate positions on issues, as distinct from supporting or opposing candidates.[33] The *Buckley* Court, as discussed above, ended up striking down the FECA expenditure limits on broader First Amendment grounds. The magic words rule,

31. 494 U.S. 652 (1990).
32. *Id.* at 660.
33. *See* Buckley v. Valeo, 424 U.S. 1, 40–44 (1976).

however, still found a use. The Rehnquist Court's *MCFL* decision applied the rule to cure any vagueness in the long-standing Taft-Hartley restrictions on corporate and union spending "in connection with" federal elections.[34] That application of the magic words rule effectively neutered the Taft-Hartley restrictions. Political strategists quickly realized that, if you really want to say "vote against candidate Y," you can get the same result by instead saying, for example, "Candidate Y is a monster who wants to club baby seals to death. Call candidate Y to say you oppose her baby seal-clubbing policy." Armed with that insight, corporations and unions during election seasons began to pour money into "issue advertisements" that promoted or attacked candidates under a thin gauze of nonelectoral issue advocacy.

In 2002 President George W. Bush signed into law the Bipartisan Campaign Reform Act, better known as the McCain-Feingold law.[35] McCain-Feingold sought to close what Congress saw as loopholes that had weakened the FECA regulatory framework. One of the law's major concerns was the "issue advertising" hole that the magic words rule had punched through Taft-Hartley's bar on corporate and union campaign spending. McCain-Feingold's *electioneering communications provision* barred corporations and unions from funding advertisements that referred to any clearly identified federal candidate and targeted the candidate's electorate within 30 days of a primary or 60 days of a general election. A sharply divided Rehnquist Court in *McConnell v. Federal Election Commission*[36] upheld the electioneering communications provision as a permissible adjunct to the Taft-Hartley bar on corporate and union electoral spending. The *McConnell* majority held that McCain-Feingold's functional definition of "electioneering communication" avoided the vagueness problem that had caused the Rehnquist Court in *MCFL* to impose the magic words rule on the Taft-Hartley expenditure limits. (The other major cluster of provisions in the McCain-Feingold law restricts "soft money," unregulated contributions to political parties that the parties can then use to help their federal candidates. *McConnell* upheld the soft money provisions as well.)

*The Precursor Decision:* FEC v. Wisconsin Right to Life. The Roberts Court, with a new majority hostile to campaign finance regulation, quickly seized an opportunity to revisit *McConnell.* Wisconsin Right to Life, an antiabortion group, had sought to run television spots just before the re-election vote for Wisconsin senator Russ Feingold (co-architect of the McCain-Feingold law). The ads urged viewers to call Senator Feingold and complain about his support for filibusters against some of President Bush's judicial nominees. The group argued that McCain-Feingold's bar on their ads violated their First Amendment

34. *See MCFL*, 479 U.S. at 249.
35. Pub. L. No. 107–155, 116 Stat. 81 (2002).
36. 540 U.S. 93 (2003).

rights. ***Federal Election Commission v. Wisconsin Right to Life* (2007)**[37] put the fledgling Roberts Court in a difficult position. A majority wanted to overrule *McConnell*. However, the principle of stare decisis—adherence to precedent—strongly discourages overruling earlier decisions, especially very recent decisions, and most especially where the shift owes wholly to a change in the Court's membership.

Chief Justice Roberts's lead opinion in *Wisconsin Right to Life* tries to thread the stare decisis needle by nullifying *McConnell* without expressly overruling it. *McConnell,* the chief justice points out, held only that McCain-Feingold's electioneering communications provision didn't *facially* violate the First Amendment. *McConnell* left open the possibility that applying McCain-Feingold to *particular* issue advertisements might go too far. This availability of as-applied challenges, says the chief justice, requires a constitutional narrowing of the "electioneering communication" definition, which *McConnell* had no occasion to perform. Accordingly, he narrows the definition: only ads "susceptible of no reasonable interpretation other than as an appeal to vote for or against a specific candidate" can count as "electioneering communications" barred by McCain-Feingold.[38] One might reasonably interpret Wisconsin Right to Life's anti-Feingold ads as addressing the judicial filibuster issue, not Feingold's re-election. Accordingly, the government could not, consistent with the First Amendment, invoke McCain-Feingold to bar the ads.

Only Chief Justice Roberts's fellow newcomer to the Court, Justice Alito, joined his substantive analysis of McCain-Feingold. The other seven justices called out the chief justice for covertly overruling *McConnell,* though they split into opposing factions as to the wisdom of doing so. Justice Souter, dissenting for himself and Justices Stevens, Ginsburg, and Breyer, flatly states the "unacknowledged result" of the chief justice's analysis: that "*McConnell*'s holding that [the electioneering communications provision] is facially constitutional is overruled."[39] He acknowledges that *McConnell* left open the possibility of as-applied challenges, but he claims the *McConnell* majority sought only to protect against improper suppression of "a genuine or pure issue ad."[40] He accuses the chief justice's "no other interpretation" test of "invert[ing]" the *McConnell*

37. 551 U.S. 449 (2007) (WRTL II). Roberts (majority (in part), plurality (in part)) (with Alito; with Scalia, Kennedy, Thomas (in part)); Alito (concurring); Scalia (concurring in part and concurring in the judgment) (with Kennedy, Thomas); Souter (dissenting) (with Stevens, Ginsburg, Breyer). The Scalia trio joined only the part of the chief justice's opinion that concludes the Court had jurisdiction to decide the case. In an earlier per curiam decision, a unanimous Court had enabled substantive review by holding that *McConnell* did not foreclose as-applied challenges to the McCain-Feingold limits on electioneering communications. *See* Wis. Right to Life v. FEC, 546 U.S. 410 (2006) (WRTL I).

38. *WRTL II*, 551 U.S. at 470 (plurality opinion).

39. *Id.* at 525 (Souter, J., dissenting).

40. *Id.* at 526 (Souter, J., dissenting).

majority's meaning and tacitly reinstating the "toothless" magic words test for corporate and union political expenditures.[41]

Justice Scalia, writing for himself, Justice Kennedy, and Justice Thomas, derides Chief Justice Roberts's strategy in even blunter terms: "This faux judicial restraint is judicial obfuscation."[42] Justice Scalia dismisses the chief justice's "no other interpretation" test as no less vague than the language of McCain-Feingold itself.[43] Justice Scalia concurs in the Court's result because he believes the electioneering communications provision violates the First Amendment. For him, though, the McCain-Feingold provision's unconstitutionality is a secondary, derivative problem. McCain-Feingold, he argues, simply built a new structure on the unconstitutional foundation of *Austin.*[44] He strongly implies that the Court should overrule not only *McConnell* but also *Austin,* thus fully invalidating the federal bar on corporate and union electoral spending.

Chief Justice Roberts's failed stealth assault on *McConnell* compelled a cleanup mission. At first, that's all ***Citizens United v. Federal Election Commission*** **(2010)**[45] appeared to be. Citizens United, a conservative nonprofit group, produced a film, *Hillary: The Movie,* which sharply criticized 2008 presidential candidate Hillary Clinton. Citizens United wanted to offer the movie through video-on-demand services during the presidential primary season. Because the group got some of its funding from business corporations, the McCain-Feingold electioneering communications provision barred the video-on-demand strategy. Initially *Citizens United* presented nothing more than a fresh opportunity for the Court to weaken McCain-Feingold by overruling *McConnell* on electioneering communications. After oral argument, however, the Court upped the ante. The justices ordered new briefing and argument on the question whether they should overrule *Austin.* Suddenly the government had to defend not just McCain-Feingold's enhancement of the Taft-Hartley bar on corporate and union electoral spending but also the bar itself. Expanding the case's blast radius from *McConnell* to *Austin* also threatened every state-level version of the Taft-Hartley bar, such as the Michigan law upheld in *Austin.*

41. *Id.* at 531 (Souter, J., dissenting).
42. *Id.* at 498–99 n.7 (Scalia, J., concurring in part and concurring in the judgment).
43. *See id.* at 495–97 (Scalia, J., concurring in part and concurring in the judgment).
44. *See id.* at 489–91 (Scalia, J., concurring in part and concurring in the judgment).
45. 558 U.S. 310 (2010). Kennedy (majority) (with Roberts, Scalia, Alito; with Thomas (in part); with Stevens, Ginsburg, Breyer, Sotomayor (in part)); Roberts (concurring) (with Alito); Scalia (concurring) (with Alito; with Thomas (in part)); Stevens (concurring in part and dissenting in part) (with Ginsburg, Breyer, Sotomayor); Thomas (concurring in part and dissenting in part). The only part of the majority opinion that the Stevens group joined, and from which Justice Thomas dissented, was the rejection of the First Amendment challenge to McCain-Feingold's disclosure and disclaimer requirements. The rest of the decision carried a 5-4 majority.

The *Citizens United* decision, heeding Justice Scalia's *Wisconsin Right to Life* admonition, overruled *Austin*. Justice Kennedy's majority opinion bristles with the language of government oppression. He describes *Austin* as holding "that political speech may be banned" and as "suppress[ing] [corporate political] speech altogether."[46] Past Supreme Court decisions on campaign finance, from *Buckley* forward, wrestled with the special problems of speech regulations in the electoral context and the distinctive character of corporate electoral speech. Justice Kennedy's opinion elides those distinctions. One remarkable passage attacks the Federal Election Commission with large chunks of text from a 1965 decision about government censorship. Justice Kennedy doesn't mention that the 1965 case dealt with a Maryland agency, unabashedly called the State Board of Censors, that regulated movies, not elections.[47] That passage exemplifies the emboldened majority's strategy of insisting that any reasonable person must view a bar on direct corporate electoral advocacy as censorship. In *Wisconsin Right to Life*, Chief Justice Roberts sought to incapacitate *McConnell* with a scalpel. In *Citizens United*, Justice Kennedy seeks to eviscerate *Austin* with a machete.

Both Citizens United, because it wanted to win its lawsuit, and the government, because it wanted to avoid the sweeping decision the Court ultimately rendered, urged the Court to avoid the explosive *Austin* question. Citizens United argued that offering *Hillary: The Movie* on demand wasn't really an "electioneering communication," because the film wouldn't reach a large enough audience; that the film didn't satisfy the "electioneering communication" definition as narrowed in *Wisconsin Right to Life;* and that on-demand video couldn't distort the electoral process and therefore should be excluded from McCain-Feingold. Citizens United and the government both argued that the Court could defuse the case by reading the bar on corporate electoral spending to exempt corporate speech, such as that of Citizens United, mostly funded by individuals. Justice Kennedy rejects all of these narrowing proposals. He emphasizes two major ideas. First, the narrowing approaches fail on their own terms, because they would require the Court to stretch or distort the relevant statutes. Second, and more novel, using any of the suggested narrowing approaches would violate the First Amendment by burdening corporate electoral spending with undue legal expense and ambiguity. "We decline," Justice Kennedy writes in rejecting the individual financing exemption, "to adopt an interpretation that requires intricate case-by-case determinations *to verify whether political speech is banned, especially if we are convinced that, in the end, this corporation has a constitutional right to speak on this subject.*"[48] The First

46. *Id.* at 319.
47. *See id.* at 335–36 (quoting Freedman v. Maryland, 380 U.S. 51, 57–58 (1965)).
48. *Citizens United,* 558 U.S. at 329 (emphasis added).

Amendment violation, he insists, lies "beyond all doubt."[49] This conclusory reasoning makes overruling *Austin* inevitable.

With concerns about the case's proper scope out of the way, Justice Kennedy turns to establishing the government's violation of Citizens United's rights. Critics of *Citizens United* have made much of the Court's conclusion that the First Amendment protects corporations. That basic idea, though, has a deep grounding in prior law. The Supreme Court more than a century ago established that corporations are legal "persons" with at least some constitutional rights.[50] *New York Times Co. v. Sullivan,*[51] one of the Court's most celebrated First Amendment decisions, protected a corporation's expression. We've seen the Roberts Court extend free speech protection to corporations in *Entertainment Merchants* (Chapter 1) and *IMS Health* (Chapter 2).

What's special about the *Citizens United* analysis of corporate free speech is the majority's expansive notion of corporate identity. FECA established, and *Austin* approved, the use of PACs to ameliorate legal restrictions on corporate and union electoral spending. A PAC is a separate legal entity, but the parent corporation can fully control and direct it; the separation inheres only in how the two entities may accumulate funds. The *Citizens United* majority, however, treats the legal separation between corporation and PAC as an existential fissure that wholly extinguishes the corporation's free speech rights. "A PAC," Justice Kennedy declares, "is a separate association from the corporation. So the PAC exemption . . . does not allow corporations to speak." Beyond that existential problem, "PACs are burdensome alternatives; they are expensive to administer and subject to extensive regulations."[52] Corporations, which only exist pursuant to government authority, thus enjoy not just the right to speak but the right to speak *with the minimum possible constraint,* even where a constraint isn't meant to stifle their speech. Even as Justice Kennedy distinguishes the corporation from its PAC, he rejects the pivotal distinction the *Austin* Court drew between a corporation and its shareholders. *Austin* held, and the government in *Citizens United* argued, that the government may bar corporations from spending their general treasury funds in elections because a corporation's political views don't reflect the views of its owners. Justice Kennedy shunts this concern aside.[53] For the *Citizens United* Court, then, a corporation cannot speak through a PAC, need not speak for its owners, and gets the strongest possible measure of First Amendment speech protection.

49. *Id.* at 336.

50. *See* Santa Clara Cty. v. S. Pac. R.R. Co., 118 U.S. 394 (1886) (widely recognized as holding that the Fourteenth Amendment's equal protection clause applies in some circumstances to corporations).

51. 376 U.S. 254 (1964) (holding that the First Amendment barred a libel judgment against a newspaper's publication of a civil rights group's advertisement).

52. *Citizens United,* 558 U.S. at 337.

53. *See id.* at 361–62.

In *Citizens United,* corporate wealth constitutes corporate identity, and the federal bar on corporate spending therefore discriminates against speakers based on identity.[54] Justice Kennedy argues that the law "silence[s] entities whose voices the Government deems to be suspect." Does he mean the corporate spending bar targets corporations because the government doesn't like corporations' ideas? No. This isn't viewpoint discrimination, Justice Kennedy avers, but rather an instance of "distinguishing among different speakers, allowing speech by some but not others."[55] We've seen Justice Kennedy make this same "speaker-based discrimination" argument in *IMS Health,* the drug detailing case. Recall that Justice Breyer, dissenting in that case, argued that the government should have power to regulate commercial actors differently than it regulates other actors, because commerce has distinctive effects on society. To deny that power, he insisted, repeats the infamous mistake of the *Lochner* era, when the Supreme Court invoked laissez faire economic theories to block government economic regulations. Justice Breyer's *Lochner* argument echoes *Austin.* The *Austin* anti-distortion rationale viewed electoral politics as the area in which the government should have its greatest latitude to curb wealthy commercial actors' influence.[56]

To justify his expansive account of corporate free speech rights in *Citizens United,* Justice Kennedy had to defuse the *Lochner* objection, which meant defeating the *Austin* anti-distortion rationale. He accordingly follows the Burger Court's *Bellotti* decision[57] on corporate referendum spending by invoking the idea that democracy requires voters to get as much political information as possible. *Bellotti* framed corporate political speech as part of "the widest possible dissemination of information from diverse and antagonistic sources."[58] Restricting corporate electoral spending, Justice Kennedy argues in *Citizens United,* diminishes public information.[59] Depriving the electorate of the information corporations want to impart denies us all "the freedom to think for ourselves."[60]

Justice Kennedy's rhetoric and reasoning, though, keep slipping from concern for democracy's needs into concern for corporations' prerogatives. *Austin,* he argues, was wrong to link the federal bar on corporate electoral spending to benefits the government confers through the corporate form, because the

54. *See id.* at 350.
55. *Id.* at 340.
56. For an extensive discussion of private money's influence on electoral politics, see TIMOTHY K. KUHNER, CAPITALISM V. DEMOCRACY: MONEY IN POLITICS AND THE FREE MARKET CONSTITUTION (2014).
57. First Nat'l Bank v. Bellotti, 435 U.S. 765 (1978).
58. First Nat'l Bank v. Bellotti, 435 U.S. 765, 790 n.29 (1978) (quoting N.Y. Times Co. v. Sullivan, 376 U.S. 254, 266 (1964)) (internal quotation marks and citation omitted).
59. *See Citizens United,* 558 U.S. at 349–50.
60. *Id.* at 356; *see also* MARTIN H. REDISH, THE ADVERSARY FIRST AMENDMENT: FREE EXPRESSION AND THE FOUNDATIONS OF AMERICAN DEMOCRACY 149 (2013) (arguing that the only alternative to political spending by wealthy interests is "an equality of ignorance").

First Amendment prohibits conditioning a government benefit on a sacrifice of constitutional rights.[61] Exempting media corporations from the federal limits on corporate electoral spending treats nonmedia speakers unfairly, deepening the law's impermissible identity-based discrimination.[62] Barring all business corporations from electoral spending unfairly disadvantages small and closely held corporations, because large corporations can exert political influence through lobbying.[63] All those arguments, whatever their merits, fly wide of the *Bellotti* public information interest. Justice Kennedy seems concerned with neither the diversity nor the antagonistic quality of electoral debates. If the *Citizens United* majority had wanted to focus on voter information, it could have issued a narrow decision that specifically exempted ideological nonprofits from the corporate spending ban. By instead going broad, the majority made *Citizens United* a case about why business corporations deserve the right to spend in elections.

At the normative core of *Citizens United,* Justice Kennedy explains that corporate political advocacy isn't just as important for democracy as other political speech—it's *more* important. He merges the public information interest into corporate prerogatives. Quoting Justice Scalia's opinion from the *McConnell* case, Justice Kennedy calls corporations "the voices that best represent the most significant parts of the economy."[64] He continues: "By suppressing the speech of manifold corporations, the Government prevents their voices and viewpoints from reaching the public and advising voters on which persons or entities are hostile to their interests."[65] (Note the crucial ambiguity of that second "their.") Justice Scalia's *Citizens United* concurrence reiterates the point, arguing that "to exclude or impede corporate speech is to muzzle the principal agents of the modern free economy."[66] Justice Scalia in *McConnell* also extolled corporate electoral spending as an essential counterbalance against government's repressive, totalizing ambitions.[67] Justice Kennedy in *Citizens United* repeats that point,[68] which echoes academic critiques of campaign finance regulation.[69] The Roberts Court's conservative majority cares more about corporate electoral speech than about ordinary speech

61. *See Citizens United,* 558 U.S. at 350–51.

62. *See id.* at 351–53. Justice Kennedy, following the Supreme Court's prevailing view, denies that the First Amendment protects media speakers more or differently than nonmedia speakers. For a contrary view, see Sonja R. West, *Press Exceptionalism,* 127 Harv. L. Rev. 2434 (2014).

63. *See Citizens United,* 558 U.S. at 355–56.

64. *Citizens United,* 558 U.S. at 354 (quoting McConnell v. FEC, 540 U.S. 93, 257–58 (2003) (opinion of Scalia, J.)) (internal quotation marks and citation omitted).

65. *Id.*

66. *Id.* at 393 (Scalia, J., concurring).

67. *See* McConnell v. FEC, 540 U.S. 93, 257–58 (2003) (opinion of Scalia, J.).

68. *See Citizens United,* 558 U.S. at 355–56.

69. *See, e.g.*, Martin H. Redish, Money Talks: Speech, Economic Power, and the Values of Democracy 86 (2001) (situating corporations as government's "rival

because corporate speech represents more important interests than ordinary speech. *Austin,* on this view, wasn't just wrong; it was backward. The *absence* of corporate influence on elections is the real distortion.

In affirming the primacy of corporate electoral speech, Justice Kennedy explains the apparent disconnect between the celebration of liberty in *Citizens United* and the deference to government authority in Chapter 3's institutional speech decisions. He acknowledges that Supreme Court rulings about speech in schools, prisons, military facilities, and public workplaces routinely treat the subjects of those institutions differently from other speakers. Those differential treatments, however, don't violate the First Amendment, because they reflect "an interest in allowing governmental entities to perform their functions." Conversely, "[t]he corporate independent expenditures at issue in this case . . . would not interfere with governmental functions."[70] For the Roberts Court, the desire of institutional subjects such as students and public workers to speak freely in institutional settings irritates a functioning democracy. In contrast, the desire of business corporations to dominate electoral debate exemplifies a functioning democracy.

As in the Chapter 1 categorical speech cases, the Roberts Court in *Citizens United* supports its desired result with a selective story about tradition. By 2010 a rich tradition might have seemed to foreclose striking down restrictions on corporate electoral spending. Federal election law for 63 years had restricted corporate spending. The Court for the 34 years since *Buckley* had let corporate spending limits stand. None of this troubles Justice Kennedy. "[N]ot until 1947," he announces, "did Congress first prohibit independent expenditures by corporations and labor unions[.]"[71] The pre-*Buckley* Court never ruled on the corporate and union electoral spending bar. In Justice Kennedy's account, however, disapproval oozes from between the lines of several decisions that *almost* struck the bar down.[72] He insists that the Court "in the wake of *Buckley*" surely would have declared the spending bar unconstitutional,[73] even though the *Austin* Court actually did the opposite. Similarly, although *Bellotti* (decided between *Buckley* and *Austin*) struck down a state bar on corporate initiative and referendum spending while pointedly distinguishing a parallel bar on corporate spending in candidate elections, the latter bar "would have been unconstitutional" had the Court ruled on it. That might sound like a kennel full of dogs that didn't bark,[74] but for Justice Kennedy it forms "a pre-*Austin*

for social authority"); JOHN SAMPLES, THE FALLACY OF CAMPAIGN FINANCE REFORM 271 (2006) (arguing that corporations should have "the means to counterbalance the power of the state").

70. *Citizens United,* 558 U.S. at 341.

71. *Id.* at 343.

72. *See id.* at 343–45.

73. *Id.* at 346.

74. *See* Sir Arthur Conan Doyle, *Silver Blaze,* in THE MEMOIRS OF SHERLOCK HOLMES 20 (Dover Pub. 2010) (1894) (discussing "the significance of the silence of the dog").

line [of precedent] that forbids restrictions on corporate speech based on the speaker's corporate identity."[75]

What of the precedential force of *Austin* itself and the doctrine of stare decisis, which had caused Chief Justice Roberts to tread so carefully in *Wisconsin Right to Life*? "[I]t must be concluded," Justice Kennedy declares in a pregnant passive voice, "that *Austin* was not well reasoned." He cites numerous grounds for that conclusion. The government's decision in *Citizens United* not to base its argument on the anti-distortion rationale "diminished" stare decisis. The *Austin* Court "abandoned First Amendment principles . . . by relying on language in some of our precedents that traces back to [an earlier precedent's] flawed historical account of campaign finance laws." Campaign practices and technology have changed since *Austin*. "No serious reliance interests are at stake," based on an understanding of "reliance" limited to private parties' interactions with commercial law and not the public's investment in legislative policy decisions about elections. "Our nation's speech dynamic is changing[.]"[76] Justice Kennedy says little about why these various factors matter, but he presents them as a wave that overwhelms stare decisis.

Justice Stevens wrote the *Citizens United* dissent, which Justices Ginsburg, Breyer, and Sotomayor all joined without additional comment. It was the last major free speech opinion of Justice Stevens's 35-year career on the Court. Coming out swinging just as hard as Justice Kennedy, Justice Stevens first contends that the Court never should have reached the question whether to overrule *Austin*. The majority, he insists, unnecessarily and improperly converted a narrow as-applied challenge into a broad facial challenge. (Recall the distinction between facial and as-applied challenges from last chapter's discussions of *Washington State Grange* and *Doe v. Reed*.) The majority's argument that it must take on the broad question to avoid chilling speech "beg[s] the question what types of corporate spending are constitutionally protected and to what extent,"[77] presumes a First Amendment crisis the majority fails to document, and exposes the decision in *Wisconsin Right to Life* as a failure. Justice Stevens also takes issue with the majority's refusal to dispose of the case on one of the narrower grounds the parties urged.

He then tears into the majority's disregard for stare decisis in overruling *Austin*. "The Court's central argument for why *stare decisis* ought to be trumped," he charges, "is that [the majority] does not like *Austin*." Justice Kennedy's attempts to explain the majority's departure from stare decisis amount to "a string of non-sequiturs[.]"[78] Nothing, Justice Stevens writes, supports Justice Kennedy's assertions that prior dissents' attacks on *Austin*,

75. *Id.* at 347.
76. *Id.* at 363–64.
77. *Id.* at 402 (Stevens, J., concurring in part and dissenting in part).
78. *Id.* at 409 (Stevens, J., concurring in part and dissenting in part).

the government's disavowal of the *Austin* anti-distortion rationale, and the absence of private transactional reliance on *Austin* somehow diminish the decision's precedential weight. "[T]he majority opinion," Justice Stevens writes, "is essentially an amalgamation of resuscitated dissents. The only relevant thing that has changed since *Austin* and *McConnell* is the composition of this Court."[79]

The bulk of Justice Stevens's dissent methodically rebuts the majority's substantive First Amendment analysis. He commends three categorical distinctions, all rejected by the majority, that underlie corporate electoral spending limits. First, corporations differ from other speakers. Business corporations, as *McConnell* made clear, threaten far more than ordinary speakers to dominate electoral debates. The corporate electoral spending limits "target a class of communications that is especially likely to corrupt the political process, that is at least one degree removed from the views of individual citizens, and that may not even reflect the views of those [shareholders] who pay for it."[80] Allowing corporations to spend through PACs fully vindicates whatever free speech rights they have in the electoral setting.[81] Second, electoral debate differs from ordinary public discussion. Justice Stevens agrees with the majority that political speech has special First Amendment significance. For him, though, "the context of election to public office" warrants special regulatory approaches.[82] Third, media corporations differ from other business corporations. Justice Stevens rejects the majority's concern that restricting corporate election spending necessarily, and undesirably, strips institutional media of First Amendment protection for editorializing. "[R]ecognition of the unique role played by the institutional press in sustaining public debate" justifies relaxing corporate electoral spending limits for media corporations.[83]

Justice Stevens defends *Austin* and corporate electoral spending limits under both the anti-corruption and anti-distortion rationales, which he sees as converging. "Understood properly," he contends, "'anti-distortion' is simply a variant on the classic governmental interest in protecting against improper influences on officeholders that debilitate the democratic process."[84] Corporate power in the electoral process, for Justice Stevens, reflects not special persuasive force but rather advantages of both wealth and organizational structure that allow corporations to dominate electoral debate without regard to the substantive merit of their arguments. Justice Stevens shakes off the conventional public-private distinction to contend that unregulated corporate dominance

79. *Id.* at 414 (Stevens, J., concurring in part and dissenting in part).
80. *Id.* at 419 (Stevens, J., concurring in part and dissenting in part).
81. *See id.* at 393 (Stevens, J., concurring in part and dissenting in part).
82. *Id.* at 394 (Stevens, J., concurring in part and dissenting in part).
83. *Id.* at 416–17 (Stevens, J., concurring in part and dissenting in part).
84. *Id.* at 464 (Stevens, J., concurring in part and dissenting in part).

of electoral debates undermines free speech values. *Austin,* he writes, "reflects a concern to *facilitate* First Amendment values by preserving some breathing room around the electoral 'marketplace' of ideas."[85] Limiting corporate electoral spending, on this view, reflects a realistic understanding of the electorate's capacity to absorb and process information from different sources.

Justice Kennedy ignores the dissent. He leaves the counterattack to concurrences by Justice Scalia and Chief Justice Roberts. (Justice Alito joined both concurrences, and Justice Thomas joined most of Justice Scalia's concurrence.) Justice Scalia rebuts Justice Stevens's argument—on the conservative majority's favorite analytic terrain—that constitutional history and tradition cut against the majority's overruling of *Austin.* Substantively, Justice Scalia argues that incorporation for profit, or for any other purpose, is a way for "individual person[s] . . . to speak *in association with other individual persons.*"[86] The chief justice tries to bolster the majority against Justice Stevens's procedural and stare decisis objections. He walks something of a tightrope, defending his resistance in *Wisconsin Right to Life* to overruling *McConnell* while also defending Justice Kennedy's maneuvering in *Citizens United* to overrule both *McConnell* and *Austin.*[87] The chief justice, echoing Justice Kennedy, derides the federal limits on corporate electoral spending as "a direct prohibition on political speech" that amount to "censorship" of everything from pamphlets and posters to newspaper editorials.[88] He seems particularly eager, as the keeper of the Court's institutional capital, to validate and sharpen Justice Kennedy's stare decisis apologia.

Four postscripts to the primary *Citizens United* holding that federal limits on corporate electoral spending violate the First Amendment:

First, *Citizens United* indirectly but essentially spawned "super PACs." *Citizens United* did not disturb the Tillman Act's ban on corporate *contributions* to federal candidates.[89] In the wake of *Citizens United,* however, the U.S. Court of Appeals for the District of Columbia Circuit held that corporations and unions, as surely as *Citizens United* now lets them make unlimited independent expenditures in federal elections, must also be free to make unlimited contributions to PACs that engage only in independent electoral spending.[90] That decision authorized what quickly became known as super PACs.

85. *Id.* at 473 (Stevens, J., concurring in part and dissenting in part).

86. *Id.* at 392 (Scalia, J., concurring). Justice Scalia's categorical equation of corporations with associations leads me to doubt the suggestion that his concurrence draws a nuanced distinction among types of corporations in assigning First Amendment rights. *See* RANDALL P. BEZANSON, TOO MUCH FREE SPEECH? 47–48 (2012).

87. *See Citizens United,* 558 U.S. at 372 (Roberts, C.J., concurring).

88. *Id.*

89. The Roberts Court declined to hear a case that challenged a state's bar on corporate contributions to electoral campaigns. *See* Iowa Right to Life Comm., Inc. v. Tooker, 717 F. 3d 576 (8th Cir. 2013), *cert. denied,* 134 S. Ct. 1787 (2014).

90. *See* SpeechNow.org v. FEC, 599 F.3d 686 (D.C. Cir.) (en banc), *cert. denied sub nom.* Keating v. FEC, 562 U.S. 1003 (2010).

Second, *Citizens United* doomed state as well as federal bans on corporate electoral spending. Two years after *Citizens United,* the same 5-4 majority (with Justice Kagan replacing Justice Stevens in dissent) summarily reversed a Montana Supreme Court decision that had upheld that state's bar on corporate electoral spending. The majority's one-paragraph per curiam opinion in ***American Tradition Partnership, Inc. v. Bullock* (2010)**[91] rejects Montana's arguments for its law because they "either were already rejected in *Citizens United,* or fail to meaningfully distinguish that case."[92] Justice Breyer's dissent both reiterates his view that *Citizens United* was wrongly decided and insists that Montana's law should survive First Amendment review even under *Citizens United,* based on the distinctive record the Montana legislature amassed to support its law. The *Citizens United* majority shrugs off the idea that different states may have distinctive insights about the effects of corporate electoral spending, even though the members of that majority elsewhere prize state autonomy.[93]

Third, the *Citizens United* majority declined to decide whether an interest in avoiding foreign influence on elections might justify limits only on foreign corporate spending.[94] After *Citizens United* the Court summarily affirmed, without opinion, a lower court decision that upheld a federal ban on foreign nationals' making contributions, or independent expenditures for "magic words" advocacy, in connection with any federal, state, or local election.[95] That decision puts to rest, for now, questions about whether the *Citizens United* bar on identity-based distinctions among campaign spenders would force the government to legalize foreign spending on U.S. elections.[96] The Court, though, gave no explanation for its decision to treat foreign nationals differently from corporations. The ban on foreign money limits the information available to voters, in direct conflict with the *Citizens United* majority's stated concern about promoting voter information.[97]

91. 132 S. Ct. 2490 (2012) (per curiam); Breyer (dissenting) (with Ginsburg, Sotomayor, Kagan).

92. *Id.*

93. *See, e.g.*, Nat'l Fed'n of Indep. Bus. v. Sebelius, 132 S. Ct. 2566 (2012) (reaching a mixed verdict on federalism-based challenges to portions of the Patient Protection and Affordable Care Act).

94. *See* Citizens United v. FEC, 558 U.S. 310, 362 (2010).

95. *See* Bluman v. FEC, 800 F. Supp. 2d 281 (D.D.C. 2011), *affd. mem.*, 132 S. Ct. 1087 (2012).

96. *See, e.g.*, Richard L. Hasen, Citizens United *and the Illusion of Coherence*, 109 MICH. L. REV. 581, 605–10 (2011).

97. *Cf.* ALEXANDER MEIKLEJOHN, POLITICAL FREEDOM: THE CONSTITUTIONAL POWERS OF THE PEOPLE 119 (1960) ("[U]nhindered expression must be open to non-citizens, to resident aliens, to writers and speakers of other nations, to anyone, past or present, who has something to say which may have significance for a citizen who is thinking of the welfare of this nation").

Fourth, one might wonder what became of labor unions in the *Citizens United* analysis. Both the original Taft-Hartley federal limits on electoral spending and the McCain-Feingold extension of those limits to "electioneering communications" applied to unions as well as corporations. The *Citizens United* overruling of *Austin* frees unions as well as corporations to spend in federal elections. The *Citizens United* majority, however, largely ignores unions beyond citing some pre-*Buckley* labor cases that expressed concern about the spending bar's application to unions, a concern whose specific focus on unions Justice Kennedy doesn't acknowledge.[98] Next chapter we'll see the Court focus intently on unions' political spending, with restrictive results that diverge sharply from *Citizens United.*

Beyond the primary holding, Justice Kennedy wrote in *Citizens United* for a different, 8-1 majority—everyone but Justice Thomas—in upholding McCain-Feingold's disclaimer and disclosure requirements. Recall from last chapter's discussion of the petition signature case, *Doe v. Reed,* that *Buckley v. Valeo* rejected a facial First Amendment challenge to the FECA requirement that federal candidates disclose their contributors. McCain-Feingold requires every electioneering communication to include a four-second disclaimer that clearly identifies who funded the communication. The law also requires any entity that spends $10,000 on electioneering communications within a calendar year to file a disclosure statement with the FEC that provides basic information about the entity's electioneering activities, including contributors' names. *McConnell* upheld those requirements against a facial First Amendment challenge.[99] Citizens United challenged the requirements as applied to *Hillary: The Movie,* arguing that the disclaimer requirement interfered with the group's message, unfairly singled out broadcast communications, and created a danger of retaliation against donors. The group wanted the disclosure requirement confined to communications functionally equivalent to express advocacy.

Justice Kennedy and the majority reject Citizens United's arguments, holding that the government's interest in informing voters about the source of political messages justifies disclaimer and disclosure requirements as "a less restrictive alternative to more comprehensive regulations of speech."[100] Citizens United, although it expressed concerns about retaliation against unpopular speakers, presented no evidence suggesting that its political messages exposed it to adverse consequences. Justice Thomas alone, as in *Doe v. Reed,* dissents. Relying once again on allegations about hostile treatment of people who publicly supported California's anti-same-sex marriage Proposition 8, Justice Thomas insists that compelled political disclosures "enable private

98. *See Citizens United,* 558 U.S. at 343–45.
99. *See* McConnell v. FEC, 540 U.S. 93, 196 (2003).
100. *Citizens United,* 558 U.S. at 369.

citizens and elected officials to implement political strategies *specifically calculated* to curtail campaign-related activity and prevent the lawful, peaceful exercise of First Amendment rights."[101]

The *Citizens United* Court's affirmation of the disclosure and disclaimer requirements rests much more firmly than its rejection of the corporate spending limits on the public's interest in political information. This part of *Citizens United* thus engages the tension between the interest in informing the electorate and the danger of chilling political speech that we saw the *Doe v. Reed* Court avoid in the arguably more difficult context of direct democracy petitions.[102] *Citizens United* portrays the requirement that campaigns and political committees disclose their contributors as the constitutionally respectable form of campaign finance regulation. However, the success opponents of regulation are enjoying in virtually every campaign finance battle has prompted challenges to disclosure laws.[103] Disclosure may yet emerge in the Supreme Court as a battleground in the First Amendment law of campaign finance.

## *McCUTCHEON*: A WHOLE LESS CORRUPTING THAN THE SUM OF ITS PARTS?

Recall that *Buckley* justifies campaign contribution limits under only one rationale: prevention of actual or apparent political corruption. "Political corruption" can mean at least two different things. It might include any exchange of money for access to, or influence over, a candidate or a political party that can influence the candidate in office. A donor might, for example, contribute to a legislator's campaign and then, after a decent interval, send a lobbyist to inform the legislator about the contributor's priorities. Alternatively, the legislator might simply come to feel beholden to the donor, or to a broader class of major donors or independent spenders. This sort of *influence corruption* doesn't entail any explicit promise of action. We might, on the other hand, understand "political corruption" to refer only to cases where the contributor gives money in direct exchange for a particular legislative vote or other action. That narrower definition describes quid pro quo corruption: one thing for another. Defining corruption to include influence provides a broad, secure constitutional basis for contribution limits. In contrast, limiting corruption to quid pro quo scenarios dramatically narrows the basis for justifying contribution

101. *Id.* at 483 (Thomas, J., concurring in part and dissenting in part).

102. The Court later declined to hear a challenge to a California law that makes tax-exempt charities reveal the identities of their major donors. *See* Ctr. for Competitive Politics v. Harris, 784 F.3d 1307 (9th Cir.), *cert. denied*, 136 S. Ct. 480 (2015).

103. *See* RONALD COLLINS & DAVID SKOVER, WHEN MONEY SPEAKS: THE *McCUTCHEON* DECISION, CAMPAIGN FINANCE LAWS AND THE FIRST AMENDMENT 196–98 (2014).

limits under *Buckley*. Quid pro quo corruption may even reduce to bribery, a crime that federal and state laws punish outside the scope of campaign finance regulation. *Buckley* didn't canonize either corruption definition.[104]

The government in *Citizens United* pressed the anti-corruption rationale as one justification for the federal limits on corporate and union electoral spending that the Court eventually struck down. Justice Kennedy mainly responds that expenditures don't cause corruption. However, he also presses the idea, consistent with his concurrence in the legislative ethics case *Carrigan* (Chapter 1), that the First Amendment and democratic values compel the Court to understand "corruption" narrowly. "Favoritism and influence," he writes, "are not . . . avoidable in representative politics. It is in the nature of an elected representative to favor certain policies, and, by necessary corollary, to favor the voters and contributors who support those policies."[105] That idea, on Justice Kennedy's account, animated the *Buckley* corruption analysis. "When *Buckley* identified a sufficiently important governmental interest in preventing corruption or the appearance of corruption," Justice Kennedy writes for the *Citizens United* majority, "that interest was limited to quid pro quo corruption."[106]

If that's right, then aren't contribution limits both superfluous, given the existence of separate bribery laws, and overbroad as a First Amendment matter? Justice Kennedy hints that his account of corruption may point to that result. "[R]estrictions on direct contributions," he asserts, "are preventative, because few if any contributions to candidates will involve *quid pro quo* arrangements."[107] He doesn't pronounce that preventative strategy constitutionally permissible. To the contrary, he maintains that even when a campaign contributor's excessive influence over a state appellate judge led the Supreme Court to make the judge recuse himself from a case in which the contributor had an interest, the facts didn't warrant "that the litigant's political speech could be banned."[108] Justice Kennedy's account of corruption meant little for *Citizens United,* and it drew little fire in the public outcry that greeted the decision. The narrower understanding of corruption, however, spelled trouble for contribution limits.[109]

104. For academic arguments in favor of an influence corruption definition, see LAWRENCE LESSIG, REPUBLIC, LOST: HOW MONEY CORRUPTS CONGRESS—AND A PLAN TO STOP IT (2011); ZEPHYR TEACHOUT, CORRUPTION IN AMERICA: FROM BENJAMIN FRANKLIN'S SNUFF BOX TO *CITIZENS UNITED* (2014). For an argument in favor of the quid pro quo definition, see REDISH, *supra* note 60, at 122–50.

105. *Citizens United,* 558 U.S. at 359 (quoting McConnell v. FEC, 540 U.S. 93, 297 (2003) (Kennedy, J., concurring in the judgment in part and dissenting in part)) (internal quotation marks omitted).

106. *Citizens United,* 558 U.S. at 359.

107. *Id.* at 357.

108. *Id.* at 360 (discussing Caperton v. A.T. Massey Coal Co., 556 U.S. 868 (2009)).

109. Election law scholars anticipated the problem. *See* Richard Briffault, *Corporations, Corruption, and Complexity: Campaign Finance after* Citizens United, 20 CORNELL J.L. & PUB. POL'Y 643, 661–63 (2011); Heather Gerken, *Lobbying as the New*

Recall that the 1974 FECA amendments included both a ceiling on how much a contributor may give any federal candidate in an election cycle (*base limits*) and a ceiling on the total amount a contributor may give all federal candidates combined in an election cycle (*aggregate limits*). The 2002 McCain-Feingold law updated and increased both the base and aggregate limits as a trade-off for the law's new restrictions on campaign finance. For the 2014 election cycle, a contributor could give any candidate a base amount of $5,200, with an aggregate limit for all candidates of $48,600. (Separate base and aggregate limits governed contributions to political committees.) Sean McCutcheon, a major donor to Republican candidates, reached the aggregate limit during the 2012 cycle and wanted to give more. McCutcheon and the Republican National Committee brought a First Amendment challenge to the aggregate limits. In ***McCutcheon v. Federal Election Commission* (2014)**,[110] the same five justices who prevailed in *Citizens United* struck down the federal aggregate contribution limits. Chief Justice Roberts's controlling plurality opinion[111] and Justice Breyer's dissent offer a vivid contrast of ideas about democratic politics, normative First Amendment theory, and campaign finance doctrine.

Chief Justice Roberts's vision of democratic politics, echoing Justice Kennedy in *Citizens United,* celebrates campaign contributors' pursuit of political influence. A concern for wealthy political actors' prerogatives, which we saw *Citizens United* mask under a surface concern for an informed electorate, emerges in the foreground of *McCutcheon*. "There is no right more basic in our democracy," the chief justice declares, "than the right to participate in electing our political leaders" by, among other means, "contribut[ing] to a candidate's campaign."[112] The specific right to donate to an unbounded number of candidates matters because contributors need latitude to advocate their policy interests. Aggregate contribution limits may force a contributor "to choose which of several policy concerns he will advance."[113] Making the contributor choose between more and larger contributions "imposes a special burden

*Campaign Finance*, 27 GA. ST. U. L. REV. 1155, 1157–59 (2011); Hasen, *supra* note 96, at 615–17; Michael S. Kang, *After* Citizens United, 44 IND. L. REV. 243, 250–52 (2010) [hereinafter Kang, Citizens United]. One argued that the new corruption language spelled "the end of campaign finance law as we knew it." Michael S. Kang, *The End of Campaign Finance Law*, 98 VA. L. REV. 1, 21 (2012) [hereinafter Kang, *Campaign Finance*].

110. 134 S. Ct. 1434 (2014). Roberts (plurality) (with Scalia, Kennedy, Alito); Thomas (concurring in the judgment); Breyer (dissenting) (with Ginsburg, Sotomayor, Kagan).

111. Justice Thomas, as in *Randall*, declines to join the *McCutcheon* plurality because he believes the Court should overrule the *Buckley* allowance for contribution limits rather than try to work within *Buckley*. *See id.* at 1462 (Thomas, J., concurring in the judgment).

112. *Id.* at 1440–41 (plurality opinion).

113. *Id.* at 1448 (plurality opinion).

on . . . participation in the democratic process." Chief Justice Roberts explicitly rejects a competing political vision based on "a generalized conception of the public good."[114] His reasoning embraces a pluralist political ideal and rejects a republican political ideal. The Supreme Court's First Amendment decisions about electoral speech have long inclined toward interest group pluralism.[115] No prior decision, however, has made the connection between normative political theory and First Amendment law so explicit.

Chief Justice Roberts's pluralist vision of democratic politics requires a First Amendment theory that privileges wealthy speakers' expressive autonomy. Focusing First Amendment analysis on expressive autonomy, as we've seen throughout the Roberts Court's First Amendment jurisprudence, requires a rigid conceptual dichotomy between private speaker and government censor. Chief Justice Roberts accordingly invokes the public-private distinction to frame *McCutcheon* as a simple case of beleaguered speaker against repressive state. He refuses to entertain the idea that campaign finance disputes may reflect conflicts between different First Amendment interests and values. Citizens' preference for an electoral system that enables broad-based participation in electoral debate amounts, for the chief justice, to nothing more than "the will of the majority [to enact] laws that restrict free speech."[116] Any "interest that may justify restrictions on individual speech" can't be a First Amendment interest but reduces under "our established First Amendment analysis" to an excuse for government censorship.[117] The chief justice especially deplores the popular backlash against *Citizens United.* "Money in politics may at times seem repugnant to some," he intones, "but so too does much of what the First Amendment vigorously protects."[118] When the chief justice declares that "those who govern should be the last people to help decide who *should* govern,"[119] he presumably means Congress, but his First Amendment theory extends the dismissal to the sovereign people.

Chief Justice Roberts's pluralist political vision and autonomy-focused First Amendment theory undergird his doctrinal holding that campaign contribution limits may remedy only quid pro quo corruption. He maintains that *Buckley* and subsequent decisions always limited the anticorruption rationale for contribution limits to quid pro quo corruption, but

114. *Id.* at 1449 (plurality opinion).

115. *See* Gregory P. Magarian, *Regulating Political Parties under a "Public Rights" First Amendment*, 44 WM. & MARY L. REV. 1939, 1946–70 (2003); *see also* KUHNER, *supra* note 56, at 154–71 (characterizing the Roberts Court's campaign finance decisions prior to *McCutcheon* as embracing interest group pluralism and rejecting republican deliberation).

116. *McCutcheon,* 134 S. Ct. at 1449 (plurality opinion).

117. *Id.* at 1450 (plurality opinion).

118. *Id.* at 1441 (plurality opinion).

119. *Id.* at 1441–42 (plurality opinion).

he suggests that *Citizens United* provides enough authority for that limitation.[120] "[G]overnment regulation," the chief justice declares, "may not target the general gratitude a candidate may feel toward those who support him or his allies, or the political access such support may afford."[121] He equates the idea of stemming "influence corruption" with the "equalization rationale" for campaign finance regulation that *Buckley* rejected.[122] On a quid pro quo theory, contribution limits must not interfere with the influence that large aggregate campaign donations can buy. Chief Justice Roberts maintains that other actual or possible campaign finance laws prevent circumvention of the base limits well enough to obviate the need for aggregate limits, at a lower cost to donors' expressive autonomy.[123] The chief justice prominently echoes Justice Breyer's concern in *Randall* for the major political parties, warning particularly against any legal theory of corruption that would weaken the parties.[124]

In striking down the federal aggregate contribution limits, Chief Justice Roberts faced a major obstacle: *Buckley* explicitly upheld the 1974 version of the aggregate limits. The *Buckley* Court held that the aggregate limits imposed only a "limited, additional restriction on associational freedom" while serving as a "corollary" of the base limits.[125] The chief justice overrules the *Buckley* Court's holding that the aggregate limits place only a marginal burden on expressive freedom.[126] In other respects, though, he follows his *Wisconsin Right to Life* playbook, claiming to distinguish the key precedent rather than overrule it. He emphasizes, repeatedly, that the *Buckley* analysis of the aggregate limits took up only "one paragraph of its 139-page opinion . . . three sentences."[127] He insists that McCain-Feingold, the source of the updated aggregate limit, "is a different statutory scheme, and the aggregate limits it imposes operate against a distinct legal backdrop." In particular, he says, federal law since *Buckley* has installed new, improved checks against the danger that large donors can circumvent the base limits. He also claims the *McCutcheon* challengers raised new legal arguments against the aggregate limits. *Buckley*, for all these reasons, "does not control here."[128] However, both Justice Thomas (approvingly) and Justice Breyer (ruefully) charge the plurality with overruling

120. *See id.* at 1451 (plurality opinion).
121. *Id.* at 1441 (plurality opinion).
122. *See id.* at 1450 (plurality opinion).
123. *See id.* at 1452–56 (plurality opinion).
124. *See id.* at 1461 (plurality opinion).
125. Buckley v. Valeo, 424 U.S. 1, 38 (1976).
126. *See McCutcheon,* 134 S. Ct. at 1448 (plurality opinion).
127. *Id.* at 1445 (plurality opinion). Chief Justice Roberts fixates on the three-sentence length of the *Buckley* aggregate limits discussion. *See id.* at 1446, 1447 (plurality opinion).
128. *Id.* at 1446 (plurality opinion).

*Buckley* on aggregate limits.[129] Thus, a majority of the Court in *McCutcheon* believes the decision takes the unprecedented step of changing the balance *Buckley* struck between expenditure and contribution limits.

Justice Breyer, dissenting for the Court's four liberals, proceeds from a republican vision of democratic politics that contrasts fundamentally with Chief Justice Roberts's pluralist vision. Justice Breyer sees campaign finance regulations as reflecting "an interest in maintaining the integrity of our public governmental institutions."[130] That integrity, in his view, requires a government that reflects the influence of all the people, not just privileged interest groups. Reaching back to Justice Brandeis's famous concurring opinion in *Whitney v. California*,[131] Justice Breyer posits a political system through which "government may be responsive to the will of the people."[132] Reaching back even further, to the Federalist Papers, he contends that our founders sought a system with "the necessary 'communion of interests and sympathy of sentiments' between the people and their representatives, so that public opinion could be channeled into effective government action."[133] Open communication between the people and their representatives yields an understanding of the common good, which in turn drives the government's policy decisions. This republican ideal rejects wealthy campaign contributors' use of money to gain disproportionate influence. "Where enough money calls the tune," Justice Breyer says, "the general public will not be heard."[134]

Justice Breyer's republican vision of democratic politics corresponds with an instrumental First Amendment theory that diverges sharply from Chief Justice Roberts's single-minded concern for wealthy contributors' expressive autonomy. Justice Breyer elaborates Justice Stevens's idea from *Citizens United* that campaign finance laws can actually advance First Amendment interests. The people, Justice Breyer explains in *McCutcheon*, convey their policy views to their representatives through "[a] politically oriented marketplace of ideas" whose effectiveness requires constitutional protection for expressive

129. *See id.* at 1464 (Thomas, J., concurring in the judgment); *id.* at 1465 (Breyer, J., dissenting).

130. *Id.* at 1467 (Breyer, J., dissenting). Justice Breyer's dissent appears to reflect the strong influence of Robert Post's May 2013 Tanner Lectures at Harvard Law School, later published as ROBERT C. POST, CITIZENS DIVIDED: CAMPAIGN FINANCE REGULATION AND THE CONSTITUTION (2014). Justice Breyer even cited Dean Post's then-unpublished book manuscript. *See McCutcheon,* 134 S. Ct. at 1468 (Breyer, J., dissenting).

131. 274 U.S. 357, 372 (1927) (Brandeis, J., concurring), *cited in McCutcheon,* 134 S. Ct. at 1467 (Breyer, J., dissenting).

132. *McCutcheon,* 134 S. Ct. at 1467 (Breyer, J., dissenting) (quoting Stromberg v. California, 283 U.S. 359, 369 (1931) (internal quotation marks omitted)).

133. *McCutcheon,* 134 S. Ct. at 1467 (Breyer, J., dissenting) (quoting James Madison, *The Federalist*, "Federalist Paper, No. 57" (J. Cooke ed. 1961) (1788)).

134. *McCutcheon,* 134 S. Ct. at 1467 (Breyer, J., dissenting).

freedom. He thus portrays the interest in maintaining government integrity as "an interest rooted in . . . the First Amendment itself." Political corruption threatens First Amendment values by "derail[ing] the essential speech-to-government-action tie."[135] Justice Breyer acknowledges the importance of the countervailing First Amendment interest in the use of money to circulate political ideas. He sees campaign finance law as presenting a difficult First Amendment conflict between the people's interest in communicating their ideas to the government and political actors' interest in communicating their ideas to the electorate.[136] That conflict belies the chief justice's schematic portrayal of a "private" electoral speech interest threatened by a "public" political integrity justification for suppressing speech.

Justice Breyer's republican political theory and instrumental First Amendment theory compel his doctrinal conclusion that the *Buckley* anti-corruption rationale for campaign finance regulation must extend beyond quid pro quo corruption to include influence corruption. He maintains that the Court from *Buckley* onward, understanding the First Amendment value of political integrity, hewed to the broader definition of corruption. *McConnell* articulated an especially strong basis for the influence definition of corruption, documenting "the web of relationships and understandings among parties, candidates, and large donors that underlies privileged access and influence."[137] *Citizens United,* Justice Breyer charges, deviated from that well-conceived and well-worn path by imposing the quid pro quo definition, and *McCutcheon* simply extends the aberration. He insists, however, that the plurality reaches the wrong result even under the quid pro quo definition, because eliminating the aggregate limits enables circumvention of the base limits. He derides Chief Justice Roberts's contrary argument as "substitut[ing] judges' understandings of how the political process works for the understanding of Congress[.]"[138] The *McCutcheon* majority, Justice Breyer concludes, "eviscerates our Nation's campaign finance laws."[139]

*McCutcheon* immediately changed the shape of electoral debate. George Soros and the Koch brothers may now give the maximum base contribution to every congressional candidate in the country. More significant than the end of aggregate contribution limits, however, is what *McCutcheon* may portend for base contribution limits.[140] Could a future decision hold that bribery laws

135. *Id.* (Breyer, J., dissenting) (internal quotation marks omitted).
136. *See id.* at 1468 (Breyer, J., dissenting).
137. *Id.* at 1469 (Breyer, J., dissenting).
138. *Id.* at 1481 (Breyer, J., dissenting).
139. *Id.* at 1465 (Breyer, J., dissenting).
140. The Roberts Court to date has avoided directly confronting the base limits. *See* Richard L. Hasen, *Election Law's Path in the Roberts Court's First Decade: A Sharp Right Turn but with Speed Bumps and Surprising Twists*, 68 STAN. L. REV. 1597, 1604–05 (2016).

suffice to deal with quid pro quo corruption and that, therefore, even base limits unjustifiably burden First Amendment rights? Chief Justice Roberts in *McCutcheon* purports to leave the *Buckley* contribution-expenditure distinction undisturbed.[141] He carefully notes that "[t]his case does not involve any challenge to the base limits[.]"[142] He repeatedly invokes the superstructure of federal contribution limits to help discredit the aggregate limits. The base limits, he says, do the major work of preventing quid pro quo corruption, making the aggregate limits unnecessary and thus unjustifiably burdensome on contributors' First Amendment rights. However, the chief justice never states or even implies that any contribution limit actually satisfies the First Amendment.[143] He has shown in other contexts, including *Wisconsin Right to Life,* a tactical knack for working indirectly or incrementally to neutralize disfavored laws.[144] Invalidating the base limits wouldn't contradict his *McCutcheon* logic for striking down the aggregate limits. To the contrary, a future decision to strike down the base limits could easily build on the *McCutcheon* justification for rejecting the aggregate limits.

Three features of Chief Justice Roberts's opinion suggest *McCutcheon* could undermine the base contribution limits. First, limiting the *Buckley* anti-corruption rationale to quid pro quo corruption leaves all contribution limits teetering on a very narrow foundation. For example, Justice Breyer charges that the quid pro quo definition tacitly overrules the part of *McConnell* that upheld McCain-Feingold's restrictions on "soft money" contributions to political parties. That *McConnell* holding, he points out, explicitly relied on a theory of influence corruption.[145] Chief Justice Roberts denies Justice Breyer's charge, but he doesn't explain how a quid pro quo theory can support the *McConnell* soft money holding.[146] Second, as noted above, Chief Justice Roberts holds that the First Amendment protects a contributor from the choice, imposed by the aggregate limits, between

141. *See McCutcheon,* 134 S. Ct. at 1445–46 (plurality opinion).

142. *Id.* at 1442 (plurality opinion).

143. In discussing regulatory alternatives to the aggregate limits, for example, Chief Justice Roberts makes clear that "[w]e do not mean to opine on the validity of any particular proposal." *Id.* at 1459 (plurality opinion).

144. *See* Shelby County v. Holder, 133 S. Ct. 2612 (2013) (indirectly overturning the Voting Rights Act's "preclearance" requirement, which made jurisdictions with a history of voting discrimination clear voting changes with the U.S. Department of Justice, by striking down the formula that determined which jurisdictions the requirement covered); Nat'l Fed'n of Indep. Bus. v. Sebelius, 132 S. Ct. 2566 (2012) (upholding the Affordable Care Act's individual mandate but striking down the law's provision for Medicaid expansion).

145. *See McCutcheon,* 134 S. Ct. at 1469–71 (Breyer, J., dissenting). Commentators argued even prior to *McCutcheon* that the *Citizens United* conception of corruption effectively dooms the soft money limits. *See* Briffault, *supra* note 109, at 661–63; Kang, Citizens United, *supra* note 109, at 252–53.

146. *See McCutcheon,* 134 S. Ct. at 1451 n.6 (plurality opinion).

contributing more money to fewer candidates and less money to more candidates. That position directly contradicts the *Buckley* principle, key to justifying contribution limits, that the amount of a contribution has only marginal First Amendment value. Third, the chief justice reiterates Justice Kennedy's claim from *Citizens United* that "the *base limits* themselves are a prophylactic measure."[147] The base limits, in this conception, don't necessarily address actual corruption. Rather, they aim to *prevent* corruption. Given that Chief Justice Roberts found the aggregate limits too speculative to satisfy First Amendment review, the prophylactic approach he ascribes to the base limits would appear similarly vulnerable.

## CONCLUSION

The managed speech account of the Roberts Court's free speech jurisprudence can illuminate *Citizens United* and *McCutcheon*. The Roberts Court's campaign finance decisions, by Kathleen Sullivan's approving lights, treat the "distribution and assessment [of speech as] nearly always best left to the citizenry rather than the government."[148] Sullivan equates the "citizenry" with a "private order" that distributes expressive opportunities through the economic market.[149] That equation captures the Roberts Court's worldview. On the managed speech account, *Citizens United* and *McCutcheon* empower corporations, wealthy individuals, and the major political parties to shape the content and form of electoral debates. These two decisions diminish the political voices of groups and individuals with more modest expressive resources.

The Roberts Court has attacked with unprecedented fervor the equalization and anti-distortion rationales for campaign finance regulation, both of which encourage more broadly inclusive, wider-ranging electoral debate. Critics of the Roberts Court's campaign finance decisions have extolled the practical viability and normative appeal of those rationales, even in the wake of *Citizens United*.[150] The equalization and anti-distortion rationales embody doubts that political debate under conditions of economic inequality, conditions the

147. *Id.* at 1458 (plurality opinion).

148. Kathleen M. Sullivan, *Two Concepts of Freedom of Speech*, 124 HARV. L. REV. 143, 176 (2010).

149. *Id.* at 155.

150. *See* Richard Briffault, *On Dejudicializing American Campaign Finance Law*, 27 GA. ST. U. L. REV. 887, 911–18 (2011); Richard L. Hasen, Citizens United *and the Orphaned Anti-distortion Rationale*, 27 GA. ST. U. L. REV. 989, 1000–05 (2011); Johanna Kalb, *J. Skelly Wright's Democratic First Amendment*, 61 LOY. L. REV. 107 (2015); Nadia Urbinati, *Free Speech as the Citizen's Right*, in POST, *supra* note 130, at 133–34; *but see* POST, *supra*, at 47–59 (arguing that the equalization and anti-distortion rationales don't answer the concern that regulating money in politics undermines the First Amendment's protection of free and open public discourse).

government helps to create, can fulfill democracy's needs and promote the First Amendment's values. Those rationales treat campaign finance regulations that counterbalance economic inequality as advancing both democracy and free speech. The Roberts Court's emphatic rejection of the equalization and anti-distortion rationales shields electoral debate from potentially disruptive outsider speech.

In the familiar managed speech mode, *Citizens United* embodies a preference for political stability over dynamism and tumult. Business corporations are government-sanctioned pillars of our economic order. By virtue of their economic primacy, they have a strong interest in bolstering existing social institutions and power arrangements. Of course corporations want to change whatever government policies oppose corporate interests. The status quo, however, generally favors corporate interests, and *Citizens United* sensibly trusts corporations not to rend the social fabric in challenging whatever exceptions may test that general rule. The role of government power in fostering corporate profits belies the arguments by opponent of campaign finance regulation that corporate spending promotes political dissent.[151] The government-corporate relationship likewise belies the complementary argument that campaign finance regulations entrench incumbents and thus promote political stability.[152]

The managed speech account of *Citizens United* provides a framework for thinking about the "corporate rights" problem that has dominated public discussion of the decision. Determining which constitutional rights a given institution should enjoy requires asking what sort of legal entity the institution is and whether that sort of entity fits the purposes of any given constitutional right.[153] That inquiry animated the Roberts Court's controversial *Hobby Lobby* decision, in which the same majority responsible for *Citizens United* held that business corporations can "exercise" religion and therefore may assert a federal statutory protection for religious exercise against adverse government regulation.[154] The result in *Citizens United* wouldn't make sense if the right to

151. *See, e.g.*, McConnell v. FEC, 540 U.S. 93, 262 (2003) (Scalia, J., concurring in part, concurring in the judgment in part, and dissenting in part) (arguing that defense of campaign finance regulations "is about preventing criticism of the government").

152. *See* Briffault, *supra* note 150, at 925–29 (contending that no substantial evidence supports the charge that campaign finance regulations advantage incumbents).

153. *See* LAURENCE TRIBE & JOSHUA MATZ, UNCERTAIN JUSTICE: THE ROBERTS COURT AND THE CONSTITUTION 111–12 (2014); MARK TUSHNET, IN THE BALANCE: LAW AND POLITICS ON THE ROBERTS COURT 263–64 (2013). A similar institutional approach may justify the corporate expenditure limits' exemptions for media corporations. *See* BEZANSON, *supra* note 86, at 39–40; Burt Neuborne, *Felix Frankfurter's Revenge: An Accidental Democracy Built by Judges*, *in* MONEY, POLITICS, AND THE CONSTITUTION: BEYOND *CITIZENS UNITED* 210–11 (Monica Youn ed., 2011).

154. *See* Burwell v. Hobby Lobby Stores, Inc., 134 S. Ct. 2751 (2014). I have criticized the *Hobby Lobby* decision's analysis of corporate rights. *See* Gregory P. Magarian, *The New Religious Institutionalism Meets the Old Establishment Clause*, *in* THE RISE OF CORPORATE RELIGIOUS LIBERTY 460–62 (Micah Schwartzman et al. eds., 2016).

spend money in elections depended on membership in a self-governing community of natural persons.[155] The Roberts Court's managed speech reasoning, however, provides a basis for giving business corporations that right to spend. If one believes business corporations make a uniquely valuable contribution to electoral debate, then their electoral speech deserves constitutional protection. The surface *Citizens United* holding that "corporations are persons" depends on a deeper belief about what kind of persons corporations are.

To this point, my managed speech story about the Roberts Court's campaign finance decisions has ignored a problem *Citizens United* may present for the story. As Chapter 6 explained, our two major political parties have long served as paladins of political stability in First Amendment doctrine. They have succeeded for decades, with the Court's active support, in bolstering the political status quo while marginalizing dissenting speakers and ideas. *Citizens United,* though, contributes to a weakening of the parties' power.[156] The *Buckley* distinction between contributions and expenditures has always advantaged independent spenders over parties, which must raise money in the electoral arena before they can spend it. The broadening of electoral spending rights in *Citizens United,* exacerbated by the subsequent emergence of super PACs, dramatically increases that advantage. The majority presumably failed to anticipate how enhancing business corporations' influence over elections would further degrade the major parties' power. Can we reconcile *Citizens United* with the Court's well-established solicitude for the major parties?

Here *McCutcheon* figures prominently in the managed speech story. *McCutcheon* in many ways parallels *Citizens United.* Both decisions valorize wealthy speakers and condemn long-standing federal election laws in the name of protecting political speech. Both embody a pluralist political theory and reject a republican political theory. Both enhance the capacity of powerful interests to manage and stabilize electoral debates. In one important respect, however, *McCutcheon* counteracts *Citizens United.* The unprecedented blow *McCutcheon* strikes against federal contribution limits helps political speakers who depend on contributions: the major political parties and their candidates. Loosening contribution limits helps the parties compete with the independent spenders emboldened by *Citizens United.* As I've noted, Chief Justice Roberts in *McCutcheon* emphasizes the parties as beneficiaries of large, diffused campaign contributions. The *McCutcheon* Court's narrowing of the anti-corruption justification for campaign finance laws also expands the parties' license to build and trade on relationships with moneyed interests.

155. *See* POST, *supra* note 130, at 69–76; Ashutosh Bhagwat, *Associational Speech*, 120 YALE L.J. 978, 1023–25 (2011); Steven J. Heyman, *The Conservative-Libertarian Turn in First Amendment Jurisprudence*, 117 W. VA. L. REV. 231, 308–11 (2014).

156. *See* TRIBE & MATZ, *supra* note 153, at 107; Kang, *Campaign Finance, supra* note 109, at 42–43.

*McCutcheon* thus helps to ensure that the major political parties can continue to function, alongside corporations and wealthy individuals, as managers and stabilizing forces in electoral debates.

Some Roberts Court critics accuse the campaign finance decisions of carrying water for conservative interest groups by prioritizing the economic self-interest of corporations and wealthy individuals.[157] Justice Kennedy's slippage into the rhetoric of expressive autonomy in *Citizens United* and Chief Justice Roberts's emphasis on that rhetoric in *McCutcheon* bolster the charge that the majority simply seeks to benefit the wealthy. A simple ideological account of these decisions, though, has only limited explanatory power. Conservatives such as Chief Justice William H. Rehnquist have supported the constitutionality of campaign finance regulation, whereas liberals such as Justice William J. Brennan Jr. have questioned the constitutionality of regulation. A managed speech analysis shows how the Roberts Court's decisions rest not on reflexive ideology but on a cogent, though contestable, First Amendment theory. The Roberts Court majority isn't (or isn't only) giving concentrations of capital pride of place in electoral debate because it wants moneyed interests to make more money. It's giving concentrations of capital pride of place in electoral debate because it believes doing so benefits electoral debate. If corporations' democratically crucial contributions to electoral debate cause them to make more money, that's just a by-product of a well-functioning democracy.

The matter of private money's role in electoral discourse plays out very differently under dynamic diversity than under managed speech. Dynamic diversity's vision of a substantively rich, broadly participatory electoral debate requires ample funding for political speech and counsels healthy skepticism about elected officials' motives in regulating elections. However, when campaign finance laws create space in electoral debate for a greater number and variety of speakers, who bring to the debate a wider range of perspectives and ideas, those laws directly and forcefully advance the central goals of dynamic diversity.

Perhaps surprisingly, a dynamic diversity analysis would converge with the Roberts Court's precise holding on the corporate spending issue in *Citizens United*. Nonprofit corporations that receive minimal funding from business corporations contribute to electoral debate without threatening to dominate it. The best reading of the federal corporate spending ban would, as the parties in the case urged, exempt corporations such as Citizens United. Because wide-ranging electoral debate can't happen without public access to political information, the dynamic diversity analysis would also follow the *Citizens*

157. *See, e.g.*, Gene Nichol, Citizens United *and the Roberts Court's War on Democracy*, 27 GA. ST. U. L. REV. 1007, 1016 (2011) ("What increasingly emerges from the Roberts Court's campaign finance decisions . . . is a foundational conclusion that the United States Constitution, ultimately, secures a power for people of wealth to use their disproportionate economic resources to get their way in our politics.").

*United* Court's reasoning and result in approving contribution disclosure rules. Beyond those modest agreements, dynamic diversity would reverse nearly everything this chapter's decisions hold. The divergence transcends the Roberts Court, reaching back to *Buckley v. Valeo* itself. Notwithstanding due caution about the motives and effects of campaign finance laws, dynamic diversity would consider as potentially valid justifications for those laws not just the anti-corruption rationale that *Buckley* approved but also the equalization rationale that *Buckley* disdained, the anti-distortion rationale of *Austin*, and the time protection rationale proposed in *Randall*. That broader constitutional basis for campaign finance laws would give contribution limits multiple grounds for withstanding legal challenges. The dynamic diversity analysis would accept Vermont's strong evidence in *Randall* that its contribution limits allowed for robust electoral discussion. In *McCutcheon*, dynamic diversity would welcome, rather than condemn, the federal aggregate contribution limits' interference with campaign money's influence over elected officials. The dynamic diversity analysis would uphold contribution limits on both anti-corruption and equalization grounds.

Dynamic diversity's embrace of the alternative justifications for campaign finance laws would dissolve the wall *Buckley* built between contributions and expenditures. Legislatures would gain latitude to impose reasonable spending limits. A dynamic diversity analysis would easily uphold most applications of the corporate spending ban struck down in *Citizens United*, and by extension would affirm the Rehnquist Court's validation in *McConnell* of the McCain-Feingold "electioneering communication" rules, under both the equalization and anti-distortion rationales. As to such candidate spending limits as the FECA rules struck down in *Buckley* and the Vermont rules struck down in *Randall*, dynamic diversity's departure from *Buckley* would require a new judicial inquiry into spending constraints' effects on the public's access to political information. Expenditure limits that let candidates spend enough to enable robust electoral debate could survive review under both the equalization and time protection rationales.

Another group of Roberts Court decisions about money and politics refines and applies the ideas we've seen in *Citizens United* and *McCutcheon*. These remaining decisions, however, present an important contrast with *Citizens United* and *McCutcheon*. Where the cases discussed in this chapter clear the way for more money to enter the electoral process, the other decisions *restrict* electoral money. The next chapter places these last tiles in the mosaic of the Roberts Court's First Amendment.

# CHAPTER 8

# Keeping Money out of Elections

## *Government Leveling and Labor Speech*

Last chapter we saw the Roberts Court invoke the First Amendment to let more money into the electoral process. *Citizens United* struck down limits on electoral spending. *McCutcheon* struck down limits on campaign contributions. Both decisions reflect the Court's managed speech approach to First Amendment law. *Citizens United* promotes corporations and *McCutcheon* promotes wealthy donors and the major political parties as responsible managers to shape and constrain electoral debate.

This chapter considers the Roberts Court's other decisions about political money. Almost all of these cases strike down more government attempts to regulate money in politics. One key factor, however, distinguishes these cases from *Citizens United, McCutcheon,* and the other cases discussed in Chapter 7. All those decisions invoked the First Amendment to stop governments from restricting money in elections. In contrast, all the major decisions in this chapter invoke the First Amendment to stop governments from *increasing* money in elections. Two decisions strike down measures designed to increase funding for candidates who face resource-rich opponents. Another group of decisions undermines the ability of public employee labor unions to amass and spend money in elections. A final decision upholds a direct restriction on campaign fundraising, though only in the narrow, specialized context of state judicial elections.

How can the same Court that so righteously liberated political money in *Citizens United* and *McCutcheon* turn around and restrict political money in these other settings? The contrast turns on managed speech reasoning about how different sorts of institutions contribute to the electoral process. This chapter's decisions reinforce *Citizens United* and *McCutcheon* by further subjecting electoral debates to wealthy speakers' control, muting less wealthy speakers' voices, and advancing political stability. Last chapter's decisions promoted responsible management of electoral debate and marginalized political dissent by clearing paths for corporations and wealthy donors to fund the electoral process. This chapter's decisions pursue those same goals by blocking paths for government and union money to fund the process. Both lines of decisions aspire to a political debate that doesn't threaten the stable continuation of existing social and political power arrangements.

## PAYING PETER TO ROB PAUL?

Before *Citizens United* confronted the central "issue advertising" provisions of the McCain-Feingold campaign finance law, the Roberts Court in ***Davis v. Federal Election Commission*** **(2008)**[1] addressed a different part of that law: the so-called "millionaire's amendment."[2] *Buckley v. Valeo*[3] extended First Amendment protection to three different types of electoral spending: by campaigns, by independent advocates (the sort of spending at issue in *Citizens United*), and by self-financing candidates. The question how to handle self-financers—wealthy candidates who can draw on vast personal fortunes to outspend their opponents—continued to vex policymakers after *Buckley*. Self-financing raises the danger that wealthy individuals can dominate electoral debates and effectively buy public offices.

The McCain-Feingold millionaire's amendment addressed the self-financing concern by relaxing federal campaign finance limits for self-financing candidates' opponents. Whenever a candidate spent $350,000 more in personal funds than an opponent, contributors could give the candidate's opponent up to three times the amount normally permitted by federal law, without regard to the federal aggregate limits (later struck down in *McCutcheon*). The opponent's party could also ignore federal limits on expenditures coordinated with the opponent's campaign, and the amendment imposed special disclosure requirements on self-financing candidates. The amendment sought to counter the effect of self-financing by making more and larger contributions available to candidates whose opponents self-financed. Empirical analysis suggests the millionaire's amendment had little practical effect in the elections it governed.[4]

1. 554 U.S. 724 (2008). Alito (majority) (with Roberts, Scalia, Kennedy, Thomas; with Stevens, Souter, Ginsburg, Breyer (in part)). Stevens (concurring in part and dissenting in part) (with Souter, Ginsburg, Breyer (in part)). Ginsburg (concurring in part and dissenting in part) (with Breyer).

2. Section 319(a) of the Bipartisan Campaign Reform Act of 2002, 52 U.S.C. § 30117(a) (2002) (formerly cited as 2 U.S.C. § 441a-1(a)).

3. 424 U.S. 1 (1976).

4. *See* Richard Briffault, Davis v. FEC: *The Roberts Court's Continuing Attack on Campaign Finance Reform*, 44 TULSA L. REV. 475, 480–82 (2009).

*Davis* strikes down the millionaire's amendment. After unanimously resolving some jurisdictional questions, the justices split sharply over the substance of the law. Justice Alito, writing for the Court's five conservatives, begins with a potentially interesting but ambiguous concession: "If [the amendment] simply raised the contribution limits for all candidates, Davis' argument would plainly fail."[5] That statement could mean either of two things. First, Justice Alito could mean that Congress may raise contribution limits across the board without causing a First Amendment problem. That meaning would be so trivial as to render the statement almost pointless. Second, he could mean that Congress may, in only those races that include heavily self-financing candidates, raise contribution limits for all candidates without causing a First Amendment problem. That meaning, as we'll see, clashes with other Roberts Court campaign finance principles.

Justice Alito finds that the millionaire's amendment burdens self-financing candidates' First Amendment rights in two ways. First, the amendment does not, in any sense, raise contribution limits "for all candidates"; rather, it subjects opposing candidates to different, unequal contribution limits (and coordinated party spending limits and disclosure requirements). It thus discriminates among candidates.[6] Second, the amendment "imposes an unprecedented penalty on any candidate who robustly exercises [the] First Amendment right [to self-finance]."[7] Justice Alito acknowledges that *Buckley* upheld the federal voluntary public financing system for presidential elections, but he distinguishes that system because it gives candidates the choice to forgo public funding and spend private money without any adverse consequence.[8] He describes the freedom to spend unlimited personal funds in pursuit of elected office as a "fundamental . . . right."[9]

Because Justice Alito finds that the millionaire's amendment burdens First Amendment rights, he subjects the law to strict scrutiny. Largely tracking the *Buckley* analysis of expenditure limits, he finds that the amendment does not promote any compelling government interest. Interestingly, Justice Alito ignores the charge, advanced by election law scholars, that Congress enacted the millionaire's amendment to protect incumbents' position against wealthy challengers.[10] He declares that the interest in avoiding actual or apparent corruption, which *Buckley* found to justify contribution limits, doesn't matter for

5. *Davis,* 554 U.S. at 737.
6. *See id.* at 738.
7. *Id.* at 739.
8. *See id.* at 739–40.
9. *Id.* at 738.
10. *See* Steven Ansolabehere, Arizona Free Enterprise v. Bennett *and the Problem of Campaign Finance,* 2011 Sup. Ct. Rev. 39, 74; Briffault, *supra* note 4, at 475; Samuel Isaacharoff, *On Political Corruption,* 124 Harv. L. Rev. 118, 135 (2010); Nathaniel Persily, *Fig Leaves and Tea Leaves in the Supreme Court's Recent Election Law Decisions,* 2008 Sup. Ct. Rev. 89, 107.

self-financers because "reliance on personal funds *reduces* corruption."[11] He states that the interest in "leveling the electoral playing field" is, as the Court held in *Buckley* (and later *Citizens United* and *McCutcheon*), flatly illegitimate. He insists that money should function in elections just like any other resource, such as celebrity or family ties. Efforts to limit private money's influence on politics, Justice Alito concludes, "use the election laws to influence the voters' choices."[12]

In dissent, Justice Stevens makes two arguments, one for himself alone and the other for all four liberal justices. On his own he calls, as in his *Citizens United* dissent, for the Court to overrule the *Buckley* First Amendment constraint on expenditure limits.[13] For all the liberals, he argues that, notwithstanding the *Buckley* strictures on expenditure limits, the millionaire's amendment should pass muster because it appropriately aimed to "reduc[e] the importance of wealth as a criterion for public office" and "counter[] the perception that seats in the United States Congress are available for purchase by the wealthiest bidder[.]"[14] Although he thinks those goals would justify the burden the majority claims the millionaire's amendment placed on First Amendment rights, Justice Stevens maintains the amendment in no way silenced self-financing candidates. In fact, the amendment "actually advances [the First Amendment's] core principles" by helping all candidates get their messages to voters.[15]

Several years after *Davis,* the Court confronted a state's somewhat similar attempt to reduce the importance of wealth in politics. Arizona, like many states, offers candidates for state office voluntary public financing. A candidate may accept public funds if she agrees to spending limits. Arizona added to its public funding law a "matching funds" provision.[16] Under that provision, if a privately funded candidate (one who had declined public funding) got more contributions or spent more of her own money than the public funding allotment, or if independent spenders spent above the public funding allotment to support her, the state gave extra funds to all publicly funded candidates in the race, topping out at about twice the original public funding allotment. The Arizona matching funds law resembled the federal millionaire's amendment from *Davis* in that both laws created legal triggers for lesser-financed candidates to get more money. The Arizona law differed from the millionaire's

11. *Davis,* 554 U.S. at 740–41.

12. *Id.* at 742.

13. *See id.* at 750–52 (Stevens, J., concurring in part and dissenting in part). Justice Ginsburg expressly declines to join Justice Stevens on this point because the parties hadn't briefed the issue. *See id.* at 758 (Ginsburg, J., concurring in part and dissenting in part).

14. *Id.* at 752–53 (Stevens, J., concurring in part and dissenting in part).

15. *Id.* at 753–54 (Stevens, J., concurring in part and dissenting in part).

16. ARIZ. REV. STAT. §§ 16–952(A), (B), (C)(4)–(5) (2007).

amendment in that any private spending, not just self-financing, triggered the Arizona law, and the Arizona law provided funds directly rather than permitting extra fundraising.

In ***Arizona Free Enterprise Club's Freedom Club PAC v. Bennett* (2011),**[17] the Roberts Court by a 5-4 vote struck down Arizona's matching funds law. Chief Justice Roberts, writing for the conservative majority, declares that "the logic of *Davis* largely controls our approach to this action."[18] In fact, the chief justice argues, the Arizona law placed a greater burden on First Amendment rights than the federal millionaire's amendment had, because the Arizona scheme gave government funding directly to candidates with less private funding, potentially benefited multiple opponents of the privately funded candidate, and countered not just the privately funded candidate's own spending but also independent spending on the candidate's behalf. Including independent spending as a trigger for matching funds both placed the trigger beyond privately funded candidates' control, because independent spenders can't lawfully coordinate with candidates, and burdened not just the candidates' First Amendment rights but also the rights of the independent spenders.[19] The core problem, though, remains the government's helping underfinanced candidates in response to private spending. "The direct result of the speech of privately financed candidates and independent expenditure groups is a state-provided monetary subsidy to a political rival."[20]

Having found that Arizona's matching funds law burdens First Amendment rights, Chief Justice Roberts subjects the law to strict scrutiny. Despite Arizona's denials, he first presumes that Arizona meant for its law to equalize the financial resources of opposing candidates. That state interest, he declares, is flatly illegitimate.[21] He then turns to Arizona's professed justification: that the matching funds scheme helps deter actual and apparent political corruption. Arizona, well aware of the Court's past holdings that contribution limits suffice to prevent corruption (see *McCutcheon*), that self-financing actually reduces the danger of corruption (see *Davis*), and that independent expenditures have no relevance for corruption (see *Citizens United*), floated a different sort of anti-corruption argument. Public financing of elections, claimed Arizona, discouraged corruption and concerns about corruption, and the matching funds system encouraged candidates to accept public financing.

17. 564 U.S. 721 (2011). Roberts (majority) (with Scalia, Kennedy, Thomas, Alito); Kagan (dissent) (with Ginsburg, Breyer, Sotomayor).

18. *Id.* at 736.

19. *See id.* at 736–40 & n.6.

20. *Id.* at 723.

21. *See id.* at 748–50. Justice Kagan, in dissent, sharply criticizes the chief justice for questioning the sincerity of Arizona's justification and for obscuring the decisive inquiry whether some constitutionally permissible interest supports the law. *See id.* at 780–84 (Kagan, J., dissenting).

The chief justice rejects the claim out of hand. Arizona's law "is unduly burdensome and not sufficiently justified," and Arizona's reasoning would require the Court to permit even stronger government incentives to accept public financing, such as quintuple matching funds or fines for refusing public money.[22]

Justice Kagan wrote the *Arizona Free Enterprise* dissent for the four liberals, her first free speech opinion after she took Justice Stevens's seat on the Court. She develops an idea Justice Stevens introduced in *Davis:* that government efforts to help underfinanced candidates actually *advance* First Amendment values by increasing the electoral information available to the public. "The First Amendment's core purpose," Justice Kagan declares, "is to foster a healthy, vibrant political system full of robust discussion and debate."[23] Arizona's matching funds system in no way limits that discussion and debate but rather "subsidizes and so produces *more* political speech."[24] The system optimizes how much scarce public money a state spends on campaign subsidies, "finding the sweet-spot"[25] by funding however much electoral information private funding can't or won't deliver. Crucially, Justice Kagan points out, "[n]o one can claim that Arizona's law discriminates against particular ideas," which would be the only viable basis for striking down a speech subsidy.[26] The *Davis* majority, in her view, directly contradicts the First Amendment by decreasing rather than increasing the volume of electoral speech.

Justice Kagan calls the *Arizona Free Enterprise* majority's rejection of Arizona's matching funds law a broad assault on government efforts to remedy market deficits in elections. "[W]hat [the law's challengers] demand," Justice Kagan explains, "is essentially a right to quash others' speech through the prohibition of a (universally available) subsidy program. [The challengers] are able to convey their ideas without public financing—and they would prefer the field to themselves, so that they can speak free from response."[27] Because Arizona's law fosters more speech, Justice Kagan concludes that it cannot possibly burden speech. Even if a burden existed, however, she would find that Arizona's anti-corruption argument justified the matching funds law. The majority, she chides, "dismisses, but does not actually answer the state's [anti-corruption] contention."[28]

Chief Justice Roberts responds to Justice Kagan's "more speech" defense of the Arizona law by claiming that matching funds "reduc[e] the speech of privately financed candidates."[29] That might be an empirical claim that matching

22. *Id.* at 753.
23. *Id.* at 757 (Kagan, J., dissenting).
24. *Id.* at 763 (Kagan, J., dissenting).
25. *Id.* at 779 (Kagan, J., dissenting).
26. *Id.* at 765 (Kagan, J., dissenting).
27. *Id.* at 766 (Kagan, J., dissenting).
28. *Id.* at 780 (Kagan, J., dissenting).
29. *Id.* at 741.

funds create incentives that actually cause privately funded candidates and independent spenders to fund less electoral speech. Alternatively, it might be a theoretical claim that matching funds reduce the quality or value of privately funded candidates' and independent spenders' speech. The chief justice starts out in empirical mode. He cites examples in the record to argue that Arizona's matching funds provision deterred private candidates and independent advocates from spending.[30] Justice Kagan, however, cites evidence that private electoral spending actually grew under Arizona's matching funds regime.[31] Chief Justice Roberts can only reply that "it is never easy to prove a negative" and that "the burden imposed by the matching funds provision is evident and inherent in the choice that confronts privately financed candidates and independent expenditure groups." Thus, "we do not need empirical evidence[.]"[32] The majority's rejection of empirical grounds for Arizona's matching funds law echoes its refusal in *Citizens United* and *McCutcheon* to credit the government's empirical justifications for campaign finance regulations.

Chief Justice Roberts shifts into theoretical mode. Building on Justice Alito's *Davis* opinion, the chief justice posits that, even if Arizona's matching fund law increased speech in the aggregate, it impermissibly made the privately financed candidate's speech "less effective." He elaborates: "[A]n advertisement supporting the election of a candidate that goes without a response is often more effective than an advertisement that is directly controverted."[33] Chief Justice Roberts doesn't just believe the First Amendment lets candidates spend as much money as they have, or can raise, to speak. He also believes the First Amendment bars government from subsidizing electoral speech in ways that devalue private electoral spending. That idea channels *Citizens United,* whose rejection of PACs as a constitutionally sufficient alternative to direct corporate spending extended the First Amendment to protect not just the freedom but the effectiveness of electoral speech. *Davis* and *Arizona Free Enterprise,* though, stretch First Amendment protection even further. *Citizens United* barred the government from making wealthy speakers choose an arguably more cumbersome way of spending their money on speech. *Davis* and *Arizona Free Enterprise* bar the government from adopting policies that may diminish the persuasive force of market-funded speech.

The chief justice tries to narrow his reasoning by emphasizing that Arizona provided matching funds "in direct response to the political speech of another,

30. *See id.* at 744.

31. *See id.* at 764 n.2 (Kagan, J., dissenting) (citing Arizona statistics on substantially increased candidate and independent spending after the matching funds law took effect); *see also id.* at 769 n.6 (challenging the sparse evidence in the record that matching funds deterred any private spending).

32. *Id.* at 746 (internal quotation marks and citation omitted).

33. *Id.* at 747 (internal quotation marks and citation omitted).

to allow the recipient to counter that speech."[34] Arizona, though, didn't stack the deck against any particular candidate, party, or ideology. Instead, Arizona promoted responsive speech wherever the market wouldn't pay for it. Justice Kagan posits that subsidies have greater First Amendment value when they promote responsive speech.[35] In any event, all government electoral subsidies and allowances for fundraising foster competitive speech that otherwise wouldn't happen. We saw in Part II's discussion of speech in government preserves that the Roberts Court does little to help marginal or underfinanced speakers access speech resources. *Davis* and *Arizona Free Enterprise* deepen that tendency by holding that the First Amendment forbids the government from interfering with market distributions of electoral funding. Just as the drug detailing case *IMS Health* (Chapter 2) protected drug manufacturers' ability to profit from their speech without regulatory burdens, *Davis* and *Arizona Free Enterprise* protect the capacity of private wealth to influence electoral debate without opposition.

In *Arizona Free Enterprise,* as in *McCutcheon,* Chief Justice Roberts focuses his First Amendment analysis far less on the imperatives of democracy than on wealthy speakers' autonomy. The chief justice asserts the central importance of electoral speech in First Amendment law. "'Leveling the playing field' can sound like a good thing," he lectures. "But in a democracy, campaigning for office is not a game. It is a critically important form of speech."[36] His broader reasoning, however, treats electoral speech as just another market resource. When free speech theorists celebrate the distinctive constitutional value of political speech, they usually emphasize the practical importance for our democratic system of a well-informed electorate.[37] *Arizona Free Enterprise* doesn't rely on that idea. Quite the contrary: Chief Justice Roberts holds that the First Amendment mandates a *less-informed* electorate whenever fuller information, funded by government, would reduce the persuasive force of a privately financed candidate's speech.[38] That holding doesn't appeal to democratic values. It appeals only to an individual's autonomous right to spend money for speech. "When it comes to protected speech," the chief justice strikingly declares, "the speaker is sovereign."[39] The people, by that logic, are subordinate.

34. *Id.* at 743.

35. *See id.* at 765 n.3 (Kagan, J., dissenting).

36. *Id.* at 750; *see also id.* at 734.

37. *See* ALEXANDER MEIKLEJOHN, POLITICAL FREEDOM: THE CONSTITUTIONAL POWERS OF THE PEOPLE (1960).

38. Likewise, these decisions belie the emphasis of a Roberts Court plurality in *Randall v. Sorrell* (Chapter 7) on electoral competition as a reason to strike down Vermont's campaign contribution and expenditure limits. *See* Briffault, *supra* note 4, at 497; Persily, *supra* note 10, at 106–08.

39. *Arizona Free Enterprise*, 564 U.S. at 754.

The bar that *Davis* and *Arizona Free Enterprise* erect against tailoring public campaign funding to the financial contours of particular elections undermines the government's ability to mount an effective scheme of public financing.[40] As Justice Kagan's dissent emphasizes, public financing without a tailoring mechanism risks either a lack of candidate interest if the lump sum is too small or a waste of public funds if the lump sum is too large. Scholars have proposed a fix for this problem that they contend comports with *Davis* and *Arizona Free Enterprise:* multiplied matching funds for small contributions.[41] The state would pay every candidate a multiple (say, five times) of every private contribution the candidate raised, up to a relatively low ceiling per contribution (say, $200). This "low-threshold matching" would encourage small donors to participate in electoral funding and would reward candidates who appeal to a broad donor base. Every candidate would have equal access to matching funds, and the system would reward, rather than discourage, private funding. Rewarding a broad base of small contributions would help ameliorate legislators' reliance on a small class of major donors, which can lead to policies that benefit that small class rather than the public at large.[42]

Whatever the policy virtues of low-threshold matching, I think its advocates underestimate the breadth of the Court's prohibition in *Davis* and *Arizona Free Enterprise.* These decisions reject the government's interests in promoting electoral competition and increasing voter information as justifications for laws that limit the expressive power of private money, even if the laws promote speech rather than restrict it.[43] Low-threshold matching would distort private financing of elections, as surely as Arizona's tailoring statute did, by favoring small contributions over large ones and by marginally incentivizing retail politics over appeals to larger donors. As the *McCutcheon* discussion last chapter showed, the Roberts Court views elected officials' service to market concentrations of wealth not as a bug of campaign finance but as a feature.

40. *See* Vikram D. Amar & Alan Brownstein, *The Voracious First Amendment:* Alvarez *and* Knox *in the Context of 2012 and Beyond*, 46 LOY. L.A. L. REV. 491, 526 (2013); Richard Briffault, *The Future of Public Funding*, 49 WILLAMETTE L. REV. 521, 535 (2013); Spencer Overton, *Matching Political Contributions*, 96 MINN. L. REV. 1694, 1695 (2012).
41. *See* Briffault, *supra* note 40, at 538; Isaacharoff, *supra* note 10, at 135–38; Overton, *supra* note 40, at 1725–30.
42. *See* LAWRENCE LESSIG, REPUBLIC, LOST: HOW MONEY CORRUPTS CONGRESS—AND A PLAN TO STOP IT (2011); Isaacharoff, *supra* note 10, at 126–30; Timothy K. Kuhner, *Consumer Sovereignty Trumps Popular Sovereignty: The Economic Explanation for* Arizona Free Enterprise v. Bennett, 46 IND. L. REV. 603, 638–39 (2013); Spencer Overton, *The Donor Class: Campaign Finance, Democracy, and Participation*, 153 U. PA. L. REV. 73 (2004); Nicholas O. Stephanopoulos, *Aligning Campaign Finance Law*, 101 VA. L. REV. 1425 (2015).
43. *See* Ansolabehere, *supra* note 10, at 63–69; Briffault, *supra* note 4, at 486–90; Kuhner, *supra* note 42, at 618–22.

In fact, the breadth of the chief justice's reasoning in *Arizona Free Enterprise* appears to threaten all public financing of campaigns, including basic lump sum grants. A candidate who accepts public funds needs those funds to overcome a financial disadvantage against a privately financed opponent. *Davis* and *Arizona Free Enterprise* cast the underfinanced candidate's disadvantage as the privately financed candidate's First Amendment entitlement.[44] Chief Justice Roberts might appear to validate lump sum public financing when he suggests in *Arizona Free Enterprise* that the state could have simply given publicly financed candidates an initial lump sum that included the full amount of potential matching funds.[45] All he concedes, though, is that the challengers didn't *claim* that hypothetical alternative would violate the First Amendment. He never holds or declares that it actually wouldn't. Likewise, he acknowledges the Court's past constitutional approval of public financing, but he never reaffirms that approval.[46] As in *McCutcheon,* the chief justice notes prior-approved campaign finance rules without blessing them, even as he opens the door to striking them down.

*Davis* and *Arizona Free Enterprise,* taken to their logical conclusion, threaten any government action that diminishes the economic market's power to drive electoral speech. When a lesser-funded candidate holds a campaign rally in a public park, or a public broadcast station sponsors a televised candidate debate, the government dampens the power of private electoral money in a manner akin to what the chief justice condemns. Justice Alito in *Davis* cites the *Buckley* admonition against "restrict[ing] the speech of some elements of our society in order to enhance the relative voices of others"[47] to doom a law that restricted no speech but merely diminished the expressive potency of private money. This reasoning overwhelms Justice Alito's ambiguous suggestion in *Davis* that Congress could have dealt with concerns about self-financing by increasing all candidates' contribution limits in races that feature self-financing candidates. Such a scheme, according to both Chief Justice Roberts and Justice Alito himself, would impermissibly reduce the expressive value of the self-financing candidate's personal wealth.

By entrenching in First Amendment law a mandate for private ordering of electoral speech, *Davis* and *Arizona Free Enterprise* sing in harmony with

44. Timothy Kuhner suggests lump sum public financing systems might survive First Amendment review after *Arizona Free Enterprise* because they "do not remove the incentive for private investment." Kuhner, *supra* note 42, at 628. My analysis here, however, suggests that distinction would make an insufficient constitutional difference to the Roberts Court.

45. *See* Ariz. Free Enter. Club's Freedom Club PAC v. Bennett, 564 U.S. 721, 746–47 (2011)

46. *See id.* at 751–52.

47. Buckley v. Valeo, 424 U.S. 1, 48–49 (1976) (*quoted in* Davis v. FEC, 554 U.S. 724, 741–42 (2008)).

*Citizens United* and *McCutcheon*. Justice Kennedy's majority opinion in *Citizens United* limits the anti-corruption justification for campaign finance laws to quid pro quo corruption precisely because he believes the First Amendment protects the ability of moneyed interests to influence public policy through electoral spending. Chief Justice Roberts's majority opinion in *McCutcheon* follows suit, extending First Amendment protection to wealthy individuals' ability to influence electoral outcomes through campaign contributions.

*Davis* and *Arizona Free Enterprise* deepen the managed speech account of the Roberts Court's campaign finance jurisprudence. These decisions give people and institutions that dominate the economic marketplace, and therefore have a strong interest in preserving existing arrangements of social and political power, managerial authority over a crucial field of public discussion. The Court's privileging of private wealth diminishes opportunities for lesser-funded speakers, who more likely favor social and political change, to contribute effectively to electoral debate. These moves aim to ensure that public discussion around elections will serve the interest of "a financially conservative, socio-economic elite"[48] in maintaining social and political stability.

## MANAGING LABOR SPEECH

Measured by sheer number of decisions, the Roberts Court's single deepest First Amendment obsession has concerned a legally obscure but practically important issue about labor unions and political money. Recall from Chapter 5, which dealt with government-subsidized speech, that the First Amendment bars the government from *compelling* people to speak contrary to their beliefs. Thus, in the *Open Society* case, the Court held that the government could not make nongovernmental organizations condemn sex work as a condition of government funding. The decisions in this section deal with a compelled speech twist on money in politics: how the First Amendment protects non-union government workers from labor contracts that require them to support unions financially.

Union members' dues pay for unions' expressive activities, including both representational activities such as collective bargaining and political activities such as canvassing for political candidates. Federal law lets unions and employers in the private sector agree to *agency shop* arrangements, under which workers who decline to join unions must pay *agency fees* in lieu of union dues.[49] (States may bar this practice by passing so-called "right-to-work" laws.)

48. Kuhner, *supra* note 42, at 640.

49. The term "agency fee" usually appears in discussions of private sector agency shop contracts, whereas the term "fair share fee" more commonly describes the same sort of fee in the public sector. The blanket term "union security provision" can also

Many states let unions that represent state government employees negotiate agency shop contracts. The Supreme Court long ago recognized that agency shop contracts promote labor peace. Agency shop contracts encourage workers to designate unions as their exclusive bargaining representatives.[50] Agency shop contracts also compensate unions for their legal obligation to represent not just members but also non-members in collective bargaining, preventing non-members from free riding on beneficial union activities.[51]

At the same time, the Court has long viewed agency fees as a form of compelled speech. For decades the justices have worried that requiring nonunion workers to fund union speech that the non-members oppose violates their First Amendment rights. The Court has avoided the potential First Amendment problem with private sector agency fees by interpreting the relevant federal labor laws to authorize the use of agency fees only to pay for unions' collective bargaining (which the cases have come to call *chargeable expenses*), not their political advocacy (*nonchargeable expenses*).[52] As to agency fees for state government workers, the 1977 Burger Court decision *Abood v. Detroit Board of Education*[53] held that the First Amendment constrains unions' uses of public sector agency fees in the same way the Court's interpretations of the federal labor laws constrain unions' uses of private sector agency fees. A subsequent Burger Court decision, *Chicago Teachers Union v. Hudson,*[54] set out procedures for implementing *Abood.* The *Abood* doctrine's distinction between collective bargaining and political advocacy protects nonunion workers from having to fund political speech with which the workers disagree. The distinction thus constrains unions' ability to finance that same speech.

Why should the First Amendment even apply to the relationship between unions and workers? Where is the state action that grounds the claim of a constitutional right? A government employer is a state actor.[55] When a public employment contract authorizes agency fees pursuant to state law, the

encompass these fees. The Roberts Court cases under discussion deal with public sector labor contracts. Nonetheless, this Court—perhaps conscious that the term "fair share fee" might cast a sympathetic light on unions—generally uses the term "agency fee." My discussion follows that form.

50. *See, e.g.*, Ry. Emps. Dep't v. Hanson, 351 U.S. 225, 233 (1956).

51. *See* Int'l Ass'n of Machinists v. Street, 367 U.S. 740, 760–61 (1961).

52. *See* Commc'ns Workers of Am. v. Beck, 487 U.S. 735 (1988) (interpreting the National Labor Relations Act (NLRA)); *Street,* 367 U.S. 740 (interpreting the Railway Labor Act (RLA)).

53. 431 U.S. 209 (1977).

54. 475 U.S. 292 (1986).

55. As to private sector agency fees, the Supreme Court has defused these questions by using statutory interpretation, not the First Amendment, to protect nonunion workers from compelled speech. Even so, the First Amendment looms over the Court's statutory constructions. The Court in *Hanson* found state action as to the RLA because the RLA preempts state labor laws. *See Hanson,* 351 U.S. at 231–32. That finding of state action undergirds the Court's interpretation of the RLA in *Street,* an interpretation the *Street* Court described as necessary to avoid the First Amendment issue. *See*

government is, in a sense, making nonunion workers pay for unions' speech. Moreover, public employers may have stronger incentives than private employers to agree to agency shop contracts, because unions can exert political pressure against public employers. On the other hand, government employers don't impose agency shop contracts unilaterally or voluntarily. Rather, they acquiesce in those contracts as a bargaining concession to unions. Still, courts have found state action in public sector agency shop contracts.

The Roberts Court has decided five cases that relate directly or indirectly to the *Abood* doctrine. The agency fee scenario might appear to present a First Amendment conflict between public employee unions' interest in mounting effective political advocacy and nonunion workers' interest in not supporting political speech they oppose.[56] Indeed, the Supreme Court long ago acknowledged that conflict, recognizing that "the [union] majority also has an interest in stating its views without being silenced by the dissenters."[57] The Roberts Court, however, has made clear that the unions have no First Amendment interest in agency fees, whereas nonunion workers have a profound First Amendment interest in avoiding them. Union advocates have criticized the key *Abood* distinction between chargeable and nonchargeable union activities as unduly formalistic, because unions coordinate bargaining and political engagement to promote workers' interests.[58] The Roberts Court inverts that critique to attack even the limited, non-political use *Abood* permits for agency fees.

*Street*, 367 U.S. at 749. Later, after invoking the First Amendment to constrain public sector agency fees in *Abood*, the Court applied the First Amendment to RLA agency fees. *See* Ellis v. Bhd. of Ry., Airline, & Steamship Clerks, 466 U.S. 435 (1984). Whatever the merits of the Court's state action reasoning in the RLA context, the NLRA *doesn't* preempt state labor laws. Yet the Court in *Beck*, without any distinct state action analysis, extended the reasoning of *Street* to the NLRA. *See Beck*, 487 U.S. at 745. For recent discussions of this line of cases, including critiques of the Court's state action analysis, see Catherine L. Fisk & Erwin Chemerinsky, *Political Speech and Association Rights after* Knox v. SEIU, Local 1000, 98 CORNELL L. REV. 1023, 1029–40 (2013); William B. Gould IV, *Organized Labor, the Supreme Court, and* Harris v. Quinn: *Déjà Vu All over Again?*, 2014 SUP. CT. REV. 133, 138–42; Benjamin I. Sachs, *Unions, Corporations, and Political Opt-Out Rights after* Citizens United, 112 COLUM. L. REV. 800, 813–17 (2012); *see also* Charlotte Garden, *Citizens, United and* Citizens United: *The Future of Labor Speech Rights?*, 53 WM. & MARY L. REV. 1, 32–39 (2011).

56. *See* Fisk & Chemerinsky, *supra* note 55, at 1063–64; Garden, *supra* note 55, at 39–46; Ciara Torres-Spelliscy, *Taking Opt-In Rights Seriously: What* Knox v. SEIU *Could Mean for Post-*Citizens United *Shareholder Rights*, 74 MONT. L. REV. 101, 114 (2013); *see also* Marion G. Crain & John D. Inazu, *Re-assembling Labor*, 2015 U. ILL. L. REV. 1791 (situating unions' speech in the First Amendment right of assembly).

57. *Street*, 367 U.S. at 773.

58. Justice Frankfurter made this point in dissent in *Street*. *See id.* at 814–15 (Frankfurter, J., dissenting). Scholars continue to press it. *See* Fisk & Chemerinsky, *supra* note 55, at 1070–71 n.247; Garden, *supra* note 55, at 38–39; Gould, *supra* note 55, at 148–49; Sachs, *supra* note 55, at 805 n.22.

Illustrating the legal truism that procedure matters more than substance, unions scored their one, very minor *Abood*-related Roberts Court victory in a case that deals with the substantive distinction between chargeable and non-chargeable expenses rather than the procedures for enforcing that distinction. ***Locke v. Karass* (2009)**[59] presented the question whether a public employee union may use agency fees from a given bargaining unit to help fund national litigation that does not directly benefit workers in that bargaining unit. Justice Breyer's opinion for a unanimous Court holds that the union may use the fees for national litigation expenses if the litigation concerns chargeable (that is, non-political) activities and if workers in all bargaining units have a reciprocal entitlement to the national union's support for their chargeable litigation expenses.[60] Justice Alito, joined by Chief Justice Roberts and Justice Scalia, wrote a concurrence to make clear that the Court's decision "does not reach the question what 'reciprocity' means."[61] If a future case imposed a strict definition of "reciprocal," unions might have trouble funding even non-political litigation.

In contrast to *Locke,* unions have lost all four of the Roberts Court's labor speech cases that consider procedural rules about agency fees or union dues. The earliest decision, ***Davenport v. Washington Education Association* (2007),**[62] presented a First Amendment claim not from nonunion workers but from a union. Washington lets public employee unions collect agency fees from nonunion workers equivalent to a member's full (chargeable and nonchargeable) union dues. Under *Abood* and *Hudson,* the union must give non-members an opportunity to avoid paying the nonchargeable portion of the fee. *Hudson* doesn't specify whether the union may require a non-member to *opt out* of paying for nonchargeable expenses or must convince the non-member to *opt in* before collecting the nonchargeable portion of the fee. Unions, of course, strongly prefer the opt-out system. Under that system, any non-member who doesn't object to paying for nonchargeable expenses pays the full equivalent of union dues. The default position favors the union. Washington voters adopted an opt-in system, barring public employee unions from spending non-members' agency fees on nonchargeable expenses unless the union first gets the non-member's affirmative authorization.[63] The Washington Education Association (WEA) challenged the opt-in rule as a violation of the union's First Amendment expressive and associational rights.

59. 555 U.S. 207 (2009). Breyer (majority) (unanimous); Alito (with Roberts, Scalia) (concurring).

60. *See id.* at 217–18.

61. *Id.* at 221 (Alito, J., concurring).

62. 551 U.S. 177 (2007). Scalia (majority) (with Stevens, Kennedy, Souter, Thomas, Ginsburg); Breyer (concurring in part and concurring in the judgment) (with Roberts, Alito).

63. WASH. REV. CODE § 42.17.760 (1993).

*Davenport* holds that unions have no First Amendment interest in agency fees. The WEA contended that *Abood* had balanced the First Amendment rights of unions and nonunion workers. That balance, the WEA maintained, barred the government from making a union get opt-in agreements before collecting the nonchargeable portion of an agency fee. Justice Scalia, writing for a unanimous Court, rejects the WEA's claim, because "unions have no constitutional entitlement to the fees of nonmember-employees."[64] *Abood* and *Hudson,* he declares, did not balance conflicting First Amendment interests. Rather, those decisions balanced nonunion public workers' First Amendment rights against the government's regulatory interest in agency shop contracts' benefits for labor relations. In denying the presence of a conflict between expressive interests, the *Davenport* Court echoes numerous other Roberts Court decisions we've encountered, including the copyright extension case *Golan v. Holder* (Chapter 2) and virtually all the other electoral speech cases discussed in this and the last two chapters. Justice Scalia also recalls the restrictive categorical speech cases (Chapter 1), the institutional subject cases (Chapter 3), and the "government speech" cases (Chapter 4) by completely removing public employee unions' interest in agency fees from First Amendment protection.

Justice Scalia rejects an alternative argument through which the WEA connected the agency fee problem to campaign finance law.[65] The union contended that Washington's opt-in system improperly barred the union from spending its money on political action. Justice Scalia dismisses this argument because the union has no constitutional entitlement to non-members' agency fees. Those fees simply reflect "the union's extraordinary *state* entitlement to acquire and spend *other people's* money."[66] Justice Scalia doesn't just subsume the union's speech interest within the government's regulatory interest; he converts the union's contractual entitlement to fees from a bargained-for government concession into a matter, entirely, of "extraordinary" government largesse. Washington tempered this largesse "to protect the integrity of the election process . . . which the voters evidently thought was being impaired by the infusion of money extracted from nonmembers of unions without their consent."[67] That inference, for which Justice Scalia cites no support, casts unions as rogue interlopers in electoral debate. It resonates with the "anti-distortion" rationale for corporate spending limits that the Roberts Court rejected in *Citizens United* (Chapter 7). Even as *Citizens United* barred the government from doing anything to keep corporate profits out of elections,

64. *Davenport,* 551 U.S. at 185.

65. Justice Breyer, joined by Chief Justice Roberts and Justice Alito, declines to join this part of the majority opinion, because he maintains the union did not properly place this argument before the Court. *See id.* at 192 (Breyer, J., concurring in part and concurring in the judgment).

66. *Id.* at 187 (footnote omitted).

67. *Id.* at 189.

*Davenport* lets the government act forcefully to keep unions' agency fees out of elections.

The WEA contended that the opt-in system discriminated against the union's speech. Justice Scalia dodges that claim by asserting that, when Washington voters adopted an opt-in system, they didn't wield regulatory power at all. Rather, they acted in a manner analogous to government management of a nonpublic forum or government subsidization of speech.[68] His reasoning recognizes the union as a speaker, but only a speaker such as the student group that lost its public forum case in *Christian Legal Society* (Chapter 4) or the law schools who lost their subsidy case in *FAIR* (Chapter 5): a subject in a government preserve. Justice Scalia assures us that here "no suppression of ideas is afoot, since the union remains as free as any other entity to participate in the electoral process with all available funds other than the state-coerced agency fees lacking affirmative permission."[69] That logic evokes the argument that corporations can participate fully in electoral debates through PACs, an argument *Citizens United* flatly rejected.

*Davenport* didn't divide the Court along ideological lines, but it foreshadows the more divisive battles to come. Justice Scalia's conception of agency fees as "state-coerced" and an "extraordinary state entitlement" suggests that *Abood* created an anomalous, suspect exception to First Amendment principles. We'll soon see the conservative justices make that suggestion a battle cry. Likewise, Justice Scalia's conflation of public employee unions with government employers carries a virus that will threaten the *Abood* doctrine's survival. If unions really have no cognizable speech interest in agency fees, and if we can really ascribe unions' bargaining for agency fees to government largesse, then *Abood* becomes easier to read as an unjust license for unions to compel nonunion workers' speech. That's exactly how the conservative majority will portray *Abood* from here on. The other agency fee decisions will follow *Davenport* in diminishing unions' capacity to participate in electoral debates.

***Ysursa v. Pocatello Education Association* (2009)**[70] begins to reveal the Court's fault lines on unions' political speech. This case, like *Davenport,* deals with how unions may collect funds from workers. *Ysursa,* though, concerns not non-members' agency fees but members' voluntary funding of unions' political activities. Idaho (a right-to-work state) lets government employees set up payroll deductions for various purposes, including payment of union dues. Union members had used the payroll deduction system not only for

68. *See id.* at 188–89.

69. *Id.* at 190.

70. 555 U.S. 353 (2009). Roberts (majority) (with Scalia, Kennedy, Thomas, Alito; with Ginsburg (in part)); Ginsburg (concurring in part and concurring in the judgment); Breyer (concurring in part and dissenting in part); Stevens (dissenting); Souter (dissenting).

paying dues but also for contributing to unions' political action committees. In 2003 Idaho enacted the Voluntary Contributions Act (VCA), which barred payroll deductions for "political activities."[71] Unions challenged the VCA as a violation of their and their members' First Amendment rights, at least as the law applied to payroll deductions for employees of local governments. Idaho conceded before the case reached the Supreme Court that the law violated free speech rights as applied to private sector employees.

Chief Justice Roberts, writing for the five conservatives, analogizes the case to *Davenport,* finding that unions have once again asserted a First Amendment right where none exists. The state's payroll deduction system for government employees, he explains, expends government resources to support speech. The First Amendment doesn't compel the government to subsidize speech. Idaho therefore needs only a rational basis for its ban on political payroll deductions, and the state's "interest in avoiding the reality or appearance of government favoritism or entanglement with partisan politics" satisfies that lenient standard.[72] The Court's recasting of an asserted free speech right as a government subsidy mirrors the treatment of institutional support for student groups in *Christian Legal Society* and government support for law schools in *FAIR.* Just like *Davenport,* the *Ysursa* majority transforms the union's speech interest into a matter of voluntary government largesse. Also like *Davenport,* the majority lets the government withhold that largesse based on a version of the anti-distortion rationale for campaign finance limits that we've seen the same majority reject in *Citizens United.*

The solo opinions in *Ysursa* of Justices Stevens, Souter, and Breyer all express concerns that Idaho in the VCA impermissibly targeted unions' political speech. Justice Breyer rejects Chief Justice Roberts's framing of the VCA as a mere withdrawal of a voluntary government subsidy. Idaho's payroll deduction system, Justice Breyer points out, predated the VCA. The new law singled out just one sort of deduction to exclude from that system.[73] Justice Breyer, characteristically, urges a proportionality analysis, asking whether the VCA imposes a disproportionate burden on unions' speech in light of the government's interests.[74] The VCA, he suggests, would exceed Idaho's asserted

71. IDAHO CODE §§ 44-2004, 2601-05 (2003).

72. *Ysursa,* 555 U.S. at 359. The chief justice shrugs off the argument that, because the state didn't directly subsidize payroll deductions for local government employees, the union had a stronger claim at the local level. States, he declares, control their political subdivisions. *See id.* at 362–64. Justice Ginsburg concurs in this basis for the Court's decision. *See id.* at 364–65 (Ginsburg, J., concurring in part and concurring in the judgment). Justice Breyer also concurs in this part of the Court's opinion, and Justice Souter approves of its reasoning, but neither finds the point dispositive. Only Justice Stevens argues that the local context may present a different legal problem from the state context. *See id.* at 373–75 (Stevens, J., dissenting).

73. *See id.* at 367 (Breyer, J., concurring in part and dissenting in part).

74. *Id.* at 368 (Breyer, J., concurring in part and dissenting in part).

interest in political neutrality if the law placed a special legal burden on unions' political speech. He finds the evidence on that crucial point unclear, but Justices Stevens and Souter hold no such doubts. Their dissents emphasize that the VCA originally applied to the private sector, where the majority's subsidized speech reasoning wouldn't apply. Justice Stevens accuses the majority of "examining the statute out of context and ignoring its initial applicability to private employers."[75] Justice Souter declares that "[u]nion speech, and nothing else, seems to have been on the legislative mind."[76] Chief Justice Roberts responds that the case as presented to the Court didn't include any claim of viewpoint discrimination,[77] a deficit that Justice Souter reluctantly acknowledges.[78]

The Roberts Court in *Ysursa* once again impedes unions' efforts to collect funds for political action. The *Ysursa* majority reiterates the *Davenport* holding that public employee unions lack any First Amendment interest in government-facilitated political speech. In a case where the state had to concede private sector unions' First Amendment interest, the Roberts Court still treats public employee unions' political speech like a government preserve, via "subsidy" here as via collective bargaining in *Davenport*. By repeating the *Davenport* claim that states have an important interest in preventing unions from distorting electoral debate, in a case about a very minimal form of state "support" for unions' political speech, the *Ysursa* majority sharpens the suggestion that unions' political speech warps rather than enhances public debate.

***Knox v. Service Employees International Union, Local 1000* (2012)**[79] returns to public sector agency fees, with a vengeance. On its surface, the case deals with an extremely narrow procedural problem. *Hudson,* the decision that sets up procedures for distinguishing collective bargaining (chargeable) from political (nonchargeable) union expenses, makes public employee unions that assess agency fees send non-members an annual notice, commonly called a *Hudson* notice. The notice discloses, based on an independent audit, what percentages of the union's budget in the prior year paid for chargeable and nonchargeable expenses. The non-members then get 30 days to object to paying the nonchargeable portion of the agency fee. Recall from *Davenport* that *Hudson* does not dictate whether non-members must opt out to avoid paying the nonchargeable portion or must opt in before the union may collect it. Different states have different rules.

75. *Id.* at 375 (Stevens, J., dissenting).
76. *Id.* at 377 (Souter, J., dissenting).
77. *See id.* at 361–62 n.3.
78. *See id.* at 377–78 (Souter, J., dissenting).
79. 132 S. Ct. 2277 (2012). Alito (majority) (with Roberts, Scalia, Kennedy, Thomas); Sotomayor (concurring in the judgment) (with Ginsburg); Breyer (dissenting) (with Kagan).

In *Knox*, the Service Employees International Union (SEIU), after assessing its regular agency fee and after the *Hudson* objection period had ended, announced an additional, special assessment entirely for political purposes. (One stated purpose of the special assessment was to defeat a ballot initiative that would have imposed an opt-in system for public employee unions to spend agency fees on political activities.) The union did not send non-members a new *Hudson* notice. However, the union charged those non-members who had filed timely objections to the original *Hudson* notice only a percentage of the special assessment corresponding to the prior year's chargeable expenses. The First Amendment claimants in *Knox* included some non-members who had filed timely objections to the original *Hudson* notice and others who had not. The timely objectors argued that they shouldn't have to pay any portion of the special assessment because it had an entirely political (and thus nonchargeable) purpose. The nonobjectors argued that the union should have given them a new chance to object to the special assessment, essentially a second *Hudson* notice.

Justice Alito's majority opinion for the five conservative justices fully sustains both groups' claims.[80] As to the timely objectors, the union violated the First Amendment by charging any portion of the special assessment. As to the nonobjectors, the union violated the First Amendment by not sending a new *Hudson* notice. Two aspects of the majority's holding stretch out in surprising directions. First, Justice Alito extends the Court's holdings not just to special assessments for political purposes, such as the SEIU assessment in this case, but to all special assessments. After *Knox*, even if a union makes a special assessment entirely for collective bargaining (chargeable) purposes, it must treat all timely objections to its original *Hudson* notice as applying to the full amount of the special assessment, and it must send nonobjectors a fresh *Hudson* notice.[81] Second, the *Knox* Court breaks new ground by finding a constitutional difference between opt-in and opt-out rules. Justice Alito holds that the First Amendment subjects all special assessments to an opt-in regime, for objectors and nonobjectors alike.[82] Both the extension of strong procedural protections to all special assessments and the requirement of an opt-in regime arguably exceed what the Court had to decide in *Knox*.

Justice Alito strongly implies, but doesn't squarely pronounce, the unconstitutionality of all opt-out systems for public sector agency fees. "Once it is

80. In *Knox*, as in *Citizens United*, the majority forgoes a procedural path that would have avoided the case's deeper constitutional issues. The SEIU tried to defuse the dispute by backing down and offering objecting non-members a full refund. Justice Alito, however, states that, because the union did not disavow its claims that its prior tactics were legal, the Court had to assume the union might try those tactics again. *See id.* at 2287–88.

81. *See id.* at 2293 n.6.

82. *See id.* at 2296.

recognized . . . that a nonmember cannot be forced to fund a union's political or ideological activities," he asks, "what is the justification for putting the burden on the nonmember to opt out of making such a payment?" *Hudson* and other decisions, he asserts, indulged opt-out systems "more as a historical accident than through the careful application of First Amendment principles."[83] By that indulgence, "our prior decisions approach, if they do not cross, the limit of what the First Amendment can tolerate."[84] Justice Alito doesn't explain what distinguishes "historical accident" from the "tradition" we've seen the Roberts Court extol as a basis for First Amendment doctrine in Chapter 1 and elsewhere. As in the campaign finance cases, the *Knox* majority appears to be laying the groundwork for a future case to strike down all opt-out rules.

Even more aggressively, Justice Alito questions the core *Abood* allowance for requiring nonunion members to contribute to the cost of collective bargaining. Unions' collective bargaining positions, he notes, "have powerful political and civic consequences,"[85] a point that challenges the central *Abood* distinction between chargeable (non-political) and nonchargeable (political) expenses. He derides unions' collective bargaining activities as "services that nonmembers may not want and in any event have not agreed to fund."[86] One might characterize union non-members in agency shops as consenting to support the union's collective bargaining activities by choosing to work under an agency shop contract. For the *Knox* majority, however, even union activities long recognized as beneficial to non-members, and thus classified under *Abood* as chargeable, raise First Amendment suspicions. Justice Alito avers that "we do not revisit today whether the Court's former cases have given adequate recognition to the critical First Amendment rights at stake."[87] In his next breath, however, he attacks the familiar *Abood* precept that agency fees rightly prevent nonunion workers from free riding on unions' collective bargaining efforts. "Acceptance of the free-rider argument as a justification," he writes, "represents something of an anomaly—one that we have found to be justified by the interest in furthering 'labor peace.'"[88] Labor peace, a basic value in labor law, sounds in Justice Alito's voice like crude foreign slang.

Justice Alito raises the First Amendment stakes, and links the *Abood* problem to *Citizens United* and other campaign finance decisions, by predicating his First Amendment analysis on "our nation's commitment to self-government."[89] The agency fee problem may seem like an esoteric, even

83. *Id.* at 2290.
84. *Id.* at 2291.
85. *Id.* at 2289.
86. *Id.* at 2295.
87. *Id.* at 2289.
88. *Id.* at 2290.
89. *Id.* at 2288.

arcane corner of First Amendment law, but Justice Alito frames agency fees as a major threat to free speech. He declares that agency shops "impose[] a significant impingement on [nonunion members'] First Amendment rights" that the Court has merely "tolerated."[90] He repeatedly emphasizes the *Davenport* holding that only nonunion workers, not unions, have a First Amendment interest in agency fees.[91] He denounces the "aggressive use of power by the SEIU to collect fees from nonmembers."[92]

Justice Alito expresses remarkable disdain not just for *Abood* and agency fees but for public employee unions themselves. He repeatedly implies, with little support from the factual record, that unions lie about the chargeability of their expenses.[93] Responding to the SEIU's argument that timely objectors to the original *Hudson* notice in *Knox* got a windfall, because the chargeable portion of that year's expenses turned out to be larger than the *Hudson* notice projected, he all but accuses the union of lying. "[T]he SEIU's understanding of the breadth of chargeable expenses," he writes, "is so expansive that it is hard to place much reliance on its statistics." He dismisses the reliability of independent audits for distinguishing chargeable expenses because "the auditors take the union's characterization [of expenses] for granted[.]"[94] In defending the Court's extension of its holding even to non-political special assessments, he suggests that courts cannot "rely on unions to advertise the true purpose behind every special fee."[95] This relentless mistrust of unions contrasts sharply with deference we've seen the Roberts Court grant to the government's factual claims in other First Amendment contexts, such as the "material aid to terrorists" case *Humanitarian Law Project* (Chapter 2) and the student speech case *Morse v. Frederick* (Chapter 3). Justice Alito also criticizes unions' role in public life, emphasizing "the budget consequences of growing compensation for public employees backed by powerful public-sector unions"[96] and referring ominously to "unions' controversial political activities."[97]

Justice Sotomayor, joined by Justice Ginsburg, agrees with the *Knox* Court's basic holding that when a union makes a special assessment solely

90. *Id.* at 2289 (internal quotation marks and citation omitted).

91. *See id.* at 2291, 2295.

92. *Id.* at 2291.

93. Justice Alito cites one questionable union statement about chargeability: the SEIU's characterization, in its brief to the Court, of "lobbying the electorate" as a chargeable expense. *Id.* at 2294. Justice Breyer, however, points out in dissent that a California statute specifically authorizes unions to claim lobbying expenses as chargeable. *See id.* at 2304 (Breyer, J., dissenting). Justice Alito also attacks the union's statement, again in its brief, that its special assessment for political purposes was "germane" to its collective bargaining activities. *See id.* at 2294–95.

94. *Id.* at 2294.

95. *Id.* at 2293 n.6.

96. *Id.* at 2285.

97. *Id.* at 2295.

for political purposes, it must spare non-members who timely objected to the original *Hudson* notice and send nonobjectors a new notice. However, she accuses the majority of reaching beyond the scope of the case to mandate an opt-in regime. She points out that the parties never briefed or argued the question whether opt-out systems ever (or always) violate the First Amendment, making the Court's decision on that question highly unusual and, she says, a violation of the Court's internal rules.[98] She especially deplores the majority's suggestions that all opt-in regimes violate the First Amendment: "To cast serious doubt on longstanding precedent . . . on our own invitation and without adversarial presentation is both unfair and unwise."[99] She also complains that the majority's overreaching leaves the full scope of its holding unclear.

Justice Breyer, dissenting for himself and Justice Kagan, defends the wisdom and workability of the procedures *Hudson* set out for handling agency fee disputes. Where Justice Alito launches his opinion from the constitutional mountaintop, Justice Breyer hikes through the administrative trenches. The key *Hudson* practice of determining chargeable union expenses through an audit, he maintains, effectively protects nonunion objectors from funding union political speech while also ensuring that unions can perform their collective bargaining function. Making the nonunion workers who in this case objected to the original *Hudson* notice pay the chargeable portion of the SEIU's special assessment, Justice Breyer says, would cause them no constitutional injury, because the audit behind that notice underestimated the chargeable portion of the union's expenses.[100] The nonobjectors, in his view, have a somewhat stronger claim, but giving them a new opportunity to avoid paying a special assessment would create administrative problems, and nonobjectors are less likely than objectors to oppose the union's political activities anyway.[101]

Justice Breyer's dissent shows that at least some members of the Roberts Court's liberal wing believe unions have a legal interest in how agency fees support their speech. Where Justice Alito portrays the agency fee issue as a one-sided constitutional dispute that entitles nonunion workers to every legal presumption, Justice Breyer delineates a complex interplay of interests that demands a more nuanced and equitable resolution. His analysis cannot easily accommodate the rigid *Davenport* holding that unions have no First Amendment interest in agency fees. Justice Breyer joined *Davenport,* and he has never advocated balancing First Amendment interests in agency fee cases. Even so, he treats the union as more than a government proxy. The union, in Justice Breyer's account, has important expressive interests, at least

98. *See id.* at 2297–98 (Sotomayor, J., concurring in the judgment).
99. *Id.* at 2299 (Sotomayor, J., concurring in the judgment).
100. *See id.* at 2302–04 (Breyer, J., dissenting).
101. *See id.*at 2304–05 (Breyer, J., dissenting).

in collective bargaining, that agency fees promote. That account complicates the public-private binary that *Davenport* imposed on the agency fee problem.

***Harris v. Quinn* (2014)**[102] continues the conservative majority's First Amendment campaign against agency fees. The case concerns a specialized class of workers: healthcare "personal assistants" who provide in-home care to disabled clients pursuant to a state program. As in *Knox*, a SEIU contract required nonunion personal assistants to pay an agency fee pursuant to *Abood*. Objecting non-members, emboldened by *Knox*, raised two First Amendment objections. First, the Court should overrule *Abood* and prohibit public sector agency fees across the board. Second, if the Court declined to overrule *Abood*, it should declare personal assistants not to be public employees and accordingly exempt them from the *Abood* allowance for public sector agency fees. The *Harris* majority takes the second, narrower path, but not before amplifying its *Knox* rhetoric about the failings of *Abood*.

In fact Justice Alito, writing once again for the majority, digs much deeper into the precedents, questioning even the pre-*Abood* decisions that upheld *private sector* agency fees.[103] Those cases, Justice Alito suggests, built a shaky foundation for *Abood*,[104] and *Abood* made matters worse. First, *Abood* paid too little attention to the heightened First Amendment stakes of public sector, as opposed to private sector, agency fees. Public employees' wages and benefits matter politically. Here, as in *Knox*, Justice Alito stresses that "state and local expenditures on employee wages and benefits have mushroomed."[105] Second, *Abood* failed to anticipate the difficulty of distinguishing chargeable from nonchargeable expenses, which Justice Alito portrays as monumental. Third, *Abood* didn't appreciate the First Amendment burdens nonunion workers would face under the procedures later announced by *Hudson*. Here Justice Alito again impugns unions' honesty in audits.

*Harris* supplements *Knox* with an important new attack on the core "labor peace" logic of *Abood*. "A union's status as exclusive bargaining agent and the right to collect an agency fee from non-members," Justice Alito declares, "are not inextricably linked."[106] He responds to the *Abood* concern that agency shops generally discourage union rivalries, noting that the particular nonunion workers who brought the *Harris* challenge didn't claim a First Amendment right to form a rival union. He points out that some federal agencies permit employees to choose an exclusive bargaining agent while imposing no agency fees. He "presume[s]" that enough personal assistants have joined

102. 134 S. Ct. 2618 (2014). Alito (majority) (with Roberts, Scalia, Kennedy, Thomas); Kagan (dissenting) (with Ginsburg, Breyer, Sotomayor).

103. *See id.* at 2627–30.

104. *See id.* at 2632–34.

105. *Id.* at 2632; *see also id.* at 2642-43 (positing the SEIU's complicity in burgeoning Medicaid expenditures).

106. *Id.* at 2640.

the SEIU to fund its activities without agency fees. He also makes an anecdotal case that unions don't benefit workers enough to justify agency fees, because state employers are "highly receptive to suggestions for increased wages and other improvements."[107] Justice Alito links this critique of the labor peace argument in the specific context of Illinois personal assistants to his broader assault on *Abood*.[108]

The majority, in *Harris* as in *Knox*, leaves its attack on *Abood* hanging in the air. Justice Alito sustains the nonunion workers' First Amendment challenge by refusing to "expand" *Abood* to cover Illinois personal assistants. The majority limits *Abood* to "full-fledged public employees."[109] *Abood* depends on "the assumption that the union possesses the full scope of powers and duties generally available under American labor law."[110] The SEIU here, Justice Alito argues, doesn't have that breadth of power. Illinois personal assistants answer primarily to their in-home clients, not to the state; Illinois treats them as public employees only for collective bargaining purposes. Illinois controls personal assistants' wages by statute. Thus, reasons Justice Alito, the union doesn't work under the legal obligation to represent non-members' interests that *Abood* said justifies the agency shop arrangement.[111] Without that *Abood* justification, the agency fee in *Harris* fails First Amendment review.

Justice Kagan, dissenting for the four liberal justices, sardonically cheers Justice Alito's failure to overrule *Abood*. "[T]he majority," she chides, "could not restrain itself from saying (and saying and saying) . . . that *Abood* does not rank on [its] top-ten list of favorite precedents," but "save for an unfortunate hiving off of ostensibly 'partial-public' employees, *Abood* remains the law."[112] She parries the majority's attacks on *Abood*. The incentive for nonunion workers to "free ride" on unions' collective bargaining efforts, she explains, belies the majority's assertion that unions can always sign up enough members to fund their activities through dues. The utility of bargaining with an exclusive representative justifies the state in negotiating and enforcing agency fees.[113] She invokes stare decisis and emphasizes the "enormous reliance interests" that *Abood* has fostered in the states.[114] As for *Harris* itself, Justice Kagan maintains that the SEIU's responsibilities to personal assistants more than suffice to activate the *Abood* rationale for agency fees.

107. *Id.* at 2641. Justice Alito makes a repeated point of naming the Democratic governor who created the challenged Illinois program: the disgraced, imprisoned Rod Blagojevich.

108. *See id.* at 2634.

109. *Id.* at 2638.

110. *Id.* at 2636.

111. *See id.* at 2636–37 & n.18.

112. *Id.* at 2653 (Kagan, J., dissenting) (internal citation omitted).

113. *See id.* at 2656–58 (Kagan, J., dissenting).

114. *Id.* at 2652 (Kagan, J., dissenting).

Justice Kagan joins her conventional defenses of *Abood* to a novel alternative justification. Recall from Chapter 3 the *Pickering* test for public employers' restrictions on employees' speech, which the Roberts Court considered in *Garcetti v. Ceballos.* Under *Pickering,* the Court performs a moderately speech-protective review when an employee speaks as a citizen about a matter of public concern, but government employers get great latitude to punish an employee's speech about private, employment-related matters. Justice Kagan likens the *Abood* justification for agency fees to the logic of *Pickering.* The *Pickering* category of "public concern" speech corresponds with a union's "nonchargeable" political expenses, as to which nonunion employees get meaningful First Amendment protection. The *Pickering* category of private, employment-related speech corresponds with the union's "chargeable" collective bargaining expenses, as to which nonunion employees get negligible First Amendment protection and thus may be charged an agency fee.[115] Justice Alito waves off Justice Kagan's *Pickering* argument. Even if the Court measured *Abood* against the *Pickering* framework, he says, everything a public employee union does is a matter of public concern, so nonunion objectors to agency fees would still deserve more First Amendment protection than *Abood* gives them. Justice Alito's expansive conception of "public concern" in this narrow context reflects the majority's conviction that making nonunion members contribute to unions does much greater First Amendment harm than punishing employees' speech.

The Court's choice in *Harris* not to overrule *Abood* may reflect the absence of five votes for going that far.[116] On the other hand, the *Harris* majority may simply have wanted to build a foundation for a later, bolder move. In early 2016 the Court heard oral argument in *Friedrichs v. California Teachers Association.* The *Friedrichs* petitioners asked the Court either to overrule *Abood* and bar agency fees altogether, or at least to mandate an opt-in rule for all uses of agency fees to fund political advocacy. Even the latter, narrower holding would have dealt a body blow to public employee unions' political advocacy.[117] Justice Scalia's sudden passing in February 2016, however, led to a pro forma affirmance of *Friedrichs* by an equally divided Court.[118]

After the Roberts Court handed down *Citizens United,* labor law scholars suggested the decision's solicitude for corporate speech might undermine constitutionally grounded limits on unions' political spending.[119] Nonunion workers who object to unions' spending agency fees on political advocacy, these scholars argued, closely parallel corporate shareholders who object to

115. *See id.* at 2653–55 (Kagan, J., dissenting).
116. *See* Gould, *supra* note 55, at 156–57.
117. *See* Fisk & Chemerinsky, *supra* note 55, at 1067–69.
118. *See* Friedrichs v. Cal. Teachers Ass'n, 136 S. Ct. 1083 (2016) (per curiam).
119. *See* Garden, *supra* note 55; Sachs, *supra* note 55.

corporations' spending general treasury funds on political advocacy. First Amendment law should therefore apply symmetrically to both groups of objectors.[120] Corporate law gives directors and executives sweeping control over political spending,[121] and the Supreme Court has long refused to extend *Abood* protection to corporate shareholders.[122] Asymmetric treatment of union and corporate dissenters matters in practical as well as theoretical terms, because corporations and unions typically oppose one another politically, and *Citizens United* strengthened corporations' hand in that conflict.[123] *Knox* and *Harris* exacerbate the asymmetry.

A managed speech account of the labor speech decisions reveals a deeper asymmetry. Public employee unions are large institutions with a major stake in public debate. In case after case, we've seen the Roberts Court empower similar institutions to channel, modulate, and manage public debate. Prominent among those speech managers are not just the corporations of *Citizens United* (Chapter 7) but also the public employer of *Garcetti v. Ceballos* (Chapter 3). As Justice Kagan points out in her *Harris* dissent, the Court's labor speech decisions loudly denounce public employers' incursions on workers' speech, but *Garcetti* gave those same employers unprecedented latitude to restrict workers' speech. The Roberts Court's labor speech decisions, by denigrating unions' role in public debate, appear to diverge not just from *Citizens United* but from the Roberts Court's managed speech paradigm.

Closer examination of the labor speech decisions, however, reveals continuity with managed speech. The decisions imply that empowering unions to manage public debate would damage, rather than promote, the stability value that underwrites managed speech. To the extent earlier Supreme Courts dismissed First Amendment concerns about agency fees, they relied on the theory that letting unions collect agency fees promotes labor peace. Agency fees, on that theory, help to bolster and justify labor law's system of exclusive representation.[124] In *Knox* and especially *Harris,* Justice Alito thoroughly rejects the

120. Professor Sachs considers distinctions between nonunion agency shop workers and corporate shareholders, finding those distinctions insufficient to defeat the parallel. *See* Sachs, *supra* note 55, at 827–58.

121. *See* Lucian A. Bebchuk & Robert J. Jackson, *Corporate Political Speech: Who Decides?*, 124 HARV. L. REV. 83 (2010).

122. *See* First Nat'l Bank v. Bellotti, 435 U.S. 765, 794 n.34 (1978). Scholars have proposed various means of bringing the two lines of doctrine into harmony. For a proposal to let shareholders opt out of corporate political spending, see Sachs, *supra* note 55, at 862–66. For an opt-in proposal, see Torres-Spelliscy, *supra* note 56, at 127–29. For arguments that the Court should loosen constraints on unions' spending of agency fees for political purposes, see Fisk & Chemerinsky, *supra* note 55, at 1085–91; Charlotte Garden, *Meta Rights*, 83 FORDHAM L. REV. 855, 895–98 (2014).

123. *See* Fisk & Chemerinsky, *supra* note 55, at 1072; Garden, *supra* note 55, at 11–16; Sachs, *supra* note 55, at 803.

124. Unions, of course, do more than just promote labor peace. *See* Fisk & Chemerinsky, *supra* note 55, at 1074–77.

labor peace theory. As a legal matter, he argues, a union's status as exclusive bargaining representative doesn't give it any right to collect agency fees from non-members. As a factual matter, unions don't need non-members' agency fees to fund the activities they claim benefit workers.[125] Moreover, Justice Alito implies that whatever gains unions make for workers hurt society. He repeatedly suggests that unions' power threatens not just nonunion workers but state budgets.[126] Especially in *Knox,* he also portrays unions as liars in the system *Abood* established for constraining agency fees. Lies, as we saw in the military honors case *Alvarez* (Chapter 1), threaten social order. The labor speech decisions portray unions as the antithesis of the stabilizing institutions the Roberts Court has elsewhere empowered to manage public discussion.

Even as the labor speech decisions marginalize unions, they promote other institutional managers of public debate. The Roberts Court's undermining of public employee unions benefits and empowers two sorts of institutions whose managerial authority we've seen the Court promote in other settings. First, these decisions help corporations, the beneficiaries of *Citizens United,* in their political struggle against unions' advocacy of positions favorable to workers. Second, despite the majority's conflation of public employee unions' interests with government employers' power, weakening unions ultimately benefits government employers in their adversarial engagement with the unions. In that sense, the labor speech decisions complement *Garcetti.* Even as the labor speech decisions reject unions' managerial prerogatives, the decisions advance managed speech.

The labor speech cases illustrate how the public-private distinction helps the Roberts Court shape First Amendment law to maximize social and political stability. The public sector agency fee scenario involves three actors: not just the government employer and the private employees, but another private actor: the union. The public-private constitutional binary, which always pits a private rights-holder against a government rights-violator, can't account for a third player. *Davenport* derives, from the government employer's state action and the nonunion workers' First Amendment interest, the absence of any First Amendment interest for the union. The author of *Davenport,* Justice Scalia, used to recognize that unions' statutory mandate to represent the interests not just of members but also of non-members amounts to a state-created burden on unions' rights, which agency fees alleviate.[127] *Davenport,* though,

125. *See* Harris v. Quinn, 134 S. Ct. 2618, 2640 (2014).

126. Justice Alito's concern about unions' destructive effect on budgets raises serious empirical questions. *See* Fisk & Chemerinsky, *supra* note 55, at 1077.

127. "In the context of bargaining, a union *must* seek to further the interests of its nonmembers . . . . Thus, the free ridership (if it were left to be that) would be not incidental but calculated, not imposed by circumstances but mandated by government." Lehnert v. Ferris Fac. Ass'n, 500 U.S. 507, 556 (1991) (Scalia, J., concurring in part and dissenting in part).

denies that the union has any cognizable expressive interest related to agency fees. The union, for the majority, devolves to a powerful repository of state-conferred power that coercively undermines non-members' First Amendment rights.[128] A private speaker becomes a government censor, in a perfect inversion of the Court's transformation of private speech into government speech in the park monument case *Summum* and the Confederate license plate case *Walker* (both Chapter 4).

The labor speech decisions have a complicated relationship with First Amendment doctrine's usual emphasis on protecting political speech. On one hand, the decisions assert, without documenting, that nonunion workers have a strong, widespread desire not to fund unions' political messages. On the other hand, the decisions treat unions' political speech as a threat, a rogue exploitation of nonunion workers and a distortion of the political process. Justice Alito repeatedly cites the political importance of public employee unions' speech as a reason not to protect that speech but to constrain it. The Court's liberals don't exactly race to the unions' defense. Justice Kagan's *Pickering* argument in her *Harris* dissent justifies agency fees not as a constitutionally salient aid to unions' political speech but merely as a permissible encroachment of government power on nonunion workers' First Amendment rights. By elevating nonunion workers' interest in not having to pay for compelled speech over unions' interest in political expression, the labor speech decisions reinforce the idea that speech matters for its economic value rather than its informational role in public debate. We've seen that idea animate both *Golan v. Holder* and the drug detailing case *Sorrell v. IMS Health* (Chapter 2).

## A SNOWBALL FIGHT IN HELL: THE ROBERTS COURT UPHOLDS A CAMPAIGN FINANCE LIMIT

Beyond the decisions about government efforts to help underfinanced candidates and the decisions about labor speech, the Roberts Court has decided one other case about money in politics. Like the other decisions in this chapter, ***Williams-Yulee v. Florida Bar* (2015)**[129] limits the flow of funds into elections.

128. The extent to which agency fees actually coerce nonunion workers remains open to question. *See* Int'l Ass'n of Machinists v. Street, 367 U.S. 740, 805–06 (1961) (Frankfurter, J., dissenting); Fisk & Chemerinsky, *supra* note 55, at 1048–57; Garden, *supra* note 122, at 896–98; *see also* Bebchuk & Jackson, *supra* note 122, at 114 (challenging the premise that nonunion workers face greater coercion than corporate shareholders to support institutional political speech); Sachs, *supra* note 55, at 827–44 (same).

129. 135 S. Ct. 1656 (2015). Roberts (majority (in part), plurality (in part)) (with Breyer, Sotomayor, Kagan; with Ginsburg (in part)); Breyer (concurring); Ginsburg (concurring in part and concurring in the judgment) (with Breyer (in part)); Scalia (dissenting) (with Thomas); Kennedy (dissenting); Alito (dissenting).

This decision is unique in the Roberts Court's canon, however, in upholding a direct government limit on electoral money. Yulee, an unsuccessful judicial candidate, challenged a Florida law that forbade judicial candidates from making personal appeals for campaign contributions. As in *McCutcheon* and *Arizona Free Enterprise*, the chief justice wrote for the Court. In this case, however, his majority includes the four liberal justices, with all four conservatives in bitter dissent. The chief justice begins with an important ruling that garners only a plurality. He finds that Florida's rule places a great enough burden on electoral speech to require the Court to review the rule under strict First Amendment scrutiny.[130] That almost makes *Williams-Yulee* one of the rare cases, alongside *Holder v. Humanitarian Law Project* (Chapter 2), in which the government prevails under strict scrutiny. Justice Ginsburg, however, refuses to join the part of the chief justice's opinion that declares strict scrutiny the proper standard of review. She writes separately to reiterate her long-standing view that, even if rigorous First Amendment constraints apply to other elections, states should have greater latitude to regulate judicial elections.[131] The conservative dissenters in *Williams-Yulee* agree with the chief justice that strict scrutiny is the proper standard of review, but they argue that Florida's law should fail under that standard.

Chief Justice Roberts finds that Florida's ban on personal solicitation by judicial candidates serves "the State's compelling interest in preserving public confidence in the integrity of the judiciary[.]"[132] Judges, he explains, need not and should not serve financial supporters' interests in the same way that (as he argued in last chapter's *McCutcheon* decision) legislators should.[133] Yulee tried to cast doubt on the state's interest by arguing that the rule against personal solicitation covered too little speech to preserve public confidence in judicial integrity. Florida lets judicial candidates' campaign committees ask for money, and it lets the candidates themselves write thank-you notes to contributors. Aren't those practices, Yulee asked, just as suspect as solicitation by the candidate? Not necessarily, responds the chief justice. Florida could fairly decide that candidate solicitations present the greatest threat to actual or apparent judicial integrity. We shouldn't punish the state for restricting less speech than it might have.[134] Turning to the "narrow tailoring" requirement

130. *See id.* at 1664–65 (plurality opinion).

131. *See id.* at 1673 (Ginsburg, J., concurring in part and concurring in the judgment) (citing Republican Party of Minnesota v. White, 536 U.S. 765, 805 (2002) (Ginsburg, J., dissenting)). Justice Breyer also wrote a brief concurrence to reiterate his familiar view that standards of review should not apply mechanically in First Amendment cases. *See Williams-Yulee*, 135 S. Ct. at 1673 (Breyer, J., concurring). Justice Breyer joined Chief Justice Roberts's opinion while also joining all of Justice Ginsburg's opinion except her explicit disavowal of strict scrutiny for judicial election laws.

132. *Williams-Yulee*, 135 S. Ct. at 1666.

133. *See id.* at 1666–68.

134. *See id.* at 1668–70.

of strict scrutiny, Yulee argued that Florida's rule barred more speech than the judicial integrity interest required. Yulee made her personal appeal for campaign donations through a Web post and a mass mailing. Perhaps face-to-face meetings between candidates and potential donors undercut judicial propriety, but mass mailings? The chief justice replies that Florida's integrity interest is categorical, the scope of the state's rule reasonable, and the distinctions Yulee's argument would require unworkable. Narrow tailoring need not mean perfect tailoring.

Justice Scalia's dissent, joined by Justice Thomas, first invokes the categorical speech cases discussed in Chapter 1 to argue that no tradition supports regulation of judicial candidates' speech in general or judicial electoral fundraising in particular.[135] He then picks apart the chief justice's formulation of Florida's compelling interest, "public confidence in judicial integrity," which Justice Scalia derides as logically sloppy and rhetorically deceptive.[136] Justice Scalia mocks the chief justice's conclusion that Florida couldn't easily have narrowed its solicitation ban to restrict less speech.[137] Arguing that Florida's ban on personal solicitations by judicial candidates doesn't substantially advance the state's putative judicial integrity interest, Justice Scalia contrasts the Court's credulity in *Williams-Yulee* with its skepticism in the military honors case *Alvarez* (discussed in Chapter 1). "Now that we have a case about the public's perception of judicial honor rather than its perception of military honor," he complains, "the Justices of this Court change the rules."[138]

Justice Scalia impugns Florida's, and the majority's, motives. The state's targeted ban on solicitation by judicial candidates, he insists, "has nothing to do with the appearances created by judges' asking for money, and everything to do with hostility toward judicial campaigning." The law seeks to undermine the very institution of judicial elections. "It should come as no surprise," Justice Scalia darkly intones, "that the [American Bar Association], whose model rules the Florida Supreme Court followed when framing [the solicitation ban], opposes judicial elections, preferring a system in which (surprise!) a committee of lawyers proposes candidates[.]"[139] He celebrates judicial elections as a noble populist response to the legal profession's elitism. The majority, Justice Scalia concludes, is compromising the First Amendment out of excessive, parochial concern for public confidence in judges.[140]

Justice Kennedy's solo dissent casts the Court's decision as enabling "state censorship" of political speech.[141] The Court's holding, he insists, simply

135. *See id.* at 1676–77 (Scalia, J., dissenting).
136. *See id.* at 1677–78 (Scalia, J., dissenting).
137. *See id.* at 1679–80 (Scalia, J., dissenting).
138. *Id.* at 1678 (Scalia, J., dissenting).
139. *Id.* at 1681 (Scalia, J., dissenting).
140. *See id.* at 1682 (Scalia, J., dissenting).
141. *Id.* at 1684 (Kennedy, J., dissenting).

reflects its belief "that in certain elections—here an election to choose the best qualified judge—the public lacks the necessary judgment to make an informed choice." Because of Florida's limitation on campaign fundraising, "broader campaign debate . . . is silenced."[142] In particular, Justice Kennedy argues, the Court's approval of Florida's solicitation ban "undermines the educational process that free speech in elections should facilitate."[143] He assails Chief Justice Roberts's strict scrutiny analysis as "literally a casebook guide to eviscerating strict scrutiny any time the Court encounters speech it dislikes."[144] Justice Alito picks up on that criticism in his brief solo dissent, deriding Florida's law as "about as narrowly tailored as a burlap bag."[145]

Chief Justice Roberts's response to the *Williams-Yulee* dissents offers interesting glosses on two recurring motifs in the Roberts Court's free speech jurisprudence: tradition and deference. In validating Florida's compelling interest in maintaining judicial integrity, the chief justice rebuffs Justice Scalia's point that no strong tradition supports bans on personal fundraising by judicial candidates. "We do not dispute that fact," the chief justice shrugs, "but it has no relevance here."[146] Tradition, he says, guides only inquiries into whether the Court should recognize new categories of unprotected speech (as discussed in Chapter 1), not determinations whether a restriction on protected speech should pass First Amendment muster. In affirming the Florida law's narrow tailoring, the chief justice notes that "most states with elected judges" have restricted personal solicitation by judicial candidates, and "[t]hese considered judgments deserve our respect."[147] That's just the sort of deference the Roberts Court has granted to numerous government restrictions on speech (most ubiquitously in Part II's government preserve decisions) but has completely denied in every one of its other campaign finance decisions.[148] *Williams-Yulee* offers no guidance about how to determine when the Court should and shouldn't defer to government judgments.

Chief Justice Roberts can't contain his annoyance at his dissenting colleagues' rhetoric. "A reader of Justice Kennedy's dissent," he snaps, "could be forgiven for concluding that the Court has just upheld a latter-day version of the Alien and Sedition Acts[.]"[149] He colorfully calls out Justice Scalia's

142. *Id.* at 1683 (Kennedy, J., dissenting).
143. *Id.* at 1684 (Kennedy, J., dissenting).
144. *Id.* at 1685 (Kennedy, J., dissenting).
145. *Id.* (Alito, J., dissenting).
146. *Id.* at 1666.
147. *Id.* at 1671.
148. *See* Briffault, *supra* note 4, at 497 (contending that the Roberts Court's campaign finance decisions, which "give[] little or no weight to the empirical findings and political values of elected decision-makers," bear "no trace of judicial modesty").
149. *Williams-Yulee,* 135 S. Ct. at 1670.

dissent for "evok[ing] nothing so much as Delacroix's painting of Liberty leading a determined band of *citoyens*, this time against a robed aristocracy scurrying to shore up the ramparts of the judicial castle through disingenuous ethical rules."[150] The irony is that Justices Kennedy and Scalia bite no harder in *Williams-Yulee* than in their prior campaign finance opinions, most of which the chief justice joined. Nothing the chief justice says in *Williams-Yulee,* however, undercuts his First Amendment objections to other campaign finance laws. His opinion crisply distinguishes judicial elections from other elections. We've previously seen the Roberts Court in the bankruptcy advice case *Milavetz* (Chapter 2) show a characteristic judicial distaste for potentially unethical speech by lawyers. Chief Justice Roberts's office makes him not just the "first among equals" on the Supreme Court but also the leader of the federal judiciary. His momentary break with the Court's other conservatives in *Williams-Yulee* almost certainly represents nothing more than situational attention to that unique duty. To that extent, Justice Scalia's criticism of this decision as a special protection for the judiciary's reputation holds water.

## CONCLUSION

The Roberts Court's campaign finance jurisprudence, most prominently *Citizens United,* has prompted widespread criticism from both academic commentators and the general public. Many of the academic critics, however, share at least one important premise with the majority opinions in *Citizens United* and *McCutcheon.* They maintain that our electoral system needs more money, not less. Money may or may not *be* speech, but money *enables* speech. A well-functioning democracy needs a lot of political speech. More spending on elections could make a positive difference for informing the electorate.[151] If our electoral system would benefit from the speech that more money could generate, we must confront the question where the money should come from. The Roberts Court in *Citizens United* and *McCutcheon* declares it should come from private wealth. Corporate money, *Citizens United* tells us, does affirmative, distinctive good for our electoral system. Corporations can give voters a lot of information relevant to elections. That information, of course, comes to voters through the filter of corporations' interest, but *Citizens United* treats that filter as precious rather than problematic. *McCutcheon* likewise extols moneyed interests' freedom to influence government through campaign

150. *Id.* at 1672.

151. *See* Ansolabehere, *supra* note 10, at 69–75; *see also* Briffault, *supra* note 40, at 537; Isaacharoff, *supra* note 10, at 134–35; Overton, *supra* note 40, at 1695.

contributions and, accordingly, eases candidates' and the major political parties' ability to amass funds from wealthy donors.

This chapter's decisions, though, show that the Roberts Court doesn't always want more money in the electoral process. This Court believes the First Amendment bars key legislative strategies for diversifying the sources of electoral money. *Davis* and *Arizona Free Enterprise* hold that private campaign spenders and donors have a First Amendment right to be free of responsive messages funded by government allowances or subsidies, at least when the private funding triggers the government's action. These decisions interpret the First Amendment to give private electoral funders the right not merely to spend on political speech but to spend under conditions that increase the likelihood their arguments will prevail. That sounds like the sort of affirmative right to reach an audience that the Court routinely denies to underfinanced speakers, especially in public forum cases (Chapter 4). *Knox* and *Harris* hold that nonunion workers deserve strong First Amendment protection from unions' efforts to spend agency fees on political causes that, the Court presumes, the nonunion workers oppose. Both of these First Amendment innovations serve to keep sources the Court disfavors from funding elections.

These are all managed speech decisions. *Citizens United* and *McCutcheon* don't let wealthy and powerful interests dominate electoral debate simply because they're wealthy and powerful. Rather, corporations, big donors, and the major political parties, with their vested interests in the social and political status quo, promote a restrained, responsible electoral discourse. The other campaign finance decisions paint a very different picture of underfunded political candidates and public employee unions. The outspent candidates of *Davis* and *Arizona Free Enterprise* can only reach audiences through the government's undermining of market forces. Their inability to get support from the market portends substantive positions unmoored from the sort of responsible authority that *Citizens United* associates with business corporations. Public employee unions, per *Davenport, Knox,* and *Harris,* deviate even more disturbingly from the market baseline. They lie to auditors, bust public budgets, and oppose the government's managerial prerogatives. In last chapter's cases, the Roberts Court used First Amendment law to enlist powerful and wealthy actors to maintain stability in electoral debate. In this chapter's cases, the Court uses First Amendment law to block the government from empowering economically marginal actors to speak in ways that might destabilize the debate.

The dynamic diversity model of constitutional speech protection understands that our electoral system needs money to pay for political speech. Dynamic diversity, however, opposes the Roberts Court's prescription that First Amendment law should empower corporations, wealthy individuals, and the major political parties to provide, amass, and direct electoral money.

Dynamic diversity favors laws that bring "more speech and more competition into the electoral system."[152] Regulations such as the McCain-Feingold millionaire's amendment and public financing systems such as Arizona's counterbalance the wealth of big spenders, big contributors, and self-financing candidates, helping underfinanced challengers respond to their political messages. Accordingly, a dynamic diversity analysis would dismiss the First Amendment challenges in *Davis* and *Arizona Free Enterprise.* Agency shop arrangements that give unions a substantial chance to collect political funds from non-members help workers' representatives effectively contest their employers' political messages. Unlike the Roberts Court, dynamic diversity would recognize cases such as *Davenport, Knox,* and *Harris* as presenting conflicts between unions' expressive interest in political advocacy and nonunion workers' expressive interest in not financially supporting political causes those workers oppose. A dynamic diversity analysis would reject the Roberts Court's empirical assumption that nonunion workers reflexively oppose unions' political agendas, to say nothing of the Court's normative view that unions distort electoral debates. At the margin of the *Abood* doctrine where this chapter's major labor speech cases reside, dynamic diversity would compel judgments in the unions' favor.

We've now considered all the Roberts Court's decisions about the First Amendment's protections for expressive freedom. We still need to weave the threads of this Court's free speech jurisprudence into a full account and to subject the decisions to a focused critique. The final chapter will undertake those tasks.

152. Ansolabehere, *supra* note 10, at 78.

# CHAPTER 9

# Managed Speech and Beyond

## *Confronting the Roberts Court's First Amendment*

We've now considered a decade in the life of the Supreme Court's First Amendment doctrine. This concluding chapter rises above the trees to survey the forest with a critical eye. In discussing the Roberts Court's decisions, I've contended that this Court has developed and ingrained a particular normative approach to First Amendment law: managed speech. This chapter first gathers the analytic threads from the case discussions to craft a thorough account of managed speech. That account emphasizes the coherence of managed speech as an approach to First Amendment doctrine. It situates managed speech in a conservative intellectual tradition that counterbalances individual freedom with control of public discussion by responsible managers.

This chapter then critiques managed speech based on my preferred normative framework for free speech law, dynamic diversity. Where managed speech seeks only to protect certain forms of private speech from government interference, dynamic diversity seeks to advance democratic public discussion. Where managed speech scorns outsider speakers and authorizes powerful actors to manage public discussion, dynamic diversity promotes a contentious discussion that outsider speakers can shake up. Where managed speech constrains public debate to preserve social and political stability, dynamic diversity unleashes public debate to enable social and political change. This chapter closes by using dynamic diversity to suggest how a future Supreme Court might improve upon the Roberts Court's approach to the First Amendment.

## THE COHERENCE OF MANAGED SPEECH

The Roberts Court's First Amendment decisions construct a sophisticated, coherent approach to constitutional speech protection. The coherence of managed speech will enable a full-bodied critique of the Roberts Court's First Amendment. The Court's decisions reveal three central tendencies of managed speech: (1) granting wealthy and powerful actors, whether governmental or private, managerial control over public discussion; (2) disregarding the expressive interests of politically, socially, and economically marginal speakers; and (3) advancing the ultimate goal of social and political stability.

*Empowering Managers of Public Discussion.* The signature feature of managed speech, the action behind the label, is the Roberts Court's reliance on a variety of institutions, both public and private, to manage public discussion. The phenomenon I'm describing transcends government success against free speech claims. To be sure, the Roberts Court when rejecting free speech claims has shown special regard for the government's managerial function. Even more distinctively, however, the Roberts Court has assigned managerial authority over important fields of public discussion to select private speakers who win their First Amendment claims. In cases that involve underlying clashes between competing expressive interests, the Roberts Court has favored the interests of large, established institutions, empowering those institutions to dominate the content or control the scope of important discussions.

The most vivid illustrations of the Roberts Court's deference to government managers emerge from the Court's "government speech" decisions: *Summum v. Pleasant Grove City* and *Walker v. Texas Division, Sons of Confederate Veterans* (both Chapter 4). The Court in these cases makes First Amendment claims disappear by reconceptualizing individuals' and institutions' expression as government messages. The Court doesn't see the religious sect's seven aphorisms in *Summum* or the Confederate apologists' license plate design in *Walker* as autonomously expressing those groups' religious and cultural values. Rather, the groups merely submitted their messages for the government's consideration, and the government chose not to embrace the messages. *Agency for International Development v. Alliance for Open Society International* (Chapter 5), in protecting the autonomy of government funding recipients against government policy mandates, restrains the government speech doctrine following *Summum*. The subsequent decision in *Walker*, however, shows that the Roberts Court remains comfortable asserting and even expanding the government speech doctrine. The union agency fee cases, led by *Davenport v. Washington Education Association* (Chapter 8), mirror the government speech doctrine by merging private unions' interest in collecting agency fees into the government's decision to contract with the unions.

Beyond the government speech cases, the theme of government as speech manager permeates the Roberts Court's other decisions about speech in government preserves. *Beard v. Banks* (Chapter 3) lets prison authorities use access to reading material as a bargaining chip and a cudgel against prisoners. *Morse v. Frederick*, the "BONG HiTS 4 JESUS" case (also Chapter 3), lets school administrators decide not only which ideas students may express at school but which ideas they may express in any place where other students are present and, more deeply, what students' expressions mean. *Christian Legal Society v. Martinez* (Chapter 4) broadly parallels *Morse* in higher education, elevating university administrators' managerial prerogatives over students' interests in forming expressive groups. *Rumsfeld v. FAIR* (Chapter 5), in turn, subordinates law school administrators' autonomy to the higher managerial prerogatives of the U.S. military.

The Roberts Court has empowered the government to manage speech even outside government preserves. Most important, *Holder v. Humanitarian Law Project* (Chapter 2) supercharges the deference to military authority seen in *FAIR*. *Humanitarian Law Project* licenses the national security state to define the scope of permissible communication between domestic speakers and whatever foreign groups the government chooses to label as terrorists. The government's interests in political propaganda and courting favor with foreign governments overwhelm political dissidents' interests in choosing what they say and to whom they speak. In *New York State Board of Elections v. Lopez Torres* (Chapter 6) the Court again favors government management, for the sake of the major political parties that constitute the government, in rejecting a challenge to the parties' nominating procedures. The Court similarly lets the government control the contours of private speech in the speech-restrictive categorical decisions (Chapter 1), most notably the copyright extension case, *Golan v. Holder.* There the Court, out of similar international comity concerns to those in *Humanitarian Law Project*, endorses an intellectual property regime that favors original creators over new creators who want to recontextualize old works. The winning government officials in all these speech-restrictive cases don't merely defeat free speech claims. Rather, they get to structure public discussion in ways that advance their managerial priorities. The government doesn't stop the discussion; it runs the discussion.

On the speech-protective side of the ledger, several important Roberts Court decisions let powerful speakers manage expressive environments where the government sought to promote rival speakers' interests. In particular, well-funded private speakers consistently get to manage speech over the heads, and sometimes to the exclusion, of lesser-funded speakers.

Private speech management by well-financed speakers appears most visibly and consequentially in the Roberts Court's parade of campaign finance decisions. *Citizens United v. Federal Election Commission* (Chapter 7) doesn't simply liberate corporations from government control. Instead, the Court valorizes the expressive interests of corporations—"the voices that best represent the most significant parts of the economy"[1]—over the interests of ordinary citizens, for whom the government sought to preserve a space in electoral debate. *Davis v. Federal Election Commission* and *Arizona Free Enterprise Club's Freedom PAC v. Bennett* (both Chapter 8) similarly prioritize the interests of self-financing and privately financed candidates over the interests of electoral rivals whose competitive viability the federal and state governments sought to bolster. *McCutcheon v. Federal Election Commission* (Chapter 7) enhances the managerial power of both wealthy donors and the major political parties. These campaign finance decisions reject the government's efforts to promote viewpoint diversity and electoral competition in favor of the Court's choice to place powerful speakers' concerns at the forefront of the discussion.

In speech-protective decisions outside the electoral sphere, the Roberts Court's solicitude for wealthy speakers takes the form of trusting successful market actors to manage speech. Most notably, the drug "detailing" case *Sorrell v. IMS Health* (Chapter 2) works an innovation in the Court's convoluted commercial speech doctrine by protecting the profit-making capacity of speech between commercial actors. *IMS Health* rejects government efforts to protect consumers from commercial deals that take place outside their view, instead letting speakers who seek profit from expression dictate the flow of commercial information. Elsewhere, *United States v. Stevens* and *Brown v. Entertainment Merchants Association* (both Chapter 1) show that this Court's rejection of new categorical First Amendment exclusions has commanded majorities only in commercial settings.

No wealthy or powerful speaker has lost a major First Amendment case in the Roberts Court. The major political parties lost in *Washington State Grange v. Washington State Republican Party* (Chapter 6), but the Court there suggested the parties simply brought a viable claim prematurely. Institutional speakers lost narrow, very weak First Amendment challenges in the little-noted cases of *Milavetz, Gallop & Milavetz v. United States* (Chapter 2) and *Tennessee Secondary School Athletic Association v. Brentwood Academy* (Chapter 3). Unions are the only class of powerful institutions to wash out as First Amendment claimants in the Roberts Court, losing in both *Davenport* and *Ysursa v. Pocatello Education Association* (Chapter 8). Unions, however, are the institutional speakers for which the Roberts Court's conservative majority has expressed the strongest distaste, as *Knox v. SEIU* and *Harris v. Quinn* (both Chapter 8) resoundingly announce.

The public-private distinction provides maneuverability for the Roberts Court to choose which institutions will manage public discussion. First Amendment law requires a strict distinction between private rights-bearers

1. Citizens United v. FEC, 130 S. Ct. 876, 907 (2010) (quoting McConnell v. FEC, 540 U.S. 93, 257–58 (2003) (opinion of Scalia, J.)) (internal quotation marks and citation omitted).

and public rights-violators that the Supreme Court has long administered in undertheorized, normatively charged ways. Managed speech doubles down on both the commitment to rigid public-private line drawing and the normative polarization of the lines. First, and most directly, the aggressive government speech reasoning of *Summum* and *Walker* frees the Court to ignore private expressive interests and validate government restrictions. In a second group of cases, the government prevails in its regulatory guise while backing one class of private speakers against another. The government victories in *Golan, Lopez Torres,* and *Davenport* represent wins for, respectively, copyright holders over new users, political party organizations over insurgent candidates, and non-union workers over unions. In all these cases, speakers whose interests the government favored triumph over speakers whose interests the government opposed. The campaign finance decisions perform a third sort of contestable public-private line drawing. *Citizens United, McCutcheon, Davis,* and *Arizona Free Enterprise* bar the government from promoting the interests of lesser-financed speakers against more powerful speakers.

*Disfavoring Outsider Speech.* The mirror image of the Roberts Court's empowering of speech managers has been its consistent rejection of First Amendment claims by outsider speakers. These are speakers, usually individuals or smaller institutions, who lack significant expressive resources, who challenge dominant institutions or views, or whose identities or beliefs place them outside the social mainstream. *Humanitarian Law Project* rejects peace activists' First Amendment challenge to the government's political isolation of designated terrorist organizations. The Roberts Court has rejected First Amendment claims from agitators on both sides of the culture war between traditional morality and LGBT rights, spurning a conservative Christian student group's desire to maintain its boundaries in *Christian Legal Society* and liberal law schools' effort to resist the military's anti-LGBT policies in *FAIR.* The Court stretches precedent to reject criminal defendants' challenge to a ban on pandering non-existent child pornography in *United States v. Williams* (Chapter 1), and it all but ignores prisoners' challenge to a punitive restriction on reading material in *Beard.* The underdog political candidate in *Lopez Torres,* the insurgent creators in *Golan* who wanted to keep works in the public domain, and the inscrutable student sloganeer of *Morse* all get the back of the Court's hand. The Roberts Court treats outsider speech as a threat to stable, orderly public discussion, a dangerous aberration rather than a desirable stimulus.

The Roberts Court has given First Amendment victories to a handful of outsider speakers. All of those victories, however, come with important caveats. The faker of military honors in *United States v. Alvarez* (Chapter 1) won his First Amendment claim, but the Court couldn't agree on a principle to justify its result. The tiny Good News Community Church prevailed in *Reed v. Town of Gilbert* (Chapter 2), but the Court's opinion speaks in such broad First

Amendment platitudes that it will probably have only limited practical effect. The rabidly anti-LGBT Westboro Baptist Church is a quintessential outsider speaker, but its First Amendment victory in *Snyder v. Phelps* (also Chapter 2) rests on narrow grounds that leave it (and other political protesters) highly vulnerable to government restrictions. The public employee speaker's victory in *Lane v. Franks* merely qualifies employees' much more important loss in *Garcetti v. Ceballos* (both Chapter 3). Even the rescue in *Open Society* of AIDS-fighting organizations from the demands of the government's anti-human trafficking policy, an encouraging counterpoint to *Humanitarian Law Project*, mainly serves to mitigate the Roberts Court's own expansion of the government speech doctrine.

The Roberts Court has actively avoided using First Amendment law to redistribute expressive opportunities among outsider speakers. The Supreme Court, dating back to the Burger and Rehnquist Courts' invalidation of claims for First Amendment access to shopping centers and weakening of the public forum doctrine, has long ignored how economic inequality skews the distribution of speakers' opportunities to reach audiences. The Roberts Court has shown even less concern than its predecessors for imbalances in power and wealth that create differences among speakers' capacities to get their messages heard. That disregard has found its most potent expression in the campaign finance decisions, especially *Citizens United* and *McCutcheon*. The same disregard marks the Court's approach to creative activity in *Golan* and to the competitive disadvantages of electoral challengers in *Lopez Torres*. The Roberts Court has eroded the major distributive device in First Amendment law, the public forum doctrine. The Christian Legal Society, the religious sect in *Summum*, and the "lost cause" nostalgists of *Walker* sought expressive access to government property, and the Court said no. For this Court, differences in expressive opportunities reflect valid market distributions that First Amendment law need not, and should not, disturb.

While showing little concern about the cost of speech, the Roberts Court has also denigrated the value of speech, particularly outsider speech, for inspiring or enabling positive social change. This Court sees no loss in stifling new uses of ideas in *Golan*, while restoring those works to copyright protection creates value by monetizing them. The Court scorns the activist groups in *Humanitarian Law Project* for believing they could teach terrorists peaceful conflict resolution, but terrorist organizations can cash out the activists' speech as violence. The withheld newspapers and magazines in *Beard* function not as aids to rehabilitation but as the cold currency of punishment. The agency fees that nonunion workers pay to public employee unions in *Knox* and *Harris* bring the unions no expressive value worth the Court's attention, but the Court grimly measures the nonunion workers' loss of freedom by their forgone dollars. The campaign finance decisions' pluralist political vision celebrates speech not as a medium for political deliberation but as a vehicle for political influence. Interactive technology matters in *Entertainment Merchants* because it makes money for the game industry. Data mining deserves protection in *IMS Health* because it makes money for the drug industry.[2] The Roberts Court values free speech less as a force of social or political dynamism than as a prerogative of economic power.

*Prioritizing Social and Political Stability.* Both the Roberts Court's assignment of powerful, trusted institutions to manage public discussion and its relentless disregard for outsider speakers serve a regime of expressive freedom that preserves social and political stability. The extent to which the Court's empowering of speech managers and rejection of outsiders' First Amendment claims actually advance stability is an empirical question, but stability emerges from the decisions as the raison d'etre of managed speech.

Managed speech embodies an effort to reconcile a serious commitment to liberty with a thoroughgoing preference for stability. Speakers win First Amendment cases when their perspectives and interests track established distributions of social power. The corporate spenders of *Citizens United,* the wealthy donors of *McCutcheon,* and the self-financing candidates of *Davis* want to contest elections, but they want to maintain the fundamental arrangements that underwrite their own power and resources. The video game industry of *Entertainment Merchants* and the drug "detailers" of *IMS Health* want to compete in the marketplace, but they don't want to upend the conditions under which the market distributes access to resources. The Roberts Court relies on economically powerful actors to promote stability.

Conversely, the government wins First Amendment cases when expressive freedom threatens to destabilize existing power arrangements. The activists of *Humanitarian Law Project* and *FAIR* challenged the authority of the national security state. The First Amendment claimants in *Beard, Morse,* and *Garcetti* challenged the authority of prison wardens, school administrators, and law enforcement. The claimant in *Lopez Torres* challenged the electoral primacy of the major political parties. Managed speech protects the prerogatives of those stabilizing institutions. The Roberts Court's disinterest in distributing expressive opportunities keeps outsider speakers from expanding public discussion in unpredictable, potentially disruptive ways.

Potentially destabilizing speakers occasionally win their First Amendment claims, but their victories never seriously threaten established order. The Westboro Baptist Church attacks the military, other religions, and the growing consensus around LGBT rights, but *Snyder* gives the church only a narrow victory that does little to enhance its expressive autonomy. The antiabortion activists of *McCullen v. Coakley* (Chapter 4) engage in classic street activism,

2. For an argument that First Amendment litigation has become a vehicle for protecting property rights, *see* Julie E. Cohen, *The Zombie First Amendment*, 56 WM. & MARY L. REV. 1119 (2015).

but the Court isolates and professionalizes their agitation by treating them as "counsellors." The Good News Church in *Gilbert* and the false hero of *Alvarez* challenge social boundaries (in very different ways), but the decisions that validate their First Amendment claims have uncertain or limited precedential force. The nonunion workers of *Knox* and *Harris* aim to destabilize public employee unions, but the Court denies the unions' stabilizing value. The AIDS-fighting groups in *Open Society* present the strongest challenge to stability of any Roberts Court First Amendment winners. They're important institutions, they defy an important government policy, and the Court grants them much greater autonomy than *Snyder* grants the Westboro Baptists, letting them carry government resources in the direction they choose. *Open Society,* though, shares with *Gilbert* an uncertain scope and a function of tidying up doctrine more than revising it.

The Roberts Court's unprecedented reliance on tradition to guide First Amendment analysis in the categorical First Amendment cases axiomatically bolsters stability. When the Court insists in *Stevens* that the government properly may restrict extreme depictions of sex but not extreme depictions of violence, it argues for continuing to do things as, in the majority's narrative, we have always done them. Tradition presents problems as a basis for legal authority, because tradition's enthusiasts tend to portray it as more easily discernible and less contested than it is. The Roberts Court's reliance on tradition doesn't escape that trap, but this Court highly prizes the stability and certainty that tradition promises.

The Roberts Court's predecessors showed much greater solicitude for speech that threatens, or enables, social and political change. The Court under conservative Chief Justice William Rehnquist showed a strong commitment to political stability in its First Amendment cases about political parties.[3] On the other hand, the Rehnquist Court handed down the most important free speech decision of the past four decades, *Reno v. American Civil Liberties Union,*[4] which promoted the unruly, decentralized development of speech on the Internet. The Rehnquist Court also let Congress fight the political influence of large-scale electoral contributors and spenders,[5] and it invoked the First Amendment to protect flag burning as a form of political protest.[6] The prior Court, under conservative Chief Justice Warren Burger, promoted stability by closing off privately owned public spaces to expressive freedom claims.[7]

3. *See* Cal. Democratic Party v. Jones, 530 U.S. 567 (2000); Timmons v. Twin Cities Area New Party, 520 U.S. 351 (1997).

4. 521 U.S. 844 (1997).

5. *See* McConnell v. FEC, 540 U.S. 93 (2003); Colo. Republican Fed. Campaign Comm. v. FEC, 518 U.S. 604 (1996).

6. *See* United States v. Eichman, 496 U.S. 310 (1990); Texas v. Johnson, 491 U.S. 397 (1989).

7. *See* Hudgens v. NLRB, 424 U.S. 507 (1976); CBS, Inc. v. Democratic Nat'l Comm., 412 U.S. 94 (1973).

The Burger Court, however, also invoked the First Amendment to protect newspapers' publication of sensitive national security information,[8] political protesters' use of language designed to shock audiences,[9] and civil rights activists' enforcement of a disruptive commercial boycott.[10] The Roberts Court has shown a deeper, more consistent appetite than prior Courts for using First Amendment law to preserve stability and stifle change.

## THE CONSERVATISM OF MANAGED SPEECH

The coherence of managed speech as a mode of First Amendment jurisprudence belies charges by some critics that the Roberts Court has simply decided free speech cases to advance the immediate electoral and policy interests of political conservatives. I don't mean to dismiss the explanatory value of that charge entirely, especially given that thorough empirical analysis provides support for it.[11] However, a simple narrative about promoting immediate advantage for political conservatives gives at best an incomplete account of this Court's First Amendment jurisprudence. The decisions' promotion of social and political stability diverges sharply from the goals of reactionary groups such as the Tea Party, which at least in its more grass-roots aspects agitates for considerable political and social change.

Managed speech reflects a deeper, more complex brand of conservatism than a simple preference for the right-wing policy views of the moment. David Brooks, a leading conservative public intellectual of the Roberts Court era, offers a conception of conservatism that helps to situate managed speech:

> [C]onservatism stands for intellectual humility, a belief in steady, incremental change, a preference for reform rather than revolution, a respect for hierarchy, precedence, balance and order, and a tone of voice that is prudent, measured, and responsible. Conservatives of this definition can be dull, but they know how to nurture and run institutions.

Brooks adds that conservatism prioritizes "self-restraint and coalition building" over "self-expression." [12] This account scratches the surface of a conservative intellectual tradition that undergirds managed speech. Two antecedents can aid in understanding the Roberts Court's effort to reconcile expressive

8. *See* N.Y. Times Co. v. United States, 403 U.S. 713 (1971).
9. *See* Cohen v. California, 403 U.S. 15 (1971).
10. *See* NAACP v. Claiborne Hardware Co., 458 U.S. 886 (1982).
11. *See* Lee Epstein et al., *Do Justices Defend the Speech They Hate? In-Group Bias, Opportunism, and the First Amendment*, http://epstein.wustl.edu/research/InGroupBias.pdf (last visited Apr. 27, 2016).
12. David Brooks, *The Incompetence Conference*, N.Y. TIMES (Oct. 13, 2015) at A25.

freedom with responsible management: the political philosophy of Edmund Burke and the First Amendment theory of Robert Bork.[13]

Burke's critique of the French Revolution[14] builds a model of ordered liberty that prefigures the enlistment by managed speech of tradition, state power, and private wealth in the dualistic mission of maintaining and tempering liberty. Burke diverged from the assumptions of our contemporary political culture in his rejection of democracy[15] and "the wildest democratic ideas of freedom."[16] Even so, he advanced a substantial account of freedom: "a scheme of liberty, soberly limited, and defined with proper qualifications."[17] Burke posited an interdependence of human freedom and social stability. He called for liberty "combined with government; with public force; with the discipline and obedience of armies; with the collection of an effective and well-distributed revenue; with morality and religion; with the solidity of property; with peace and order; with civil and social manners."[18]

Tradition, for Burke, lay at the heart of a wise account of liberty. "All the reformations [England has] hitherto made," he wrote, "have proceeded upon the principle of reference to antiquity; and I hope . . . that all those which possibly may be made hereafter, will be carefully formed upon analogical precedent, authority, and example."[19] The Roberts Court echoes this commitment to tradition, most vividly in the categorical analysis that protects speech in *Stevens* and *Entertainment Merchants* while licensing speech restriction in *Golan*, *Williams*, and *Nevada Commission on Ethics v. Carrigan* (Chapter 1).

Burke also extolled state power. "The people of England," he wrote, "look upon the legal hereditary succession of their crown as among their rights, not as among their wrongs; as a benefit, not as a grievance; as a security for their liberty, not as a badge of servitude."[20] Like the Roberts Court in *Humanitarian Law Project,* Burke condemned claims of right that presumed to question the state's authority to preserve itself. "If civil society be the offspring of

13. Another candidate for the oddly alliterative roster of managed speech's conservative intellectual forebears is James Burnham, who in the mid-twentieth century prophesied, with striking normative ambivalence, an age of managerial control over society. *See* James Burnham, The Managerial Revolution: What Is Happening in the World (1941).

14. Edmund Burke, Reflections on the Revolution in France (Conor Cruise O'Brien ed., 1986) (1790).

15. *See id.* at 146 (disparaging "democratists" and positing "the many fallacies that lurk in the generality and equivocal nature of the terms 'inadequate representation'").

16. *Id.* at 155.

17. *Id.* at 374.

18. *Id.* at 90–91; *see also id.* at 151 ("[T]he restraints on men, as well as their liberties, are to be reckoned among their rights.").

19. *Id.* at 117; *see also id.* at 121 (describing the virtue of "considering our liberties in the light of an inheritance").

20. *Id.* at 111; *see also id.* at 102–06 (defending the British monarchy), 144 (defending institutions associated with the monarchy).

convention," he insisted, "that convention must be its law.... [H]ow can any man claim, under the conventions of civil society, rights which do not so much as suppose its existence? Rights which are absolutely repugnant to it?"[21] Accordingly, he questioned the right of radical authors "to exist, and so be permitted to act."[22]

Burke similarly relied on property to help regulate liberty. Foreshadowing *Citizens United*, he advocated disproportionate representation in government for large concentrations of property. Considering the relative political power of the Houses of Commons and Lords, Burke contrasted the "vigorous" nature of "ability" with the "sluggish, inert, and timid" character of "property." He insisted that property "never can be safe from the invasions of ability, unless it be, out of all proportion, predominant in the representation. It must be represented too in great masses of accumulation, or else it is not rightly protected."[23]

Undergirding Burke's account of constrained liberty is a normative preference for social and political stability. Burke celebrated "the peace, quiet, and security of the realm"[24] and condemned the French revolutionaries for "invert[ing] order in all things."[25] Likening social to familial order, he argued that would-be reformers "should approach to the faults of the state as to the wounds of a father, with pious awe and trembling solicitude."[26] Burke didn't entirely reject political and social change, but he merged "the two principles of conservation and correction" to identify "regenerat[ion]" of established institutions as the only proper aim of change.[27] Burke harbored deep skepticism about the capacities of human reason. He lauded established institutions for their "conformity with nature," and he invoked that ideal of nature "to fortify the fallible and feeble contrivances of our reason."[28] Burke's grave concern about "the ignorance and fallibility of mankind"[29] denies the constructive capacity of public debate. The Roberts Court's free speech jurisprudence echoes that denial.

In contemporary First Amendment theory, the major antecedent for the Roberts Court's free speech jurisprudence is a 45-year-old article by

21. *Id.* at 150.
22. *Id.* at 186.
23. *Id.* at 140.
24. *Id.* at 101; *see also id.* at 103 (extolling "the unity, peace, and tranquility of this nation").
25. *Id.* at 161.
26. *Id.* at 194
27. *Id.* at 106.
28. *Id.* at 121; *see also id.* at 156 (criticizing liberals "so taken with their theories about the rights of man, that they have totally forgot his nature"), 171 (lamenting the assault on venerable social norms by "this new conquering empire of light and reason").
29. *Id.* at 376.

conservative legal titan Robert Bork.[30] Writing in the shadow of increasingly violent protests over the Vietnam War and racial discrimination, Professor (later Judge and nearly Justice) Bork argued that Justices Holmes and Brandeis were entirely wrong to insist that the Constitution should protect advocating violent overthrow of the government.[31] First Amendment law, Bork posited, may only protect "the system of government which the judge is commissioned to object and maintain." Thus, judges lack proper authority to protect any speech that challenges "the premises of our system concerning the ways in which [political] truth is defined." For Bork, speech that advocated revolution or other unlawful action served not to inform the public or to provoke debate but only to "destroy[] the premises of our political system and the means by which we define political truth."[32] Bork grounded his ideas about the First Amendment in a broader constitutional theory that insisted on his conception of "neutral principles" as the only legitimate basis for judicial overruling of legislative decisions.[33] Like the Roberts Court, Bork strove to reconcile a substantial measure of constitutional speech protection with an overarching commitment to tradition and established structures of authority. Concern for stability animates Bork's call for restraining First Amendment law within settled bounds of ordered political engagement.

*Humanitarian Law Project* shows the Roberts Court's inheritance from Bork's approach to First Amendment rights. I contended in Chapter 2 that *Humanitarian Law Project* clashes with *Brandenburg v. Ohio,*[34] the 1968 decision that fully established First Amendment protection for advocacy of unlawful action. Bork derided *Brandenburg* as unprincipled.[35] The salience of Bork's brand of conservatism for managed speech, however, transcends the problem of advocating unlawful action. I explained in Chapter 7 how *Citizens United* promotes stability by empowering corporations as managers of electoral discourse. Corporate power, in the vision of *Citizens United,* serves to insulate political debate from the unpredictable influence of unruly dissenting voices. Corporations, along with the major political parties, order and structure electoral debate. These stabilizing institutions enable electoral debate, but the constraints their power imposes on the debate ensure that it won't stray too far from the political status quo. That

30. *See* Robert H. Bork, *Neutral Principles and Some First Amendment Problems*, 47 IND. L.J. 1 (1971).

31. I discuss the Holmes and Brandeis positions in connection with the development of categorical exclusions from the First Amendment (Chapter 1) and the *Humanitarian Law Project* case (Chapter 2).

32. Bork, *supra* note 30, at 30–32.

33. *See id.* at 1–20.

34. 395 U.S. 444 (1969).

35. *See* Bork, *supra* note 30, at 34–35.

reasoning from *Citizens United* simply extends to powerful private institutions Bork's ideas about how the state can and should constrain public discussion.

## FROM MANAGED SPEECH TO DYNAMIC DIVERSITY

Through the lens of dynamic diversity, the Roberts Court's First Amendment looks deeply flawed. Dynamic diversity embodies two core values. The idea value seeks to maximize the range of views and information present in public discussion. The participation value seeks to maximize the number and variety of people engaged in public discussion. Several speech-protective Roberts Court decisions promote dynamic diversity's values to some meaningful extent: *Entertainment Merchants, Snyder, Town of Gilbert, Open Society,* and *McCullen*. All those decisions, however, are narrow in effect or equivocal in reasoning. Meanwhile, the Roberts Court has handed down multiple important decisions in each of this book's three categories of free speech cases—private speech, government preserves, and electoral speech—that strongly discourage or impede the diversification of ideas and participants in public discussion. From a dynamic diversity perspective, this Court has underprotected speech in too many private speech cases and far too many government preserve cases while overprotecting certain speakers the Court favors, mainly in electoral speech cases.

The Roberts Court's refusal to expand categorical exclusions from the First Amendment in *Stevens* and *Entertainment Merchants*, along with the plurality opinion in *Alvarez*, unites managed speech and dynamic diversity. Categorical exclusions from First Amendment protection constrain public debate at the ground level of free speech doctrine. They embody a speech-restrictive consensus that undervalues outsider speech and dissent. Behind the favorable results in *Stevens* and *Entertainment Merchants*, however, tensions emerge. First, those decisions carry limited value for dynamic diversity. Even *Entertainment Merchants*, where Justice Scalia's rhetoric makes the Roberts Court's strongest statement about the constructive power of speech, merely reaffirms established First Amendment speech protection. More important, the decisions ground their approach firmly in tradition. Dynamic diversity, with its emphasis on speech as a vehicle for social and political change, sees little use for tradition as a basis for First Amendment law. When the Roberts Court's fealty to tradition leads it to sustain categorical limits on the First Amendment's scope, especially in *Golan*, the tension with dynamic diversity expands from methodology to substance. For dynamic diversity, disputes between copyright holders (or their heirs) and new users presents a conflict between important speech values, with greater weight on the side of speakers who deploy old materials in the service of new ideas. Dynamic diversity requires a nuanced assessment of the conflicting interests, an assessment the Roberts Court's fixation on tradition causes *Golan* to evade.

The Roberts Court's private speech balancing decisions present deeper problems for dynamic diversity. *Humanitarian Law Project* lets the government suppress exactly the kind of speech dynamic diversity most deeply values: dissent from a strong public consensus on issues of national security and terrorism. By dynamic diversity's lights, political dissenters greatly benefit public discussion by offering oppositional ideas for public consideration. That benefit can't happen if we follow managed speech in restricting public debate to ideas that pose no threat of unsettling established order. The capacity of public debate to spur political change should embolden First Amendment law, not define its limits. We trust the Supreme Court, insulated from day-to-day politics, to defend political dissenters against the majority's anxious power. *Humanitarian Law Project* betrays that trust. In contrast, *IMS Health* protects a sort of speech that has little value for dynamic diversity, commercial sales pitches, while undermining a government effort to protect consumers from potential market distortions that evade public scrutiny. The decision confirms how far the priorities of managed speech diverge from dynamic diversity.

From the perspective of dynamic diversity, *Snyder* stands with *Entertainment Merchants* among the Roberts Court's finest First Amendment decisions. If we want to encourage the greatest possible variety of participants and ideas in public discussion, then we need First Amendment law to protect marginal, dissident, outsider voices. The rhetoric of *Snyder* tells speakers at the margins of public debate to go ahead and post their online provocations or organize their protest marches. It puts all of us who think we're in the mainstream on notice that we'll have to confront weird, disconcerting, offensive ideas when we venture into public debate. Likewise, the *Gilbert* Court's rejection of a clumsily content-based sign regulation should discourage some laws that limit the range of ideas in public discussion. However, the narrow scope of *Snyder* and the uncertain effect of *Gilbert* leave these cases far less beneficial to dynamic diversity than *Humanitarian Law Project* is detrimental.

The Roberts Court's decisions about the First Amendment in government preserves undercut dynamic diversity at almost every turn. The key institutional speech cases *Beard, Morse,* and *Garcetti* diminish public debate by denying First Amendment protection to entire classes of speakers who live, study, or work under government institutional control. These decisions remove ideas from public debate by disregarding institutional subjects' distinctive, often oppositional insights and perspectives. Prisoners occupy a unique, fraught place in society that the rest of us, whatever our views on crime and punishment, could stand to think and learn more about. Public school students become smarter and better citizens by pushing back against school authority, even if they don't always know what they're pushing toward. Public employees perform a valuable service when they call out government corruption or mistakes, either on the job or in public. The Roberts Court sacrifices on the altar of managerial control all the benefits these groups bring to public debate.

Dynamic diversity's aim of broadening the ranges of ideas and participants in public discussion points toward a First Amendment regime that doesn't merely bar government from restricting speech but requires, or at least presses, the government to promote speech. Making public property and public funds available for speech is the least the government can do. The Roberts Court, led in this area by its liberal wing, has reduced those scraps of redistributive First Amendment doctrine to even less than they were before. The government speech doctrine of *Summum* and *Walker* doesn't merely restrict speech that dynamic diversity values; it conceptually devours that speech. The last thing First Amendment law should do, from the perspective of dynamic diversity, is convert independent speech, especially the speech of religious and political outsiders, into a mere dissonant note for the government to squelch. *Christian Legal Society* takes an interesting problem about how best to encourage exchanges of ideas and flattens it into another paean to managerial authority. *FAIR*, like *Humanitarian Law Project*, brusquely subordinates political dissent to military power.

The funding and subsidy cases yield two more decisions that advance dynamic diversity. The skepticism in *McCullen* about the tailoring of Massachusetts's abortion clinic buffer zone law may mark the Roberts Court's single most positive advance in First Amendment law. Can that skepticism, though, protect dissent in future cases that don't involve antiabortion "counsellors"? Similarly, *Open Society* may signal a move toward greater protection for publicly funded speakers against the government's desire to attach policy strings. How much of the distance between *Open Society* and the speech-restrictive *FAIR* decision, though, owes to a passing imperative to keep the government speech genie in its bottle? These decisions offer reasons for hope, tempered by causes for doubt.

The Roberts Court's electoral speech cases offend dynamic diversity as deeply as the government preserve decisions do, but by different means. Except for *IMS Health*, all the decisions I've criticized up to this point have rejected First Amendment claims. In the campaign finance field (with *Williams-Yulee v. Florida Bar* (Chapter 8) the lone, qualified exception), the Roberts Court has scarcely met a First Amendment challenge it hasn't liked. Dynamic diversity requires public discussion, centrally including electoral debates, to engage the widest possible range of participants and ideas. The Roberts Court's campaign finance decisions sabotage those goals.

*Citizens United* and *McCutcheon* assert that the First Amendment, above all, is about letting wealthy people and entities convert their market success into expressive influence. Moneyed interests comprise one particular segment of the electorate. They tend to favor public policies that perpetuate the conditions under which they amassed their wealth. A First Amendment doctrine that lets moneyed interests maximize their political influence crowds out lesser-financed ideas and speakers, particularly ideas and speakers that challenge prevailing social and economic policies. *Citizens United* and *McCutcheon* thus contradict both the idea value and the participation value of dynamic diversity. The Burger Court started us down this road, but the late Rehnquist Court had shifted campaign finance law toward dynamic diversity's values. The Roberts Court's decisions erode those values beyond anything the Burger Court imagined.

*Davis* and *Arizona Free Enterprise* cut even deeper. In those cases, governments tried to counter electoral advantages conferred by private wealth and provide voters with fuller information about candidates. The decisions strike down those efforts to increase electoral competition and voter information. Through a dynamic diversity lens, the Court's reasoning is almost impossible to fathom. Like *IMS Health, Davis* and *Arizona Free Enterprise* treat pursuit of monetary advantage as a central First Amendment value, blocking government efforts to decrease the influence of private wealth in elections. Just as *Davis* and *Arizona Free Enterprise* keep government from countering private wealth, the Court's assault on public sector agency fees in *Knox* and *Harris* disables unions' efforts to counter corporate power. *Lopez Torres* likewise enhances the electoral influence of the major political parties. Our duopolistic political system, which drives politically marginal voices into smothering coalitions, presents deep problems for dynamic diversity, which wants those voices engaged and their ideas audible.

Managed speech, as embodied in the Roberts Court's First Amendment jurisprudence, strongly undermines both the idea value and the participation value of dynamic diversity. Dynamic diversity seeks a broadly participatory public discussion. Managed speech lets select government actors and powerful speakers manage the content and scope of public debates. Dynamic diversity prioritizes First Amendment protection for political dissenters and other outsider speakers, both to broaden participation in public discussion and to bring new ideas into the discussion. Managed speech largely ignores or rejects First Amendment claims from dissenters and outsiders, fearing that those speakers might disrupt orderly discussion. Dynamic diversity views the capacity of speech to foster social and political change as central to the constitutional value of free expression. Managed speech places paramount value on maintaining a regime of expressive freedom that preserves social and political stability. From the perspective of dynamic diversity, the Roberts Court's elaboration of First Amendment doctrine along managed speech lines has made public discussion less free and robust than it should and could be.

## TOWARD THE NEXT FIRST AMENDMENT

If dynamic diversity opposes most of what the Roberts Court has done to First Amendment doctrine, what would dynamic diversity have the Court do differently? This book has looked back on a decade of the Roberts Court's free speech jurisprudence. It closes by looking forward. Justice Antonin Scalia's sudden passing in February 2016 deprived the Supreme Court of one of its leading intellectual voices. Justice Scalia played a major role in the development of managed speech. His departure reminds us that the Court's makeup changes continuously and sometimes dramatically. This final section offers some thoughts about how a potential new Court, in the nearer or further future, might productively develop the next First Amendment. I'll first propose some general shifts in how the Court approaches First Amendment decisions. I'll then briefly outline new directions in several specific areas of First Amendment law.

*General Approaches to First Amendment Law*. The Roberts Court has made some positive contributions to First Amendment doctrine, even from the largely critical perspective of dynamic diversity. The Court has issued a handful of speech-protective decisions in the private speech and government preserve categories that have at least the potential to increase the variety of participants and ideas in public discussion. However, as the last section explains, the Roberts Court's managed speech approach to the First Amendment mostly sets those goals back. This Court's commitment to a First Amendment that preserves social and political stability clashes with dynamic diversity's vision of a First Amendment that enables social and political change. To advance dynamic diversity, a new Court should approach First Amendment law on fundamentally different premises.

First and foremost, a new Court should shift its center of First Amendment gravity from powerful and well-financed speakers to dissenters and outsider speakers. The paladins of First Amendment law in the 1920s were communists and anarchists; in the 1940s, Jehovah's Witnesses; in the 1960s, activists for racial justice. All of those groups, in different ways, spoke from outside the social and political mainstreams. In contrast, the leading First Amendment paladins over the past 45 years have been corporations and commercial interests. Their dominance has peaked on the Roberts Court, whose emblematic First Amendment decision is *Citizens United*. Religious speakers might count as a second group of Roberts Court First Amendment paladins, given their victories in *Snyder, Gilbert*, and *McCullen*. Religious speakers, however, have a less prominent and weaker record of success than commercial actors, having lost important free speech challenges in *Summum* and *Christian Legal Society*.

The next First Amendment should, within a broadly inclusive scope, prioritize strong First Amendment protection for dissenters and outsider speakers.

Street protesters, muckraking journalists, and campus agitators need more of the Court's attention. Speakers who lack substantial expressive resources, who challenge the power of entrenched institutions, and who resist and critique broadly popular ideas deserve stronger First Amendment protection. Managed speech has mostly left these speakers out in the cold. The next Supreme Court should encourage the constructive power of speech to change society for the better. The Roberts Court has treated speech that challenges the status quo as a threat to social order, most prominently in *Humanitarian Law Project* and also in such cases as *Morse, FAIR*, and *Lopez Torres*. A new Court should tap into the optimism of the Warren Court's *New York Times Co. v. Sullivan,*[36] which extolled the democratic virtue of broad-based public debate; the Burger Court's *Cohen v. California,*[37] which treated even profane expressions of political anger as valuable contributions to public discussion; and the Rehnquist Court's *Reno v. American Civil Liberties Union,*[38] which celebrated the Internet's democratization of speakers' abilities to reach broad audiences.

The Roberts Court, in contexts from *Golan* to *Christian Legal Society* to the campaign finance decisions, has sustained and exacerbated the Supreme Court's long-standing tendency to hide collisions of expressive interests behind a rigid public-private distinction. That tendency ignores the reality that private actors, not just the government, can suppress speech in ways that threaten First Amendment values. A new Court should confront conflicts between expressive interests forthrightly. Templates for adjudicating clashes between expressive interests exist.[39] The Warren Court in *Red Lion Broadcasting v. Federal Communications Commission*[40] upheld the broadcast fairness doctrine based on the people's interest, grounded in the First Amendment, in hearing varied perspectives on public issues. The Rehnquist Court in *Bartnicki v. Vopper*[41] invoked the First Amendment to bar legal liability for broadcasting an illegally taped conversation about a labor dispute, after weighing the First Amendment conflict between the public's informational interest and speakers' interest in confidentiality. Justice Breyer's pragmatic balancing approach to the First Amendment, expressed in his separate opinions in such cases as *Alvarez* and *Gilbert,* offers a useful starting point for resolving collisions between expressive interests.

36. 376 U.S. 254 (1964).
37. 403 U.S. 15 (1971).
38. 521 U.S. 844 (1997).
39. Elsewhere I have proposed that courts resolve collisions of First Amendment interests by deciding which resolutions better promote widespread participation in public debate. *See* Gregory P. Magarian, *The Jurisprudence of Colliding First Amendment Interests: From the Dead End of Neutrality to the Open Road of Participation-Enhancing Review*, 83 Notre Dame L. Rev. 185, 249–63 (2007).
40. 395 U.S. 367 (1969).
41. 532 U.S. 514 (2001).

These broad conceptual shifts in the Supreme Court's approach to First Amendment law would affect numerous areas of doctrine. Here I sketch changes a new Court could make in three areas that have particular importance for dynamic diversity: the mass media, money in politics, and access to expressive resources.

*The Mass Media*. The past two decades have brought an explosion in the social, political, and economic importance of the mass media and mass culture.[42] The Roberts Court's First Amendment decisions, though, largely ignore the First Amendment issues, both familiar and novel, that attend the information age. Citizens United challenged the government's refusal to let it show *Hillary: The Movie* on pay-per-view television, but the Court's *Citizens United* decision draws greater rhetorical fuel from the challenged law's asserted effect on book publication.[43] *Snyder* declines to consider the Internet portion of the Westboro Baptist Church's anti-LGBT screed. The information age has intensified concerns about defamation and media encroachments on privacy, but only in *Snyder*, a case involving a nonmedia defendant, has the Roberts Court come near those issues. *IMS Health* flirts with making a major statement about "big data," but the Court ultimately roots its decision in less fraught doctrinal ground. The Roberts Court has liberally invoked the First Amendment to protect corporations, but just one Roberts Court free speech decision, *Federal Communications Commission v. Fox Television* (Chapter 1), directly involves media corporations, and that decision makes no First Amendment law.

The dearth of mass media decisions from the Roberts Court doesn't reflect any absence of legal controversies that warrant the Court's attention. In fact, the contemporary mass media present numerous important legal problems. Three First Amendment media issues that a new Supreme Court could productively engage are press freedom, control of information channels, and morals regulations.

*Press Freedom*. As Lee Bollinger eloquently argues, a free, vigorous press remains an essential feature of a thriving democratic society.[44] Journalism matters deeply for dynamic diversity. The mass media's function of gathering and disseminating information about public issues directly advances dynamic diversity's idea value. In the age of blogs and social media, the mass media also advance dynamic diversity's participation value. Remarkably, one could read the Roberts Court's decisions, blink, and never know the First Amendment

42. Significant discussions in the legal literature include YOCHAI BENKLER, THE WEALTH OF NETWORKS: HOW SOCIAL PRODUCTION TRANSFORMS MARKETS AND FREEDOM (2007); LAWRENCE LESSIG, CODE VERSION 2.0 (2006); Jack M. Balkin, *Digital Speech and Democratic Culture: A Theory of Freedom of Expression for the Information Society*, 79 N.Y.U. L. REV. 1 (2004).

43. *See* Citizens United v. FEC, 558 U.S. 310, 349 (2010).

44. *See* LEE C. BOLLINGER, UNINHIBITED, ROBUST, AND WIDE-OPEN: A FREE PRESS FOR A NEW CENTURY (2010).

bars the government from abridging "the freedom of speech, *or of the press.*"[45] This Court's major attention to what people used to call the fourth estate is the derision in *Citizens United* of the media's exemption from the late federal ban on corporate electoral spending. First Amendment doctrine had moved far toward abandoning journalists before Chief Justice Roberts arrived,[46] and the Court's continuing neglect surely owes in part to the increased challenges of identifying "the press" amid the Internet's diffusion of information sources.[47] Still, the failure of any Roberts Court First Amendment decision to consider, let alone vindicate, a press claimant's speech interests marks the most glaring omission from this Court's free speech jurisprudence.

The press continues to grapple with important legal problems, both familiar and novel. Police often block reporters' efforts to cover volatile events on the streets.[48] Journalists, in the absence of a federal "press shield" law, continue fighting to protect their confidential sources from legal exposure. In fact, the Roberts Court in 2014 refused to hear a high-profile appeal from a *New York Times* reporter who faced a contempt citation for refusing to identify a source relevant to a federal criminal case.[49] This era's most urgent free speech issue for the press arises from the massive leaks to news organizations of sensitive government documents by WikiLeaks, Edward Snowden, and others.[50] Those disclosures raise similar questions about public information and national security to the Nixon-era Pentagon Papers Case,[51] but they bring those questions into our fraught and technologically accelerated present. The next Supreme Court should confront press freedom issues, with strong emphasis on the continuing democratic salience of the press. As for the challenge of

45. U.S. CONST. amend. I (emphasis added). For discussions of the distinctive relevance of the press clause, see C. EDWIN BAKER, MEDIA, MARKETS, AND DEMOCRACY 193–213 (2002); Sonja R. West, *Press Exceptionalism*, 127 HARV. L. REV. 2434, 2439–43 (2014).

46. *See, e.g.*, Cohen v. Cowles Media Co., 501 U.S. 663 (1991) (rejecting a newspaper's argument that the First Amendment should shield it against a civil action by a source whose identity it revealed); Branzburg v. Hayes, 408 U.S. 665 (1972) (rejecting journalists' argument that the First Amendment should shield them against law enforcement demands for disclosure of their confidential sources' identities).

47. *See* West, *supra* note 45, at 2456–62 (proposing guidelines for legally identifying "the press" in contemporary media circumstances).

48. One vivid example is police suppression of journalists during the 2014 protests in Ferguson, Missouri. For a useful compilation of materials, see Newseum Institute, *Ferguson Resources*, http://www.newseuminstitute.org/news/exchange/ferguson-resources/ (last visited May 19, 2016).

49. *See* United States v. Sterling, 724 F. 3d 482 (4th Cir. 2013), *cert. denied sub nom.* Risen v. United States, 134 S. Ct. 2696 (2014).

50. *See, e.g.*, Jonathan Peters, *WikiLeaks, the First Amendment, and the Press*, HARV. LAW & POL'Y REV. (Apr. 18, 2011), http://web.archive.org/web/20110422201541/http://hlpronline.com/2011/04/wikileaks-the-first-amendment-and-the-press/ (last visited May 19, 2016).

51. N.Y. Times Co. v. United States, 403 U.S. 713 (1971).

defining "the press" in the Internet age, a new Court should take a functional approach, expanding the press clause's protection to encompass whatever people and institutions gather and disseminate news.

*Control of Information Channels.* Another critical First Amendment concern about the contemporary mass media is structural. Who materially and economically controls the public's access to information has always been a matter of great First Amendment concern, but the Supreme Court has never addressed the concern vigorously. If relatively few companies control the channels of communication, the diversity of both participants and ideas in public discussion comes under grave threat. In the old media era, this concentration concern inspired government regulations to disperse ownership of newspapers and broadcast stations.[52] That issue still matters, because the old media ownership structure hasn't disappeared. On the new media landscape, the concentration concern drives the debate over "net neutrality," the legal prohibition of Internet service providers (ISPs) from providing faster or less expensive access to favored sources or types of information. The Federal Communications Commission's Open Internet Order enshrines net neutrality, for now, in federal law.[53] ISPs have argued that the order violates the First Amendment by dictating the terms on which ISPs may, in effect, "publish" information. Consumer advocates and other supporters counter that the order advances First Amendment values by ensuring the public's unconstrained access to information. Net neutrality exemplifies the need, discussed above, for a new Supreme Court to look past a rigid public-private distinction and resolve conflicts between expressive interests. Under the dynamic diversity model, the Court should secure net neutrality in order to broaden speakers' access to audiences and audiences' access to information.

*Morals Regulations.* The Supreme Court's long-standing allowance for the government to punish "obscenity"[54] continues, directly and through its underwriting of other legal restrictions on sexual content, to restrain important segments of the mass media. The subjectivity of that categorical exclusion, which bases criminal liability for speech on local community standards, has always run against the grain of First Amendment law. *Stevens* and *Entertainment Merchants* admirably limit categorical exclusion as a means of diminishing the First Amendment. However, as Chapter 1 explains, those decisions' fixation on tradition reinforces, rather than weakens, the justification for obscenity bans. The Roberts Court, in fact, refused to hear a challenge to a federal

52. *See* C. EDWIN BAKER, MEDIA CONCENTRATION AND DEMOCRACY: WHY OWNERSHIP MATTERS (2007).

53. *See* Protecting and Promoting the Open Internet, 80 Fed. Reg. 19,737 (2015) (to be codified at 47 C.F.R. §§ 1, 8, 20); *see also* United States Telecom Ass'n v. FCC, No. 15-1063 (D.C. Cir. June 14, 2016) (upholding the FCC's order against legal challenges).

54. *See* Miller v. California, 413 U.S. 15 (1973). Chapter 1 discusses *Miller* and obscenity in conjunction with the Roberts Court's categorical First Amendment decisions.

ban on Internet obscenity.[55] The Internet's globalization of information has blurred the "community" boundaries that structure the obscenity doctrine. At the same time, our society's rapid advances in LGBT rights have eroded the traditional, restrictive sexual morality that provides the doctrine's normative lifeblood. Formally interring the obscenity exclusion would sound a clearer warning against pernicious content-based regulations than the Roberts Court's rhetoric in *Gilbert*. At a minimum, a new Supreme Court should decouple the desirable results in *Stevens* and *Entertainment Merchants* from the Roberts Court's inappropriate and counterproductive tradition rationale.

*Money in Politics*. No Roberts Court decision has prompted such fervent criticism as *Citizens United*. Even on dynamic diversity principles, however, *Citizens United* gets some important things right. First, the Court rightly emphasizes the overriding importance of political speech in our democratic system and, accordingly, places special emphasis on political speech in First Amendment doctrine. Second, the Court rightly includes money's role in facilitating speech, including electoral speech, within the scope of First Amendment concern. Reaching an audience requires resources, and the First Amendment would protect almost nothing if it categorically ignored restrictions on the resources that enable speech. Legislatures have incentives to stifle electoral debate by entrenching incumbents or by depriving voters of access to information, and those dangers compel some First Amendment review of campaign finance laws. Finally, *Citizens United* Court reaches the correct *result* in the specific legal dispute before it. To bar Citizens United, an ideological nonprofit group with minimal corporate funding, from circulating a political video would unjustly and unwisely constrain electoral debate.

Unfortunately, *Citizens United* doesn't stop with Citizens United. The decision's uncompromising protection for corporate electoral spending, combined with letting big contributors spread their money across the electoral map in *McCutcheon* and restricting public funding in *Davis* and *Arizona Free Enterprise*, effectively places wealthy and powerful speakers in charge of electoral debate. Unregulated private money in elections creates hazards for a well-functioning democracy: not just the danger of corruption that the *McCutcheon* Court narrows to include little if anything more than outright bribery, but letting moneyed interests drown out lesser-financed speakers; turning elected officials into professional fundraisers; and arguably reducing the informational value of campaign speech even as its volume, in both senses of the word, increases. The Roberts Court's conviction that corporations and wealthy donors deserve to dominate elections and that only their money can protect us from government wilts under a dynamic, inclusive vision of democratic politics.

55. *See* Nitke v. Gonzales, 413 F. Supp. 2d 262 (S.D.N.Y. 2005), *cert. denied*, 547 U.S. 1015 (2006).

On the dynamic diversity model, a new Supreme Court should reverse the course of *Citizens United* and the Roberts Court's other campaign finance decisions. The new Court should scrap the stability-bolstering assumptions that undergird those decisions and promote the benefits to democracy when more ideas reach the electorate and more people discuss them. Such an approach to campaign finance, like the approach I advocate above to net neutrality, would require a nuanced mixture of deference and oversight. Something like the intermediate scrutiny that applies to "expressive conduct" regulations[56] or, again, Justice Breyer's proportional First Amendment methodology would provide a fruitful starting point for the new doctrine. In evaluating particular regulations, the Court could consider a range of factors, including whether the sort of regulation at issue has a history of biasing debates in incumbents' favor or undercutting voter information; the regulation's foreseeable effects on speakers' ability to reach audiences; whether a present societal consensus favors the regulation, and on what grounds; and the relative competence of the legislature and the Court to assess the regulation's costs and benefits.

Under that sort of approach, all the major campaign finance regulations the Roberts Court has struck down should have survived substantially intact. The corporate spending ban in *Citizens United,* the aggregate contribution limit in *McCutcheon,* and the public leveling formulas in *Davis* and *Arizona Free Enterprise* all put reasonable constraints on the dominance of private wealth in electoral debate. Those regulations enhance electoral competition and allow a wide variety of participants and ideas into electoral debate. The approach I propose would shift the *Buckley v. Valeo*[57] contribution-expenditure equilibrium by substantially permitting limits on electoral expenditures, as long as the limits didn't prevent electoral speakers, especially opponents and critics of incumbent officials, from effectively communicating with voters. Elections are purposive democratic processes. Whatever First Amendment salience the autonomy to spend as much as one desires might have in other contexts, it has none in elections.[58] First Amendment law in the campaign finance setting should enable and encourage rules that optimize the range of participants and ideas in electoral debate.

*Access to Expressive Resources.* Access to public expressive resources is the most important distributive element in our system of constitutional speech protection. Public space is the fallback resource for people who lack other means to reach an audience. The public forum doctrine has never done enough

56. *See* United States v. O'Brien, 391 U.S. 367 (1968).

57. 424 U.S. 1 (1976).

58. For arguments that the First Amendment should apply differently to elections than to other expressive arenas, see C. Edwin Baker, *Campaign Expenditures and Free Speech*, 33 HARV. C.R.-C.L. L. REV. 1 (1998); Frederick Schauer & Richard H. Pildes, *Electoral Exceptionalism and the First Amendment*, 77 TEX. L. REV. 1803 (1999).

to open public expressive space, and the problem has only gotten worse. Over the past two decades, police across the country have honed tactics to suppress, discourage, and punish public political activism.[59] Restricting political protesters at public events to remote, constricting "free speech zones" has become common practice.[60] These assaults on public expression pose a dire threat to First Amendment rights. The Roberts Court, however, has done almost nothing to restore expressive rights in public places. Instead, *Summum* and *Walker* let the government speech doctrine corrode the public forum, and *Christian Legal Society* subordinates public forum principles to institutional power. Even *McCullen*, with its welcome skepticism about the breadth of government regulation in the public forum, carves out special protection for antiabortion "counselors" by denigrating the larger category of "protesters."

A new Supreme Court should revitalize and enhance the public forum. First, the Court should restrict the government speech doctrine. First Amendment law benefits from the insight that government interacts with private speakers when it participates in public discussion.[61] That insight, however, should raise a warning sign about the vulnerability of private speech rather than an opportunity for suppressing it. The government speech principle should limit the First Amendment's reach only where both private speakers and the government understand that the government is engaging the speakers to convey a specific, defined message. Second, the Court should recalibrate the balance between managerial authority and expressive rights in the public forum. The Court should treat free expression not as an inconvenient encroachment on public spaces but as a primary purpose of those spaces. It should acknowledge and safeguard the distinctive expressive value of public spaces for lesser-funded speakers. It should, as Justices Breyer and Kagan urge in their *Gilbert* concurrences, reject government property regulations that exclude distinctive views or ideas. Every public forum case should prompt a *McCullen*-style probe of the government's justifications for limiting public speech. Cases such as *Christian Legal Society* should turn not on simple deference to the government's managerial authority but on a deeper analysis of whether institutional leaders are making competent, credible efforts to advance free speech.

Then the new Court should look beyond the public forum doctrine. Even at its speech-protective zenith, that doctrine only thinly embodies what should be a stout goal of First Amendment doctrine: widely distributed access to expressive resources. A half-century ago, Jerome Barron argued forcefully that

59. *See* Kris Hermes, Crashing the Party: Legacies and Lessons from the RNC 2000 (2015).

60. *See* Timothy Zick, Speech out of Doors: Preserving Liberty in Public Places 61–62 (2009).

61. *See* Mark G. Yudof, When Government Speaks: Politics, Law, and Government Expression in America (1983).

the Court should recognize a First Amendment right of access to mass media.[62] The Internet has radically transformed the media landscape, making electronic communication available to nearly everyone. Barron's plea for access rights, however, remains relevant. Even the Internet has a power structure that concentrates the capacity to reach wide audiences, as the net neutrality debate demonstrates. More important for present purposes, shared physical space remains a uniquely valuable expressive resource. People still live and interact in the physical world. Face-to-face communication, as *McCullen* recognizes, can be the most effective way to convey important messages to desired audiences. That expressive resource, however, has suffered not just from government managerial constraints but also from private property's crowding out of public spaces. We no longer go to Main Street; we go to malls called "Main Street."

A new Supreme Court should promote distribution of expressive resources through three doctrinal moves:

*The Public Forum as Government Duty.* The Court should treat the distribution of government property and money for expressive uses not as a mere government prerogative but as a government duty. Although the Court lacks a mechanism for affirmatively compelling the government to distribute expressive resources, conceiving distribution as a government duty would change the assumptions the Court brings to public forum and subsidized speech cases. The Court should expand on the speech-protective reasoning of *McCullen* and *Open Society* to construe both the public forum and speech subsidies as providing the greatest reasonable degree of expressive autonomy for speakers. Just as the Court should let the government enhance public discussion through public financing of lesser-funded political candidates, it should make the government enhance public discussion through liberally construed access to public property and subsidies.

*Expressive Private Spaces.* The new Supreme Court should prudently expand the First Amendment access principle to the private sphere. Just as the campaign finance problem compels allowance for the benefits government regulation can bring for free expression, the public forum problem compels remediation of the constraints private power can impose on free expression. *Amalgamated Food Employees Union v. Logan Valley Plaza*[63] extended First Amendment rights to a private shopping center. The *Logan Valley Plaza* Court reasoned that the shopping center had replaced the function of the town square and should therefore provide the town square's expressive opportunities. The Burger Court abandoned *Logan Valley Plaza* because private

62. *See* JEROME A. BARRON, FREEDOM OF THE PRESS FOR WHOM? THE RIGHT OF ACCESS TO MASS MEDIA (1973); Jerome A. Barron, *Access to the Press—A New First Amendment Right*, 80 HARV. L. REV. 1641 (1967).

63. 391 U.S. 308 (1968).

shopping centers don't fully replicate public spaces.[64] A new Supreme Court should revive and revitalize the *Logan Valley Plaza* doctrine, based not on a mere descriptive comparison of public and private spaces but on a deeper normative principle of expressive access. The First Amendment should reach privately owned property that is open to the general public and that replicates the expressive value of public space. Expressive resources that enable broad participation in public discussion have migrated to the private sphere to an extent undreamed of when the Supreme Court abandoned *Logan Valley Plaza.* Dynamic diversity counsels that expressive rights should follow them. Otherwise, the private sphere's crowding out of public space will negate expressive freedom as surely as the government speech doctrine does.

*Heightening Electoral Competition. Lopez Torres* opens a small window into the many ways our electoral system blocks insurgent candidates from challenging entrenched officials. The problem is even worse for minor parties. The one thing about which our two major parties reliably agree is maintaining their institutional power. Their control over the federal and state governments lets them make election laws that weaken competition within the major party structures and doom challenges from outside. Those laws include the sort of rigid nominating processes seen in *Lopez Torres,* limits on the openness of primary elections as suggested in *Washington State Grange,* single-member legislative districts with plurality voting, restrictive ballot access rules, high hurdles for access to televised candidate debates, and bans on minor parties' co-nominating major party candidates. Policy goals other than stifling competition may justify some of those measures. The Supreme Court, however, has for decades used First Amendment law to rubber-stamp the major parties' efforts to avoid regulation and stifle competition. A new Court should review anticompetitive election laws much more critically. The Court should recognize that vigorous electoral competition, and the robust debate it fosters, is crucial for our democratic system.

## CONCLUSION

The Supreme Court under Chief Justice John Roberts has built a formidable approach to First Amendment, comprehensible through the analytic lens of managed speech. Managed speech, as elaborated in the Roberts Court's decisions, is no cheap exercise in right-wing hackwork. Rather, it embodies a sophisticated fusion of Burke's institutionally anchored conservatism with Bork's ideas about properly constrained expressive freedom. Managed speech provides substantial protection for expressive autonomy. That protection,

64. *See* Hudgens v. NLRB, 424 U.S. 507 (1976).

however, comes with debilitating limits. By placing a high premium on social and political stability, managed speech encourages a public discussion where a limited number of speakers exchange a limited range of ideas. By enlisting powerful government and private managers to keep public discussion within responsible boundaries, managed speech discourages spontaneity and dampens vitality.

Dynamic diversity is the antithesis of managed speech. Dynamic diversity seeks to broaden the range of participants and ideas in public discussion, with the ultimate aim of enabling social and political change. Our political discourse often posits an opposition between robust constitutional speech protection and social goals of equality, inclusion, and progress. Dynamic diversity, though, extols free speech as a medium for pursuing those goals. The dynamic diversity model underwrites a sharp critique of the Roberts Court's First Amendment. Dynamic diversity largely disfavors this Court's free speech decisions across the spectrum of private speech, government preserves, and electoral speech. Although a handful of Roberts Court decisions advance the values of dynamic diversity, the Court's First Amendment jurisprudence as a whole erodes those values. A First Amendment jurisprudence oriented toward dynamic diversity would focus not on management by powerful institutions but on protection for dissenters and outsider speakers. It would acknowledge and confront conflicts between expressive interests, and it would nurture the constructive, creative power of free expression.

The Supreme Court's elaboration of constitutional protection for expressive freedom contributes to a thriving, humane democracy. First Amendment law has always been politically contingent. The doctrine shifts and evolves under each era's Court, yielding a succession of new First Amendments. That continual regeneration seems to me both inevitable and broadly desirable. I don't fault the Roberts Court for casting First Amendment doctrine in a new, distinctive mold. I just find the mold normatively unappealing. This Court, in my view, has given us a First Amendment that is ambitious, coherent, and mostly lamentable. Others will disagree, and I hope this book will serve to inform and sharpen their points of view. Understanding the Roberts Court's free speech jurisprudence through the lens of managed speech should help people with many and varied normative commitments to discuss how the next Supreme Court can ingrain the strengths of the Roberts Court's First Amendment while transcending its failings.

# APPENDIX

# Roberts Court Free Speech Decisions and Holdings

## PART I

### Chapter 1

*United States v. Stevens* (2010) (Roberts majority): the First Amendment bars the federal government from indiscriminately banning depictions of violence against animals.

*Brown v. Entertainment Merchants Association* (2011) (Scalia majority): the First Amendment bars a state from banning the sale of violent video games to minors.

*Golan v. Holder* (2012) (Ginsburg majority): the federal government may, without regard to the First Amendment, restore copyright protection to material that had previously passed out of copyright protection and into the public domain.

*United States v. Williams* (2008) (Scalia majority): the federal government may, without regard to the First Amendment, criminalize the pandering of non-existent child pornography if the panderer believes, or intends to cause the receiver to believe, that the panderer is pandering child pornography.

*Nevada Commission on Ethics v. Carrigan* (2011) (Scalia majority): a state may, without regard to the First Amendment, ban a public official from voting on or advocating about a matter as to which the official has a conflict of interest.

*FCC v. Fox Television Stations, Inc.* (2012) (Kennedy majority): [no direct First Amendment holding; the Court holds that the federal government's ban on the broadcast of "fleeting expletives" was unconstitutionally vague].

*United States v. Alvarez* (2012) (Kennedy plurality): the First Amendment bars the federal government from flatly banning false claims about receipt of military honors.

## Chapter 2

*Snyder v. Phelps* (2011) (Roberts majority): the First Amendment restricts a state's power to impose tort liability for intentional infliction of emotional distress on a speaker who spoke about a matter of public concern.

*Holder v. Humanitarian Law Project* (2010) (Roberts majority): even under the most stringent standard of First Amendment review, the federal government may criminalize giving expert advice and training about peaceful conflict resolution to foreign groups that the government designates as terroristic.

*Sorrell v. IMS Health, Inc.* (2011) (Kennedy majority): the First Amendment bars a state from restricting the use of particular information for commercial purposes while permitting use of that information for other purposes.

*Milavetz, Gallop & Milavetz v. United States* (2010) (Sotomayor majority): the First Amendment does not bar the federal government from prohibiting debt relief agencies from advising their clients to incur more debt or from making them identify themselves to potential clients as debt relief agencies.

*Reed v. Town of Gilbert* (2015) (Thomas majority): the First Amendment requirement of content neutrality bars a state from imposing content-based restrictions on the display of signs.

# PART II

## Chapter 3

*Beard v. Banks* (2006) (Breyer plurality): the First Amendment balancing test that applies to prisoners' speech permits state prison officials to withhold reading materials from high-security prisoners for the purpose of motivating better behavior.

*Morse v. Frederick* (2007) (Roberts majority): a public high school may, without regard to the First Amendment, discipline a student for displaying a message, off school property but during a school event, that school officials interpret as advocating illegal drug use.

*Tennessee Secondary School Athletic Association v. Brentwood Academy* (2007) (Stevens partial majority): the First Amendment does not bar a state high school athletic association from prohibiting a private school that joins the association from using "hard sell" recruiting tactics.

*Garcetti v. Ceballos* (2006) (Kennedy majority): a state employer may, without regard to the First Amendment, discipline an employee for speech created in the course of the employee's job duties.

*Lane v. Franks* (2014) (Sotomayor majority): First Amendment protection for public employee speech extends to an employee's speech outside the course of employment that conveys information learned in the course of employment.

*Borough of Duryea v. Guarnieri* (2011) (Kennedy majority): the rule that the First Amendment protects only public employee speech about matters of public concern extends to speech an employee styles as a petition to the government for redress of grievances.

## Chapter 4

*Pleasant Grove City v. Summum* (2009) (Alito majority): the First Amendment does not bar a state from choosing which permanent monuments to display in a public park, because when a state accepts a monument for display, the monument becomes government speech.

*Walker v. Texas Division, Sons of Confederate Veterans* (2015) (Breyer majority): the First Amendment does not bar a state from approving some proposals for specialty license plates while rejecting others, because the contents of license plates are government speech.

*Christian Legal Society v. Martinez* (2010) (Ginsburg majority): the First Amendment does not bar a state university from requiring student organizations, as a condition of official recognition, to accept as members any students who wish to join.

*McCullen v. Coakley* (2014) (Roberts majority): a state's imposition of a "fixed buffer zone" around abortion clinics is content neutral and thus subject only to intermediate scrutiny, but the law fails intermediate scrutiny because the state could have accomplished its content-neutral ends in ways that restricted less speech.

## Chapter 5

*Rumsfeld v. Forum for Academic and Institutional Rights* (2006) (Roberts majority): a federal requirement that universities give U.S. military employers the same access to on-campus interview resources available to any other employer does not implicate any First Amendment interest.

*Agency for International Development v. Alliance for Open Society International* (2013) (Roberts majority): the First Amendment bars the federal government from requiring, as a condition of receiving federal funds, that recipients endorse a government policy outside the scope of the funding program.

# PART III

## Chapter 6

*New York State Board of Elections v. Lopez Torres* (2008) (Scalia majority): the First Amendment does not bar a state from requiring political parties to choose their candidates for judicial offices by a vote of elected delegates at party nominating conventions.

*Washington State Grange v. Washington State Republican Party* (2008) (Thomas majority): the First Amendment does not flatly bar a state from requiring general election candidates to be chosen through a nonpartisan primary where candidates may choose a party preference to identify them on the ballot.

*Doe v. Reed* (2010) (Roberts majority): the First Amendment does not flatly bar a state from disclosing to the public the identities of people who signed a petition to place a direct democracy measure on the election ballot.

## Chapter 7

*Randall v. Sorrell* (2006) (Breyer plurality): (1) The First Amendment bars states from setting such low limits for political campaign contributions that candidates cannot effectively communicate their positions to the electorate. (2) The First Amendment continues to bar states from limiting electoral spending.

*Federal Election Commission v. Wisconsin Right to Life* (2007) (Roberts partial majority): the First Amendment bars the federal government from restricting corporate and union election advertising unless the advertisement is susceptible of no reasonable interpretation other than as a call to support or oppose a particular candidate.

*Citizens United v. Federal Election Commission* (2010) (Kennedy majority): (1) The First Amendment bars the federal government from restricting corporate and union election advertising. (2) The First Amendment does not bar the federal government from making corporate and union advertisers in elections disclose their identities.

*American Tradition Partnership v. Bullock* (2012) (per curiam): Montana presented no justifications for restrictions on corporate and union election spending that the Court had not considered and rejected on First Amendment grounds in *Citizens United.*

*McCutcheon v. Federal Election Commission* (2014) (Roberts plurality): the First Amendment bars the federal government, at least in the presence of a restriction on the amount of money a campaign contributor may give to any single candidate, from restricting the aggregate amount the contributor may give to all candidates.

## Chapter 8

*Davis v. Federal Election Commission* (2008) (Alito majority): the First Amendment bars the federal government from increasing statutory limits on campaign contributions and coordinated expenditures for a particular candidate because the candidate's opponent spends personal funds over a certain amount.

*Arizona Free Enterprise Club's Freedom Club PAC v. Bennett* (2011) (Roberts majority): the First Amendment bars a state from increasing public funding for a particular candidate or candidates because an opposing candidate who has declined public funds raises funds, spends, or benefits from independent spending at some level above the base amount of public funding.

*Locke v. Karass* (2009) (Breyer majority): the First Amendment does not bar a public sector union from using agency fees to fund non-political litigation that does not benefit workers in the bargaining unit from which the fees were collected, provided that workers in all bargaining units have a reciprocal entitlement to the national union's litigation resources.

*Davenport v. Washington Education Association* (2007) (Scalia majority): a state may, notwithstanding the First Amendment, adopt an "opt-in" system that makes a public sector union get a non-member's affirmative consent before the union may collect from the non-member the portion of an agency fee that funds the union's political advocacy.

*Ysursa v. Pocatello Education Association* (2009) (Roberts majority): a state may, notwithstanding the First Amendment, exclude political contributions from the scope of a payroll deduction system used to deduct funds for various purposes from public employees' paychecks.

*Knox v. Service Employees International Union, Local 1000* (2012) (Alito majority): when a public sector union makes a special fee assessment after collecting its regular agency fee, the First Amendment (1) requires the union to get the affirmative consent of a non-member who did not timely object to paying the percentage of the regular fee that funded the union's political advocacy before the union may collect from such non-member the same percentage of the special assessment, and (2) requires the union to get the affirmative consent of a non-member who timely objected to paying the percentage of the regular fee that funded the union's political advocacy before the union may collect from such non-member any portion of the special assessment.

*Harris v. Quinn* (2014) (Alito majority): the First Amendment bars a public sector union from collecting agency fees from non-members who are not "full-fledged" public employees.

*Williams-Yulee v. Florida Bar* (2015) (Roberts partial majority): the First Amendment does not bar a state from prohibiting personal appeals for campaign contributions by judicial candidates.

# INDEX